Public Budgeting
in Theory and Practice

Public Budgeting in Theory and Practice

Fremont J. Lyden
University of Washington

Marc Lindenberg
INCAE, *Nicaragua*

Longman
New York & London

PUBLIC BUDGETING IN THEORY AND PRACTICE

Longman Inc., 1560 Broadway, New York, N.Y. 10036
Associated companies, branches, and representatives
throughout the world.

Developmental Editor: Irving E. Rockwood
Editorial and Design Supervisor: Frances A. Althaus
Production Supervisor: Ferne Kawahara
Manufacturing Supervisor: Marion Hess
Composition: A & S Graphics, Inc.

Library of Congress Cataloging in Publication Data

Lyden, Fremont J.
   Public budgeting in theory and practice.
   Bibliography: p.
   Includes index.
   1. Budget.   I. Lindenberg, Marc.   II. Title.
HJ2009.L9 1983   350.72′2   82-14847
ISBN 0-582-28350-7

Printing: 9 8 7 6 5 4 3 2 1   Year: 91 90 89 88 87 86 85 84 83

Manufactured in the United States of America

To the Memory of George Anderson Shipman
1903–1982

Contents

Foreword

Public budgeting involves the drama of politics. Public budgeting requires sound technical approaches. These are very different dimensions of a process that is of fundamental importance to public policy, administration and politics. These dimensions are uniquely and effectively captured and balanced in this text.

Students and faculty will quickly appreciate the contribution that Fremont J. Lyden and Marc Lindenberg have made to the study of public budgeting. The dilemma presented by existing texts has been that either they provide exciting insight into the political struggles that are the essence of much of budget formulation and adoption or they explain the techniques and approaches used in establishing, presenting and implementing a budget. Professors Lyden and Lindenberg will leave students neither unversed in how to compile or analyze a governmental budget nor fearful of the seemingly strange world of struggle, negotiation and compromise in which budgeting occurs. This is a unique text that provides both techniques and political insight.

This is a sophisticated introduction to public budgeting. Some students will value the material and discussion presented here as the first step in pursuing the study of one or more aspects of public budgeting in considerable depth. Others will use this text for general preparation for work in the public sector. The breadth of topics covered and the depth of that coverage will serve the needs of both groups.

The authors make good use of some rich examples of budgetary data and forms. These examples are from all levels of government, and they illustrate a wide variety of processes and issues. In addition, there are exercises included in many of the chapters that are pedagogically invaluable. Experiential learning is effective learning, and it is highly appropriate to include that in a text on a subject like budgeting. In short, all of what one hopes to find in a text on a specialized subject is present here.

Dennis L. Dresang

Introduction

An Approach to the Study of Budgeting

Most books on public budgeting are written from either an institutional or a political-environment point of view. In the former, attention is given to the way organizational and legal instruments work—how the budget office is organized, who performs economic analyses, how appropriation bills are constructed and interpreted, and so forth. Political texts on budgeting focus on the political process by which budgets are formulated and executed—how the public translates its desires for public action into political issues, how legislatures deliberate and act upon such issues, what political roles the executive plays in this process. Neither of these perspectives reflects the way the executive branch of government perceives the budget as a working tool for developing and carrying out program efforts. This text looks at budgeting from this executive perspective and consequently is titled the *theory* and *practice* of budgeting. The institutional and political-environmental considerations are not ignored but are viewed as they seem relevant from the executive's programmatic point of view.

From this perspective, the budget is seen as an assembly of information required for the making of policy and resource decisions. Specific techniques are used in the formulation and administration of budgets. These techniques—such as line item budgets, performance budgets, program budgets, and other ways of assembling budget information—are explained in the text in sufficient detail to allow the reader to implement them. Instructions for implementing some techniques cannot be provided because legal requirements differ for different jurisdictions. In these instances—such as the reprogramming, transferring, or impounding of funds—the effects of using the procedures in budgetary decision making are described. In short, this book is concerned with the *practice* of budgeting, with the mode of presentation being either prescriptive or descriptive.

But it is not intended to serve primarily as a "how-to-do-it" manual. Techniques are of little value unless one knows how and when to use them. One must have some analytic framework, explicit or implicit, for thinking about how techniques can be employed to contribute appropriately to decision making. Analytic models, sometimes referred to loosely as theories, have been suggested throughout the text to help the reader understand the contributions that budget techniques can make to decision making, as well as to illustrate the consequences of using such techniques inappropriately.

In the first chapter three techniques for structuring the budget—administrative, consolidated cash, and national income accounts—are explained. A theoretical framework is suggested to help the reader understand the decision-making significance of each. This framework postulates several policy issues, each of which may be classified as related primarily to one of three analytic categories. Policy questions concerned with (1) the activities to be employed in programs (administrative), (2) the financial transactions involved in paying for the resources used in programs (fiscal or cash flow), and (3) the economic impact of government spending (economic) all require different ways of assembling budgetary information. To deal with each of these policy issues one must be able to reframe the budget into executive, fiscal, and economic formats. These three different ways of organizing the budget constitute the scheme used for ordering the discussions of budgeting in the remainder of this text.

In Chapter 2 the concept of the Executive Budget is explored. First, the historical development of governmental spending is traced, showing the changing responsibilities that federal, state, and local governments have assumed over time in the performance of different governmental functions. The procedure that provides the structure for decision making in government budgeting, the budget cycle, is set forth, indicating what roles are played, when, and by what different actors in the formulation of a budget. Finally, consideration is given to the constraints that exist in the exercise of discretion—controllable and uncontrollable expenditures—in budgetary decision making.

Indirect as well as direct programmatic consequences ensue from public expenditure activities. Fiscal and Economic Budget perspectives are discussed in Chapter 3 in terms of such indirect consequences. The economic and financial theories underlying each are presented and related to operational budget questions.

In Chapters 4 and 5, four different techniques for representing the Executive Budget—objects of expenditure, performance, PPB, and ZBB—are identified. A theoretical framework, James Thompson's decision-making taxonomy, is then employed to show the contribution each technique can make to budgetary decision making. Finally, cases are included at the end of each chapter to give the reader a chance to employ the technique discussed in real-life problem-solving contexts.

Having identified in Chapters 4 and 5 the different ways of structuring the Executive Budget, Chapter 6 turns to a consideration of the array of rational controls and behavior strategies used in the actual process of making budgetary decisions. Both traditional budgetary control devices—such as fixed ceilings and workload measurement—and systems analysis tools—such as benefit-cost and cost-effectiveness analysis—are discussed.

In Chapter 7 we turn to a discussion of the techniques used in making investment decisions in budgeting. Since capital facilities are not consumed during the budget year, expenditures for such purposes must be justified in terms of economic investment criteria, that is, the costs and benefits of using financial resources for one purpose rather than another over time. Since governments have unique responsibilities for the provision of many basic capital facilities in society—roads, bridges, battleships, and the like—

considerable space is given in this chapter to explaining the techniques appropriate for decision making in this important area of budget formulation.

The first seven chapters concentrate on the expenditure side of budgeting. In Chapter 8 we look at the other side of the coin: revenues. The chapter is organized around such questions as where do revenues come from, who bears the burden of financing government, how much money is needed to finance government operations, and what are the major patterns of intergovernmental fiscal relations. As in the other chapters, this subject is presented as it applies to all three levels of government. Although a considerable amount of material is covered in this chapter, the appropriate budget techniques (here, kinds of revenue sources) are, as in previous chapters, discussed in terms of explanatory theoretical formulations (e.g., ability to pay or benefits received).

From the foregoing discussion one can see why this text is titled the *theory* and *practice* of budgeting. A concerted effort has been made throughout the volume to provide explanations about how to employ budget techniques (practice) and what consequences (theory) are likely to follow from employing each technique. Cases have been included following most chapters to allow the reader to see how *theory* and *practice* questions must be joined in real-life situations.

One final explanatory note should be added. The federal government provides the major base of reference throughout much of the text. This practice has not been followed because more budget decisions are made at the federal level than at state or local levels. Obviously the opposite is true. Yet there are fifty different state and thousands of different local systems of government. All have been and continue to be influenced by federal governmental practices. Moreover, in recent years the federal government has become a major source of income for state and local governments. Even if they operate differently from the federal government in some respects, it behooves them to understand how federal budgeting is carried on, if only for the sake of protecting their sources of outside income.

This attention given to federal practices does not mean that other units of government have been ignored when they can provide better examples of budgetary practices than the federal government. Thus state and local practices receive prominent attention in Chapter 3 where cash flows and debt management are discussed and again in Chapters 7 and 8 where capital budgeting and sources of revenue are considered. This generic approach to budgeting supported by applications at specific levels emphasizes the continuity of budgeting in government and stresses the multifaceted perspective one must take to understand public budgeting adequately as a field of study and practice.

No single approach to a subject as complicated as public budgeting will ever satisfy the needs of everyone. What a text should do is to act as a catalyst for more in-depth explorations by the reader into all relevant facets of understanding. A list of selected references has been included at the end of each chapter in this text to provide the reader with some guides for embarking on such an intellectual journey. It is hoped that the approach taken in this book will encourage the reader to pursue such a course of action.

Chapter 1

What Is a Budget?

LBJ's Budget Hits Record $135 Billion

DETROIT FREE PRESS

1968 Budget Hits Record $172.4 Billion

UNITED PRESS INTERNATIONAL

$169.2 Billion Budget Provides $73 Billion for Defense and Limited "Great Society" Rises

NEW YORK TIMES

THREE KINDS OF BUDGETS

Above are but three of the newspaper headlines that attempted to announce to the American people the size of President Johnson's 1968 budget.[1] How could three reputable news sources report such widely divergent totals? The answer: All were correct. The $135 billion reported by the *Detroit Free Press* refers to what was then called the Administrative Budget; the $172.4 billion announced by the United Press International represents the budget from a cash consolidated perspective; the $169.2 billion reported by the *New York Times* reflects the budget from a national income accounts viewpoint. But which one was the *real* budget, the one that tells us what the President really proposes to spend? According to Figure 1.1, this would seem to be the $135 billion—"Expenditures in 1968." Yet the President was asking Congress for authority to spend $144 billion, only $95.7 billion of which would actually be spent in fiscal year 1968. The remaining $39.3 billion to be spent in 1968 would come from unspent authorizations enacted in prior years. And the remaining $48.3 billion of the $144 billion Congress was being asked to authorize would not be spent until later. This spending lag reflects the fact that it may take several years to produce some goods purchased (e.g., the construction of a nuclear submarine or the building of a highway). The government must obligate itself to pay for such purchases when it engages a provider to furnish the product, not when the product is ready for use.

Yet even the $135 billion does not include all federal funds to be paid out in fiscal year 1968. An additional $37.4 billion would be paid out to recipients of federal trust funds (e.g., social security, highways). These funds were not included in the Administra-

1

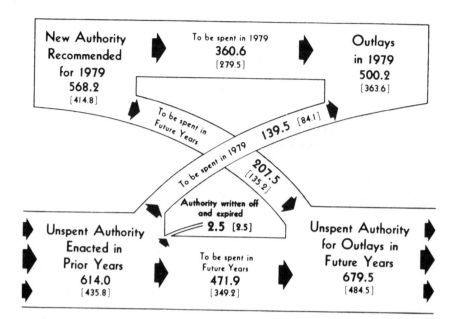

New Authority Recommended for 1979
568.2
[414.8]

To be spent in 1979
360.6
[279.5]

Outlays in 1979
500.2
[363.6]

To be spent in Future Years
139.5 [84.1]

To be spent in 1979
207.5 [135.2]

Authority written off and expired
2.5 [2.5]

Unspent Authority Enacted in Prior Years
614.0
[435.8]

To be spent in Future Years
471.9
[349.2]

Unspent Authority for Outlays in Future Years
679.5
[484.5]

FIGURE 1.1   Relation of Budget Authority to Outlays— 1979 Budget. (*From* The Budget of the United States Government, Fiscal Year 1979, *p. 241*)

NOTE: Figures in brackets represent federal funds only ($ in billions). The difference between the total budget figures and federal funds shown in brackets consists of trust funds and interfund transactions between fund groups.

tive Budget because the payments to be made would depend upon the number of recipients eligible during the year for the amounts authorized under existing law, not on the overall amount Congress may deem appropriate. Still, such expenditures represent federal spending just as much as goods and services purchased. So, if one includes these expenditures, the 1968 budget would be $172.4 billion, the amount reported by UPI.

This budget representation, usually referred to as the cash consolidated budget, measures the flow of cash between the public and the government as a whole in terms of checks issued and payments received. Net expenditures (i.e., gross expenditures minus gross receipts) from loan transactions are also included. While this may be the best indicator of the financial status of federal transactions, it fails to reflect adequately the budget's economic impact on society. Say the government contracts with Boeing to build fifty guided missiles. This transaction will not show up as a governmental expenditure until checks are written to pay Boeing for the missiles. Long before that time, Boeing will have gone into the money market to borrow funds for beginning the production process. And it will purchase goods and services to set up production assembly lines. All this economic activity will have occurred before the government writes a check to Boeing in return for the delivered missiles. This example, of course, is a gross oversimplification of reality. Any large undertaking will undoubtedly involve progress payments for portions of the work completed. Even so, payments will still lag behind the actual economic activity involved in producing the work. Therefore, by the time checks are written and expenditures appear in the consolidated budget the economic impact of the expenditures will have already been felt in the economy. To avoid this, one may record budget expenditures on an accrued rather than a cash basis. That is, one may show expenditures when liabilities are incurred (when government legally obligates itself) rather than when a check is written for a completed product.

The national income accounts (NIA) budget is presented in this form. Since this budget is concerned with recording all products contributed to the gross national product (GNP) by the government, gross receipts and expenditures of government and enterprises (rather than net expenditures) are included. The rationale for following this procedure is that a government enterprise activity like TVA is making productive contributions to the GNP and consequently all its transactions should be included in the budget. Also, the NIA budget excludes government loans on the grounds that such transactions are basically exchanges of one asset for another rather than expenditures for currently produced goods and services. The budget of $169.2 billion reported by the *New York Times* reflects this NIA budget perspective.

Prior to 1932 there was only one concept of "the budget," which included general, special, and emergency and trust accounts.[2] In his 1932 budget message President Hoover separated trust funds from other expenditures and, in effect, created the Administrative Budget. Primary attention continued to center on the Administrative Budget for several years. Yet as early as the 1940s and '50s economists and budget analysts were increasingly urging that greater attention be given to the cash consolidated view of the budget. By this time the trust funds created by the social security legislation of the 1930s were beginning to constitute a significant proportion of federal income. Surpluses built up in these funds were regularly borrowed, at a given rate of interest, of course, to meet the depository needs of the Treasury.

Also, with the passage of the Employment Act of 1946 and the creation of the Council of Economic Advisers, increased attention was given to the economic effect of the federal budget on the rest of the economy. Consequently, by 1964 it seemed only natural for attention to shift from the Administrative Budget to a cash consolidated version of the budget, with increasing attention also given to the effect of the budget on the gross national product as reflected in the national income accounts version of budgetary activity.

From 1964 to 1968 all three ways of representing the budget were presented and prominently discussed in the budget document. Besides being confusing, this practice tended to result in stress being put on whichever perspective depicted the budget in its most favorable light. For example, it could be argued that President Johnson directed primary attention in his 1968 budget to the NIA version because the budget deficit shown by this version was smaller ($−2.1 billion) than that appearing in either the Administrative ($−8.1 billion) or the cash consolidated ($−4.3 billion) budget.

At any rate, concern became so widespread over the use of multiple presentation approaches that the President created a Commission on Budget Concepts to study the problem. This commission issued a report in October 1967 that recommended that the budget be presented in terms of a unified format.[3] The format recommended was something of a compromise. Included were nearly all receipt and expenditure items covered by the cash consolidated budget, but they were reported on an accrual (when liability incurred) basis rather than when cash was actually transferred (bills paid–cash received).

TABLE 1.1. Budget Concepts: The New and the Old

	The Budget	NIA Budget	Consolidated Cash Budget	Administrative Budget
I. Coverage				
Receipts				
Regular taxes	Included	Included	Included	Included
Trust fund taxes	Included	Included	Included	Included
Receipts from market-oriented activities	Excluded from receipts, netted against expenditures or outlays	Excluded from receipts, netted against expenditures	Includes some in receipts	Includes some in receipts
Expenditures				
Regular agencies	Included	Included	Included	Included
Trust funds	Included	Included	Included	Excluded
Loans	Excluded from expenditure account; included in total budget outlays	Excluded	Included (net on expenditure side)	Included (net on expenditure side)
Other				
Participation certificates	Treated as borrowing	Excluded	Treated as reduction of payments	Treated as reduction of expenditures
Seigniorage	Excluded from receipts, treated as a means of financing the deficit	Excluded	Excluded from receipts, treated as a means of financing the deficit	Treated as receipt item
Federal home loan banks and land banks	Excluded	Excluded	Included	Excluded
District of Columbia	Excluded	Excluded	Included	Excluded
II. Accounting				
Basis Receipts	Accrual[a]	Combination, cash and accrual	Cash collections	Cash collections
Expenditures	Accrual[b]	Deliveries	Cash payments—checks cashed	Cash payments—checks issued

SOURCE: Federal Reserve Bank of Cleveland, *Economic Review*, March 1968.

[a] At present on a cash collection basis, but are expected to be on an accrual basis in the future.

[b] At present on a checks issued basis, but are expected to be on an accrual basis in the future.

This form of reporting, the commission argued, would make the federal budget more useful for studying its impact on the economy. As in the cash consolidated budget, the proposed unified budget would include net government loans, but they would be clearly distinguished from other federal expenditures. Government enterprises would also be reported on a net rather than a gross basis, so as not to inflate the government budget with essentially businesslike transactions.

The commission's proposals were substantially adopted as the official budget format beginning with fiscal year 1969 (presented in January 1968). Table 1.1 compares the three formats then in use with the format adopted. Since then, however, several changes have been made in the unified budget presentation.[4] The accrual basis of presentation has been abandoned for the more familiar cash basis. A single term, outlays, has been introduced to represent total spending, and it includes both expenditures and net lending (loans minus loans repaid). Also, the old concept of the Administrative Budget, abandoned in 1968, has been reintroduced into the budget document under the name Federal Funds. (The major federal fund included is the general fund, which is derived from general taxes and borrowing.) Although total outlays include both Federal Funds and Trust Funds, the deficit (or surplus) associated with each is shown separately. See the following glossary of terms currently used in the federal budget.

GLOSSARY OF BUDGET TERMS*

AUTHORIZATION   Basic substantive legislation enacted by Congress that sets up or continues the legal operation of a federal program or agency. Such legislation is normally a prerequisite for subsequent appropriations, but does not usually provide budget authority (see below).

BUDGET AUTHORITY (BA)   Authority provided by law to enter into obligations that will result in immediate or future outlays. It may be classified by the period of availability (1-year, multiple-year, no-year), by the timing of congressional action (current or permanent), or by the manner of determining the amount available (definite or indefinite). The basic forms of budget authority are:

Appropriations—budget authority provided through the congressional appropriation process that permits federal agencies to incur obligations and to make payments.

Borrowing authority—statutory authority not necessarily provided through the appropriations process, that permits federal agencies to incur obligations and to make payments from borrowed moneys.

Contract authority—statutory authority, not necessarily provided through the appropriations process, that permits federal agencies to enter into contracts or incur other obligations in advance of an appropriation.

BUDGET RECEIPTS   Money, net of refunds, collected from the public by the federal government through the exercise of its governmental or sovereign powers, as well as gifts, contributions, and premiums from voluntary participants in federal social insurance programs closely associated with compulsory programs. Excluded are amounts received from strictly business-type transactions (such as sales, interest, or loan repayments) and payments between government accounts. (See offsetting receipts.)

BUDGET SURPLUS OR DEFICIT (−)   The difference between budget receipts and outlays.

CONCURRENT RESOLUTION ON THE BUDGET   A resolution passed by both Houses of Congress, but not requiring the signature of the President, setting forth targets or binding congressional budget totals for the federal government.

---

*These definitions are consistent with those contained in the booklet "Terms Used in the Budgetary Process" published by the General Accounting Office in July 1977.

Reprinted from *The United States Budget in Brief, Fiscal Year 1980* (Washington, D.C.: GPO), pp. 86–88.

CONTINUING RESOLUTION   Legislation enacted by Congress to provide budget authority for specific ongoing activities when a regular appropriation for such activities has not been enacted by the beginning of the fiscal year.

CONTROLLABILITY   In the President's budget this refers to the ability of the President to control budget authority or outlays during a fiscal year without changing existing substantive law. The concept "relatively uncontrollable under current law" includes outlays for open-ended programs and fixed costs, such as interest on the public and social security and veterans benefits, and outlays to liquidate (pay for) prior-year obligations.

CURRENT SERVICES ESTIMATES   Estimated budget authority and outlays for the upcoming fiscal year at the same program level as and without policy changes from the fiscal year in progress. To the extent mandated by existing law, estimates take into account the budget impact of anticipated changes in economic conditions (such as unemployment or inflation), beneficiary levels, pay increases, and benefit changes. The Congressional Budget Act of 1974 requires that the President transmit current services estimates to the Congress. The current services estimates for 1980 are published in Special Analysis A of the 1980 budget.

DEFERRAL   Any action or inaction by an officer or employee of the United States that temporarily withholds, delays, or effectively precludes the obligation or expenditure of budget authority. Deferrals may not extend beyond the end of the fiscal year and may be overturned at any time by either House of Congress.

FEDERAL FUNDS   Funds collected and used by the federal government for the general purposes of the Government. There are four types of federal fund accounts: the general fund, special funds, public enterprise (revolving) funds, and intragovernmental funds. The major federal fund is the general fund, which is derived from general taxes and borrowing. Federal funds also include certain earmarked collections, such as those generated by and used to finance a continuing cycle of business-type operations.

FISCAL YEAR   The yearly accounting period for the federal government, which begins on October 1 and ends on the following September 30. The fiscal year is designated by the calendar year in which it ends; e.g., fiscal year 1980 is the fiscal year ending September 30, 1980. (Prior to fiscal year 1977 the fiscal year began on July 1 and ended on the following June 30.)

GOVERNMENT-SPONSORED ENTERPRISES   Enterprises with completely private ownership, such as federal land banks and federal home loans banks, established and chartered by the federal government to perform specialized functions. These enterprises are not included in the budget totals, but financial information on their operations is published in a separate part of the appendix to the President's budget.

IMPOUNDMENT   Any action or inaction by an officer or employee of the federal government that precludes the obligation or expenditure of budget authority provided by the Congress (see deferral and rescission).

OBLIGATIONS   Amounts of orders placed, contracts awarded, services rendered, or other commitments made by federal agencies during a given period, that will require outlays during the same or some future period.

OFF-BUDGET FEDERAL ENTITIES   Organizational entities, federally owned in whole or in part, whose transactions belong in the budget under current budget accounting concepts but which have been excluded from the budget totals under provisions of law. While these transactions are not included in the budget totals, information on these entities is presented in various places in the budget documents.

OFFSETTING RECEIPTS   Collections deposited in receipt accounts that are offset against budget authority and outlays rather than being counted as budget receipts. These collections are derived from other government accounts or from government activities that are of a business-type or market-oriented nature. Offsetting receipts are classified as (1) intragovernmental transactions or (2) proprietary receipts from the public.

OUTLAYS Values of checks issued, interest accrued on the public debt, or other payments made, net of refunds and reimbursements.

RESCISSION Enacted legislation canceling budget authority previously provided by the Congress.

SUPPLEMENTAL APPROPRIATION An appropriation enacted as an addition to a regular annual appropriation act. Supplemental appropriation acts provide additional budget authority beyond original estimates for programs or activities (including new programs authorized after the date of the original appropriation act) for which the need for funds is too urgent to be postponed until the next regular appropriation.

TAX EXPENDITURES Losses of tax revenue attributable to provisions of the Federal income tax laws that allow a special exclusion, exemption, or deduction from gross income or provide a special credit, preferential rate of tax, or a deferral of tax liability affecting individual or corporate income tax liabilities.

TRUST FUNDS Funds collected and used by the federal government for carrying out specific purposes and programs according to terms of a trust agreement or statute, such as the social security and unemployment trust funds. Trust funds are not available for the general purposes of the government. Trust fund receipts that are not anticipated to be used in the immediate future are generally invested in interest-bearing government securities and earn interest for the trust fund.

Two other new developments have been introduced into the current budget scene. First, the off-budget agency has come into existence. The two major ones are the Postal Service and the Federal Financing Bank. As the term "off-budget" implies, none of these agencies is included in total budget outlays. Their financial activities are reported on in supporting tables.[5] Nevertheless, they are federally sponsored ventures, and their expenditures have grown from $100 million in 1973 to $21 billion in 1981—a significant amount to be excluded from the budget. The budget is, of course, underestimated by the amount of these off-budget outlays. The Executive and Congress have on several occasions expressed concern about the practice of excluding such outlays from the budget.[6] And as noted in Table 1.2, the 1983 budget projects that off-budget outlays will be reduced to $11 billion by 1985. Even $11 billion is not an insignificant amount, though; so it seems that one must continue to give consideration to off-budget outlays when analyzing government outlays.

TABLE 1.2. Outlays of Off-Budget Federal Entities (In billions of dollars)

Off-budget Federal Entity	1981 (actual)	1982 (estimate)	1983 (estimate)	1984 (estimate)	1985 (estimate)
Federal Financing Bank	21.0	16.2	12.1	11.0	7.8
Rural Electrification and Telephone revolving fund	a				
Rural Telephone Bank	.1	.2	.2	.2	.2
Strategic Petroleum Reserve account		2.8	2.8	2.3	2.2
Postal Service fund	.1	.6	.7	.9	.8
U.S. Railway Association	−.3	−.1	− a		
Synthetic Fuels Corporation					
Total	21.0	19.7	15.7	14.3	11.0

SOURCE: *Budget of the United States, Fiscal Year 1983*, pp. 6–9.

a $50 million or less.

The second new wrinkle in budget reporting is the tax expenditure. The Congressional Budget and Impoundment Control Act of 1974 (P.L. 93-344) requires a listing of all tax expenditures in the budget document. The act defines a tax expenditure as "revenue losses attributable to provisions of the Federal tax laws which allow a special credit, a preferential tax rate, or a deferral of tax liability."[7] Tax expenditures are, then, tax breaks given to some taxpayers or corporations to encourage certain activities or assist certain groups. They include such things as individual deductions for charitable contributions and medical expenses, tax credits to corporations to encourage certain kinds of business activities (such as the search for new oil resources), and the exclusion of unemployment compensation from taxable income.[8] It is clear from these examples that tax expenditures involve no transfer of funds from the government to the private sector. Rather, the Treasury forgoes the income it would otherwise have collected. In effect, while the term really describes a subsidy to some individual or corporation, such action *implies* an expenditure of government funds by virtue of the loss of tax income that results. The calculation of such tax expenditures is still rather tentative, but current budget presentations do list all tax expenditures thus far identified with the estimated loss attributable to each. For example, Table 1.3 shows the revenue losses that can be attributed to some of the tax expenditures listed in the *Special Analysis G* of the 1983 federal budget. Two additional pages are required in the document to tabulate revenue losses from all tax expenditures. From the items included in Table 1.3 it can be seen that billions of dollars* are lost each year by the tax expenditures presently authorized under federal tax policy. This is not to say, of course, that these projected revenue losses are estimates of the increase in federal receipts that would accompany the repeal of the special provisions that give rise to the tax subsidies.[9] Since many subsidies are enacted as incentives to encourage various kinds of private spending and investment, one could expect a dampening of efforts in these areas if such activities became subject to ordinary tax rates. Thus the removal of a price support from a particular commodity could be expected to lead to higher production of other, still protected (price supported) commodities and a decrease in production of the formerly protected commodity. Yet the multiplicity of subsidies that now exist raises serious questions about the need for tax reform.

BUDGETS AND POLICY QUESTIONS

So where has our discussion taken us? It would seem that in spite of the presidential commission's earnest efforts to develop a single unified budget, we still have substantial reporting in the federal budget in terms of the Administrative Budget, the cash consolidated budget, and the national income accounts budget perspectives. It should be obvious from this discussion that there can be no single, unified budget format because several kinds of policy decisions must be made in developing and approving a government budget, each of which requires a somewhat different arrangement of the financial data involved. At least five different kinds of policy decisions appear relevant. Each may be posed in the form of a question:

*Estimated at over $200 billion in the 1983 budget.

TABLE 1.3. Revenue Loss Estimates for "Tax Expenditures" by Function (In millions of dollars)

Description	Fiscal Years		
	1981	1982	1983
National defense			
Exclusion of benefits and allowances to Armed Forces personnel	1,735	1,885	1,940
Exclusion of military disability pensions	155	165	170
International affairs			
Exclusion of income earned abroad by United States citizens	610	985	1,285
Deferral of income of domestic international sales corporations (DISC)	1,595	1,465	1,490
General science, space, and technology			
Expensing of research and development expenditures	1,550	380	−810
Credit for increasing research activities	15	405	580
Energy			
Expensing of exploration and development costs:			
Oil and gas	3,525	4,065	4,530
Other fuels	25	25	30
Excess of percentage over cost depletion:			
Oil and gas	1,865	1,965	1,695
Other fuels	380	380	425
Capital gains treatment of royalties on coal	100	105	95
Exclusion of interest on State and local government industrial development bonds for certain energy facilities	*	5	15
Residential energy credits:			
Supply incentives	150	205	260
Conservation incentives	425	415	410
Alternative, conservation and new technology credits:			
Supply incentives	180	235	290
Conservation incentives	220	285	315
Alternative fuel production credit	25	55	50
Alcohol fuel credit[1]	5	20	35
Energy credit for intercity buses	5	5	5
Natural resources and environment			
Expensing of exploration and development costs, nonfuel minerals	45	50	55
Excess of percentage over cost depletion, nonfuel minerals	385	405	440
Exclusion of interest on State and local government pollution control bonds	715	835	970
Tax incentives for preservation of historic structures	60	80	75
Capital gains treatment of iron ore	20	20	20
Capital gains treatment of certain timber income	585	600	615
Investment credit and seven-year amortization for reforestation expenditures	5	10	15
Agriculture			
Expensing of certain capital outlays	525	545	560
Capital gains treatment of certain income	425	460	375
Commerce and housing credit			
Dividend and interest exclusion	1,335	2,185	475
Exclusion of interest on State and local industrial development bonds	1,200	1,650	2,185

TABLE 1.3. Revenue Loss Estimates for "Tax Expenditures" by Function (In millions of dollars)

Description	Fiscal Years		
	1981	1982	1983
Commerce and housing credit			
Exemption of credit union income	−25	5	40
Excess bad debt reserves of financial institutions	325	250	515
Exclusion of interest on life insurance savings	4,060	4,535	4,805
Deductibility of interest on consumer credit	8,675	9,285	9,355
Deductibility of mortgage interest on owner-occupied homes	20,145	23,030	25,490
Deductibility of property tax on owner-occupied homes	9,125	10,065	10,635
Exclusion of interest on State and local housing bonds for owner-occupied housing	685	920	1,245
Expensing of construction period interest and taxes	755	745	645
Capital gains (other than agriculture, timber, iron ore and coal)	17,965	18,315	14,390
Deferral of capital gains on home sales	1,160	1,070	1,200

SOURCE: *Special Analysis G*, Budget for Fiscal Year 1983, p. 34.

1 What proportion of the goods and services produced by the whole economy should government consume in carrying out its functions?
2 What should be the relationship between government expenditures and government receipts?
3 How should the burden of the costs of government be shared?
4 How much of the goods and services should be used to accomplish each governmental purpose?
5 How can operating objectives be achieved at the lowest possible costs?

As indicated in Figure 1.2, the first question must be answered primarily from the perspective of the national income accounts budget, which we may call the Economic Budget. The second and third questions relate equally to the Economic Budget and to what might be called the Fiscal Budget, which is based on the cash consolidated presentation and provides information on monetary options available for maintaining an effective cash flow of funds.

The last two questions reflect the rationale upon which the Administrative Budget was constructed, and can more properly be referred to as the Executive Budget. These questions deal with programmatic questions involved in constructing a budget and consequently provide information on what mix of resources is to be used to carry out governmental activities in order to accomplish program goals. As suggested by Figure 1.2, economic and fiscal implications involved in decisions made about program priorities (question 4) and operating efficiency (question 5) cannot be ignored, since both decision areas will be affected by fiscal constraints (such as borrowing limits or timing on the availability of receipts) and economic consequences of governmental activity. In the federal government the Council of Economic Advisers will normally play the lead role in dealing with question 1, the Treasury Department and the Federal Reserve with question 2, and the Office of Management and Budget with questions 3, 4, and 5. The arrows on the left-hand side of the chart, though, indicate that many of these organizations are involved, in one way or another, in dealing with nearly all of these questions, each from a different perspective. Counterpart organizations can be found in

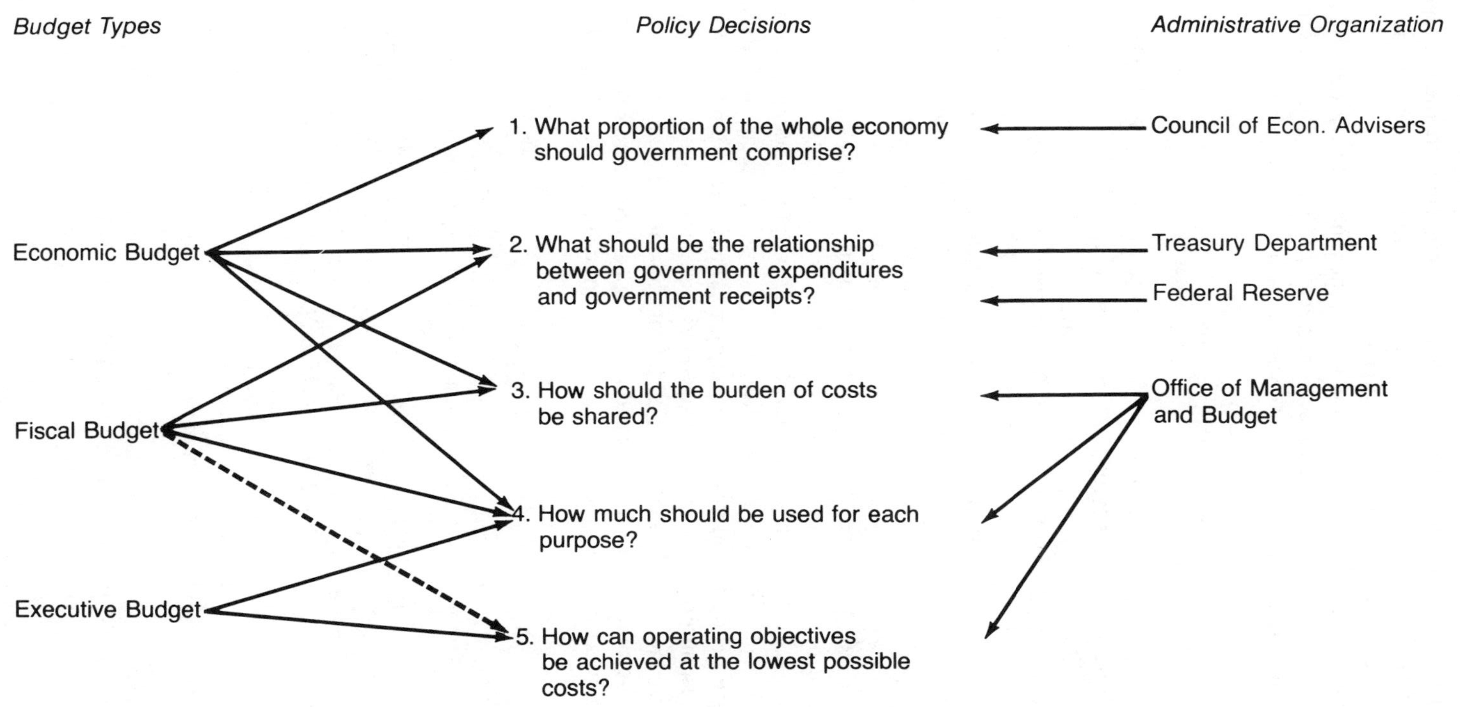

Budget Types　　*Policy Decisions*　　*Administrative Organization*

Council of Econ. Advisers

Treasury Department

Federal Reserve

Office of Management and Budget

1. What proportion of the whole economy should government comprise?

2. What should be the relationship between government expenditures and government receipts?

3. How should the burden of costs be shared?

4. How much should be used for each purpose?

5. How can operating objectives be achieved at the lowest possible costs?

Economic Budget

Fiscal Budget

Executive Budget

FIGURE I.2　Types of Budgets and Policy Decisions.

11

state and local governments (many of which have even renamed their budget offices OMBs after the federal model), which play similar roles in constructing their economic, fiscal, and executive perspectives of the budget.

If we can conclude, then, that these five policy questions will typically be dealt with from the viewpoints of the Economic, Fiscal, or Executive Budget formats, the next step is to set forth the frame of reference employed by each.

SUMMARY

This chapter has been concerned with the definition of a public budget. It was pointed out that there is no one way of classifying the components of a budget to meet all the needs of decision makers. Different classifications are needed to reflect the program content, the economic impacts, and the fiscal impacts of the budget. The administrative, the national income accounts, and the cash consolidated classifications have been developed to serve these different needs. Each approach, however, yields a different budget total, leading to endless confusion in budget presentations. In the late 1960s the President appointed a commission to study the problem. A compromise unified budget approach was proposed by this body and accepted by the President and Congress. Supplementary data are still provided in the federal budget, though, on each of the three—administrative, cash consolidated, and national income accounts—bases so that questions dealing with different kinds of policy issues can be related to the most appropriate classification.

Which budget configuration you will want to employ, then, will depend upon whether you are primarily interested in program content, economic impact, or fiscal impact. The most appropriate format for considering program questions we have labeled the Executive Budget. The formats most useful for considering economic or fiscal issues are the Economic Budget and the Fiscal Budget respectively. The Executive Budget is discussed in the next chapter, the Fiscal and Economic Budgets in Chapter 3.

NOTES

1. President's Commission on Budget Concepts, *Staff Papers* (Washington, D.C.: GPO, 1967), p. 40.

2. The discussion on budget concepts presented here draws primarily on materials presented in the commission's *Staff Report*, pp. 93–116.

3. *Report of the President's Commission on Budget Concepts* (Washington, D.C.: GPO, 1967).

4. David J. Ott and Attiat F. Ott, *Federal Budget Policy*, 3rd ed. (Washington, D.C.: Brookings Institute, 1977).

5. *The United States Budget in Brief, Fiscal Year 1980* (Washington, D.C.: GPO, 1979), p. 80.

6. *Budget of the United States, Fiscal Year 1983*, pp. 6–8.

7. *Special Analyses, Budget of the United States, Fiscal Year 1980* (Washington, D.C.: GPO, 1979), p. 183.

8. See *Special Analyses*, ibid., pp. 183–211.

9. *Special Analysis G*, Budget for Fiscal Year 1983, pp. 13–14.

Chapter 2

The Executive
Budget Perspective

The Executive Budget is the arrangement of the budget so as to accentuate what government does, what activities it undertakes. In a sense, it is the citizen's budget, the way the citizen thinks of government spending, and is presented in this format in the *Budget in Brief*, the popularized treatment of the budget intended for general consumption. And it is the government agency's budget, the culmination of the process involved in proposing, reviewing, prioritizing, and reprioritizing what the government agency wants to accomplish and how it intends to go about doing so. As noted in the previous chapter, trust funds were excluded from the federal Administrative Budget in the 1930s because they were not subject to the same kind of review by appropriation committees as other expenditures. Both receipts and expenditures were established by law, with the amount of revenues and expenditures occurring each year governed by the number of persons eligible for the programs involved. Only by changing the law could the volume of revenues collected or expenditures incurred be changed. Moreover, from the 1930s to the 1960s the Social Security Fund, largest of the trust funds, was continually expanding as more persons were included under the law. By the 1970s, though, this situation had changed. In 1975 expenditures actually exceeded income, resulting in a deficit in the fund. This occurred for several reasons:[1] Inflation caused benefits to increase faster than expected; unemployment caused revenues to fall behind faster than expected; claims for disability payments were rising faster than expected; a faulty benefit formula enacted in 1972 exaggerated the deficit, and a falling birthrate was changing the demography of the country. Whereas prior to the 1970s social security legislation was directed primarily to expanding benefits, since then more attention has necessarily been given to keeping the fund out of the red. To accomplish this end, employee and employer contributions have been increased so steeply that serious consideration is now being given to the partial financing of this fund from general revenues. Consequently, trust fund questions are now closely related to the Executive Budget, and thus are appropriate to include in constructing this budget.

Also, when discussing the Administrative Budget in the previous chapter, the concept was considered strictly in terms of the way it has been employed in the federal government. But total governmental spending in the United States must be considered from the viewpoints of the Executive Budgets of the 50 states and over 27,000 local government units as well. So any discussion of the government budget as a spending instrument in the American economy must be viewed in terms of the Executive Budgets of all governmental units, not merely that of the federal government.

HISTORICAL DEVELOPMENT

The United States is a federal system. The powers of the national government are enumerated in Article 1, Section 8 of the Constitution, which states, in part: "Congress shall have the Power to lay and collect taxes, Duties, Imports and Excises, to pay Debts and provide for the Common Defense and General Welfare of the United States." All powers not delegated to the national government nor prohibited to the states are assumed to reside in the states (residual powers). Local governments, on the other hand, are creations of state government and consequently are legally subordinate to and dependent for their authority upon state governments.

Significant changes have occurred in the spending roles played by each level of government over the two-hundred-year history of the United States. During the first fifteen years of the republic, the national government vigorously exercised its spending powers: refunding successfully the debts of both the Confederation and the states, establishing a system of federal excises, and creating a Bank of the United States. Despite these early actions, the states soon began to gain strength, with the divisiveness resulting therefrom eventually culminating in the Civil War. During the latter part of the nineteenth century neither the federal nor the state governments played major roles in performing the civil (domestic) functions of government. By 1902 over 70 percent of the expenditures for civil government were being made by local governments. With the coming of the Great Depression in the 1930s, however, and the increasing interdependence of the working populace, both state and national governments began to play greater roles in providing civil functions, such as public highways, employment services, public housing, and flood control. Thus, by 1980 local expenditures had decreased to less than 50 percent of total general expenditures for civil functions, while the federal government was assuming nearly 50 percent of such costs:[2]

Level of Government	% of Civil Expenditures	
	1929	*1980*
Federal	15.2	46.8
States	18.5	21.1
Local	66.3	31.1

But even this presentation understates the increasing role of the national government in civil affairs. It is true that from the perspective of who disburses monies for final payment, the national government paid for less than 47 percent of the civil expenditures in 1980; but when viewed from *where the money originated* to pay these bills, the national government contributed nearly 60 percent:[3]

	% of Civil Expenditures, 1980	
Level of Government	Disbursing Level	Originating Level
Federal	46.8	59.8
State and local	53.2	40.2

These figures show the increasing role of the federal government as an indirect rather than direct participant in domestic government expenditures through the use of grants-in-aid to other governments.

State and local governments have remained the dominant spending units in education, highways, and health-hospital functions. Each area has not increased at an equal pace, though. A recent Brookings study, for example, shows that health-hospital expenditures increased 196 percent from 1962–1972, education expenditures 157 percent, and highways by only 84 percent (Table 2.1).[4] Nor were the reasons for the expenditure

TABLE 2.1. **Increase in Expenditures of State and Local Governments by Selected Funds, 1962–72**

	% Increase 1962–72	% Distribution of Increase by Generating Factor		
		Workloads	Prices	Scope-Quality
Education (local schools)	157	10	59	32
Highways	84	32	81	−18
Health-Hospitals	196	37	55	9
Welfare	314	−6	16	90

SOURCE: Henry Owen and Charles Schultze, eds., *Setting National Priorities: The Next Ten Years* (Washington, D.C.: Brookings, 1976), p. 379.

increases for each function the same. Eighty-one percent of the increase in highway expenditures resulted from high prices and 37 percent from increased workloads, both of which were, unfortunately, accomplished at the expense of the quality of work performed (−18 percent). For education and health-hospitals, price increases also accounted for more than half of the expenditure increases. But 37 percent of the remainder of the health-hospital increases was due to increased workloads, with only 9 percent due to increasing the scope and quality of the services. Over a third of the education increases, on the other hand, resulted from upgrading the scope and quality of the services with only 10 percent resulting from increased workloads.

The federal government continues to play an increasing role in the provision of welfare services, the fourth civil function. Here again, though, as the following data from another Brookings study reveal, state and local governments remain the dominant performing units, with the federal government providing increasing proportions of the resources required through grants-in-aid:[5]

	% of Public Welfare Expenditures by:			
	Government Making Final Disbursement		Government Originating Expenditure	
	State-Local	Federal	State-Local	Federal
1958	98.7	1.3	51.1	48.9
1968	87.7	12.3	39.6	60.4
1973	87.4	12.6	42.6	57.4

Going back to Table 2.1, we note that state-local welfare expenditures increased by 314 percent from 1962 to 1972. Ninety percent of this increase reflected improvements in the quality of services offered. Workload levels decreased (−6 percent), indicating that the War on Poverty conducted during this period could claim some degree of success.

THE EXECUTIVE BUDGET AS A DECISION-MAKING PROCESS: THE BUDGET CYCLE

A question one might logically ask, then, is: How are policy decisions that change the direction on emphasis of budget expenditures made? Further, are only certain parts of the budget amenable to such policy changes, or is it possible to change the whole configuration of budget expenditures to reflect changes in policy priorities? The following section first discusses what parts of the budget are most amenable to change. Then the process by which budgetary decisions are made is examined to determine which actors play decision roles at what stages of the decision-making process.

How were these spending decisions made? How much discretionary control did Congress and other legislative bodies have on spending priorities? Much attention has been directed to these questions at the national level of government in recent years. A distinction has been drawn between controllable and uncontrollable outlays. Controllability refers to the ability of the President and Congress to control budget authority or outlays during the fiscal year without changing substantive law. Outlays for open-ended programs and fixed costs, such as interest on the public debt, social security and veterans benefits, and outlays to liquidate prior-year obligations are defined as relatively uncontrollable under current law. Controllable outlays, on the other hand, include such items as salaries and wages, general expenses (e.g., heating, supplies, maintenance), and new programs.[6] The proportion of the federal budget classified as relatively uncontrollable has risen from 59 percent in 1967 to 75 percent in 1982.[7]

But it is questionable how useful the controllable-uncontrollable distinction really is. As LeLoup shows in Table 2.2, to translate controllability into potential discretion one needs to know what proportion of the budget is classified as controllable and uncontrollable respectively and what proportion of each could realistically be cut in a given year. Personnel costs are not all that controllable in the short run. Freezing new hires, deferring salaries, and rolling back retirement—such options are not really very politically viable possibilities. Real discretion is thus reduced to control over about 10 percent of the budget in any given year, with defense spending representing a primary component.

This control is also shared by a number of actors at different stages of the budget process. The federal budget procedure, as depicted in Figure 2.1, is typical of the process that occurs in most states and large cities. In the spring of the year operating agencies review their current operations and begin to project their program objectives, policy issues, and resource requirements for the coming fiscal year. While this is going on, the Office of Management and Budget (OMB) issues instructions and policy guidance on material to be developed for the spring planning review. Through the latter part of April and all of May, OMB discusses program developments and management issues with the agencies and compares total outlay estimates with revenue estimates. In

June OMB issues technical instructions on the preparation of the annual budget and provides guidance to the agencies in their compilation of detailed estimates. OMB then communicates to agency heads the government-wide policies and assumptions upon which their estimates are to be premised and issues budgetary planning targets to individual agencies. From July through September the agencies develop and compile estimates based on these criteria and submit their formal estimates to OMB. In September, October, and November the agencies submit their budget requests to OMB, which in turn holds hearings on each agency's request and decides whether requests are acceptable. OMB prepares budget recommendations for the President, and in December notifies agency heads of the President's decisions. OMB prepares the budget for submission to Congress and drafts the President's message to accompany the document. The President revises and approves the budget message and transmits the recommended budget to Congress in January.

Passage of the 1974 Congressional Budget and Impoundment Control Act has added other requirements that affect the process, as indicated in Figure 2.2. Two months before the President presents his budget to Congress (November 10), a current services budget must be submitted. This budget estimates the budget authority and outlays required to continue government policies and programs for the coming fiscal year under existing legislation and current economic assumptions. It is intended to provide an estimate of the spending levels required without program changes or new programs, and thus the resources needed for maintaining present program commitments.

The Joint Economic Committee of Congress considers the current services budget and reports on its analysis to the Senate and House budget committees by December 31. After the President has submitted his budget to Congress in late January, the two budget committees begin consideration of a first budget resolution, whose purpose is to set targets for expenditures and resources to guide subsequent congressional budget decisions. After holding hearings, the budget committees prepare the first budget resolution, which must be acted upon by both houses by May 15. Thereafter, from May 15 to September 15, Congress completes action on all budget and spending authority (appropriation) bills. Hearings are held by committees in both houses. Legislative committees and subcommittees must consider bills giving government the authority to act in specific ways—to build a dam, to sell government land, to subsidize farm crops, and so forth. Appropriation committees and subcommittees meet to determine how much money will be spent on such authorized activities. Legislation is then drafted by both legislative and appropriation committees and submitted to the House and Senate for action. Similar actions are taken by revenue committees to authorize the collection of taxes and other forms of revenue.[8]

All of this emerging legislation is constantly monitored by the Congressional Budget Office (CBO) to keep the two houses posted on whether the cumulative dollar value of such proposed actions is remaining within the constraints set by the first budget resolution.

By September 15 each house adopts a second budget resolution to reflect the actions it has taken on the legislative, appropriation, and revenue bills. Another ten days are allowed for reconsideration of disagreements between the two houses. By September 25 the two houses are to reach agreement on a common resolution, which is sent to the

TABLE 2.2. Translating Budgetary Controllability into Potential Discretion

	Classified "uncontrollable" (F/Y 1977 = 77%) **LEAST CONTROLLABLE**			Classified "controllable" (F/Y 1977 = 23%) **MOST CONTROLLABLE**		
Examples:	**Fixed Costs** • interest on national debt • Public Housing loans	**Long-term Contracts** • weapons systems • highway construction	**Payments to States & Individ.** • A.D.C. and welfare programs • social security • Medicare, Medicaid • revenue sharing	**Salaries, Wages and Benefits** • military benefits • civilian salaries	**General Expenses & Operations** • automobiles • supplies • heating and utilities • maintenance	**New Programs, Research & Grants** • cancer, energy research • military procurement • state and local grants for nutrition, health, and education • Amtrak
Approximate Share of Total Budget (A)	12%	18%	47%	14%	5%	4% = 100%

18

How Controlled? (Reduced)

• default	• defer payment in short run	• change authorization • raise recipient costs • reduce eligibility • restrict automatic increases	• hiring freeze—personnel reduction • reduce or defer salary increases • decrease government retirement share	• reduce consumption • defer resupply and maintenance	• cut appropriations • phase down research • terminate project in early stages
Proportion that realistically could be cut in a given year. (P)					
0%	0–2%	5–10%	5–10%	10–20%	25–50%
approximate DISCRETION (A×P)					
0%	0–.4%	2.5–5.0%	.7–1.5%	.5–1.0%	1.0–2.0% = 10%

SOURCE: Lance LeLoup, *Budgetary Politics* (Brunswick, Ohio: Kings Court, 1977), pp. 68–69.

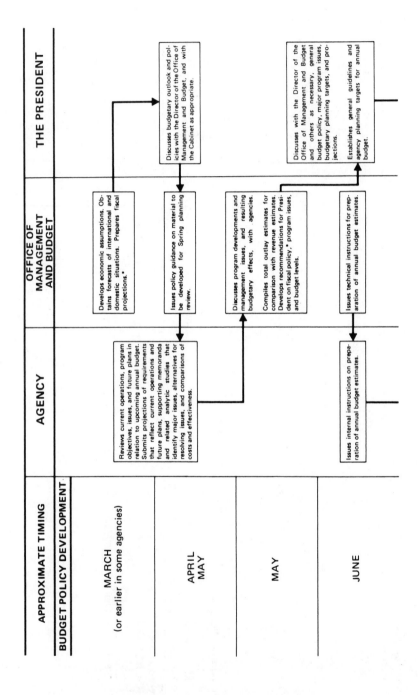

APPROXIMATE TIMING	AGENCY	OFFICE OF MANAGEMENT AND BUDGET	THE PRESIDENT
BUDGET POLICY DEVELOPMENT			
MARCH (or earlier in some agencies)	Reviews current operations, program objectives, issues, and future plans in relation to upcoming annual budget. Submits projections of requirements that reflect current operations and future plans, supporting memoranda and related analytic studies that identify major issues, alternatives for resolving issues, and comparisons of costs and effectiveness.	Develops economic assumptions. Obtains forecasts of international and domestic situations. Prepares fiscal projections.*	
APRIL MAY		Issues policy guidance on material to be developed for Spring planning review.	Discusses budgetary outlook and policies with the Director of the Office of Management and Budget, and with the Cabinet as appropriate.
MAY		Discusses program developments and management issues, and resulting budgetary effects, with agencies. Compiles total outlay estimates for comparison with revenue estimates. Develops recommendations for President on fiscal policy,* program issues, and budget levels.	Discusses with the Director of the Office of Management and Budget and others as necessary, general budget policy, major program issues, budgetary planning targets, and projections.
JUNE	Issues internal instructions on preparation of annual budget estimates.	Issues technical instructions for preparation of annual budget estimates.	Establishes general guidelines and agency planning targets for annual budget.

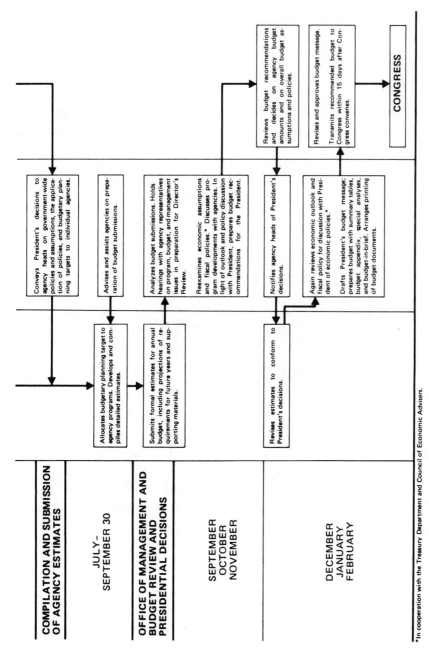

COMPILATION AND SUBMISSION OF AGENCY ESTIMATES

JULY–
SEPTEMBER 30

OFFICE OF MANAGEMENT AND BUDGET REVIEW AND PRESIDENTIAL DECISIONS

SEPTEMBER
OCTOBER
NOVEMBER

DECEMBER
JANUARY
FEBRUARY

Conveys President's decisions to agency heads on government-wide policies and assumptions, the application of policies, and budgetary planning targets to individual agencies.

Advises and assists agencies on preparation of budget submissions.

Analyzes budget submissions. Holds hearings with agency representatives on program, budget, and management issues in preparation for Director's Review.

Reexamines economic assumptions and fiscal policies.* Discusses program developments with agencies. In light of outlook and policy discussion with President, prepares budget recommendations for the President.

Notifies agency heads of President's decisions.

Again reviews economic outlook and fiscal policy for discussion with President of economic policies.*

Drafts President's budget message; prepares budget with summary tables, budget appendix, special analyses, and budget-in-brief. Arranges printing of budget documents.

Allocates budgetary planning target to agency programs. Develops and compiles detailed estimates.

Submits formal estimates for annual budget, including projections of requirements for future years and supporting materials.

Revises estimates to conform to President's decisions.

Reviews budget recommendations and decides on agency budget amounts and on overall budget assumptions and policies.

Reviews and approves budget message. Transmits recommended budget to Congress within 15 days after Congress convenes.

CONGRESS

*In cooperation with the Treasury Department and Council of Economic Advisers.

FIGURE 2.1   Formulation of President's Budget. *(From Office of Management and Budget, 1977)*

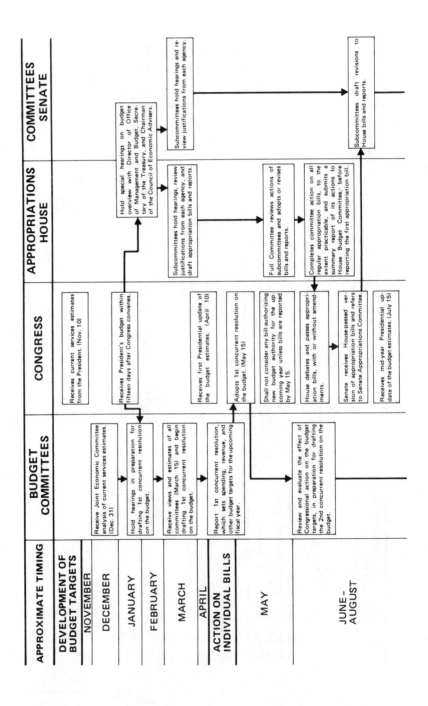

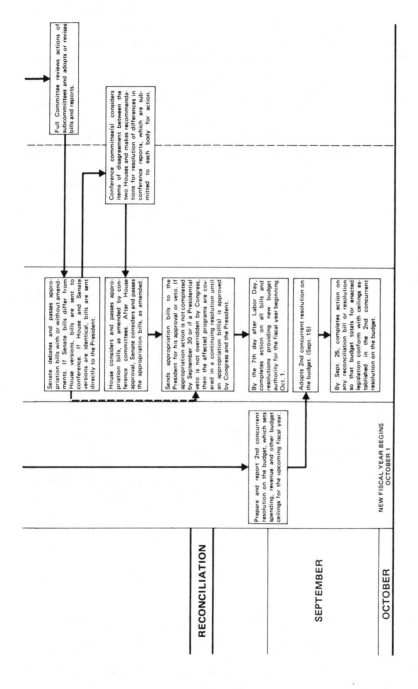

Full Committee reviews actions of subcommittees and adopts or revises bills and reports.

Conference committee(s) considers items of disagreement between the two Houses and makes recommendations for resolution of differences in conference reports, which are submitted to each body for action.

Senate debates and passes appropriation bills with or without amendments. If Senate bills differ from House versions, bills are sent to conference. If House and Senate versions are identical, bills are sent directly to the President.

House considers and passes appropriation bills, as amended by conference committees. After House approval, Senate considers and passes the appropriation bills, as amended.

Sends appropriation bills to the President for his approval or veto. If appropriation action is not completed by September 30 or if a Presidential veto is not overridden by Congress, then the affected programs are covered in a continuing resolution until an appropriation bill(s) is approved by Congress and the President.

By the 7th day after Labor Day, completes action on all bills and resolutions providing new budget authority for the fiscal year beginning Oct. 1.

Adopts 2nd concurrent resolution on the budget. (Sept. 15)

By Sept. 25, completes action on any reconciliation bill or resolution so that budget totals for enacted legislation conform with ceilings established in the 2nd concurrent resolution on the budget.

Prepare and report 2nd concurrent resolution on the budget, which sets spending, revenue and other budget ceilings for the upcoming fiscal year.

RECONCILIATION

SEPTEMBER

OCTOBER

NEW FISCAL YEAR BEGINS
OCTOBER 1

FIGURE 2.2 Congressional Budget Process. *(From Office of Management and Budget, 1977)*

President. When signed by the President, the measure becomes the final budget resolution. If the appropriation measures required to operationalize the resolution are not enacted by October 1, the beginning of the new fiscal year, continuing resolutions must be passed—allowing government agencies to continue spending at their last year's levels—until new appropriations have been enacted. In the absence of such action, the wheels of government come to a grinding halt.

To confuse things further, three budgets are worked on simultaneously: last year's, this year's, and next year's. This situation is even more serious for state governments where the legislature does not remain in session throughout the year. Figure 2.3, for example, depicts this process for Alaska. We see that reporting and auditing on last year's (1976) budget goes on from July to February of the current 1977 fiscal year; while the 1977 budget is being administered and the 1978 budget is being prepared, submitted, and amended. The Alaska budget operates on a July 1 to June 30 fiscal year basis, as do many other state and local governments. Yet some governments operate on a calendar year basis, and others begin and end on still other months of the year. The federal budget, which operated for many years on a July 1 to June 30 cycle, now runs from October 1 to September 30, so as to give Congress more time to consider the budget document submitted to them by the President in January.

The complex decision-making process reflected in the budget cycle has led many scholars to assert that budgetary decisions are made on an incremental basis. As Wildavsky says,

> The beginning of wisdom about an agency budget is that it is almost never actively reviewed as a whole every year in the sense of considering the value of all existing programs as compared to all possible alternatives. Instead, it is based on last year's budget with special attention given to a narrow range of increases or decreases.[9]

More specifically, he asserts that decision strategies in budgeting are all premised on the agency's historical budget base, and involve (1) defending the base: guarding against cuts in the old programs; (2) increasing the base: inching ahead with existing programs; and (3) expanding the base: adding new programs.[10] In a historical study of fifty-six federal agencies over the 1947 to 1963 period, he and two colleagues found that 83 percent of the agencies' budgets deviated by less than 15 percentage points from levels consistent with six decision rules they developed reflecting the above three categories.[11] They consequently concluded that each new budget was primarily an "added on" or incremental change over its predecessor. Sharkansky, Crecine, Gerwin, Hoole, and others have arrived at similar conclusions in studying state, local, school district, and international governments.[12]

Charles Lindblom argues that incremental decision making is inevitable because (1) it is usually not possible to distinguish between means and ends, thereby making means-ends analysis impossible; (2) it is never possible to identify all outcomes and alternative policies for accomplishing results; and (3) good policy is therefore that which various analysts can, for whatever reason, agree upon. Note that these postulates of incrementalism run directly contrary to the assumptions of logic upon which planning and programming are based. If Lindblom is correct, the development of elaborate program-based budgets would seem to be an exercise in futility.

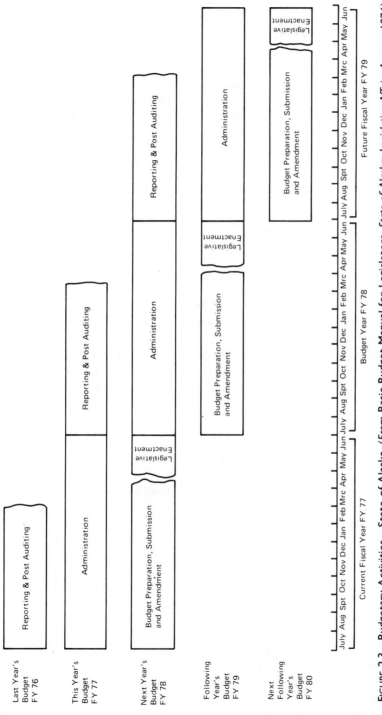

FIGURE 2.3 Budgetary Activities — State of Alaska. (From Basic Budget Manual for Legislators, State of Alaska: Legislative Affairs Agency, 1976)

25

Yet other research studies indicate that the budgetary process may not be as incrementally controlled as Wildavsky and others claim. Natchez and Bupp analyzed Atomic Energy Commission (AEC) budgets covering a fifteen-year period.[13] They found that while the total budget increased on an incremental basis from year to year, significant changes in program priorities were, at the same time, recurring within the total budget. These priorities were not set as national priorities by administrators with national constituencies, but were established "at the operating levels of federal bureaus—by program directors sensitive to their own clienteles."[14] They conclude, therefore, that the incrementalists, by concentrating on the underlying regularities of the administrative process, miss the real policy changes that occur within the total budget. This conclusion is reinforced by John Wanat's historical study of the budgetary process of the Labor Department from 1968 to 1972.[15] Wanat found that total budget incremental increases from year to year in Labor could be explained solely by mandatory expenditure requirements; the department's policy changes occurred in the allocation of discretionary funds—those not frozen by statutory requirements.

As LeLoup has noted, such controllable portions of the budget are not always as controllable as the term implies; on the other hand, not all uncontrollables are beyond some control either (see Table 2.2). The resulting effective control one can exercise over some 10 percent of the budget may not be too unreasonable. If one is to maintain any long-range program stability, it is doubtful that much more than 10 percent of the budget can be open to programmatic change each year.

Thus it would seem that incremental decision making is built into the budget process, but discretion is exercised over a significant enough portion of the budget to allow for planned program change. Moreover, this is not necessarily change over and above base requirements but may actually involve changing the base itself.

SUMMARY

In this chapter the concept of the Executive Budget has been discussed. First the historical development of the budget was considered, tracing the relative roles of local, state, and federal governments in civil expenditures. The factors contributing to the growth of civil expenditures for different functions—health, education, highways, and welfare—were explored.

The decision-making process upon which such decisions are made was then considered. How much of the budget is subject to change? What kinds of expenditures are uncontrollable? The roles played by different executive and legislative actors were identified in the frame of the budget cycle.

Finally, the affect of the budget cycle on decision making was considered. Does the structured character of the budget cycle requirements cause all decisions to be based on incrementalism, or can discretion be exercised such that the budget can be used as an instrument of policy change? The research studies on both sides of this question are summarized, and it is concluded that both incremental and nonincremental decision making occur in the budget process.

NOTES

1. Martha Derthick, "How Easy Votes in Social Security Came to an End," *Public Interest* 54 (Winter 1979): 95.
2. Advisory Commission on Intergovernmental Relations, *Significant Features of Fiscal Federalism, 1979–1980 Edition* (Washington, D.C., M-123, October 1980), p. 4.
3. Ibid., pp. 4 and 6.
4. Henry Owen and Charles Schultze, eds., *Setting National Priorities: The Next Ten Years* (Washington, D.C., Brookings Institution, 1976), p. 379.
5. James A. Maxwell and J. R. Aronson, *Financing State and Local Government* (Washington, D.C.: Brookings Institution, 1977), p. 24.
6. *Bureau of the United States Government*, Fiscal Year 1983 (Washington, D.C.: Government Printing Office, 1982), pp. 6–31 to 6–39.
7. Ibid., pp. 9–46 to 9–47; *Budget of the United States*, Fiscal Year 1976 (Washington, D.C., Government Printing Office, 1975), pp. 354–355.
8. For an in-depth discussion of the congressional role in the budget process, see Dennis Ippolito, *Congressional Spending* (Ithaca: Cornell University Press, 1981).
9. Aaron Wildavsky, *The Politics of the Budgetary Process* (Boston: Little, Brown, 1974), p. 15.
10. Ibid., pp. 102–3.
11. O. A. Davis, M. A. Dempster, and Aaron Wildavsky, "A Theory of the Budgetary Process," *American Political Science Review* 60 (September 1966).
12. Ira Sharkansky, "Agency Requests, Gubenatorial Support and Budget Success in State Legislatures," *American Political Science Review* 62 (December 1968); John Crecine, *Government Problem Solving* (Chicago: Rand McNally, 1969); Donald Gerwin, *Budgeting Public Funds: The Decision Process in an Urban School District* (Madison: University of Wisconsin Press, 1969); Francis Hoole et al., "Incremental Budgeting and International Organizations," *American Journal of Political Science*, May 1976.
13. Peter B. Natchez and Irwin C. Bupp, "Policy and Priority in the Budget Process," *American Political Science Review* 67 (September 1973).
14. Ibid., p. 963.
15. John Wanat, *Introduction to Budgeting* (North Scituate, Mass.: Duxbury Press, 1978).

BIBLIOGRAPHY

Fenno, R. F., Jr. *The Power of the Purse: Appropriation Politics in Congress*. Boston: Little, Brown, 1966.
Fisher, Louis. *Presidential Spending Power*. Princeton: Princeton University Press, 1975.
Haveman, Joel. *Congress and the Budget*. Bloomington: Indiana University Press, 1978.
Ippolito, Dennis S. *Congressional Spending*. Ithaca: Cornell University Press, 1981.
LeLoup, Lance T. *Budgetary Politics*. Brunswick, Ohio: King's Court Communications, 1977.
Maxwell, James H., and Aronson, J. R. *Financing State and Local Government*. Washington D.C.: Brookings Institution, 1977.
Musgrave, Richard A., and Musgrave, P. B. *Public Finance in Theory and Practice*. New York: McGraw-Hill, 1980.
Pfiffner, James P. *The President, The Budget and Congress: Impoundment and the 1974 Budget Act*. Boulder, Colo.: Westview Press, 1979.
Schick, Allen. *Congress and Money*. Washington, D.C.: Urban Institute, 1980.
Wildavsky, Aaron. *The Politics of the Budgetary Process*. Boston: Little, Brown, 1979.

Chapter 3

Fiscal and Economic Budget Perspectives

The Executive Budget, as noted in the previous chapter, focuses on the cost of programs undertaken by government. But the budget must also be assembled in ways that reflect the fiscal and economic implications of such government expenditures. In this chapter attention is directed to perspectives appropriate for viewing the budget as a fiscal instrument and as an economic document. Discussion of the fiscal type of budget is relevant to all levels of government, but is especially critical to an understanding at the state and local levels. At these levels expenditure decisions are much more constrained by revenue and debt considerations than at the federal level. Consequently, the transactional or cash-flow perspective must be kept in mind constantly when formulating and administering the budget. Many of the illustrations used in discussing the Fiscal Budget therefore focus on state and local practices.

THE FISCAL BUDGET

This way of depicting the budget might also be called the treasurer's budget because its rationale centers on the receipt and disbursement of funds over the course of the budget year. Different sources of revenue—taxes, fees, utility billings, and so on—will be received into the Treasury at different times of the year. Receipts from income taxes come in once a year or on a pay-as-you-go basis. Property tax income probably will be paid once a year or, in some cases, twice a year. Sales tax receipts may come in quarterly. Other fees, such as building permits, will vary with the volume and rate of activity being taxed (e.g., housing construction permits).

The disbursement of funds will also occur in spurts and starts over the course of the budget year. Personal services disbursements will vary with turnover and vacancy rates, each of which is also likely to vary considerably from department to department or occupation to occupation, based on the supply and demand requirements of the market. Total payroll costs, on the other hand, may remain fairly constant and predictable for the budget year as a whole. Construction-oriented agencies, like the Corps of Engineers or a state highway department, will also have to anticipate varying construction costs on a seasonal basis.

The Fiscal Budget is thus normally presented on a cash consolidated or income received–bills paid basis. The major cash flow and cash utilization objectives of a Fiscal Budget are, as summarized by Moak and Hillhouse:

1   To have sufficient cash available when it is required. If borrowing is necessary, the need for arrangement of loans can be anticipated in order that the cash proceeds will be on hand when needed.
2   To plan the cash stream so as to minimize and, if possible, to eliminate the necessity for short-term borrowing.
3   To assure that any excess of cash income over cash outgo, not required as a working balance, is temporarily invested. The goal is optimum investment of idle cash and bond proceeds so that investment earnings can make an important contribution to the budget. One test of efficient financial administration is the ability to "put cash to work." The better the cash forecast, the longer the time frame of the investment; the longer the investment, the greater the rate of interest in most circumstances.
4   To schedule the investment of bond proceeds to meet the periodic demands of contractors as construction progresses since bonds must often be sold in full prior to letting the contract.[1]

The provision of a consolidated cash account in the Treasury that involves the comingling of the receipts of various governmental funds into a common bank account greatly facilitates flexible cash flows. Here all revenues are pooled, but records are kept on what the entitlements are of each fund to the cash on hand. The assests of one fund may thus be used temporarily to cover deficits of other member funds. Use of the consolidated cash account must be carefully monitored to ensure that there are always sufficient reserves in a sufficiently liquid state to meet all current needs and that cash loans from one fund to another include interest for the use of the funds.

In the 1940s and '50s trust fund surpluses in the U.S. Treasury were consistently "borrowed," at a given fixed rate of interest, to meet bills coming due in the General Fund account. More recently, as surplusses in some of the trust funds have diminished, CBO director Alice Rivlin has suggested that short-run old age insurance fund deficits could be met on a temporary basis by borrowing from the General Fund or from one of the other trust funds.[2]

But what happens if there is insufficient money in the Treasury to pay all bills when they come due? This contingency must be anticipated and provided for in the Fiscal Budget either by the accumulation of reserves or by engaging in short-term borrowing. The former assumes cashing in funds currently invested or drawing down on cash reserves. The latter involves entering the money market by issuing revenue anticipation notes; that is, funds are borrowed to pay current operating expenses pending the imminent receipt of tax revenues.

Treasury funds, whether one is directing attention to the federal, state, or local level of government, are kept in commercial banks. The U.S. Treasury maintains its account in the Federal Reserve System, state and local governments in one or more commercial

TABLE 3.1. Federal, State, and Local Debt, Selected Years 1929–81

Fiscal Year	Gross Federal Debt	Total State Debt	Total Local Debt	Gross Federal Debt	Total State Debt	Total Local Debt
	Amount (in billions)			*As a Percent of GNP*		
1929	$16.9	$2.3	$14.2	16.9	2.3	14.2
1939	40.4	3.5	16.6	46.1	4.0	18.9
1949	252.8	4.0	16.9	96.6	1.5	6.5
1954	270.8	9.6	29.3	74.5	2.6	8.1
1959	284.7	16.9	47.2	60.4	3.6	10.0
1964	316.8	25.0	67.2	51.4	4.1	10.9
1969	367.1[a]	39.6	94.0	40.6	4.4	10.4
1970	382.6	42.0	101.6	39.8	4.4	10.6
1971	409.5	47.8	111.0	40.2	4.7	10.9
1972	437.3	54.5	120.7	39.3	4.9	10.9
1973	468.4[b]	59.4	129.1	37.8	4.8	10.4
1974	486.2	65.3	141.3	35.8	4.8	10.4
1975	544.1	72.1	149.1	37.5	5.0	10.3
1976	631.9	84.4	155.7	38.9	5.2	9.6
1977	709.1	90.2	167.3	38.0	5.1	9.4
1978	780.4	102.6	117.9	37.4	5.1	8.8
1979	833.8	111.7	192.4	35.4	4.9	8.4
1980	914.3	122.0	213.6	35.6	4.8	8.5
1981 Est.	995.1	135.5	235.0	34.9	4.8	8.5
	Percent Distribution			*Annual Percent Change*[c]		
1929	50.6	6.9	42.5	—	—	—
1939	66.8	5.8	27.4	9.1	4.3	1.6
1949	92.4	1.5	6.2	20.1	1.3	0.2
1954	87.4	3.1	9.5	1.4	19.1	11.6
1959	81.6	4.8	13.5	1.0	11.9	10.0
1964	77.5	6.1	16.4	2.2	8.1	7.3
1969	73.3	7.9	18.8	3.0	9.6	6.9
1970	72.7	8.0	19.3	4.2	6.1	8.1
1971	72.1	8.4	19.5	7.0	13.8	9.3
1972	71.4	8.9	19.7	6.8	14.0	8.7
1973	71.3	9.0	19.7	7.1	9.0	7.0
1974	70.2	9.4	20.4	3.8	9.9	9.5
1975	71.1	9.4	19.5	11.9	10.4	5.5
1976	72.5	9.7	17.9	16.1	17.1	4.4
1977	73.4	9.3	17.3	12.3	6.9	7.5
1978	73.6	9.7	16.8	10.1	13.7	6.3
1979	73.3	9.8	16.9	6.8	8.9	8.2
1980	73.1	9.8	17.1	9.7	9.2	11.0
1981 Est.	73.0	9.8	17.2	8.8	9.4	10.0

SOURCE: ACIR staff compilation based on U.S. Bureau of the Census, *Governmental Finances*, various years; Office of Management and Budget, *Special Analysis, Budget of the United States Government, 1982*; U.S. Treasury Department, *Treasury Bulletin*, July 1981; and ACIR staff estimates.

[a] During 1969, three government-sponsored enterprises became completely privately owned, and their debt was removed from the totals for the federal government. At the dates of their conversion, gross federal debt was reduced $10.7 billion.

[b] A procedural change in the recording of trust fund holdings of Treasury debt at the end of the month increased gross federal debt by about $4.5 billion.

[c] The percent changes indicated for years prior to 1970 are annual average changes since the previous year shown.

banks located within their respective jurisdictions. The cost of short-run borrowing depends on the going rate of interest in the money market, although the Federal Reserve has some limited control over the availability of credit and consequently of the cost of borrowing.

In recent years a large proportion of the national debt has been held in short-term loan instruments—Treasury bills, certificates, and notes—which are marketable and can consequently be bought and sold readily, at rediscount rates, to cover short-term needs. Other short-term loan instruments, such as those issued by the National Mortgage Association, the Home Loan Banks, and Federal Land Banks, are also frequently available. At the state and local levels short-term needs may be met, as noted earlier, by the issuance of tax anticipation notes.

The operation of the Fiscal Budget needs to be closely monitored, a fact clearly evidenced by New York City's fiscal crisis in 1975. Not that New York City was not warned. The Advisory Commission on Intergovernmental Relations (ACIR) issued a report in 1973, after surveying the financial health of thirty major U. S. cities.[3] According to their report, "the most important single factor in throwing a city into financial crisis is its inability to pay off short-term loans that accumulate over a period of several years."[4] The report identified six "warning signs" to help cities spot fiscal trouble:[5]

1   An imbalance of revenues and expenditures in operating funds
2   A pattern of current expenditures exceeding current revenues by small amounts over several years
3   An excess of current operating liabilities over current assets
4   Outstanding short-term debt at the end of the fiscal year
5   A high and rising (1 percent or more) rate of delinquency on property tax payments
6   A sudden substantial decline in assessed values

F. John Shannon, ACIR's assistant director for taxation and finance, has said that several of these warning signs "were clearly there as far as New York City was concerned."[6]

The Fiscal Budget is concerned with the management of long-term as well as short-term debt. Total government debt reached $1.365 trillion in 1981; 71.9 percent was federal debt and the remaining 27 percent state and local government debt. In aggregate amount, government debt has been growing rapidly since 1929. But the proportion of the annual GNP consumed by government debt has been declining since 1949. As Table 3.1 indicates, the proportional decline in government debt has been due to the federal debt increasing at a slower rate than the GNP since 1949. State and local debt has continued to consume a relatively consistent proportion of the GNP since 1964. Thus, although the magnitude of total government debt in 1981 seems to be staggering, it must be viewed in terms of an economy that produced a gross national product in that year of nearly $3 trillion.

This is not to suggest that government debt should be ignored. Congress consistently sets ceilings on the federal debt, and most states have established constitutional or legislative controls over their local governments. State controls, however, frequently tend to constrain attempts to develop good debt management in local governments. These limits are usually based on assessed property values in the jurisdiction; that is a

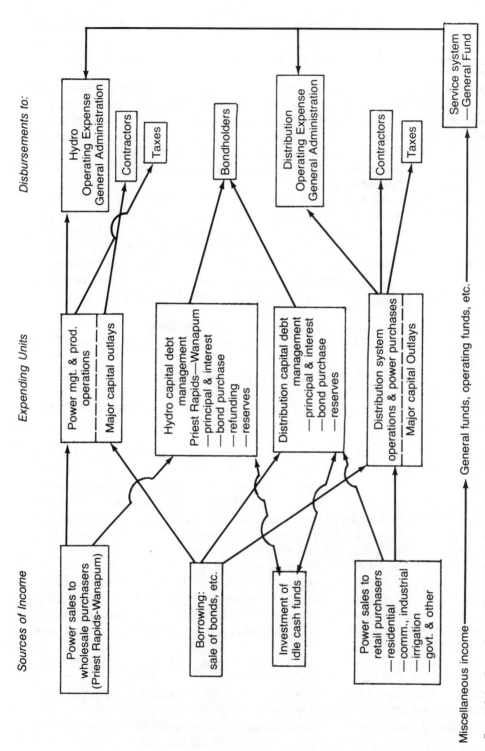

Sources of Income   Expending Units   Disbursements to:

FIGURE 3.1   Grant County Public Utility District Financial System: Fund Flows. *(From George A. Shipman and Fremont J. Lyden, Design for the Future, Ephrata, Wisc.: Grant County, Public Utility District, 1972)*

local government may borrow up to an amount equal to a certain percentage of the value of its assessed property. This method of debt control has its origins in the 1850s when local governments were simple and communities were more homogeneous than they are today. Tax experts have long recommended that the measurement base be shifted from property values to the revenue potential of the borrower.[7] While such a change would certainly represent an improvement, the local debt situation has become too complex to be controlled safely and effectively by formalized debt limits. A more rigorous analytical approach to the problem should be developed, which would give consideration to the varying characteristics of local governments in terms of their revenue-generating capacities, the economic stability of their environments, the cumulative debt burden incurred by overlapping jurisdictions, the possibility of phasing spending programs so as to maximize economic impact on the local economy and so forth.[8] The machinery for administering such an ambitious program does not exist in most jurisdictions. The ACIR report on the financial health of cities discussed earlier in the chapter does recommend the creation of a state agency responsible for monitoring and improving local financial management functions. Such an agency could certainly administer a local debt-control program.

What should be kept in mind when visualizing the Fiscal Budget is the cash flow of funds: from the sources of income available, to the expending units, to the recipients of disbursed funds. Figure 3.1 is a funds flow depiction of a public utility district (PUD) in the State of Washington. This special district government generates hydroelectric power, distributes electric power throughout the county, and sells the remainder to other customers in Washington, Oregon, California, and elsewhere. The PUD receives no tax revenues; all of its income must come from power sales, borrowing, and investment of idle cash funds. Bonds are sold for capital improvements in power generation (hydro capital debt) and power distribution facilities (distribution capital debt). The hydro debt has provisions for refunding; and so the market on such issues is monitored, with repurchases made when the market price drops below par. An active balanced investment program is monitored for all reserves.

Checking accounts are maintained in banks throughout the county for the disbursement of funds to vendors, employees (both covered under operating expense), contractors, tax collectors, and so forth, as indicated in Figure 3.1. Savings accounts are also maintained in the same banks. Weekly transfers are made of any excess balance in checking accounts to the interest-bearing savings accounts. By constructing a funds flow chart such as the one depicted in Figure 3.1, it is possible to identify how revenues, expenditures, and borrowing may be planned in the Fiscal Budget with some assurance that funds will be available when needed and at the lowest operating cost possible.

THE ECONOMIC BUDGET

The Economic Budget is the macroeconomic budget. It is constructed so as to show what part of the gross national product is used by households, businesses, governments, and the rest of the world (i.e., sources outside of the American economy). Prior to the Great Depression of the 1930s, little consideration was given to the question of macroeconomics. It was assumed that the laws of supply and demand would operate to maintain economic stability. There were, of course, upturns and downturns in business activity, which led to periods of business failures and unemployment. But, it was assumed, the demand-supply requirements of the market could be counted on to reverse these circumstances before long. Government's effect on the operation of the economy was viewed as negligible.

Then the depression arrived. People waited for the recovery, but it failed to come. Some economists urged that government spending be used as pump priming. Inject just enough government funds into the economy to get production moving again; then back off and let the market law of supply and demand take over again. John Maynard Keynes, an English economist, argued that such governmental action was useless. He asserted that recessions occur because of an economy's failure to consume all that it produces. Business produces goods and services, paying out wages, rentals, and profits in exchange for the resources needed to produce such goods and services. Persons receiving these wages, rentals, and profits use this income to purchase the goods and services produced. As long as all that is produced is purchased, business continues to produce. But if some income is not spent or if some goods are not sold, a surplus of goods already produced leads to a cutback in the production of goods and services for the future. With less production, fewer employees will be needed, less capital equipment will need to be maintained, and so on. With less income, consumers will be able to buy even less of the goods and services being produced, resulting in a further cutback in production. This action will result in even less income to consumers and the production cutback spiral continues:

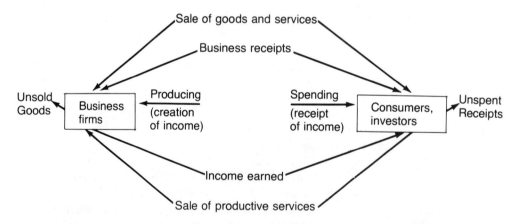

The only way this kind of spiral could be reversed, according to Keynes, was for "someone" to step in and inject monies into the economy sufficient to compensate for the unspent receipts and unsold goods. This could be accomplished by government spending. But unlike pump priming, the role of government here would be a continuing one, compensating for whatever the spending deficiencies were in the economy.

In some instances, of course, consumers and investors will try to spend more than they receive for producing current goods and services. When this occurs, they will dissave (buy on credit), which will raise the prices of existing goods and services. The result will be inflation. In this situation government can compensate for the imbalance by removing some of the consumer's effective purchasing power through tax increases or spending cuts. Thus, compensating theory would have the government (1) increase government spending and decrease taxes during periods of recession and unemployment, and (2) decrease government spending and increase taxes during periods of inflation.

Government certainly does have the ability to influence the operation of the rest of the economy. Table 3.2 shows that the percent of the gross national product *purchased* by federal, state, and local governments has not changed much since 1954. If one looks, however, at what percent of the GNP is *consumed* by government, the proportion has been rising steadily from 25 percent in 1950 to 35 percent in 1977. Thus the relative role of government in the economy has not been changing through the purchases it makes, but in terms of its other expenditures. Growth in these other expenditures, as may be noted in Figure 3.2, has occurred primarily in terms of transfer payments from the federal government to individuals (e.g., social security benefits, veterans pensions, unemployment compensation), grants to state and local governments (e.g., general revenue sharing, block grants, categorical grants), and aggregate expenditures of state and local governments.

Since the passage of the Employment Act of 1946 and the resulting creation of the Council of Economic Advisers, federal decision makers have become increasingly sensitive to the need for monitoring the economy and for instituting compensatory policies and automatic fiscal stabilizers to anticipate and alleviate economic dislocations.

State and local governments have not shown a comparable interest in the concept of the Economic Budget, primarily because their ability to borrow is severely restricted, they lack the tools of monetary policy available to the federal government, and they cannot engage in planned deficits for fiscal purposes. In recent years, though, they have been significantly affected by the countercyclical actions taken by the federal government. In 1974 Congress enacted a countercyclical public service employment program (CETA, Title VI) for state and local governments. Intended as antirecession aid, the legislation provided money only when the national unemployment rate reached at least 6 percent. Many local governments welcomed the additional revenue, but when the na-

TABLE 3.2. Government (federal, state and local) Purchases and Expenditures as Percent of GNP, Selected Years 1950–77

Year	Percent of GNP Purchases	Percent of GNP Expenditures
1950	14	24
1954	21	25
1958	21	26
1962	21	28
1966	21	28
1970	22	31
1974	22	31
1977	21	35

SOURCE: *ECM Report of the President* (Washington, D.C.: GPO, January 1978).

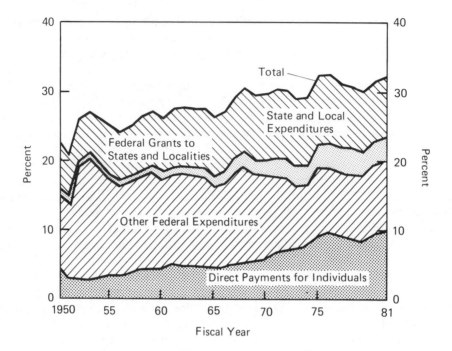

FIGURE 3.2   Government Expenditures as a Percent of GNP. (*From* Special
Analysis G, Budget of the United States, Fiscal Year 1983)

NOTE: The ending dates on several activities may vary. For example, the liability for audit
for some programs may extend for many years after a fiscal year ends. The reporting
requirement may vary by individual program.

tional unemployment rate fell below 6 percent in 1978, they had become so dependent on
this source of income that the loss of CETA funds posed a major financial problem. "It is
disastrous," said John Heim, Buffalo's Commissioner of Administration and Finance.
"Without doubt, our single most agonizing problem is how to cope with this loss."[9] Over
the previous two and a half years over $3 billion in antirecession financial assistance had
been distributed to state and local governments. It is easy to absorb such funds in the
downturn of the business cycle but difficult to part with them when conditions improve
and such income has been institutionalized into the budgets of local governments.

Compensatory policies began to draw increased critics in the 1970s as unemployment
and inflation both increased at the same time. How does one compensate for such a
condition? Keynesian economists argued that compensatory politics were still applicable,
but the economy had been subjected to a series of externally induced crises—the OPEC
oil embargo, world grain shortages, international monetary devaluations—in the 1970s,
which had temporarily interfered with the normal production-spending habits of the
domestic economy. The monetary theorists, led by Milton Friedman, replied that the
unemployment-inflation situation may well be the result of following the compensatory
policies of Keynes. By underestimating the number of transactions generated by the
government expenditures fed into the economy, the Keynesians had injected more pur-

chasing power into the economy than its productive capacity could handle. The result: inflation. To solve this problem, the monetarists proposed tax increases, reduced government spending, and a return to a balanced budget. Eventually government fiscal policies (compensatory spending and taxing) would be replaced by monetary tools (i.e., control over the volume and use of money in circulation). Few politicians found such a solution attractive, since it involved tolerating extended periods of high unemployment and low business growth before governments' diminished role would facilitate the operation of monetary policy. Consequently, governments continue to experiment with the use of both compensatory and monetary policies hoping that some combination of the two will yield the magic formula.

With the election of Ronald Reagan to the Presidency, supply-side economics made its entrance onto the policy scene. Supply-side economists—such as Laffer,[10] Gilder,[11] and Wanniski[12]—argue that our present economic woes are not the result of an inadequate demand for goods and services in the market, as the Keynesians tell us. On the contrary, our present difficulties stem from an inadequate supply of goods resulting from the siphoning of resources away from the production process to feed the expanding service programs of government.

A continual decline in the productivity of the American economy is cited as the consequence of this practice. Indeed, when compared with the productivity levels achieved by other developed industrial nations (see Table 3.3), the American economy has performed poorly in recent years. The solution to this problem, according to Reaganomics, is to cut government spending and reduce taxes. Such action, it is argued, will free up resources for increased private investment in capital facilities and thereby lead to increased production.

Although supply-side economics is espoused by only a minority of the members of the economics profession, increasing numbers of economists are beginning to question the applicability of the reigning Keynesian paradigm. Martin Feldstein suggests that economists have become so mesmerized by the Keynesian explanation that few have examined its premises in the light of current, as contrasted with 1930's, conditions.[13] For example, during the Great Depression, Feldstein argues, established family breadwinners were without jobs for long periods of time. In contrast, in 1979 the unemployed were typically young, had not lost their previous job (but were youngsters looking for their first job or were returning to the work force after a period when they were neither

TABLE 3.3 International Comparison of Manufacturing Productivity (average annual growth in output per hour, 1950–79)

	1950–79	1950–67	1967–73	1973–77	1977–78	1978–79
United States	2.4	2.6	2.9	2.2	0.5	1.5
Japan	8.5	9.5	10.0	4.2	7.9	8.3
Canada	3.9	4.1	5.1	4.8	4.7	0.8
France	5.2	4.9	6.1	5.1	4.9	5.4
West Germany	5.7	6.1	5.3	5.0	3.4	5.2
Italy	6.0	6.4	7.2	3.3	3.0	2.2
United Kingdom	2.7	3.0	4.2	0.6	1.2	2.2

SOURCE: *U.S. Bureau of Labor Statistics.*

working nor looking for work), and were unemployed for very short periods of time (most of them for four weeks or less). Also, during the Great Depression there was little concern with stimulating capital plant development since much unused capital plant capacity existed. In contrast, today America's capital plant is old and outmoded, much of it in need of replacement.

While supply-side economics may or may not provide the basis for constructing a new economic paradigm more applicable to contemporary society, it has certainly served the purpose of questioning the appropriateness of all currently propounded economic dogmas. Until something better comes along, the pragmatic use of "what works" will undoubtedly continue to be the primary guide for governmental decision making.

THE DESIRE FOR FISCAL CONSTRAINT

Even before Reaganomics, double-digit inflation raised the battle cry for fiscal constraint at all levels of government. In July 1978 a national Gallup poll found that 81 percent of the respondents favored a constitutional amendment requiring Congress to balance the budget every year. By March of 1979, 29 of the necessary 34 states had approved some form of resolution asking Congress to call a constitutional convention for the purpose of proposing such an amendment.[14] Many states placed restraints on the growth of property taxes or provided tax relief for taxpayers on fixed incomes. California's Proposition 13 placing a constitutional limitation on property taxes led the way; but in the same year, 1978, eight other states enacted constitutional amendments to limit the taxing or spending power of state and/or local government.[15] In 1979 Michigan adopted one of the tightest constitutional lids in the country, the Headlee Amendment. It applies to both state and local governments and can be lifted only when a majority of qualified voters approve.[16]

Federal, state, and local governments were all attempting to exercise tight controls over their budgets. Consequently, an almost bewildering array of proposals was being debated in legislative chambers across the country, some aimed at expenditure controls, others at tax controls, still others at developing a balanced budget. In view of the many different ways explored in this and the previous chapter for viewing a budget, each way quite valid from a particular policy perspective, it would seem obvious that the concept of a balanced budget would be difficult to define to everyone's satisfaction. Even if one could reach such agreement, it is even more doubtful that a budget could in fact be kept in balance over time. Senator Edmund Muskie has observed, for example, that a mere 1 percent increase in unemployment would automatically (without congressional action) cost the U.S. Treasury $20 billion in lost revenues and increased welfare cost.[17] Inflation also affects outlays for many programs. Thirty percent of all outlays from the federal budget are for entitlement programs (e.g., social security, civil service retirement) that are explicitly indexed to inflation. Outlays for these indexed programs increase by $1.9 billion for each 1 percent increase in the Consumer Price Index (CPI).[18] For these and other reasons, forecasting deficits in advance has become a perilous occupation. In Table 3.4 the deficits estimated in January each year from 1975 to 1981 are shown and compared with the actual deficits incurred during each of those years. Thus in 1975 a $34.7 billion deficit was forecast in the budget; the actual deficit for the year was $43.6. In 1980

TABLE 3.4. Estimates of Future Budget Deficits (in billions of dollars)

Estimate for Fiscal Year	Estimate Published in January of:							Actual Deficit
	1975	1976	1977	1978	1979	1980	1981	
1975	−34.7							−43.6
1976	−51.9	−76.0						−66.5
1977	−30.6	−43.0	−57.2					−45.0
1978	−19.6	−22.8	−47.0	−61.8				−48.8
1979	0.4	9.6	−11.6	−60.6	−37.4			−27.7
1980	25.0	40.6	13.4	−37.5	−29.0	−39.8		−59.6
1981		75.5	26.1	8.6	−1.2	−15.8	−55.2	−57.9
1982			28.6	45.2	37.8	4.8	−27.5	
1983				76.2	72.7	24.5	−8.0	
1984					106.5	81.6	32.0	
1985						158.6	84.7	
1986							138.2	

SOURCE: *Budget of the U.S. Government*, Fiscal Years 1976 to 1983. Estimated surplus expressed as positive numbers.

a deficit of $39.8 billion was projected. The actual deficit turned out to be $59.6 billion. Long-range predictions were, of course, even less accurate. In 1976 it was estimated that the budget would have a $40.6 billion surplus in 1980; in fact, a $59.6 billion deficit was incurred in 1980.[19] To maintain a balanced budget under such volatile economic circumstances would require heavy overtaxing and the maintenance of large working balances in the Treasury.

How, then, is one to evaluate all these possible approaches to fiscal constraint? Shannon and Wallin have developed a classification scheme for categorizing each of these different approaches based upon the different strategies that could be taken for politically implementing them.[20] In Table 3.5 we see that current policies (i.e., moderate tax reductions, slowdowns in government expenditures, gradual reductions in government deficits) are classified as Ad Hoc Adjustments. A more systematic set of control strategies would involve the use of Indirect Statutory means. Income taxes could be indexed (i.e., standard deductions and personal exemptions could be readjusted at the same rate as changes in the price level) to counter the effects of inflation. On the expenditure side, sunset legislation could be passed, requiring Congress to evaluate the effectiveness of all existing programs periodically and to eliminate those failing to pass the test. In fact, 35 states already have passed some form of sunset legislation. Since 1976 a total of 1500 agencies have been reviewed under the sunset process. Almost one out of every five agencies has been terminated, one in three modified and less than one-half recreated with little or no change. In a recent survey conducted by Common Cause, 23 of the 35 states reported increased government efficiency and public accountability as benefits resulting from sunset legislation.[21] Problems were reported also, of course. One-half of the states complained that sunset reviews were too time-consuming. Many states lacked adequate measurement information on agency performance; over half of them indicated that lack of measurement information has been a major problem.

An even more rigorous strategy for exercising fiscal constraints would be to resort to Direct Statutory controls, limiting taxes or expenditures to some specific percentage of

TABLE 3.5. A Classification of Various Proposals for Introducing Greater Fiscal Restraint at the Federal Level

Type of Restraint (Fiscal Policies)	Character Of Restraint (Political Implementation Strategies)			
	Ad Hoc Adjustments (Current Policy) IA	Indirect Statutory Controls (Strengthened Political Accountability) IB	Direct Statutory Controls IC	Direct Constitutional Controls Subject to Extraordinary Majority Rule ID
Income Tax Controls	Ad hoc moderate tax reductions.	Indexation to prevent unlegislated tax rate increase due to inflation.[a]	Statutory income tax limits tied to specified percentages of a national income measure (Kemp-Roth and Jarvis tax proposals)	Income tax collections tied to specified percentages of a national income measure, unless restrictions lifted with *extraordinary majority* approval in both houses.
	IIA	IIB	IIC	IID
Expenditure Controls	Slowdown in expenditure growth—no major new initiatives, most existing programs funded at current service levels. Some program reductions.	"Sunset" legislation that requires Congress to evaluate systematically the effectiveness of existing programs.[a]	Statutory spending limits tied to specified percentages of a national income measure (Kemp-Roth and Jarvis tax proposals).	Expenditures tied to specified percentages of a national income measure, unless restriction lifted with *extraordinary majority* approval in both houses (National Tax Limitations Committee proposal).
	IIIA	IIIB	IIIC	IIID
Balanced Budget Controls	A gradual reduction in budget deficits.	If President and Budget Committees submit unbalanced budgets, they must also submit balanced budget alternatives (Long Amendment).[b]	Statutory mandate for balanced budget (Dole proposal)	Deficits prohibited unless approved by *extraordinary majority vote* in both houses (Most common of the Constitutional proposals).[c]

SOURCE: John Shannon and Bruce Wallin, "Restraining the Federal Budget: Alternative Policies and Strategies," *Intergovernmental Perspective* 5, no. 2 (Spring 1979): 9. From ACIR staff analysis.

NOTE: Moving from left to right, the restraints become more restrictive or more difficult to alter or both.

[a] ACIR recommendation.

[b] Public Law 96-5—beginning with the fiscal year 1981, Congress must consider a balanced budget resolution.

[c] Certain proposals for amending the Constitution are even more restrictive—S.J. Res. 18 (Sen. Thurmond) also contains a provision for repayment of the national debt; S.J. Res. 16 (Sen. Wallop) requires that revenues after the third year exceed expenditures by at least 5% for the next 20 years.

the national income. For example, the Louisiana, Oregon, Utah, and Washington legislatures all passed laws in 1979 limiting state spending to the growth rate of personal income in the state.[22] One could ensure that such constraints could not be ignored by a legislative body by writing them into the Constitution and providing that they could be overridden only by an extraordinary vote of both houses.

Almost all of these strategies would impede or prevent the use of compensatory or anticyclical tools of fiscal policy. Yet, unless the Ad Hoc Adjustments indicated in Table 3.5 result in returning lost purchasing power to the taxpayer, it is probable that legislators will be forced to consider more direct means—statutory or constitutional—of accomplishing fiscal constraints.

SUMMARY

In this chapter the philosophies underlying the fiscal and economic perspectives of the budget have been discussed. The Fiscal Budget centers on the cash flow of funds—how budgets are financed within the monetary world. The Economic Budget focuses on the impact of public actions on the operation of the rest of the economy. Since the Great Depression, government has assumed increased responsibility for insuring continued employment and economic growth in the economy. While the economic dogmas upon which such public policies are based have changed over time, the responsibility for stable economic conditions continues to be a preoccupation of government. And the budget continues to be a major instrument for accomplishing such public policy direction.

CASE STUDY

A case study is presented at this point to illustrate how the fiscal and economic perspectives discussed in this chapter enter into the dynamics of the political decision making process. Since there is little agreement among professional economists about which economic philosophy best describes how the economy operates, there is little likelihood that an "objective" report can be produced that will be accepted with equal confidence by all political decision makers. Consequently, the question arises as to what the appropriate role of the economic adviser should be in the decision-making process. One way of grasping the significance of this question is to examine the problems that arose in this respect when the Council of Economic Advisers was created. The case that follows describes how the Council role evolved in the national political environment. The reader should give consideration to the following questions: Should the Chief Executive and the legislature each have its own economic advisers? If so, how can one give any professional credence to any economist's interpretation or prediction of economic behavior? Could consultants outside of government (university professors or nonprofit researchers) act as economic advisers in a more neutral sense? Why or why not? How can economic advice on the operation of the Economic of Fiscal Budget be related to the programmatic decisions required in the development of the Executive Budget?

CASE STUDY

The President's Economic Advisers

Corinne Silverman

IN 1946, in accordance with the Employment Act passed that year, three economists were named members of the Council of Economic Advisers and installed in the Executive Office of the President. Their principal duty was to advise President Truman on economic matters and to prepare reports which the President would consider in drawing up his annual economic message to the Congress now required by the new act.

As the CEA began its work, there were many who hoped it would strengthen the quality and rationality of economic decision-making in the government by injecting at the White House level the advice of three professional economists. The three men who were appointed to inaugurate the CEA had similar hopes, but they soon found themselves confronted with procedural problems which raised questions about the extent to which, and the manner by which, professional expertise can be effectively incorporated in the making of major policy decisions in a political democracy.

The three economists differed on some major economic policy matters. This made it harder for them to resolve their difference on one of the important procedural problems they confronted. This was the question of whether the three CEA members should testify before congressional committees on economic matters after they had rendered advice privately to the President. Was their role solely that of privy adviser to the chief executive or should they also serve as advocates of the policies he finally decided to pursue? If the President ignored his advice, was a CEA member nevertheless obliged to support White House policies at congressional hearings at the expense of his professional conscience? How neutral and confidential could a professional adviser of the President be and still exercise effective influence on policy-making within the executive branch and in the governmental process as a whole?

The three economists who faced these issues were Edwin G. Nourse, Leon H. Keyserling, and John B. Clark.[1] As the first members of the CEA they were conscious that their actions would set precedents for their successors. This case study describes their actions and then goes on to show how their first successor under the Eisenhower administration—Arthur F. Burns—attempted to resolve the same problems in 1953-1954.

The Employment Act of 1946

As the Second World War drew to a close, many economists of all types—government officials, labor union and trade association economists, bank advisers, and academicians—issued predictions of a postwar depression. The general tenor of their analyses, which were accepted in the main by government officials, was that the layoffs from defense plants, disappearance of overtime wages, and the unemployment of returning veterans, would result in a sharp fall in personal incomes. This in turn would restrict consumer purchasing power and result in a business spiral into depression. Predictions of unemployment ranged from 8,000,000 to the Federal Reserve Bulletin's 20,000,000.[2] It was in this atmosphere that the Employment Act was debated and passed, becoming law on February 20, 1946. The congressmen sponsoring the bill saw it as a means of asserting the responsibility of government to promote full employment. They hoped that one of the long-run results of the Act would be an unprecedented peacetime total of 60,000,000 jobs.

[1] This case was reviewed by the three members of the first Council of Economic Advisers. Some of their comments appear as footnotes to the text.

[2] *Keyserling comments:* "I think you should add that there were some economists who did not expect large unemployment after World War II, and that I was among them."

ICP Case Series number 48. Copyright © 1959 by the Inter-University Case Program. Reprinted by permission.

However, the economists' predictions soon proved wrong. There was an unexpectedly smooth transition from wartime to peacetime production. By May 1946 total employment had risen to 55,000,000 from the war-end level of 52,000,000. Only 2,000,000 were unemployed. Consumers rushed to buy the cars, houses, and washing machines they had been waiting for. It appeared that a major postwar economic problem was not to be unemployment but inflation.

But the Employment Act was by no means obsolete. The Act had been cast in a larger frame than guaranteeing full or maximum employment. It had been conceived fundamentally as an expression of a new consensus about government responsibility for the economy—a consensus achieved after the debates and trials-and-errors of the thirties.

The Act had received much of its support in Congress because few disagreed with its basic premises: first, that the country could not afford, nor would public opinion accept, another great depression; and second, that positive government action could and should prevent extended periods of economic distress. Debate in Congress had centered on the more difficult questions of when the government should take action, how much government action was possible or desirable, and what kinds of policies would be effective in which situations.

The final declaration of policy of the Employment Act was a cumbersome sentence of over 100 words, riddled with many qualifications resulting from legislative compromises:

> The Congress hereby declares that it is the continuing policy and responsibility of the Federal Government to use all practicable means consistent with its needs and obligations and other essential considerations of national policy, with the assistance and cooperation of industry, agriculture, labor, and state and local governments to coordinate and utilize all its plans, functions, and resources for the purpose of creating and maintaining, in a manner calculated to foster and promote free competitive enterprise and the general welfare, conditions under which there will be afforded useful employment opportunities, including self-employment for those able, willing, and seeking to work, and to promote maximum employment, production, and purchasing power.
>
> *(Public Law 304, 79th Congress, Sec. 2)*

Apart from the underlying thesis that the federal government was to assume some kind of responsibility for the economic health of the country, this declaration of policy was all things to all people—and indeed the Employment Act passed the Senate unanimously. Those interested in fostering government planning read in loud tones the phrase which enjoined the government to "coordinate and utilize all its plans, functions and resources. . . ." Those who tended more to laissez-faire saw in italics the phrase " . . . in a manner calculated to foster and promote free competitive enterprise. . . ." What the role of the government was to be under the Act would emerge only from the way in which the purposes of the new legislation were carried out.

The New Obligations of the Federal Government

Although the Act was ambiguous as to the scope and nature of the new policy obligations of the government, it was clear about the machinery to be established. The Act called upon the President to present an annual Economic Report to Congress in addition to the traditional State of the Union and Budget messages. It also established the Council of Economic Advisers in the Executive Office of the President, and a Joint Committee on the Economic Report in the Congress. The Joint Committee was to receive the President's economic message and to report to the House and Senate its own recommendations on each of the major proposals in the President's message.

The Council's principal tasks were to assist the President in drawing up his new annual message, to advise him on economic trends, to appraise current economic policies, and to develop and to recommend to the President national economic policies. The Council was also to collect from existing governmental agencies statistical information on economic developments and trends.

There had been considerable debate in Congress on whether a separate Council was desirable. The Treasury Department already reported directly to the President on the state of the economy and recommended fiscal policies. The Bureau of the Budget also reported to the

President on the effect of current and proposed economic policies, including the impact on the economy of the total federal budget. However, neither of the two agencies wished the other to be designated as the top adviser and co-ordinator of economic policies, and so a separate Council of Economic Advisers was established.

In the next year or two the Executive Office of the President was to be expanded further by the creation, for example, of the National Security Council and the re-location in the Executive Office of the Joint Chiefs of Staff. But the Council of Economic Advisers had to break new ground in deciding whether it would act solely as privy adviser to the President with no dealings with Congress on policy issues, or whether it would follow the example of the Bureau of the Budget. The Bureau was also part of the Executive Office,[3] but it had a single head and its director had always worked closely with congressional committees and testified at congressional hearings in support of presidential policies.

The Members of the Council

The Employment Act was passed in February 1946. President Truman offered positions on the Council to a number of economists, but it was not until July 25, 1946 that he received three acceptances. Edwin G. Nourse accepted the position of Chairman, Leon H. Keyserling became Vice Chairman, and John D. Clark filled the third place. The Act did not specifically invest the Chairman with any extra powers or duties. None of the three had met before being nominated to the Council.

Edwin G. Nourse was then 63. He had taught at a number of universities until 1923 when he became associated with The Brookings Institution, a non-profit research foundation in Washington. He became director of Brookings'

[3] The Executive Office of the President may be divided into (1) the President and his personal staff, and (2) the other more formal agencies such as the Bureau of the Budget and the CEA. Traditionally, there is a confidential relationship between the President and his personal staff. Unlike CEA appointments, the President's appointments of his personal staff aides and of the Director of the Bureau of the Budget do not require Senate confirmation.

Institute of Economics in 1929, and was vice president of The Brookings Institution at the time his appointment to CEA was announced. He had served as president of the American Farm Economic Association in 1924 and of the American Economic Association in 1942, and he had been chairman of the Social Science Research Council from 1942 to 1945. He was generally regarded as middle-of-the-road to conservative. Politically, Nourse claimed he was "non-political" and "non-partisan." His father had been a member of the Prohibition Party, and Nourse himself had voted only twice in presidential elections, once for a Republican and once for a Democrat. (Since the 1920s, as a resident of the District of Columbia, he had been unable to vote.)

John D. Clark, then 62, was generally considered to be the most conservative of the three. He had had a rather unusual career, starting as a lawyer, at one time serving as counsel for the Midwest Refining Company. Then he became vice president of Standard Oil of Indiana. Successful in business, he decided to turn to teaching. He resigned from Standard Oil, returned to college, and received a Ph.D. in economics in 1931. He taught economics for ten years at the University of Denver and at the University of Nebraska, and then he became dean of the College of Business Administration at the University of Nebraska. Sandwiched between these academic posts was a short stint as a Democratic representative in the Wyoming Legislature. During the 1940s he was appointed to a number of political committees or commissions. His political activities in Wyoming had brought him close to Wyoming's Democratic Senator Joseph O'Mahoney, one of the co-sponsors of the Employment Act, and he was regarded by some as the Senator's protegé. Clark did not consider himself a "conservative" economist, and his position on questions pondered by the Council of Economic Advisers seemed to confirm this estimate of himself.

Leon H. Keyserling, only 38 when he was appointed to the Council, had a reputation as one of Washington's "boy wonders." His professional training had been in both law and economics. He had received a degree from Harvard Law School, and he had also completed two years of graduate courses in economics at Columbia University. He entered government service as a lawyer for the Agricultural Adjustment Administration in 1933 and almost immediately became legislative assistant to New York's Democratic Senator Robert F. Wagner. He remained associated with Wagner until 1937 when he became general counsel of the U. S. Housing Authority. He rose to be acting administrator of the Authority and then general counsel of the National Housing Agency. During this period Keyserling had his fingers in almost every pie baking in the New Deal ovens. He became involved in the drafting of the National Industrial Recovery Act, various public works, farm, and banking acts, the Social Security Act, and the National Labor Relations Act. He also did staff work on economic questions for a number of congressional committees. As direct qualifications for nomination to the Council of Economic Advisers, Keyserling had assisted in drafting the bill which ultimately became the Employment Act of 1946; and he had maintained close connections with Senator Wagner, one of the co-sponsors of the original bill. Also, Keyserling had attracted attention when he won the second prize of $10,000 in the Pabst Brewing Company's postwar employment essay contest in 1944.[4]

These background sketches do not shed any light on the personalities of the three men, nor on how they fit together. There were people who had the opportunity to assess the members: the Council had a professional staff of twenty or so economists; also there were liaison personnel between the Council and the White House, the Bureau of the Budget, the Federal Reserve Board, and the Treasury Department. This case will draw on the recollections of four such persons.

Commentator A described the Council members this way:

> Nourse's reputation with us was that he was a

[4] One of Keyserling's theses in this essay was that planning and the development of economic policies should be a joint executive-legislative function. He suggested the establishment of a continuing American Economic Committee. This committee, Keyserling wrote, should be composed of representatives from the Senate, House, Cabinet, industry, labor, and agriculture.

wise man with scholarly achievements. His views on policy were limited: he had been in agricultural economics most of his life. He was relatively conservative—not when viewed on the spectrum of economists, but when viewed as an appointee of a Democratic administration. He was personally liked and respected.

> He was also known as relatively inflexible on substantive economic matters. This was the major reason why there were difficulties. He was willing to recognize political realities—for example, the Democratic platform might have said something about price supports which Nourse was not in favor of, but he was willing to go along. However, he chafed under it. He was not used to the kind of policy-making where there is discussion and dissension over policy, then a decision is made, and thereafter the ranks close behind the decision.

> Keyserling had no difficulty with this problem, partly because his views were nearer the President's, partly because he was by training a lawyer and government official. Keyserling was regarded as a hard working man with a somewhat abrupt and sometimes abrasive manner.

> Clark was the dark horse. He turned out to be a man who had spent most of his life in business and had just about retired. He had a vigorous mind and unorthodox ideas. He suffered from the narrowness of his background. He was the easiest personality of the three.

> On administrative policy issues the Council often split with Keyserling and Clark against Nourse. But it is very important to remember that on economic questions they agreed about eighty percent of the time.

Commentator B observed:

> Nourse was a formalistic thinker. That's one reason why he and Keyserling didn't get along very well. Keyserling didn't have a Ph.D. in economics so Nourse sometimes acted as though he didn't know anything about economics. Of course Keyserling resented this attitude.

This latter observation was repeated in substance by several persons close to the Council. It may or may not have been accurate. But the fact that others placed this interpretation on Nourse's opinion of Keyserling made for strain between the two.

Relations with the White House

The Council members were formally appointed in August 1946. By October a staff had been recruited, and CEA offices were set up in the Executive Office Building, near the White House. The Bureau of the Budget is also located in this building.

The Council's first substantive task was preparing the draft of the President's first economic message to Congress—the draft containing the Council's analysis of "foreseeable economic trends" and its suggestions for national economic policy and program.

Here, the newness of the Council presented difficulties. The CEA had no regular channels for co-ordinating its proposed recommendations with those in the drafts of the other two messages which were to be presented to Congress in the first week of January—the State of the Union and the Budget messages. The procedure this first year was somewhat disorganized, with co-ordination coming only the last two weeks in December through the joint efforts of the Council and members of the staff of John Steelman, the Assistant to the President.

In the following years a rift developed within the White House staff between John Steelman and Clark Clifford, the President's legal counsel. In time, each of the CEA members, along with many other government officials, found he was relying on a different person to serve as a channel of communication with the President. Nourse felt Steelman was more receptive to his way of thinking; Keyserling had more of a bond with Clifford. Clark found easier access through influential members of Congress. On economic questions to be discussed in presidential messages co-ordination was effected by the establishment of work groups comprised of staff members from the White House office, the Bureau of the Budget, and the CEA. Many of these staff people had been trained in the Bureau of the Budget. The work groups, forming a network of people who knew each other and had worked together, not only bridged the cleavage between Steelman and Clifford, but connected the Bureau of the Budget, the Treasury, the CEA, and the White House, as well as any department concerned with a major economic matter that would be mentioned in a presidential message.

Keyserling and Clark had no difficulty with this system. Nourse, however, had been disturbed by the extent to which responsibility for the draft of the first economic message had been delegated by the President to members of

the White House staff. In 1953, quoting from a diary which he kept during his Council years, Nourse referred to an interview he had had with the President in November 1946, during the preparation of the first draft of the economic message:

> There was nothing in this half-hour interview which in any way suggested that the President was interested in the content of the work our staff was doing or in the conclusions toward which we were moving. . . .

Writing in his diary in 1947, Nourse again expressed dissatisfaction:

> While he has accepted the material which we have presented to him for use in the Economic Reports and passed it on without material change and with only minor omissions, there is no clear evidence that at any juncture we have had any tangible influence on the formation of policy or the adoption of any course of action or feature of a program.[5]

And, Nourse wrote:

> . . . When it came to using the Council as an intellectual staff arm of the Presidency . . . the President was quite evidently at sea.

These relationships between the Council members and the President were seen by Commentator A in this way:

> There was really no basis for Nourse's feeling that the Council was rejected by the President. The White House took the Council members very seriously. Their views were sought and listened to on every occasion they should have been. But Nourse may have wished the Council was something it was not and couldn't

[5] *Keyserling comments:* "Dr. Nourse's habitual assertions that he was not accorded the utmost considerate treatment by President Truman is in my opinion one of the most extreme cases of unfair treatment of a President by a disgruntled former official on record. Dr. Nourse could see the President whenever he wanted to. The President gave him a great deal of time. . . . Dr. Nourse was simply unable to adjust himself to the nature and the problems of the Presidency. He could never understand that the President of the United States has too many things to do to engage in long bull sessions on economics of the kind that take place at The Brookings Institution. He could never understand that the President must delegate, must have confidence in his principal officers, and that these officers have no just cause for complaint when the President not only remains accessible to them but also accepts practically everything that they recommend to him."

hope to be. It was set up as a separate, advisory agency with no control or power.[6] It was not part of a regular flow of procedures and documents. The Council had to make new connections or else wait until people came to consult it—things did not flow across its path in the same way as things routed through the Bureau of the Budget. One of the original ideas had been to give the responsibility to the Bureau of the Budget, making the Council a special section within the Bureau. If that had been done, the Council would have had a more direct way of having its views made effective through influencing the budget.

However, the Council did have the initiative when it came to the draft of the economic message. That was a device for approaching issues on the Council's terms. There the Council didn't have to wait to see whether it was invited in.

The real question in determining whether anyone paid proper attention to the Council is whether it was consulted in time to have its views considered, and whether it had access to the information it needed to formulate its views. On these scores the Council had no complaints.

Commentator C saw the relationship between them this way:

> It was all a matter of temperament. The President was a man who knew his limitations. He knew he was not a scholar. He was a politician. He was somewhat awed by expertise. He just couldn't sit down and jaw with a man with the scholarly reputation and mien of Dr. Nourse. Nourse, on the other hand, wanted to sit down and "ponder" problems with the President.

And Commentator D observed:

> That's the way Truman worked. You had to work through his subordinates. Nourse never really accepted this, so the other members of the Council were sometimes able to outflank him by using White House staff channels more effectively.

[6] *Nourse comments:* "I did wish for the Council to be something it was not—that is, a purely advisory agency of the highest professional competence and political detachment. But the implication of this passage—that I wished it to be an agency of 'control or power' is completely erroneous, as is abundantly shown in other parts of this document."

Clark comments: "Mr. Keyserling and I wanted the Council to be a powerful influence in devising and securing the understanding and acceptance of sound economic policies to save prosperity."

Relations with Congress

The Employment Act had provided that the Joint Committee on the Economic Report, aided by a professional staff, should review the President's economic message and present a report of its own to Congress. The Joint Committee was composed of seven senators appointed by the president of the Senate, and seven representatives appointed by the speaker of the House. The party composition reflected roughly the party division in each of the two houses. The first Joint Committee included many of the senators and representatives who had played an active role in the debate and passage of the Employment Act. Democratic Senator Joseph O'Mahoney, who had been one of the co-sponsors of the bill, was expected to be the Committee's first chairman. However, the Republicans gained a majority in Congress in the 1946 elections, and Senator Robert A. Taft became chairman.

The President delivered his first economic message in January 1947, but the members of the Joint Committee were occupied primarily with problems attendant on the shift of party control. They did not hold extensive hearings on the 1947 message or prepare more than a mimeographed report of a few pages. Although the Joint Committee began to hold hearings during 1947 on a variety of subjects, the issue of the relationship of the Council of Economic Advisers to congressional committees arose first with the Senate Foreign Relations Committee.

In June 1947, Secretary of State George C. Marshall delivered his famous Commencement Address at Harvard, suggesting a program of economic aid to Europe. That same month President Truman set in motion three studies on the impact of a foreign aid program upon the domestic economy. One of these studies was made by the Council of Economic Advisers, which submitted its report to the President in October of that year.

The next month the Foreign Relations Committee scheduled hearings on the European Recovery Plan and tentatively scheduled appearances before the Committee by the Chairman of the CEA. When Nourse was advised by the Committee secretary of the proposed invitation, he explained that he would be "embarrassed by a formal invitation to testify" and that he had taken the position that Council members should not appear, even before the Joint Committee on the Economic Report.

Nourse stated that he had taken this position to protect the relationship between Council members and the President. He had explained his position to his colleagues and to the President: the Joint Committee on the Economic Report might try to draw Council members into a discussion of policy positions taken by the President in his economic message. Some of these policy positions might not have followed the drafted recommendations of the Council. Or, the Council members might disagree among themselves as to the advisability of some of the President's positions. To date, there had been no major divergence between the Council and the President, and only minor disagreements among Council members, but, Nourse explained, either situation might arise in the future and cause embarrassment both to the President and the Council members. It would be wise, he felt, to establish precedents to prevent such mutual embarrassment.

The President indicated to Nourse, when the subject was first raised, that he agreed that the Council should protect itself against such situations, but he added that at the same time the Council should not remain aloof from the work of the Joint Committee.

Neither of Nourse's two colleagues were happy with the Chairman's position. Clark, for one, argued that a "policy of aloofness from congressional committees" such as Nourse suggested would impede "the machinery set up by the Employment Act of 1946 to secure congressional approval of economic policies recommended by the President upon the advice of the Council of Economic Advisers." When the issue arose on the question of testifying before the Senate Foreign Relations Committee, Nourse's point of view was accepted by the Committee. Keyserling and Clark deferred to this view although they disagreed with it.

From time to time, the members of the CEA were invited by various congressional committees to testify on economic matters, and in each instance Nourse's view prevailed, and invitations were declined. By 1948 the issue of testifying or not had become a source of considerable tension among the Council members.

The President Recalls Congress

This was an election year. Harry Truman, regarded by many as a "caretaker" and President only by accident, was almost alone in feeling he had any chance of being re-elected. In July, President Truman, when accepting the Democratic nomination, made a surprise announcement to the convention: he was going to call back into session the Republican-controlled 80th Congress to consider his eight-point emergency program for inflation control. Inflation was still a serious problem, and Truman seized on this tactic to dramatize his idea that responsibility lay with Congress.

Keyserling and Clark were firmly convinced Council members should testify before congressional committees at the special session. Clark felt the Council was on probation, since the House Appropriations Committee had just cut the Council budget sharply. Clark still had ringing in his ears the words of the report of the Appropriations subcommittee:

The testimony of this agency was lamentably weak. There was strong sentiment in the committee for the complete elimination of all funds for the agency. . . . There is little evidence of any important results from its work of interpretation, and it takes the position that its views and recommendations are confidential except to the President, unless released by him.

Nourse did not agree with Keyserling and Clark that their reduced budget was a result of their refusal to testify. He interpreted it as a reflection of the Republican majority's antagonism to President Truman and his advisers, and its dislike of the Employment Act.

The issue of Council members testifying was finally resolved. Nourse described the decision process this way: "After numerous telephone conversations with Mr. Steelman, Mr. Clifford, Mr. [Paul] Porter[7] and Mr. [Robert] Turner,[8]

[7] Paul Porter had been the last head of the wartime Office of Price Administration. He was at that time one of Truman's principal campaign advisers and was co-ordinating presentations to congressional committees at the special sessions.

[8] Robert Turner had been director of the Foreign Division of the War Production Board during World War II, had been a staff member of the Office of War Mobilization and Reconstruction, and was then assistant to John Steelman. He was one of the principal liaison men between the White House staff and the CEA.

and with lengthy conferences on the *Williamsburg* [the President's yacht] between the President, the White House aides, and Mr. Porter, and after positions had been taken and reversed, as I recall it, four times within the week, the President's final decision was given me in his letter of August 13." The letter read:

Dear Dr. Nourse,

Mr. Paul Porter has raised with me the question of whether I would regard it as appropriate for members of the Council of Economic Advisers to testify before Congressional committees concerning the anti-inflation program I have recommended to the Congress.

As you know, I have considered from time to time in the past the question. . . . I am aware of the difference between your views on this subject and the views held by your colleagues on the Council. I respect these varying views, which I am sure all of you hold most conscientiously.

Under these circumstances, it seems that the wisest course in the present instance is to permit the members of the Council to be guided by their own convictions. Accordingly, I do not wish to induce any member of the Council to testify if he feels it inappropriate for him to do so; nor do I wish to restrain any member from testifying if he feels that to be an appropriate part of his duties.

I am informing Mr. Porter of this letter, with the expectation that he will make arrangements for testimony by the members of the Council if any testimony is to be presented by them.

Sincerely,

/s/ Harry S. Truman

Keyserling appeared before the Senate Banking and Currency Committee a few days later. Nourse was invited to appear but was excused by the Committee chairman. This became the practice during the rest of 1948, and in 1949. Keyserling and Clark appeared before several committees; Nourse was invited, but he declined and was excused.[9]

Nourse's Letter of Resignation

Immediately after the election of 1948 Nourse submitted his resignation to President Truman. He wrote two drafts of his resignation. The first draft, which he never sent to the President, included the thought that if the Council was "in any way to be assigned a political role or to be allowed to stray over into political activities or lay itself open to political influences, you would want an entirely different kind of chairman, and I would want to be relieved of the position at once. . . ." In the second draft—the one the President received in December 1948—Nourse said principally that in view of his age and the hard work and tensions involved in the job, he hoped he could be relieved soon.

The President did not respond to the letter of resignation, and Nourse did not actually resign until a year later. However, during the year the issue became more and more a source of bitter argument among the Council members. Nourse clung to his view that any appearances before Congress meant that the Council was taking on a political role. Keyserling and Clark were convinced that it was the duty of the Council to be the President's economic ambassadors to and tutors of Congress.

Tensions grew, also, over the kinds of public speeches both Nourse and Keyserling were making. Nourse had taken the position that he did not want to be forced into criticizing the President before congressional committees. Yet, Keyserling pointed out, Nourse did not seem to hesitate to criticize the President's position in public speeches. Nourse's reply was that he

[9] *Keyserling comments:* "The important thing is that I refrained from appearing before Congressional committees during the first year of the Council operations, and thus made the concession to Dr. Nourse of being bound by his views, although they were the minority view. I would have been willing to do this throughout the period of our joint service on the Council. But even though I made this concession, Dr. Nourse persisted in making a public issue of it, which was entirely inappropriate on a matter of Council procedure, and which violated his own profession of desire to avoid public controversy. He made a speech on this subject to the National Planning Association before I had ever testified. He carried stories on the disagreement into the public press. He imputed political motivation to his colleagues. I frequently pointed out to him how entirely unreasonable and inconsiderate this was, in view of the concession which the other members of the Council at that time were making to his views. But he persisted in this course of personal attack and disparagement in public forums, and it was this which led me ultimately to the view that nothing was to be gained by refraining further from appearing before Congressional committees, a position which I believed to be correct in substance, and which in fact was held by a majority of the Council."

could choose his own ground in making speeches, but he could not choose which questions to answer in congressional hearings. In turn, he criticized Keyserling for appearing before such partisan groups as the Americans for Democratic Action. Public appearances, Nourse felt, should be limited to academic, civic, business, labor, or agricultural organizations. (The organizations before which Nourse had appeared included such groups as the Controllers Institute of America, the U. S. Chamber of Commerce, the Executives Club of Chicago, and the Illinois Tech Alumni Association.) For his part, Keyserling felt the audience was less important than the content of the speech. Early in 1949 Nourse received considerable press attention for his public criticism of a pending presidential proposal. Keyserling wrote Nourse a memorandum pointing out that his own actions had never drawn attention for such a reason. Nourse replied that on several occasions in the past he had been "deeply concerned" when Keyserling or Clark had made speeches conveying the impression that their personal professional views were in fact the positions of the Council.

Economic Differences

The separate economic orientations of the two men also made for difficulties. These professional differences began to be felt late in 1948 and during 1949. A split first developed over the moot question of how much the nation could spend on national defense without increasing inflationary pressures to a dangerous extent. Nourse took the position that a thirteen billion dollar defense program was close to the outer limit of safety—presumably a safety defined in terms of economic stability. Keyserling argued that the economy could stand a substantial increase in the defense effort if this should prove necessary for national security. President Truman asserted his desire for a fifteen billion dollar ceiling on defense spending—much closer to Nourse's position than to Keyserling's—and the defense budget was held under that limit until the outbreak of the Korean War shot defense expenditures to $22 billion in 1951 and $45 billion in 1952.

Another source of disagreement among the

Council members began to be felt during 1949 when production, employment, and prices all declined. By mid-June 1949 unemployment was over 3,000,000. The government policy Nourse favored was allowing the recession to find its own bottom. He opposed expansion of the government expenditures as a means of pumping buying power into the economy. Inflationary deficit spending by the government, he believed, was not the way to cope with the recession. Keyserling favored more aggressive anti-slump policies.[10] In his mid-year economic message to Congress, President Truman said, "We cannot have prosperity by getting adjusted to the idea of a depression." The President went on to repeat his January requests including improved supports for farm income, an increase in the minimum wage, more unemployment and old age assistance. He specifically rejected any increase in taxation. This program of increased benefits with no additional revenue portended a budget deficit for the coming year.

A Single Head?

In January 1949 the first of the Hoover Commission reports appeared—the Report on General Management of the Executive Branch. (Under the chairmanship of former President Herbert Hoover, the non-partisan Commission prepared a series of reports aimed at improving the administrative efficiency of government departments. It recommended specific reorganization plans.) The Hoover Commission's comments and recommendations concerning the CEA reflected much of the general feeling that the Council's problems were at least partly tied to its organizational structure. The Report recom-

[10] *Nourse comments:* "There is a faulty implication of *laissez faire* in saying: 'Nourse favored allowing the recession to find its own bottom. . . .' The fact was that I was urging on both labor and management that they had a responsibility for working out sound wage and price adjustments for checking recession and quickening recovery rather than looking to the government for the inflationary devices of deficit spending."

Keyserling comments: "An increase in expenditures without an increase in tax rates does not necessarily portend a budget deficit if it produces sufficient economic recovery to enlarge tax receipts through an enlarged national income. This is standard economics."

mended that the CEA be replaced by an Office of the Economic Adviser and that it have a single head:

> . . . at least potentially it is handicapped by being a multiheaded body, with the requirement that its members be confirmed by the Senate.
>
> To put a full-time board at the head of a staff agency is to run the risk of inviting public disagreements among its members and of transplanting within the President's Office the disagreements on policy issues that grow up in the executive departments or in Congress. It also makes cooperation with related staff agencies more difficult.[11]

In 1949 the Council broke with another practice. Previously, in its quarterly reports to the President on economic policies, or in its annual and mid-year drafts of presidential economic messages, the Council members had attempted to reconcile differences of opinion and present a single viewpoint to the President. However, in the preparation of the draft of the President's mid-year report in 1949, Nourse found he differed with his colleagues to such an extent that he wrote a minority report.

Finally, on September 9, 1949 Nourse wrote Truman that "if the work of the Council is to be kept from serious demoralization," he felt he should tell his colleagues that he wished to retire so that they could get on with the job of preparing the draft of the 1950 economic message. This time Nourse's resignation was accepted, and he left the Council on November 1. Leon Keyserling became Acting Chairman and subsequently was appointed the second Chairman.

Commentator C said of Nourse's resignation:

> Nourse . . . wanted to avoid a possible difficult situation which actually never was a real situation. Nourse, so far as I could tell, diverged from the President's position only on very minor points. But Nourse felt the Council members were confidential advisers.

[11] *Keyserling, comments:* "It is significant that the Hoover Commission's recommendation was preceded by discussions between representatives of that Commission and Dr. Nourse, but no effort was made to obtain the views of the other members of the Council. Further, Dr. Nourse never informed the other members of the Council of his discussions on this point, which is to my mind one example of his improper concept of the relationships among the three members of the Council."

Keyserling felt they were arms of the President. Like other agencies, they were established by Congress to do a certain job and were confirmed in their positions by Congress. They were, he felt, accountable to Congress.

But behind those positions was another factor—the personalities of the two. Nourse didn't like the limelight. Keyserling loved it.

Many public sources attributed Nourse's resignation more to a combination of reasons. The influential British weekly, *The Economist,* reported on October 29:

> The open split in the Council between Dr. Nourse on the one hand, and Mr. Keyserling and Dr. Clark on the other, has for over a year made it likely that Dr. Nourse would resign. Their disagreement is merely the latest of a series over economic policy and practice which has plagued Washington since the scope and responsibilities of government began to grow under the impact of the great depression nearly twenty years ago.
>
> .   .   .   .
>
> It was in a speech last week that Dr. Nourse most bluntly outlined the reasons for his determination to press his resignation and made it inevitable that the President should accept it . . . his bitterest criticism was reserved for the apparent willingness to accept deficit financing as a "way of life." . . .
>
> . . . That [the CEA] should split was perhaps inevitable, but is nevertheless regrettable. Dr. Nourse is far from a proponent of *laissez faire,* but he has a caution as to the extent of government activity which is not shared by the other two members. . . . He likewise holds the conviction that a council appointed to advise the President should do exactly that and no more, while the other two believe its functions should include open advocacy . . . [of] policies felt to be appropriate. The proper character of the new organization has therefore also been an issue.

The *Washington Post* sympathized editorially with Nourse's view that the Council should be politically neutral. But, the *Post* went on,

> . . . we think that Dr. Nourse seriously impaired his influence with the President by delivering speeches in which he openly criticized some Administration policies and made it quite plain that he did not agree with the views of his colleagues on various important issues. If he had stuck to his thesis that a presidential adviser should reserve his opinions for the council table, it is our belief that he would have been more effective as a dissenter, and might still be in a position to render useful service as a member of the Advisory Council.

As Keyserling Saw It

In 1952 Leon Keyserling, then Chairman of the CEA, was testifying before a subcommittee of the Joint Committee on the Economic Report. He was asked by Senator Paul Douglas to explain exactly what his position was on this issue: was not the Council primarily an adviser to the President, Douglas asked, and if this was true could Council members be frank with Congress? Keyserling answered with this statement:

It is . . . clear that the members of the Council are employees of and advisers to the President, and that they are not employees of and advisers to the Congress in the same sense.

But this does not mean, in my opinion, that the members of the Council cannot or should not testify before, cooperate and consult with, and in a sense give advice to, committees of the Congress, just as this is done by heads of other agencies in the executive branch, and even other agencies in the Executive Office of the President. . . .

. . . In all of these cases . . . none of these officials, except in rare instances, makes available to the public or to the Congress the nature of the advice he gives to the President while he is assisting and advising the President in the preparation of such Presidential messages and the recommendations contained therein; and likewise, it is only in rare instances that such officials make it known to the public or even to the Congress if there is a variance between the advice they give to the President and the extent to which the President follows that advice. . . . Nonetheless after the Presidential message in question and the recommendations contained therein are sent to the Congress . . . it has been practically the universal custom and is entirely appropriate for those officials whose statutory responsibility makes it clear that they have been advisers to the President in the field covered by such Presidential message and recommendations to appear before such congressional committees, to discuss and analyze the matters involved, and in fact to amplify and support the recommendations made by the President and the analysis underlying it. In addition, it has been the almost universal custom and entirely appropriate for such officials to appear before congressional committees and to make analyses and give advice in the fields in which they operate under statute, even when this has not been preceded by a Presidential message. . . .

In appearing before committees of the Congress in this role, I cannot see where the Council of Economic Advisers is doing any different or appearing in any different light from what is done by heads of other agencies working in different fields. . . . Certainly, the distinction cannot be that members of the Council deal with economic problems, because many heads of many other agencies deal with economic problems, or even predominantly with economic problems.

That this construction of the Council's role is correct is supported by the legislative history of the Employment Act, by the expressed views of some of the legislative sponsors of the Act, by the fact that the Joint Committee on the Economic Report and other congressional committees have frequently invited the members of the Council to appear before them for this purpose, and by the fact that doing so is in accord with the Council's responsibilities as defined by the President. More important, it is in accord with the whole tenor of the American system of government, and I believe it a good and healthy thing that public officials should be subjected to the questioning and testing of their views by congressional committees, particularly when these public officials have been appointed and confirmed under acts of Congress to deal with the very subject matters which these committees are considering and to help in the preparation of the very reports and recommendations which the President sends to these committees.

The next phase of the question is whether the members of the Council are in a position to express themselves frankly and fully to congressional committees, in view of the fact that they are advisers to the President, and in view of the fact that the advice and recommendations that they give to the President may at times not be exactly the same as the advice and recommendations which the President transmits to the Congress. There has been considerable interest in this subject, and I am glad of this opportunity to express my views.

I believe that members of the Council of Economic Advisers are in exactly the same position, with respect to expressing themselves frankly and fully before congressional committees, as any other agency heads of integrity who had advised the President in important fields in which the President makes recommendations to the Congress. Under our system, no responsible official in such a position, while working for the President, parades before the public or before congressional committees the differences of viewpoint that there may be between himself and the President on matters under consideration by the Congress. If these differences are minor in character, the responsible public official does not feel entitled to the luxury of self-satisfaction of having the President agree with him in every detail; government could not function if that were expected. But if the President, in his recommendations to the Congress, were to depart from the analysis and advice given him by the official in question to the extent that it could be regarded as a fundamental repudiation of that official's views, the official of integrity should resign where under all the circumstances he believes it in the national interest to do so. But it seems to me incorrect to say that a public official in this kind of job can place himself in open conflict with the President for whom he works, and at the same time stay on the job. Obviously, also, a man of integrity should resign if the President for whom he works should ask him to go before a congressional committee or anywhere else and stultify himself by making analyses or supporting policies which this official believes to be against the national interest.

The view has been expressed in some quarters, that members of the Council of Economic Advisers, in order never to be faced with a choice based upon the situation described above, should solve the problem by advising the President but by refusing to appear before congressional committees to analyze and support those recommendations by the President to the Congress which are in accord with the advice they have given him. I can see no more reason why the members of the Council should duck their basic responsibilities by so doing than why other officials should thus avoid their responsibilities. Under our system, if it is to function and if congressional committees are intelligently to process reports and recommendations sent to them by the President, there must be and there always has been someone from the executive branch available and ready to come before the congressional committees and to work with them in the customary fashion. With respect to analyses and recommendations sent by the President to the Congress in those areas of economic policy which are the province of the Council as defined by statute, if the members of the Council are not the proper persons to come before the congressional committees for this purpose, then who are the proper persons?

If my analysis is at all correct, it seems to me that for a member of a congressional committee to raise a question about my freedom to be frank, or whether I agree with the recommendations made by the President, or whether after the President has sent up recommendations I am estopped from expressing my own views, is the same as asking that question of the head of some other statutory agency of government appearing before a congressional committee.

My own answer to the question is as follows: I always have and always will try to speak frankly and deal fairly with congressional committees. I ask the

subcommittee to assume what is in fact the truth, that the analyses and recommendations which I make to it are consistent with the analyses and recommendations which I make to the President. So long as the recommendations made by the President to the Congress conform in the main to the recommendations which I have given him, I feel privileged and duty-bound in appearing before a congressional committee to give my reasons for supporting those recommendations. If the President were to fundamentally repudiate my views as to what is in the nation's economic interest, and were to send recommendations to the Congress in basic conflict with them, then I would resign. That situation has not arisen. At all times, consequently, I hope this subcommittee will feel that the analyses and recommendations I present to it represent my honest convictions. I would not present them if they did not.

As Nourse Saw It

Nourse explained his point of view this way:[12]

One of the most important considerations, I felt, was for us to build the precedents properly. The Executive Office was only seven years old, and the Council was a completely new agency. I felt I should think ahead carefully. I was impressed that other people would have to sleep in the bed I was making.

I felt there were, theoretically, three levels on which the Council could operate. The first would be for us to draw up abstract economic analyses. The second would be for us to make our analyses, taking into consideration the impact on the various institutional structures of the country—the labor institutions, the banking setup, and so forth. This I considered to be economically realistic, and this is what I attempted to do. The third level would be to make analyses taking into account the different pressure groups which bear on an issue and try to make analyses which would be accepted by them. This, I felt, was none of our business. This was the role of the politician. Keyserling and Clark disagreed with me.[13]

[12] Based on a transcript of a recorded interview, July 1958.

[13] *Keyserling comments:* "No evidence can be brought to bear to support the allegation that either Clark or I took positions in which we did not substantively believe. . . . Dr. Clark and I did, of course, take account of the practicality of policy recommendations from the viewpoint of their institutional acceptability, and this is within the proper scope of economics in the public service. . . . Dr. Nourse's statement . . . that Keyserling and Clark wanted to be policy makers is also categorically false.

The sharpest difference between me and my colleagues was that I differentiated clearly between economic analysis and political synthesis. Keyserling and Clark wanted to be policy makers. But I saw the Council as an apex of economic thought, with us processing problems for the President's consideration. Our role was to give the President a notion of how professional economic thought was dividing on a question, and then give him our best judgment on it. If the President, for political considerations, formulated a policy that led to bad economic policy, the role of the Council was then to show him the least bad way to apply bad policy. I made this point in my speech before the American Philosophical Society. I said

". . . the economist must be spiritually capable of bringing the choicest pearls of scientific work to cast before the politically motivated and politically conditioned policy makers of the executive branch. He must be prepared to see these carefully fabricated materials rejected or distorted, and still carry on the same process of preparation and submission again tomorrow, unperturbed and unabashed. He must all the while be aware that his professional brethren and the public will hold him accountable for the final compromised product while he, by virtue of his relationship with the Executive Office, is estopped from saying anything in explanation or vindication of his own workmanship."[14]

Now that is where the problem came in testifying before Congress. If we were all in agreement—we three and the President—we could go up and explain to Congress what the economic needs were and how the decisions had been arrived at. But you'd be establishing a precedent. What happens when a policy comes up which you don't think is good economics—and they're bound to come because the President can't be expected always to follow the advice of the Council when he takes into account

all factors in the political decision-making process. What would I do then? That was the question I was asking. Do I go ahead as a professional economist and argue for the President's position? That came up and I said, "I can't do that." That, in my judgment, was an entirely different role from the one I envisioned as a member of the President's Council.

Take my situation. Suppose the President took a position for, say, selective price or wage controls and that I have to go before Congress and defend it. Then some smart senator on the Joint Committee like O'Mahoney, Douglas, Sparkman—there were plenty of them—says, "That's a very interesting case you make for this policy, Dr. Nourse. Now I notice that on page 486 of your book, *America's Capacity to Produce*, you deplore government controls in these words. Now, do you think the situation has changed?" What am I going to do? Someone else might make a forty-minute speech showing how conditions had changed. I couldn't operate on that basis.

I felt, as I read the Act, that the Congress had provided for dual implementation—we were to advise the President and the Joint Committee was to advise Congress. There was no necessity for us to go before Congress. Congress had its own advisers with their own staff.

Mr. Keyserling, though, felt we were responsible in a sense to Congress, partly because we had had senatorial confirmation, partly because as the President's advisers we should speak for him, and partly because he wanted to wield that influence. On the first score, I had always felt that the situation would be clarified if we did not need senatorial confirmation. We weren't presiding over any action programs. On the second score, although we were the President's advisers he didn't always follow our advice. Our advice was only one factor he took into account. On the third score, I was content being "schulmeister" to the White House. I didn't feel I needed the larger class on the Hill also.

Of course, I wasn't completely happy with the relations we did have with the President. There was never a time when I called Matt Connally, the President's appointment secretary, when there was the slightest difficulty in getting an appointment. He would say, "Will fifteen minutes be all right?" And I would say, "No, I need a half hour." Then Connally would say, "Well, we've got a lot of cash customers this morning; we'll have to move some of them around." And they were moved. There was never more than a day's lapse before I was sitting at the President's desk, and that was excellent. But when I got there, the President was always very gracious, friendly and nice—too nice, in fact. He wasn't busi-

---

We recognized that policy had to be determined by the President. We, of course, sought to urge him to adopt the policies in which we believed, but so did Dr. Nourse, and so would anyone else in our position. Further, Dr. Nourse went all around the country making speeches to all kinds of groups, urging upon them the policies in which he believed. Sometimes he did this before the President had made a determination of policy, and sometimes, after the President had made a determination of policy, Dr. Nourse made speeches to the contrary. Clark and I believed this to be inappropriate for reasons fully set forth in your quotation of my views."

14 Edwin G. Nourse, *Proceedings of the American Philosophical Society* (R.A.F. Penrose, Jr., Memorial Lecture), Vol. 94, No. 4, 1950.

ness-like enough. He'd tell me what happened on his walk that morning, or tell me chit-chat about his family—wasting minutes of this precious appointment. As I think back, I can honestly say that I think I never had a real intellectual exchange with the President, that I was opening my mind to analysis with him, that he was following me. And the situation wasn't much better when I sent him reports. On the occasion when we turned in a majority and minority report the President took them and said, "Thank you for making this report. I'll study it with great care." But the next day he saw Clark Clifford in the morning and he said, "Well, I asked these guys for a report, and they gave me two reports. You take them and see if you can make anything out of them." You see, that was the frustrating part of it. I felt there was little opportunity to become more effective.

But the important thing was to establish the Council as a professional body immune from political influence. And, in fact, if the Council could pass from one administration to the next with some continuity of personnel, I felt that would firmly establish the precedent. As I said once or twice before, "It will take time for successive Presidents to learn how to use a nonpolitical advisory staff agency effectively. It will take time for successive Council members to learn how to bring the most competent and realistic analysis of economic problems simply and effectively to the President's aid."

Blough's View

After Keyserling became Chairman, Council members appeared frequently at congressional hearings. The new Council member appointed to fill the vacancy left by Nourse's resignation was Dr. Roy Blough, then professor of economics and political science at the University of Chicago. Blough joined in these appearances but differed from Keyserling on the kinds of testimony a Council member should give. This emerged publicly at the 1952 subcommittee hearing referred to above, when Senator Douglas asked Blough whether he advised Congress to cut expenditures by five billion dollars or whether he preferred not to answer. In reply Blough stated:

. . . I consider myself completely at liberty to discuss with Congress economic trends and developments, the effects and implications of governmental policies, and the different ways in which various policy objectives can be achieved. I am very pleased to have an opportunity to do this, and I try to do

it in as objective a manner as my basic attitudes permit. However, . . . a definite recommendation on expenditures, it seems to me, is advice that I can more properly give to the Executive than to Congress.

Blough subsequently enlarged on this statement to the effect that the advisory relationship to the President clearly precludes the Council member from openly expressing views adverse to the President's recommendations. Accordingly, Blough felt, it is unwise for a Council member to serve as an advocate of administration programs. Congressmen will not receive his frank opinion on matters of policy, but they should be able to rely on the objectivity of his statements as an economist.

The CEA Under Eisenhower

In January 1953, when Republican President Dwight Eisenhower took office, he inherited an unusual situation. In 1952 the Congress, uncertain whether the Council should be continued, had provided it only enough money to function for nine months. Thus, Council funds were due to run out in March 1953. In February 1953 Sherman Adams, the Assistant to the President, advised the Chairman of the House Appropriations Committee that President Eisenhower considered it important that the Council continue to function, and asked that the Committee consider a supplemental appropriation to carry the Council through the rest of the fiscal year.

At the same time, President Eisenhower asked Dr. Arthur F. Burns if he would serve as Chairman of the Council of Economic Advisers. Burns was at that time professor of economics at Columbia University and director of research of the National Bureau of Economic Research. Burns thought back over some of the difficulties in CEA operations during the Truman administration and looked ahead to the kind of CEA on which he would be serving if he accepted the appointment. He advised the White House that he would accept the nomination provided he had the right to review the other two appointments. His condition was met. Early in March his nomination was presented to the Senate, which confirmed it on March 18. A few days later Congress approved the Supplementary Appropriation Act which provided only for the establishment of one Economic Adviser to the President and appropriated $50,000 for this Adviser and a small staff.

The CEA's forty-member economic and clerical staff was almost entirely dispersed. Only two or three economists remained.

Burns considered his first task to be an evaluation of the structure of the Council as it had functioned in the Truman administration. In the course of his evaluation he concluded that many of the CEA's difficulties had resulted from defects in the legislation. He agreed with the Hoover Commission finding that the Council had been handicapped "by being a multi-headed body" whose three members had held identical powers and responsibilities. The Chairman, as such, had no added powers at all. All administrative problems had to be decided by all three members.

The second defect which Burns detected in the basic legislation was the absence of established channels between the Council and other agencies within the government. This deficiency had caused at least two problems: (1) It had been difficult for the Council to influence the making of economic policy throughout the government. (2) There had been many accusations of "intrigue" between Council members and officials of other agencies. Burns felt that if there had been any "intriguing," one reason was the necessity to by-pass the blocks in the institutional arrangements. He therefore proposed a reorganization of the Council, which was approved by the President and which became Reorganization Plan Number 9, approved by Congress on August 1, 1953. This plan placed administrative responsibility for the CEA in the Council Chairman, who also had the sole responsibility for reporting to the President. The position of Vice Chairman was abolished.

In his letter transmitting the Reorganization Plan to Congress, President Eisenhower indicated that he was also asking the heads of several departments and agencies, or their representatives, to serve as an Advisory Board on Economic Growth and Stability under the chairmanship of the Chairman of the CEA. This was in line with Burns' notion that regular channels of communication between government agencies should be institutionalized. Burns' original idea had been to have an economic cabinet. This cabinet, under the chairmanship of the CEA Chairman, would have been composed of the Chairman of the Federal Reserve Board, the Secretary of the Treasury, and other Cabinet-level officials with major responsibility in the economic field. However, Burns recommended that rather than leap directly to this high-level economic cabinet, it might be well to try the idea first with an advisory board composed of officials from the policy-making level immediately below that of Secretary.

In June 1953 the Advisory Board on Economic Growth and Stability was set up with Burns as Chairman. The other seven members were under-secretaries, assistant secretaries, and officials of similar rank from the departments of the Treasury, Agriculture, Commerce, and Labor, and the Bureau of the Budget and the Federal Reserve Board. The White House was represented by Gabriel Hauge, an Administrative Assistant to the President with responsibility for briefing the President on details of economic matters.

Burns now had a Council reconstituted on his terms: administrative responsibility was centralized in the chairman; there was an interagency board for co-ordinating economic policy under CEA direction; the two other members of the Council were men specifically approved by Burns. (In September 1953 Burns was joined on the Council by Dr. Neil H. Jacoby, Dean of the School of Business Administration at the University of California at Los Angeles, and in December by Dr. Walter W. Stewart of the Institute for Advanced Study in Princeton.)

Burns also had strong backing from the President. Eisenhower repeatedly told his Cabinet members that he wished them to consult the CEA Chairman on all important economic matters and policies. While this did not give Burns veto power, of course, it lent weight to his position and provided him with another channel for putting forward his views. Besides consulting with the heads of departments and agencies individually, Burns attended Cabinet meetings regularly and participated in debates on economic issues.

Under the Reorganization Plan Burns alone was responsible for reporting to the President on the workings of the CEA and on economic policy recommendations. Burns had a scheduled weekly meeting with Eisenhower, generally attended also by Hauge. Burns made it clear to his two colleagues, however, that although he had sole administrative responsibility for procedural matters, he considered that all three members of the CEA shared equally the responsibility for advising on substantive economic problems.

Burns also discontinued the practice of having the Council issue separate annual economic surveys. These were now made part of the President's economic messages.

The problem of the relationship of the CEA to Congress arose immediately. During the hearings before the Senate Banking and Currency Committee on the confirmation of Burns as CEA Chairman in March 1953, Senator John Sparkman put a question to Burns: "Is it your feeling that you should testify before a congressional committee, or will you keep yourself aloof from congressional committees?"

Burns replied: "Senator Sparkman, it is perfectly plain to me that the Congress has the full right to call upon any citizen within or outside the Government to testify at any time. . . . My own personal . . . inclination would be to stay out of the limelight, make my recommendations to the President, indicate to him what the basis for the recommendation is . . . and then having done that, to remain eternally quiet."

Burns' Position

Burns later gave considerable thought to the position he should take. To a large extent he agreed with Nourse's feeling that it would be difficult for an economic adviser to maintain his usefulness to the President if he had to answer all questions put to him by a political group. However, he felt Nourse had carried this position too far. There were several categories of aid which could be given without interfering with his advisory relationship to the President. First, there might be a request for the CEA to aid the Congress in understanding the Employment Act of 1946. Such a request would call upon Council members in their function as administrators of an Act passed by Congress, and it would be completely appropriate for Council members to testify freely.

Secondly, a congressional committee might wish testimony on some technical problem, such as an analysis of the statistical units of all government departments. This too would be a legitimate request which should be honored. Third, Council members certainly should appear before the Appropriations Committee to defend budget requests for the Council itself.[15]

The difficulty arose when an invitation was proffered by a congressional committee dealing with economic conditions and policy. Here, Burns felt, there were at least two major dangers in testifying.

First, in some cases the President had to adopt policies that he didn't like and that I didn't like. He had to do it for reasons of overall political policy, but his heart was bleeding over it. What should I do before a committee of Congress in such a case? Should I criticize the President when I happen to know that he shares my views? Would that be fair? In any case, how could I criticize the President publicly and still remain a useful member of his administration? On the other hand, how could I say to a congressional committee that something is sound when I believed otherwise?

The other major danger in testifying is that once an adviser takes a strong position in public, he is apt to become a prisoner of that position. I wanted to give the President the fullest benefit of my knowl-

[15] *Nourse comments:* "With these three propositions I am, of course, in complete agreement. I only wish I had been smart enough to differentiate these cases as explicitly as Burns has done from the fourth issue—the one on which I took my stand. Naturally, I appeared before Senate and House committees to defend the Council's budget. When, in May 1947, Senator Taft, as chairman of the Joint Economic Committee, extended us an invitation to meet with that committee to discuss interpretation of the Employment Act and, in a broad way, means for its implementation, I unhesitatingly accepted. The Committee's report had been made several months before. The session was well along on the legislative program, and our discussion was entirely free of debate over policy recommendations of the President or specific issues then involved in Congressional debate. We cooperated fully on the staff level in inquiries initiated by the Joint Economic Committee as to 'statistical gaps' and if, at any time, we had been invited to join with the committee in mutual conferences within this field, I am sure I would have been glad to participate. Not having the statistical competence that Burns had, I was not in a position to exercise the leadership in this important area which he subsequently contributed."

edge and thought. Hence I wanted to be free to advise the President one way one day, and yet be able if necessary to go in the next day and say, "I've been thinking it over. What I told you yesterday was wrong. I overlooked some important points. What really ought to be done is thus and so."

Burns decided that he ought to testify despite these dangers, because good citizenship required it. He also decided that he would express to the congressional committee, if it dealt with economic policy, a preference as to the method of testifying. Burns preferred that he be permitted to testify in executive session with no transcript made of the remarks. But if the congressional committee would not agree to this method, Burns decided, he would testify anyway. "Maybe I'd have to resign after I got off the stand, but that would be one of the chances I knew I would be taking."

In 1954 the Joint Committee on the Economic Report called upon Burns to testify. At that time the Republicans controlled Congress, and Republican Jesse Wolcott was Chairman of the Joint Committee. Wolcott and the Committee with its majority of Republicans acceded to Burns' request that the testimony be taken in executive session with no transcript.

The election of 1954 resulted in the Democrats gaining control of Congress, and in 1955 Democrat Paul Douglas was Chairman of the Joint Committee with its new Democratic majority. Again, Burns was asked to testify, and again he expressed his preference. Douglas replied that although he would agree to an executive session, he would want a transcript made of the testimony. However, Douglas went on, this transcript would not be part of the public record. Burns replied that if a transcript were to be made at all, he would want the transcript made public. So in 1955 the testimony was given in executive session, and the transcript was made a part of the printed record.

The next year Douglas was still Chairman, and Burns again expressed his original preference. This time some Democrats on the Joint Committee voted with the Republicans, and Burns' testimony was taken in executive session with no transcript made.

So Burns established his policy. He would clearly express his preference to the congressional committees dealing with economic issues.

If the committee in question accepted his preference, that was all to the good. However, if the Committee insisted on different terms, Burns would accept those terms.

There was another major change in the workings of the Employment Act in the first years of the Eisenhower administration. The Joint Congressional Committee, which up to this time usually issued partisan majority and minority reports, issued a unanimous report in 1954 and again in 1955. By 1956 there were those who felt that the Joint Committee was no longer "a fifth wheel" and that its hearings and reports were as significant as those of the CEA.

Burns resigned from the Council in December 1956 and returned to his post as professor of economics at Columbia University, becoming at the same time president of the National Bureau of Economic Research. In 1958, looking back over his years as Chairman, and evaluating his policy against that of the first Council members, Burns said:

> Keyserling took an extreme position and in the process ignored a vital distinction. Cabinet officers are directly responsible to Congress. Their responsibilities are largely defined by Congress. But the Council is not an administrative agency. It is advisory only—advisory to the President by law, and advisory to the Presidency by practice.
>
> Nourse also took a rigid position. To the extent that the Council had duties defined by law it is responsible to Congress and must answer to it—that is why I placed no conditions on my testifying on proposed changes of the Employment Act or on the statistical gathering functions of the government or on the defense of the Council's budget.
>
> But I want to add this: if there had only been the type of Council that Keyserling envisaged, I never would have accepted the appointment. I would have taken it for granted that the Council Chairman must, as a practical matter, support the President's views at public hearings, and I would not place myself in that position. But because there had been a Nourse I could conceive of there being a practical alternative and could try to find it. So Nourse did more than make my job easier by taking the position he did; because there had been a Nourse my job was possible.

Not everyone agreed that Burns had solved the problems. Harvard economist Alvin H. Hansen, for one, considered that Burns' solution had been to sidestep the dilemma Nourse had feared by restricting his activities "more nearly, though not quite exclusively" to assisting and advising the President. Hansen felt that Burns had not really met the question (raised earlier by Keyserling) that the Democratic members of the Joint Committee posed in this manner in the committee's Supplementary Report of March 1955: "A sound and consistent position for the Council must be agreed upon, either it acts solely as an anonymous professional body advising the President or as the spokesmen before Congress and the public for the President's economic analyses and programs. If the first alternative is adopted, then some other spokesman for the President's overall economic position must be established."

NOTES

1. Lennox L. Moak and Albert M. Hillhouse, *Concepts and Practices in Local Government Finance* (Chicago: Municipal Finance Officers Association, 1975), pp. 198–99.

2. "Social Security Funding in Peril, Says Agency," *Seattle Daily Times*, August 8, 1979, p. 1.

3. Advisory Commission on Intergovernmental Relations (ACIR) report released July 1973, as reported in *National Journal* 7, no. 45 (November 8, 1975).

4. Ibid., p. 1543.

5. Ibid.

6. Ibid.

7. B. U. Ratchford, "A Formula for Limiting State and Local Debts," *Quarterly Journal of Economics* 51 (1936): 71–89; and *Proceedings of the Fifty-First National Tax Conference*, 1958, pp. 215–229.

8. Moak and Hillhouse, *Local Government Finance*, pp. 285–86.

9. *National Journal* 10, no. 46 (November 18, 1978), p. 1858.

10. Jude Wanniski, "Taxes, Revenues and the Laffer Curve," *Public Interest* 50 (Winter 1978).

11. George Gilder, *Wealth and Poverty* (New York: Basic Books, 1981).

12. Jude Wanniski, *The Way the World Works* (New York: Simon and Schuster, 1978).

13. Martin Feldstein, "The Retreat from Keynesian Economics," *Public Interest* 64 (Summer 1981).

14. By 1982 a total of 31 states had passed such a resolution.

15. Richard L. Lucier, "Gauging the Strength and Meaning of the 1978 Tax Revolt," in *Managing Fiscal Stress*, ed. Charles H. Levine (Chatham, N.J.: Chatham House, 1980), pp. 123–36.

16. Advisory Commission on Intergovernmental Relations, "Michigan Implements Its Headlee Amendment," *Intergovernmental Perspective*, Spring 1980, p. 20.

17. John Shannon and Bruce Wallin, "Restraining the Federal Budget: Alternative Policies and Strategies," *Intergovernmental Perspective*, 5 no. 2 (Spring 1979): 10.

18. Robert D. Behn, "The Receding Mirage of the Balanced Budget," *Public Interest* 67 (Spring 1982): 120.

19. Ibid., p. 123.

20. Shannon and Wallin, "Restraining the Federal Budget," p. 9.

21. "Survey Shows Sunset Legislation Benefits," *Public Administration Times* 5: 7 (April 1, 1982), p. 8.

22. Jane F. Roberts, "States Respond to Tough Challenges," *Intergovernmental Perspective* 6, no. 2 (Spring 1980): 18.

BIBLIOGRAPHY

Advisory Commission on Intergovernmental Relations. *The Condition of Contemporary Federalism: Conflicting Theories and Collapsing Constraints*. Washington, D.C.: A-84, August 1981.

Aronson, J. Richard. *Management Practices in Local Government Finance*. Washington, D.C.: ICMA, 1975.

Behn, Robert D. "The Receding Mirage of the Balanced Budget." *Public Interest* 67 (Spring 1982): 118–30.

Feldstein, Martin. "The Retreat from Keynesian Economics." *Public Interest* 50 (Winter 1978).

Garrarty, John A. *Unemployment in History*. New York: Harper & Row, 1979.

Gilder, George. *Wealth and Poverty*. New York: Basic Books, 1981.

Levine, Charles H. *Managing Fiscal Stress*. Chatham, N.J.: Chatham House, 1980.

Moak, Lennox, and Hillhouse, Albert. *Concepts and Practices in Local Governmental Finance*. Chicago: Municipal Finance Officers Association, 1975.

Shapiro, Robert J. "Politics and the Federal Reserve." *Public Interest* 66 (Winter 1982): 119–39.

Studenski, Paul, and Krooss, H. *Financial History of the United States*. New York: McGraw-Hill, 1963.

Wanniski, Jude. *The Way the World Works*. New York: Simon and Schuster, 1978.

Chapter 4

Design of the Executive Budget: From Objects to Performance

In Chapters 2 and 3 we discussed the historical and theoretical foundations for viewing the budget from differing policy perspectives. We now return to a more detailed consideration of what we called the Executive Budget, beginning with the different ways information may be classified in constructing this budget. For the Executive Budget, decisions must be made about what we hope to accomplish (ends) and what resources (means) we intend to employ. How do such decisional requirements relate to the methods developed for classifying expenditures in budgeting practice? The James Thompson means-ends typology is utilized to identify the four major kinds of decisions that have emerged in budgeting. Two budget formats—the objects of expenditure and the performance based—are then discussed in terms of this frame of reference to clarify the different contributions each makes to decision making.

A HISTORICAL VIEW

The budget occupies such a central position in the management process today that we are apt to forget how recent an invention the managerial budget actually is in American government. In the statute creating the Treasury Department, Congress made it the specific duty of the Secretary of the Treasury "to propose and report estimates of the public revenue, and the public expenditures." (1 Stat. L. 65). In 1800 another statute directed the Secretary "to digest, prepare, and lay before Congress . . . a report on the subject of finance, containing estimates, and plans for improving or increasing the revenues." (2 Stat. L. 79).

During the formative years of the federal government, relations between Congress and Cabinet officials were quite informal. As Henry Jones Ford observes, ". . . all of the branches of government were bunched together in their quarters so that intercourse was ready and easy without formal arrangements. . . ."[1] By the time Jefferson became President, this informality began to break down, not as the result of any substantial increase in the size of the government but because of emerging policy conflict. Washington's

Federalist party was successfully challenged in the 1800 election by the new Democratic Republican party of Jefferson and Madison. With the emergence of a two-party Congress, the policy perspectives of the two branches began to diverge. The consequent frictions often led to the use of detailed appropriations to restrict executive discretion.

Throughout the nineteenth century the Secretary of the Treasury continued to report the expenditure requirements of each department to Congress, but the function was primarily clerical with no attempt made to criticize, alter, reduce, or coordinate the separate requests. The needs of each department were then considered on a piecemeal basis by Congress.

Several circumstances occured during the later years of the nineteenth century and the early years of the twentieth that led to the perceived need for a Executive Budget. Business enterprises began to grow in size and complexity to the extent that the manager could no longer coordinate his organization by personally monitoring work operations. The more formalized tools of scientific management and financial control, such as time and motion studies, work measurement, and unit costing, were consequently developed to augment if not replace the ad hoc personalized methods previously relied upon by the manager.

Also, by the latter part of the nineteenth century, the graft and corruption that had developed in government from the political spoils system were beginning to lead to budget deficits and the deterioration of government services. Reform groups arose to decry the moral deterioration fo the political environment. Taxpayers began demanding efficiency and economy in the operation of government. At the National Conference on Good Government in 1896, it was reported that 245 organizations, among them the Civil Service Reform League, the National Municipal League, and the Citizens Union, were active throughout the country.[2]

All of these efforts emphasized the need for some mechanism that could establish accountability in government. As early as 1899 the National Municipal League proposed the use of the budget for this purpose. In that year the league drafted a model municipal corporation act that recommended the adoption of a budget system under the direct supervision of the mayor.[3] In 1906 the New York Bureau of Municipal Research was established. The bureau's first study, published the following year, revealed the lack of facts available to citizen and public official alike on the financial operation of the New York City Health Department. "No one had the facts for determining how much money was needed for governmental services, how much money was available, or how intelligent decisions might be made for appropriating money to competing municipal services."[4] Appropriations were passed by New York's Board of Estimates without any reference to revenues or expenditures. If monies available were insufficient, special revenue bonds were issued. In view of these circumstances, the bureau recommended that the Board of Estimates require that all future budgets (1) clearly indicate the specific purposes for which money was being expended, and (2) classify expenditures to reveal which specific appropriations were made for specific needs and work to be done.[5] The bureau's proposals were adopted for the City's Health Department, and the executive control philosophy underlying the proposals was soon extended to several other City functions.

It is not surprising, of course, that the origin of the Executive Budget should be found at the local level of government. As noted in Chapter 2, the vast majority of the civil functions of government were still being performed by towns and counties at the turn of the century. Similar concerns about the development of an executive-type budget, however, also began to appear at the federal level during the early years of the twentieth century. Deficits were incurred in two of the four years of President Theodore Roosevelt's second term. Congress did pass the antideficiency acts in 1905 and 1906, intended to curb agencies from spending beyond their budget allocations, but these legislative measures dealt with only one aspect of much larger problems associated with generally lax and inadequate financial practices. In March 1909 the Senate appointed a special committee to investigate the deficits. After study and deliberation, that committee concluded that adoption of the management systems and methods developed by business could lead to efficiency and economy in government.[6] In December 1909 President Taft requested an appropriation of $100,000 "to enable the President to inquire into the methods of transacting public business." This request was granted by Congress the following June, and the President created the Commission on Economy and Efficiency.

In 1912 the commission's report, *The Need for a National Budget*, was transmitted to Congress, along with a special message by the President urging that a national budget system be established as an instrument of executive management and control. The political environment in Congress in 1912, however, was one of hostility to any presidential initiatives. With the election of a new President later in the year, an improvement in business conditions, and the introduction of the personal income tax as a new source of revenue, further consideration of the proposed national Executive Budget was delayed until after World War I. The Taft Commission report, though, if not immediately acted upon by the federal government, was influential in the adoption of Executive Budgets by many cities and states. Subsequently the commission's recommendations also laid the foundations for the passage of the Budget and Accounting Act of 1921. President Wilson, in fact, recommended the enactment of a national budget system in 1919, but he vetoed the bill Congress developed to implement the recommendation. Congress included in the bill the establishment of a General Accounting Office to be headed by a Comptroller General appointed by, but not removable by, the President. Wilson argued that appointment and removal power could not be constitutionally separated. Wilson's successor, Warren Harding, was not troubled by this provision, and the Budget and Accounting Act became law on June 10, 1921, in much the same form as it had been vetoed earlier by Wilson.

All of the Executive Budgets enacted in the early years of the century called for a classification of accounts that would ensure accountability and executive control. But what classification system would accomplish these ends? To answer this question we need to know what kinds of information are required; and information requirements can be identified only if we know what kinds of financial decisions the manager must make. We know, first, that he has to make decisions about the procurement of goods and services. Second, he must make decisions about to whom to allocate these resources in the organization. What subordinates are to be given the responsibility for directing the use of which resources? Third, the manager must make decisions about what amount (volume and quality) of activity effort the organization should be expected to accomplish in relation to the resources it has available. Finally, the manager will be expected to show what, if any, differences the activity efforts undertaken by his agency will make on society. How much do such efforts contribute to the solution of society's problems?

MEANS AND ENDS

Note that the first three kinds of decisions—those dealing with procurement, delegation of authority, and the measurement of work effort—are all concerned with the *means* of accomplishing the agency's mission. The fourth kind of decision, on the other hand, is directed at the *ends* of the agency, that is, its mission and goals. One might reasonably expect that the information requirements of this fourth decision would be different from those required for the first three. But can we even assume that the first three kinds of decisions necessarily require budgeting information assembled in the same fashion? Procurement decisions certainly require information identifying the goods and services to be purchased. Assignment of spending responsibilities, though, will be allocated on the basis of the hierarchial design of the organization. And workload decisions will require information about the unit costs of the end products produced by the organization. Thus it appears that each of these four kinds of decisions have different informational requirements.

If each has different information requirements, are the four decisions related to each other in any systematic fashion? It has been observed that the first three deal with means, the fourth with ends. James Thompson has developed a conceptual scheme for distinguishing different kinds of decisions based upon agreement or lack of agreement among decision makers about ends to be accomplished and the means that could be employed to accomplish such ends.[7] Following this line of reasoning, one arrives at a fourfold classification of decisions:

		Ends	
		Agreement	*Disagreement*
Means	Agreement	1	3
	Disagreement	2	4

In decisions where there is agreement about both ends and means (i.e., number 1 above), Thompson suggests that the only question at issue is the proper combination of resources to be used. We need only sort through the various possible resource combinations until we arrive at the one that makes the most efficient and economical use of the resources required to accomplish the agreed upon work necessary to attain the agreed-upon goal. Thus, the purchase of bond paper by a government agency will depend upon which supplier offers the lowest bid price for the specified product. In this example, agreement exists about the end, paper for typing, and about the means, the appropriate size, quality and texture requirement of production. The only question at issue is which supplier can employ its resources the most efficiently and thereby underbid its competitors. Many type 1 decisions are much more complicated, or course. If GSA, for instance, is to locate warehouses in fifty cities across the country, where should each warehouse be located? There is no disagreement about ends: Locations should provide the quickest access to all users. And there is no disagreement about the means to be used: multiple-use warehouses and conventional transportation facilities. If there are thousands of users scattered throughout the country, a mathematical technique such as linear programming would probably have to be employed to arrive at the fifty most accessible cities to all users. In some cases the problem will be so complex that a computational solution will be too costly or time-consuming, and simplifying assumptions will have to be introduced to arrive at an answer. In all type 1 decisions, however, computational solutions are theoretically possible.

For Thompson's type 2 decision, there is agreement about the ends to be accomplished but not about the means most appropriate to achieve such ends. Two doctors examine a patient. Both agree that the patient has cancer. But one doctor recommends surgery, the other chemotherapy treatment. Here there is no disagreement about the end sought: the elimination of the cancer. But there is disagreement about the means sought to accomplish the end. Or take a different example of a city attempting to decide whether it should provide for garbage collection itself or contract out for the service. Either way the end to be accomplished, the collection of garbage, is the same. But there is disagreement on how the task should be performed. One might argue that this is a type 1 decision. The choice should be made according to who can provide the service the cheapest. But the costs of garbage removal will vary with the volume collected. Therefore the question is not who can offer the lowest bid for providing garbage service for a year, but who can collect all garbage at the lowest cost per pound collected. Thus a type 2 decision requires information on the relationship between resources used (input) and volume of activities performed (outputs).

In Thompson's type 3 decision there is disagreement about the end to be accomplished, but not disagreement about the most appropriate means available for achieving the different ends that are being proposed. This kind of decision is found most frequently in the process involved in setting priorities on the relative importance of different programs competing for scarce resources. Such decision making is characterized by bargaining and tradeoffs that allow for the accomodation of competing needs. These decisions thus require information set forth in alternative spending packages so that various compromise possibilities can be considered. For example, what are the relative priorities for building a new hospital, a sanitary treatment plant, or an expanded jail facility in a given community? There are acknowledged designs available for constructing each, but there may be lack of agreement about which ends—personal health, environmental health, or public safety—should command primary attention.

Type 4 decisions, those on which consensus is lacking on both means and ends, pose a dilemma that Thompson suggests can be overcome only through inspiration, perhaps by referral to a frame of reference quite alien to the conventional perspectives being expressed about means and ends. One might, for example, suggest solving the urban transportation problem by the introduction of Buck Rogers' type space belts. Gone would be the need for huge capital investments in highways, automobiles, tracks, and the like. But also the social and economic consequences of such a radical shift in transportation modes may lead to a redefinition of the role of transportation in societal life, as well as a rethinking about the appropriate means of transportation. Budgetary decisions of this type are normally resolved in the political arena with competing actors using both means and ends information to justify their respective program preferences.

On the basis of the foregoing discussion we may identify the criterion most appropriate for dealing with each of Thompson's four types of decisions:

		Ends	
		Agreement	Disagreement
Means	Agreement	1. Computational decisions. *Criterion:* Mix of resources (inputs).	3. Compromise decisions. *Criterion:* Mix of resources (inputs); or impacts (differences made).
	Disagreement	2. Judgment decisions. *Criterion:* Input-output data.	4. Inspirational decisions. *Criterion:* Responsible org. unit.

For computational decisions, one would prefer a classification of the resources to be purchased (i.e., mix of resources). Judgment decisions would require a classification of activities by the outputs to be accomplished and the resources needed to achieve such outputs. Since in judgment decisions there is no consensus on the best means of employing resources to accomplish an agreed-upon goal, output-based costs would be the most appropriate way of justifying the use of resources.

Type 3, compromise decisions, like type 1 decisions, are probably best served by a budget classification based on the resources to be purchased. Since there is no agreement on ends to be accomplished, justifications are likely to be made on the basis of the efficient use of resources with ends left purposefully vague. Such an approach will minimize ideological conflict and conce: • ate attention on agreed-upon resource use.

The budget classification most likely to be useful for making type 4, inspirational decisions, would be based on the organizational units performing the work. Since these decisions will most likely be made on the basis of charismatic identification with (faith in) the performers, budget allocations on a lump-sum basis would be most appropriate.

Viewed in the context of Thompson's typology, we may now ask what budget classifications can be used for representing budget expenditures in ways that will allow us to employ the appropriate decision criterion for each different type of decision. This is not to suggest that any government agency can use only one criterion for all the decisions it makes. But the political culture within which each agency operates will usually identify the major types of decision perspectives deemed appropriate by the decision makers involved. Consideration of the values implicit in each of the types of decisions the agency makes should then, of course, be reflected in the methods the agency employs to classify its expenditures.

THE OBJECTS OF EXPENDITURE BUDGET

An objects of expenditure classification is one in which the different kinds of goods and services to be purchased or otherwise acquired (e.g., lease, donation, grant) are itemized. Political reformers at the turn of the century sought a system of budget classification that could expose and control the graft and corruption then prevalent at all levels of government. What was needed was a uniform classification of accounts that could be audited objectively to ascertain whether monies were being expended for the purposes intended by law. The ideal classification for the purpose was based upon goods and services purchased. All government agencies purchase essentially the same kinds of goods—personal services, travel, building rental or depreciation, desks, typewriters, and so forth. Thus, it should be possible for all agencies to adopt the same expenditure categories, and therefore for auditors to apply the same criteria in auditing the expenditures of all agencies.

The procedure employed for the formulation and evaluation of such a budget is frequently referred to as line item analysis. In fact, the objects of expenditure budget is often called a line item budget for this reason. Thus in the following example there are six line items:

	Objects of Expenditure	1979	1980
1.	Wages/Salaries	$198,000	$250,000
2.	Other Personnel Costs	19,900	25,000
3.	Rentals	25,000	25,000
4.	Travel	48,000	36,000
5.	Supplies and Materials	35,000	38,500
6.	Debt Service	30,000	30,000

In most agencies Personal Services (Wages/Salaries, Other Personnel Costs) constitute over 50 percent of the budget. Consequently, much effort goes into estimating these costs. In the above example, an increase of $52,000 is projected in Wages/Salaries from 1979 to 1980. Is this due to an increase in the work force? If so, will the increase be permanent, or will it decline again in future years? To answer such questions we must start by knowing how many *positions* the agency is authorized and what the actual *paid employment* is estimated to be in 1979 and 1980. Since paid employment includes terminal leave payments for separated employees as well as persons currently in pay status, one may also want to have statistics on the *working force* (i.e., employees actually on the job).

"Average number of positions" and "paid employment," when multiplied by average wage and salary rates, may provide sufficient information about the manpower requirements of stable agencies, but not for expanding or declining agencies. Here one will want to know the beginning, average, and ending number of positions and employees paid. If seasonal variation is involved in the agency's work (e.g., construction during summer months), the highest and lowest employment during the year should also be considered. The following example should illustrate how these measures can be used to explain a Wages/Salaries budget request:

	Expanding Agency		Declining Agency	
	Positions	*Pd. Emp.*	*Positions*	*Pd. Emp.*
Beginning	985	902	1100	1010
Average	1071	975	1060	965
Ending	1100	1000	1015	920
Highest	1100	1003	1100	1010
Lowest	985	902	1015	900
Total Auth.	1140		1114	

For the expanding agency, Paid Employment at the beginning of the year is projected to be the same, 902, as the Lowest Paid Employment during the year. Similarly, for the declining agency, Paid Employment at the beginning of the year is the same, 1010, as Highest Paid Employment during the year. Average Paid Employment in the expanding agency is 975, but by the end of the year, 1000 employees are projected to be on the rolls. Thus employment is projected to expand throughout the year. The Highest Paid Employment during the year is estimated to be only 1003, though, so there appear to be few seasonal employees accounting for the expansion.

In the declining agency, on the other hand, 920 employees are estimated to be on the rolls at the end of the year; but the Lowest Paid Employment during the year is projected at 900, indicating some seasonal decline in employment during the year. In both agencies, the total number of positions authorized is greater than the total number of positions authorized at any one time because some positions will be filled for only part of the year.

Calculation of personnel costs also involves estimating the number of promotions, ingrade pay increases, vacancies, and so forth, likely to occur during the year. Explorations of the budgeted amount requested for Wages/Salaries consequently requires a sizable backup of manpower statistics, data that will not be available unless generated by rigorous manpower planning.

The same kind of analytical process is involved in the analysis of every line item of expenditure. The estimates of rental requirements may therefore require consideration of such factors as:

- The possible availability of free public quarters
- The possible alternative of rental or purchase
- The services to be covered by the rental agreement (e.g., sometimes including all or excluding certain services)
- Differences in the quantity of office space required for different employees— executive vs. clerical, office vs. field, etc.
- Variations in rental and utility rates occurring over different geographic areas (e.g., high rates in cities, low in rural areas)

Thus the cost of each object of expenditure is calculated on the basis of the agency's past use of the resource, the availability of the resource, and projected resource needs for the agency in the future. Referring back to Thompson's typology of decisions, the objects of expenditure budget is seen to be appropriate for agencies concerned with computational decisions (agreement on means and ends). It may also be the most politically viable budget format for agencies that have controversial missions. Managers, however, tend to seek control over programs by evaluating results, or at least outputs, produced rather than by monitoring resources purchased and stored (inventory). In a sense, perhaps managers tend to see all decisions as type 2, judgment decisions. They assume that they will be evaluated as managers by how well they exercise discretion in managing resources to accomplish tangible results (outputs). Society has also tended to agree that the professional manager should be evaluated in terms of this frame of reference. Consequently, the objects of expenditure budget, originally designed by political reformers to improve the operation of government, has come under severe criticism for not providing the budgetary information needed to ensure managerial control.

THE PERFORMANCE BUDGET

The origin of the performance or program budget (the terms are frequently used interchangeably) goes back to the turn of the century. The Taft Commission of 1912 called for a functional or work-based classification of budget expenditures. And in 1913–15 the Borough of Richmond, New York City, experimented with a system of cost data budgets developed by the New York Bureau of Municipal Research. Detailed classifications were devised for three public works functions: street cleaning, sewage, and street maintenance. Physical units of work, such as miles of streets flushed, were set forth in the budget, together with the unit costs, total costs, and a distribution of outlays by object of expenditure for each of the subfunctions. These schedules, further classified on a quarterly basis, were written into the appropriation acts and legislated by the Board of Aldermen. The resulting budget was highly inflexible and soon abandoned.[8]

Interest continued, however, in the performance/program budget, especially at the local level of government where a functional division of work complemented the rationale of the performance budget. The first attempts at comprehensive performance budgeting came in the 1930s—in the U.S. Department of Agriculture under William A. Jump, and in the newly created Tennessee Valley Authority. These efforts were reinforced by the work of the President's Committee on Administrative Management, which concluded that the President needed to exercise a more systematic planning and managerial direction over the Executive Branch. In 1939, when the Bureau of the Budget was transferred from the Treasury Department to the newly established Executive Office of the President, the bureau became the major management staff of the Chief Executive. The budget began to be viewed more as a planning and work programming instrument than as a device for financial control. But the objects of expenditure classification upon which the budget document was then based provided little guidance for exercising managerial direction over the performance of work. Development of a budget based on program or performance, designed to serve as a financial depiction of government work plans and policies, therefore began attracting considerable attention in the bureau and in the more planning-oriented federal agencies. By 1949, when the Hoover Commission recommended the adoption of a performance budget, many agencies were well acquainted with this form of budget presentation.

A Definition

What exactly is a performance budget? The Hoover Commission, which is frequently given credit for coining the term, defines it this way:

> Such a document which we designate as a "performance budget" would analyze the work of government departments and agencies according to their functions, activities or projects. It would concentrate attention on the work to be done or service to be rendered, rather than the things to be acquired, such as: personal services, supplies, materials and equipment. A performance budget, moreover, would facilitate congres-

sional and executive control by clearly showing the scope and magnitude of each Federal agency. It could also show the relationship between the value of work to be done and the cost of the work, a measurement which cannot be made under the present system.[9]

If one is to develop a budget based upon projected performance, the following must be done:

1 Identify the *work activities* (e.g., conducts interviews, types letters, makes inspections)
2 Identify a *work or output unit* for each activity (e.g., one interview conducted, one letter typed, one inspection completed)
3 Identify *input units* for each major resource to be used (e.g., person hours for personal services, miles for travel)
4 Calculate the *cost per work or output unit* (cost of resources divided by volume of activities)
5 Multiply cost per work or output unit by the projected activity workload for the year

Of course, there are problems with implementing this set of requirements. Does one identify *every* work activity performed by the agency? Some early experimenters in work measurement assumed so, but their efforts became so bogged down by the volume of recordkeeping necessitated by such an approach that employers soon abandoned these efforts. This result can be avoided by identifying only the key activities that most directly reflect the major scope and direction of the agency. For example, a clerk types letters, but also sharpens pencils, corrects typing errors, assembles multipaged letters and reports, and so on. The purpose of the work, though, is the typing of letters; all the other activities merely contribute to the typing task.

Output Units

The identification of work or output units for each activity used can also lead to confusion. To be countable, the output units must be homogeneous. In the example above, the output unit for the activity, typing, is: a letter typed. But what if the length of the letters to be typed varies? Some letters may be one page long, others two or more pages in length, still others less than a page. If such is the case, the tabulation of all letters typed will indicate little about the volume of work actually performed. Perhaps a more satisfactory output unit will be: a page typed. This measure could be used for all letters that are one or more pages in length (assuming all are approximately equal in terms of vocabulary used and format employed). Only letters shorter than a page would require a separate output unit, perhaps: a paragraph typed.

Input Units

Input units are somewhat simpler to develop. Such units are designed to facilitate the quantification of each resource to be used to carry out each activity. Thus, for personal services, wages and salaries are paid for time expended. A legitimate input unit would therefore be: a person-hour worked. For travel the input unit could be: miles traveled;

for heat, gallons of fuel used, and so on. Some resources, such as miscellaneous office supplies (pencils, paper, erasers, carbons, and so forth), may be too varied or inexpensive to merit the development of separate input units for each. A summary estimate of such resources (such as "office supplies"), based on past experience and projected future requirements, is an acceptable way of handling these items.

Variable and Fixed Costs

Calculation of the cost per unit of work produced involves the identification of variable costs, that is, costs that increase or decrease with the increase or decrease of outputs. The cost of medications used in treating patients in a hospital will vary with number of dosages administered. Yet the cost of employing a cook to prepare meals will not vary with number of meals prepared. A cook will be needed whether the hospital has ten or twenty patients. Only when bed occupancy rises to, perhaps, thirty patients does a second cook have to be hired, and then the two cooks will be able to provide meals for all patients until bed occupancy goes up to, say, fifty, when a third cook will have to be employed. In this instance, then, the resource (cooks) does not vary in direct relation to variations in output (number of meals served). Such costs are referred to as fixed or step-function costs (increasing only with block increases in output).

The best way to determine whether costs are or are not variable is to plot the outputs and inputs identified for any particular activity over a given performance period. Say one is trying to determine whether there is a direct relation between the number of signs painted (output) in a highway maintenance shop and the person-hours required to do so (input):

	Signs Painted	Person-Hours	Person-Hours per Output Unit
March	200	43	.21
April	140	27	.19
May	300	51	.17
June	210	31	.15

Here we see that more signs are being painted per person-hour each succeeding month during the four-month period surveyed. The relationship between changes in outputs and changes in inputs for sign painting is thus not stable enough to be an acceptable variable cost for performance budget purposes. One may find, upon investigation, that the painters used were learning the skill over this period of time, and therefore as their skill level increased, their productivity also increased. Or one may find that there was no change in the skill level of workers, but the signs painted in the later months were simpler and consequently took less time to paint. In the former case, one would use different input units for journeyman painters and apprentice painters. In the latter instance, where the instability of the relationship was due to the different kinds of products being produced (signs), different output units would be used for each different kind of sign painted.

Once all variable costs have been calculated, fixed or step-increase costs plus overhead (which provide general support for the whole budget, e.g., procurement, accounting, warehousing) are added. One may develop a percentage formula for distributing

TABLE 4.1. Performance Budget for a Customer Accounting Department

1. What are the activities of the Department?
   Reading of meters
   Billing of customers
2. Develop work (output) units for each activity:
   Meter reading: 18,000 meters read per month
   (This function will be used for the remainder of this example.)
   Customer billing: 19,000 customers billed per month
3. Estimate the output to be accomplished in the coming fiscal year for meter reading activity:
   Meter reading = 18,000 × 12 = 216,000
4. Determine the inputs (resources) needed to accomplish this output:
   a. Determine inputs required—personal services, vehicles, materials, supervision, overhead, leave
   b. Develop input units for measuring each input:
      Personal services   Man-hours worked
      Vehicles   Miles traveled
      Materials   None
      Supervision   None
      Overhead   None
      Leave   None
   c. From past experience, estimate cost per input unit:
      Personal services $4.00 per hour
      Trucks $.10 per mile
      Supervision   10% of other personal services
      Overhead   20% of all direct costs
      Leave   Man-days (20 days vacation, 12 days sick)
   d. From past experience, determine number of work units (WI) per input unit (IU):
      Personal services   24 meters per man-hour
      Vehicles   2.25 meters per mile
   e. Calculate estimated input from projected output (216,000 meters):
      Est. WUs ÷ $\dfrac{WU}{IU}$ = Est. Input

      Personal services = 216,000 ÷ 24 = 9,000

      Vehicles = 216,000 ÷ 2.25 = 96,000
   f. Calculate estimated expenditures for each input:
      Estimated input × $\dfrac{C}{IU}$ = Est. expenditure

      Pers. serv. =   9,000 × $4.00 = $36,000
      Vehicles   = 96,000 × $ .10 = $ 9,000
   g. Calculate the unit cost (UC) per function by dividing the estimated expenditures for all inputs by the estimated output:
      Est. expend. ÷ Est. no. WUs = unit cost
      $64,340 ÷ 216,000 = $0.298

Inputs	Input Unit	Est. Input	$\dfrac{C}{IU}$	$\dfrac{WU}{IU}$	Est. Expend.
Pers. serv.	MH	9,000	$4.00	24	$36,000
Vehicles	Mile	96,000	1.0	2.25	9.600
Materials	—	—	—	—	1,000
Supervision (10%)	—	—	—	—	3,600
			Direct costs:		$50,200
Overhead (20%)					10,040
Leave (20 vac., 12 sick)					4,100
	Total costs, meter reading activity:				$64,340

TABLE 4.1. *continued*

5. Follow same process as in 4 to calculate inputs for other activities.
6. Set up master performance budget schedule for all activities deriving unit costs and expenditures from input calculations:

Activity	WU	UC	No. WUs	Expenditures
Meter reading	Meters	.298	216,000	$64,340
Billing	Bills			
		Total expens.		

SOURCE: George A. Shipman and Fremont J. Lyden, *Design for the Future*. Ephrata, Wash.: Grant County, Public Utility District, 1972.

overhead costs to each of the activity categories—such as 10 percent to activity A, 30 percent to activity B, and so forth—or overhead may be collected under a single heading such as "administration."

The specific steps required to develop a performance budget are set forth in greater detail in Table 4.1. The information thus collected can then be arrayed in the manner shown in Table 4.2.

UNIT COSTS

There are problems, of course, in using unit costs for the construction of a performance budget. Price changes due to inflation, the introduction of product substitutes into the market, strikes, shipping delays, and other market-related phenomena may cause the composition of unit costs to change suddenly and frequently. Since the major resource used by many government agencies is personal services, it may be argued that performance budgets should be constructed on a work measurement rather than a unit cost basis.

TABLE 4.2. Performance Budgeting

	Work Units	Input Units Req.	Cost per Input Unit	Input Cost per Work Unit	Estimated Expenditures
100 0AA Maint.					
100.1 Intake interviews	(No. interviews conducted)	————————			
100.11 Personnel		(Work hours) —— $ ———	$ ———	$ ———	
100.12 Travel		(Miles) ———— $ ———	$ ———	$ ———	
100.13 Materials		none			
100.2 Home Visits		Total Est. Expends. for interviews:		$ ———	
100.21 Personnel	(No. home	————————————			
100.22 Travel	visits)				
100.23 Materials		(Work hours) —— $ ———	$ ———	$ ———	
		(Miles) ———— $ ———	$ ———	$ ———	
		none			
		Total Est. Expends. for home visits: ——— $ ———			

In other words, the only input unit related to output units would be the person-hour. The cost of all other resources used (e.g., equipment, fuel) are estimated, based on past experience. If analysis reveals that the cost of some of these resources varies directly with person-hours, a percentage formula may be developed for future projection of such costs.

Why, one may ask, are not more budgets that purport to be performance budgets constructed on either a unit cost or work measurement basis? The federal budget was converted from an objects of expenditure to an activity-based budget in 1951 as the result of a Hoover Commission recommendation. Since 1951, then, the federal budget has shown expenditure estimates by activities, but with no indication of how these estimates were systematically developed from input-output analysis. Frequently illustrative outputs, designated as Main Workload Factors, are depicted. In the Appendix to the Budget for Fiscal Year 1979, the Forest Service shows the following output estimates for Forest Land Management:[10]

Activities	1977 Actual	1978 Est.	1979 Est.
1. Timber sales (no.)	145,000	145,000	146,000
2. Timber harvested (billion bd. ft.)	10.5	10.5	10.3
3. Special use permits (no.)	54,000	55,000	55,000

Yet there is no indication how these output estimates are used to develop the expenditure estimates for fighting forest fires, preventing forest fires, controlling insects and diseases, and so forth, all of which are shown as activities under Forest Land Management.

Burkhead has referred to such budgets as performance reporting budgets.[11] The reader can see how much is budgeted for each activity and can get some idea how the funds requested relate to planned outputs. But no attempt is made to explain how the cost estimates were built up from the projected outputs.

In many instances, in fact, it is difficult to identify discrete output units for all or even most of the activities. Even in those cases where this can be done, some may argue that the recordkeeping chore of maintaining such a budget could cost more than the result would be worth. Consequently, most so-called performance budgets, whether developed at the federal, state, or local level, have tended to be what Burkhead refers to as performance reporting budgets rather than true performance budgets.

A CRITIQUE OF PERFORMANCE BUDGETS

Some of the reluctance exhibited toward the development of true performance budgets may be attributed to the criticisms often made of this form of budget: (1) It measures only volume and not quality of work performed, (2) it diffuses organizational responsibility for work performed, and (3) it encourages inefficient procurement practices.

It is true that an output unit measures the *volume* of work performed. But there is no reason why work quality units cannot also be developed to coincide with each output unit. Examples might be:

Activity	Output Unit	Quality Unit
1. Water supply	Gallons consumed	Water quality index
2. Rodent control	Reduction of rats	Number of rat bites reported
3. Library	Number of volumes loaned	Number of volumes requested, but not available; waiting lists
4. Immunization	Number of persons immunized	Decline in rates of smallpox, measles, etc.

In each case the quality measure acts as a control on the output measure to assure that work volume is not being achieved at the expense of work quality.

Quality units can also be combined with output units to derive productivity indices. Table 4.3 illustrates the use of this procedure. Tons of solid waste collected is the output unit. Street cleanliness ratings and consumer satisfaction are chosen as quality measures. Multiplying the output for 1970 (90,000) times the cleanliness rating (2.9), times the expressed level of consumer satisfaction (85 percent), divided by the cost yields an index of .185. If this measure is compared with the productivity measurement for 1971, a decrease in productivity of 14 percent is noted. This occurs in spite of the fact that output increased by 10,000 tons from 1970 to 1971. The decrease in productivity is thus

TABLE 4.3. Illustrative Productivity Measurement Presentation: Solid Waste Collection Example

Data	1970	1971	Change
1. Tons of solid waste collected	90,000	100,000	$10,000
2. Average street cleanliness rating[a]	2.9	2.6	−0.3
3. Percent of survey population expressing satisfaction with collection[b]	85%	80%	−5
4. Cost (current)	$1,200,000	$1,500,000	+$300,000
5. Costs (1970 dollars)	$1,200,000	$1,300,000	+$100,000

Productivity Measures	1970	1971	Change
6. Workload per dollar (unadjusted dollars)	75 tons per thousand $	67 tons per thousand $	−11%
7. Workload productivity (1970 dollars)	75 tons per thousand $	77 tons per thousand $	+3%
8. Output index: $\frac{(1)X(2)X(3)}{(4)}$ (unadjusted dollars)	0.185	0.139	−25%
9. Productivity index: $\frac{(1)X(2)X(3)}{(5)}$ (1970 dollars)	0.185	0.160	−14%

SOURCE: Harry P. Hatry and Donald M. Fisk, *Improving Productivity and Productivity Measurement in Local Governments*, The National Commission on Productivity, 1971, p. 19.

[a] Such rating procedures are currently in use in the District of Columbia. The rating in line 2 is presumed to be based on a scale of "1" to "4", with "4" being the cleanest.

[b] The figures in line 7 indicate some improvement in efficiency, but line 6 suggests that cost increases such as wages have more than exceeded the efficiency gains. Productivity has gone down even further on the basis of decreases in the street cleanliness ratings and decreased citizen satisfaction. However, such indices have to be studied carefully and interpreted according to local circumstances to be fairly understood.

the result of the lower cleanliness rating (3.6) and the lower consumer satisfaction level (80 percent) in 1971.

Another criticism frequently made of performance budgets is that they diffuse the identification of organizational responsibility by lumping together all contributions to the performance of each kind of activity, regardless of where such efforts originate in the organization. Figure 4.1 depicts a bureau consisting of four divisions that are responsible for three activities—A, B, and C. But only activity C is performed solely within one division. And even the total budget of that division is greater than the cost of performing activity C because the division also contributes to the performance of activities A and B. Consequently, how can the four division heads be held responsible for the budgets of

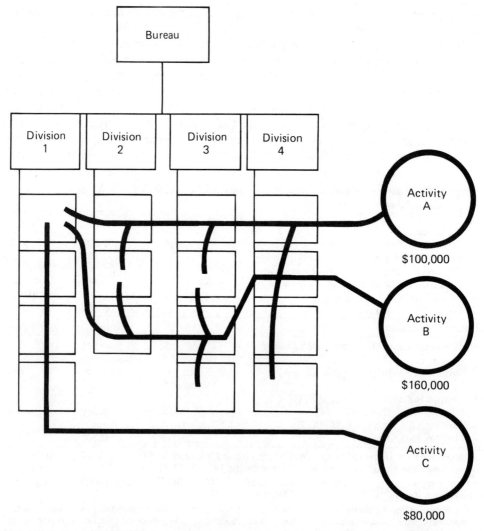

FIGURE 4.1 Performance Reporting in an Organization. (*From* Performance Reporting, *Washington, D.C.: U.S. Treasury Department, May 1950)*

$85,000, $75,000, $91,000, and $89,000 allocated to them? The answer, of course, is through matrix reporting, that is, a cross-classification of activity expenditures by organizational units, depicted as follows:

	Act. A	Act. B	Act. C	Total
Division 1	$1,000	$4,000	$80,000	$85,000
Division 2	25,000	50,000	—	75,000
Division 3	35,000	56,000	—	91,000
Division 4	39,000	50,000	—	89,000
Total	$100,000	$160,000	$80,000	$340,000

Division 1 will be held responsible for providing $1000 of the resources for the performance of activity A and $4,000 for activity B. Yet output control for activity A can be accomplished by relating the volume (and quality) of output to be accomplished to the $100,000 of inputs budgeted for this activity.

The criticism that performance budgeting can lead to inefficiency in the procurement and use of resources is based on the fact that this kind of budget makes it difficult to determine how much of each type of resource is being ordered by the whole agency. Objects of expenditure required for activities A, B, and C may look something like this:

	Pers.	Travel	Supplies	Equipment	Total
Act. A	$80,000	$5,000	$7,000	$8,000	$100,000
Act. B	90,000	15,000	10,000	45,000	160,000
Act. C	75,000	100	3,000	1,900	80,000
	$245,000	$21,100	$20,000	$54,900	$340,000

If the supplies purchased for activity A are no different from those required for activities B and C (e.g., paper, file folders, typewriter ribbons), lumping all the orders together will allow the agency to take advantage of quantity discounts. Also, the agency will be able to maintain centrally housed inventories, thus making supplies more readily available to users throughout the organization when needed.

But the need for an objects of expenditure budget for procurement purposes does not mean that these costs cannot be cross-classified to reflect performance. As noted, many cities and counties have long used functional classifications in budgeting. Since financial auditing is based on goods and services purchased, such governments frequently report expenditures on both an objects of expenditure and a functional (performance) basis.

It would therefore appear that most of the criticisms voiced about performance budgeting are less serious than they first appear. But is performance budgeting worth the effort? In a study of the work-measurement-based performance budget system employed by the City of Los Angeles, Eghtedari and Sherwood found that executive control was strengthened by this form of budgeting, but City Council decision making was not particularly affected.[12] Perhaps the finding of a more in-depth study of five federal agencies conducted by James Jernberg shed some light on the question of legislative decision making.[13] Jernberg did a content analysis of the questions raised by members of the appropriations subcommittees reviewing the requests of the Federal Prison System, the Immigration and Naturalization Service, the Internal Revenue Service, the Forest Service, and the National Park Service. When comparing the questions asked these agencies by their respective subcommittees before and after the federal budget was changed from an objects of expenditure to a performance budget in 1951, he found that agencies like the Forest Service and National Park Service, traditionally associated with work performance, were monitored more often by their subcommittee on performance expectations after 1951 than before. The Federal Prison System and the Immigration and Naturalization Service had traditionally been monitored by their subcommittee on the basis of their demonstrated capabilities and the reliability of the data they provided the subcommittee. For these agencies, then, although they were also required to change to a performance budget in 1951, their subcommittee continued to evaluate them in terms of the capability and reliability criteria provided by the objects of expenditure supplementary budget. The fifth agency, the Internal Revenue Service, had traditionally been monitored by its subcommittee on how impartially and honestly they executed the law. After 1951, their subcommittee continued to use these criteria, which required information about the staffing and supervision of employees. Such information was also more readily available from an objects of expenditure than a performance based budget. Thus Jernberg concludes that the kind of information a legislative body uses to evaluate an agency budget depends upon how the agency's mission has traditionally been perceived. If the agency's mission has traditionally been perceived as related to work output, the performance budget may provide a better basis than the objects of expenditure budget for decision making. If, on the other hand, other criteria are more directly associated with the agency's mission—such as honesty and impartiality for a revenue collection agency—the performance information provided by the performance budget may not be particularly useful. We would therefore expect a legislative body to welcome a performance-based budget for evaluating some agencies, but would continue to use information provided by other budget formats for monitoring other agencies. This would explain the somewhat ambivalent response of legislators to the use of performance budgets.

SUMMARY

The budget formats discussed in this chapter—objects of expenditure and performance—are most useful in providing the information required to make two kinds of decisions: computational (type 1) and judgment (type 2). The computation decision assumes there is agreement on both the ends to be accomplished and the means to be employed. The only decision to be made is what combination of resources can achieve these results most efficiently. The objects of expenditure provides the information needed.

The judgment decision (type 2) assumes agreement over the ends to be accomplished but lack of agreement on the appropriate means to employ. The performance budget, providing information on outputs, inputs, and the relationship of the one to the other (unit costs), contains the information required to determine what activities (means) using how much of what resources (inputs) will best accomplish the agreed-upon ends.

Neither of the two budget formats discussed in this chapter provides the kind of information needed for dealing with compromise (type 3) and inspiration (type 4) decisions. In the past, budgets constructed on an objects of expenditure or an organizational unit basis have appeared to be most useful for dealing with such decisions because both tend to allow the protagonists to define ends according to their own tastes, therefore minimizing controversies. When large amounts of public funds are expended for programs where there is lack of agreement over the ends to be accomplished, however, type 3 and type 4 decisions require program justification in terms of demonstrated differences to be made in society. Thus, in the 1960s the defense and the antipoverty programs both required a budgeting classification based upon impacts made in society. The PPB and ZBB formats discussed in the next chapter evolved to fulfill this need.

CASE STUDY

While one budget design or another may seem to be more useful than others when viewed in abstract terms, the real utility of any format can be judged only by how it contributes to or obstructs in the making of organizational decisions. In the case that follows, Seven Letters, the city manager, the water superintendent, and the budget officer all seem to be speaking different languages. Why? Is each viewing the question from a different budget perspective? If so, which actors are seeing the budget more as an instrument for recording resources required (objects of expenditure)? Which see it as a tool for showing work to be done (performance)? Why should those who hold one perspective have difficulty communicating with those holding other perspectives? How do hierarchical questions (line vs. staff, department vs. department, department vs. city manager) affect the different ways the problem is viewed? Could budget redesign change the context in which these actors communicate with each other? How would the city engineer have worded his request to the budget officer if the budget had been constructed on a performance basis? How would the budget officer have responded? What budget format would be most useful to the city manager if he is expected to play a role in resolving the problem?

CASE STUDY

Seven Letters: A Case in Public Management

Edwin O. Stene

THE case that follows is in the management area, although it brings into sharp focus some broad theoretical problems of hierarchy and staff-line relationships and it touches on the problem of performance budgeting. It presents the "What do you do now?" type of problem; it also can be considered with a view to analyzing and explaining behavior in large-scale organizations. Again, it may be considered as an illustration of concepts of authority or bureaucracy, or as supporting ideas of how government should be administered.

The names used in the case are disguised, but the problem is a real one, and the letters were actually written by city officials. The case, presented for discussion purposes, is not intended to represent either correct or incorrect administrative practices.

Cast of Characters:

Clyde Perham, city manager.

H. P. Robertson, director of the City Water Department, an officer appointed by and responsible to the city manager.

Mark B. Mason, chief engineer and superintendent of production in the City Water Department, appointed by the director of the Water Department under civil service regulations. Mason is a registered professional sanitary engineer who has held the post in the Water Department for many years.

R. J. Herrington, superintendent of purification, also appointed by the director of the Water Department under civil service regulations, but immediately responsible to the chief engineer. His office is at the pumping plant about two miles from City Hall.

Paul A. Harper, chief of the Office of Budget and Allotments, a staff agency of the manager. Harper, a man of about 30, has held the position for less than two years and has been employed in the office for about four years.

Roger Graham, assistant in the Office of Budget and Allotments, under appointment by Paul Harper. Graham has been employed for less than a year. He is still under civil service probation, but has been recommended for final appointment.

All offices are in the City Hall except that of Mr. Herrington. The Office of Budget and Allotments is near the Manager's Office; the Water Department Offices are located in a different section of the building.

The exchange of letters will indicate the subject matter of telephone conversations between the two agencies. However, two items not disclosed by the letters have been reported by Roger Graham: (1) the Office of Budget and Allotments has noted that excesses of personnel costs over estimates in the past have been accounted for almost entirely by overtime work; and (2) Graham visited the purification plant after his first telephone conversation with Herrington, and is of the opinion that overtime work at the plant can be virtually eliminated if the additional personnel are employed.

First Letter, February 5

Date : February 5, 1953
To : Office of Budget and Allotments
From: Water Department
Re : Additional Personnel

Attention Mr. Paul A. Harper

Dear Sir:

I am writing for approval to employ additional personnel in the Purification Section of

Reprinted with permission from *Public Administration Review*, vol. XVII (1957), no. 2.

the Water Department. The classifications and number of each that we are requesting are as follows:

Water Plant Attendant—4 additional
    Permanent
General Laborer**—4 additional
    From April 15 to November 1
Water Laboratory Technician—1 additional
    Permanent—either full time or part time, dependent on the qualifications and availability of applicants

The explanation of our needs for these additional men is fairly well set out in Mr. R. S. Herrington's memo of February 2, which is attached to this memorandum. I, therefore, will not go into any further detail at this time but will be glad to furnish more information if you require it.

    Yours very truly,

    MARK B. MASON
    Chief Engineer and Superintendent

Approved:
  H. P. Robertson, Director

Memo Attached to Letter of February 5

Date : February 2, 1953
To   : Mr. Mason
From: R. J. Herrington
Re   : Increase in operating personnel

Dear Sir:

I would like to recommend that the present operating personnel in the Purification Section be increased to the extent that there are two chemical attendants on each shift at the Chemical Bldg.; there is a laborer on each shift in the filter room during the summer months, and that an additional laboratory technician be provided in the laboratory. This will require 4 additional chemical attendants, 4 laborers, and 1 laboratory technician.

Chemical Bldg.

At the present time the operating personnel at the Chemical Bldg. consists of one treat-

ment foreman and one chemical attendant on each shift, except in the case of the 7-3 shift where there is an extra chemical attendant part of the time, namely Sat. & Sun.

The water treatment foreman is now spending approximately 3/4 of his time in collecting samples, making analytical determinations, and in calculation of doses. This leaves insufficient time to look after the operation of basins, equipment, etc. When trouble develops either the samples do not get collected or the analyses are made in such haste that the results are inaccurate. At the present time more frequent analyses should be performed on the raw water. During periods of peak consumption or peak hardness more frequent analyses should be performed on the various phases thru the plant. With the expanding plant there will be more sample and check points.

The chemical attendant at present is occupied in tending chemical feed machines, checking on boilers and allied equipment, and the handling of bulk chemicals that are fed by hand. During periods of maximum operation, it is impossible to give the feed machines sufficient attention.

The operations at the Chemical Bldg. are fast becoming decentralized, such as carbon feeders, CO_2 production, and primary basins.

A second chemical attendant on each shift at the Chemical Bldg. will provide the additional manpower to cover the above situations for the present time. The time of the extra chemical attendant would be split about equal between the collection of samples along with basin operations and the application of chemicals.

Filter Plant.

The filter operator is now spending between 5 to 6 hours per day washing filters. It requires approximately 30 minutes to surface wash a filter and 15 minutes to back wash. Washing filters without surface washing over extended periods is not advisable as evidenced by condition and performance of filters at the end of such period.

As the filter plant approaches its maximum capacity, it will be necessary that the filter operator devote his entire time to operation and manipulation of filters.

The addition of a laborer to each shift in the filter plant during the period May thru Oct. for surface washing filters will be necessary.

Laboratory.

The present laboratory personnel can no longer absorb any additional work. In recent years there have been increases in bacteriological examination and chemical analyses of the water in the distribution system. The testing of materials has been expanded. At present the laboratory is not doing anything but routine work. It is no longer possible to investigate all complaints and guide visitors thru the plant properly. Some additional control analyses are required on raw water.

The addition to the laboratory of a trained man such as a college student on a part time basis would adequately fill the present needs and at the same time afford us the opportunity to be in constant touch with the latest methods and developments in chemical and bacteriological analyses.

This man could work evenings, which would alleviate otherwise crowded working conditions.

Very truly yours,

R. J. HERRINGTON

RJH:mwp

The receipt of these letters by Paul Harper was followed by two telephone calls made by Roger Graham, to whom the Water Department Budget work had been assigned.

First Graham called Mark Mason to explain that the Budget Office needed more detailed information before it passed upon the requests. The nature of the information desired is described in later correspondence. At the close of the conversation Mason and Graham agreed that Graham should call Herrington, and also that he might visit Herrington at the plant to get a first-hand picture of the situation.

Graham then called Herrington and explained to him the nature of the information needed. Herrington agreed to prepare a more detailed memorandum, which he would route through Mason.

Second Letter, March 10

Date : March 10, 1953
To : Mr. Mason
From: R. J. Herrington
Re : Increase in operating personnel, filter plant

Dear Sir:

The addition of a laborer on each shift in the filter plant during the peak months was requested in order to provide sufficient manpower to properly surface wash, with fire hose, the filters. This operation requires approximately 30 minutes per filter. The filter operator will also be provided with sufficient time for making constant filter performance checks. In order to produce between 150-160 MG per day, all filters will have to operate at peak performance continuously.

During the summer 1952 the maximum filtered was about 135 MGD or the capacity of the primary settling basin flumes. At this time washing of filters occurred when the above rate was no longer able to be maintained.

In the coming summer if sufficient water is available for filtration of 150-160 MGD, an individual avg. filter rate of 6.3 MGD for 150 MGD and a rate of 7.0 MGD for 160 MGD will have to be maintained with all filters in service. With an avg. of 22 filters in service this rate will be 6.7 MGD for 150 MGD and 7.3 MGD for 160 MGD.

The length of filter runs is affected by pH of the applied water, turbidity or suspended matter in applied water, retention time available in the final basins, and the elevation of the final basins. Surface washing of filters also has a bearing upon the length of filter runs.

As all of the above mentioned items are apt to be critical at various times, it is difficult to estimate the number of washings that will be required for filtration of 150-160 MGD.

With final basin elevation of 33.0' or less, filters will have to be washed at 3.0-4.0 head loss. With a minimum final elevation maintained at 35.0' the head loss could be extended to 5.0 to 6.0' prior to washing.

Caustic water applied to filters tends to increase head losses very rapidly causing vapor locking of filters.

The amount of turbidity or suspended matter applied to the filters depends very largely upon the retention time available in final basins. At these high rates the bulk of the suspended matter, either carried over from Secondaries or that formed as a result of chemical reactions, must be filtered out.

In view of the above facts it is estimated that each filter will have to be washed every 24 hours for 150 MGD rate and between 15-20 hours for 160 MGD rate.

Very truly yours,

R. J. HERRINGTON

RJH:mwp

—————————

Two telephone calls occurred between the second and third letters. Subject matter of the conversation again is indicated in the letters that follow.

The first call was made by Graham to Herrington, at which time Graham explained that the information set forth in the second letter was incomplete and enumerated the items of further information desired. Graham understood that Herrington agreed to prepare another memo, which would again be routed by way of Mason. (See item 5 in fifth letter).

The second interoffice telephone call was made by Mason to Harper. The purpose of the call is indicated in the third letter and in the seventh letter (item 6.)

Third Letter, March 19

Date : March 19, 1953
To   : Mark B. Mason, Chief Engineer
       and Supt., Water Department
From: Office of Budget and Allotments
Re   : Additional Personnel

On February 5, 1953, your request for additional personnel in the Purification Section came to this office. The staff member from this office in a conversation with you informed you he desired further information in order to evaluate the request and believed he had secured your verbal permission to contact the Superintendent of Purification for this desired information. He proceeded to contact the Superintendent of Purification and talked with him regarding the request. He asked that certain details be incorporated in a memo, sent to you for approval, and then forwarded to him. A memo, handled in that manner, was received in this office March 10, 1953. As it did

not contain all of the information requested, another phone call was made to the Superintendent of Purification asking him if he would supply the information and forward through the same channels.

If you desire that all requests for information be sent to you in writing and permission to contact your subordinates on similar matters also be requested and approved in writing, we shall be glad to do so.

Therefore, in response to your telephone call of today, we request that the following information be forwarded to this office:

(1) A description of the job duties that will be performed by the additional Water Plant Attendant on each shift.
(2) Will this reduce overtime for this operation?
(3) Will there be a continuing need for General Laborers to work on these shifts?
(4) How many samples of water are taken on each shift and at what points and/or additional points will they be taken per shift?
(5) Data on the number of chemical analyses being made at present, in the immediate future, and time needed to make these tests.
(6) In general any other information that will in any way support your request for additional personnel requested.

Perhaps we may explain our position by pointing out that, based upon present minimum salaries, the yearly cost of this additional personnel would be $30,940 or over a 10 year period $309,400. Such an addition to fixed operating expense should receive careful consideration. I know you will agree with this.

P. A. Harper
Director

gml

cc: H. P. Robertson, Director of Water

Fourth Letter, March 25

Date : March 25, 1953
To   : Office of Budget and Allotments
From: Water Department
Re   : Additional Operating Personnel—
       Purification Division

Attention Mr. P. A. Harper, Director

Dear Paul:

I am starting this letter with some hesitation. I have a high regard for you and several of the members of your staff with whom I am acquainted. Therefore, I am embarrassed by making what seems to be a personal attack on you and the members of your staff when my real target is the sort of bureaucratic system that puts you and your staff in a position of authority (without responsibility) that in my opinion you are not qualified by experience, training and numbers to carry out.

When I phoned the other day to ask that you put your request for information into written form I stated that I did not believe that your people knew what they were doing in the case of our request for additional operating personnel in the Purification Section. The letter, dated March 19, that you sent me confirms my opinion.

Your first question asking for "a description of the job duties that will be performed by the additional Water Plant Attendant on each shift" indicates that all of the time spent on this subject to date by both your staff and mine has been completely wasted.

Let me list some of the things that have happened that should have produced the answer to the above as well as all the other information that you request in your March 19 letter.

(1) On February 5 I wrote a short memo to you transmitting a two page typewritten letter from our Superintendent of Purification stating what additional personnel he needed and why. He wrote exactly 24 typewritten lines about the Water Plant Attendant position and indicated fairly well what the duties would be.

(2) A few days later your Mr. Graham phoned to say that he wanted to visit the plant in regard to our request for additional personnel. We then continued to talk at some length about the *need* and *duties* of the additional men. We talked about these matters to such an extent that I thought Mr. Graham had obtained all the information he wanted and was not going to visit the plant after all.

(3) Following this, two phone calls were made by Mr. Graham to the Superintendent of Purification. Each one was fairly long, 10 minutes or so, and both were concerned about the additional operating personnel.

The first phone call resulted in another full page memo from the Superintendent of Purification and the second phone call was for the purpose of requesting still another memo. It was at this point that I protested. It seems to me that by this time you should know what we are going to do with the extra men.

Your second question "Will this reduce overtime for this operation?" seems to be superfluous. It is obvious that any overtime caused by a shortage of personnel would be reduced by the addition of more personnel.

Your third question "Will there be a continuing need for General Laborers to work on these shifts?" is in about the same category as the question on overtime. If the occasion arises, as it has in the past and as it undoubtedly will in the future, where more personnel are required than are available in the operating force, then General Laborers will be used as necessary.

Your next questions imply that you have a working knowledge of our operating procedures that is belied by your first question. If I thought you could make use of the answers to these questions I would obtain the information for you. I do not believe that you are well enough acquainted with the problems and procedures of operating a Purification Plant to warrant my bothering the Superintendent of Purification with a request for data on these items.

In regard to your closing paragraph wherein you point out that the additional cost to fixed operating expense should receive careful consideration, I want to say that I heartily agree with you. In fact, I believe that I have considered the cost even more carefully than you have. According to my figures the yearly cost based upon present minimum salaries for the additional operating personnel would be only $19,040 instead of the $30,940 quoted in your March 19 memo.

A letter of this type is not complete if it does not contain recommendations for correcting the complaint. For that reason I suggest that the following steps be taken.

If the system as it now exists is to continue I suggest that you obtain an adequate number of qualified people to work with our department and who will have the time and ability to study and understand our needs and to take effective action when it is necessary. Our experiences with your Department have left us with a feeling of harassed frustration. We are hesitant about attempting to obtain needed personnel because we know from past experience that in most cases we will spend weeks and months—sort of like dangling from the end of a string before getting an answer. There have of course been some exceptions. This would not be too impossible a situation if the matter would end in your department. After you have finally made a decision, we quite often have to go through the same song and dance with the Personnel Department. There should not be so many obstacles put in our path. You should give us better and more understanding service than you have in the past.

If you cannot operate as described above then I suggest that you concern yourself only with the budget side of the problem. If the budget appears to be strained by the additional personnel you should notify us accordingly and *we* would decide then either to give up some other budgeted item or to give up the additional personnel.

You could supplement this type of activity by making periodic surveys of our operations to see if we were overstaffed or not and if we were making effective use of our personnel.

I like this latter suggestion much better than the first because I can see where you could produce a real service much easier than you could under the first suggestion.

I stated at the beginning that I hesitated to write this letter. It is embarrassing to me to have to do so. It will probably cause a commotion. I heard a sermon last Sunday that was entitled "Use a Little Honey." The moral was that you can catch more flies with honey than you can with vinegar. I wish that I was clever enough to have been able to coat this letter with a generous layer of honey because I have no desire to start a fight or to harm anyone or to embarrass anyone. But I do want to get a condition straightened out that I do not believe is fair, or proper or necessary.

Maybe this letter will accomplish that purpose.

Yours very truly,

MARK B. MASON
Chief Engineer and Superintendent

MBM-t
cc: City Manager Perham
      Mr. Robertson

Fifth Letter, April 13

Date : April 13, 1953
To   : Mark B. Mason
From: Office of Budget and Allotments
Re   : Additional Personnel—Purification
           Section

I sincerely hope that you will not hesitate, in the future, to notify me if you are dissatisfied in any way with the services of this department. It is my intent and I believe also that of the City Manager, that this department be primarily a service department assisting line departments to operate as expeditiously as possible within the overall framework of municipal government. Not being perfect, we sometimes fail in this endeavor.

To a certain extent you are correct when you state that we are unqualified by experience, training, etc., to judge your requests. Therefore, it is necessary that we ask questions. We try not to judge any request on a technical basis, rather we attempt to get the technically qualified person to explain the problem to us so that we understand and can make a cogent recommendation to the Manager. If a satisfactory and understandable explanation is not presented, we feel this to be an indication that the request is not too well thought out and needs further work.

As to your suggestions for improving the situation, I agree heartily with you that little would be accomplished by our maintaining a balance sheet and at certain dollar signs saying stop. That is most unrealistic and is of little or no help to a department. Insofar as possible we try to actually survey field conditions when investigating a request, but during the past two months the preparation of the Annual Budget has made this mostly impossible.

As to the specific items in your memo of March 25, 1953:

(1) On February 8, your memo and the attached memo from the Superintendent of Purification was received in this office.

(2) Later a member of this office phoned you. He talked with you about the request, a visit to the plant, and of making contact with the Superintendent of Purification.

(3) Subsequently, a phone call was made to the Superintendent of Purification and the request was discussed with him. The Superintendent was asked

that certain details be incorporated in a memo, sent to you for approval, and then forwarded to this office.

(4) A memo, handled in this manner, was received in this office March 10, but it contained only part of the information requested. Thus, the call for another memo.

(5) A second phone call was made to the Superintendent of Purification, asking him to supply the work-load data and to forward it through the established channels. During the conversation it was mentioned that the cost of the additional personnel would be partially offset by savings in overtime and use of present personnel. It was requested that an estimate of these possible savings be included in the memo.

(6) As to the questions included in our memo of March 19th:

(a) *A description of the job duties that will be performed by the additional Water Plant Attendant on each shift?*

We understood that the additional person on each shift would perform a combination of jobs now partly performed by the present Water Plant Attendant and partly by the Water Treatment Foreman. It was felt that possibly the combining of job duties would bear upon a question of proper job classification.

(b) *Will this reduce overtime for this operation?*

We were seeking confirmation of the telephone conversation with the Superintendent of Purification. I am in no position to assume anything. I must know.

(c) *Will there be a continuing need for General Laborers to work on these shifts?*

Again, seeking confirmation of the telephone conversation. This would directly affect the request for additional people for this position. There have been occasions when part-time help have been kept longer than authorized.

(d) *How many samples of water are taken on each shift and at what points and/or additional points will they be taken per shift?*

This information would supply us with a basis for evaluating the need for extra personnel and how much.

(e) *Data on the number of chemical analyses being made at present, in the immediate future, and time needed to make these tests?*

This is again needed for an evaluation of needs. There was no detail of this nature included with original budget requests.

(f) *In general any other information that will in any way support your request for additional personnel?*

We were trying to obtain any other information that would aid us in evaluating your request.

(g) Lastly, and to my great chagrin, I find that you are correct when you state that the cost of your request will be $19,040 instead of $30,940. This certainly is the one area where I should be right, but wrong I am. Next time I will not use that slide rule!

I personally do not like honey. I much prefer the straightforwardness you have exhibited. Both you and I will make mistakes, but neither of us has anything to be ashamed of or to conceal. Therefore, I re-emphasize my desire that you communicate directly to me any impression of delay or impropriety you may have in the future.

In conclusion, I should appreciate it if you would send me the information requested in my memorandum of *March 19, 1953* in order that this matter may be closed out at the earliest possible date.

P. A. Harper
Director

gml
cc: Clyde Perham, City Manager
    H. P. Robertson, Director of Water

Sixth Letter, April 15

Date : April 15, 1953
To   : Office of Budget and Allotments
From: Water Department
Subject: Additional Operating Personnel—
         Purification Division

Attention Mr. P. A. Harper, Director

Dear Paul:

Your letter of April 13 brings to mind a dog I once knew named Rover. Rover's owner would hold out a biscuit to the dog and say, "Roll over, Rover!"

Rover would roll over, but his owner, still holding out the biscuit would then say, "Now bark, Rover."

Rover, eyeing the biscuit expectantly, would say, "Bow Wow!"

The owner would then say, "Bark again, Rover." And Rover would again say, "Bow Wow!"

This went on for some time until one day when Rover, after having said "Bow Wow" several times, laid down on the ground and would never roll over or say Bow Wow again.

Unlike Rover, I will undoubtedly have to

roll over and say Bow Wow many times in the future. However, I have only a couple of Bow Wows left for the case of the additional operating personnel at the Purification plant.

In regard to the first five questions of your March 19 memo, I have nothing to add to what has already been said.

In regard to your sixth question, I should tell you that if we cannot fill the additional positions the following will certainly occur:

1) It will be impossible to produce the quantity of water that our plant will otherwise be able to produce by this June. An amount that we hope will be at least as great as the demand.

2) It will be impossible to control the quality of the water at the high demand rates expected this summer and most of the time thereafter. Loss of control of quality may or may not be detrimental to the public health.

3) Loss of control of quality will be accompanied by a loss of control of chemical costs. This is very vital when you consider that the cost of chemicals alone for this current fiscal year has averaged about $1,700 per day.

Yours very truly,

MARK B. MASON
Chief Engineer and Superintendent
MBM-t
cc: Mr. Perham
Mr. Robertson

Seventh Letter, April 28

Date : April 28, 1953
To : H. P. Robertson, Director of Water
From: Office of Budget and Allotment
Re : Additional Operating Personnel—
Purification Division

You undoubtedly have copies of the communications sent to me by Mr. Mason, dated March 25 and April 15, in response to my memos to him, dated March 19 and April 13.

A brief restatement of the development of this situation follows:

(1) On February 8, Mr. Mason's memo and that attached memo from the Superintendent of Purification were received in this office.

(2) Later a member of this office phoned Mr. Mason. He talked with him about the request, a visit to the plant, and of making a contact with the Superintendent of Purification.

(3) Subsequently, a phone call was made to the Superintendent of Purification and the request was discussed with him. The Superintendent was asked to incorporate certain details in a memo, send the memo to Mr. Mason for his approval, and have it forwarded to this office.

(4) A memo, handled in this manner, was received in this office March 10, but it contained only part of the information requested. Thus the call for another memo.

(5) A second phone call was made to the Superintendent of Purification, asking him to supply the work-load data and to forward it through the established channels.

(6) On March 19, Mr. Mason contacted me by phone and expressed his desire that all requests for information be sent to him in writing and that requests for permission to contact his subordinates on similar matters be submitted to him for his written approval.

(7) My memo to Mr. Mason (March 19) was sent in response to his telephone request.

A copy of this and my subsequent memo were sent to you.

It would appear that Mr. Mason will not or cannot furnish this office with the information that we feel is essential if we are to properly evaluate his request and make recommendation to the Manager. If, as Mr. Mason states, the lack of personnel requested will deprive the City of water it could otherwise have, the request should be approved. But if this is true, there must be reasons and this is what we are trying to determine.

I would appreciate it if you would send me the information requested in my memorandum of March 19, 1953, to Mr. Mason, or any other information that you believe pertinent to the request for additional personnel.

I have no desire to engage in a running fight with any individual or department. This department has a certain job to do in the overall administration of the City's activities. Sometimes differences of opinion result. This is inevitable. Usually through mutual cooperation these differences can be resolved in a satisfactory manner. If you have any suggestions as to how this spirit of cooperation can be enhanced, I will be only too glad to discuss it with you at your convenience.

P. A. Harper
Director

gab
cc: Clyde Perham, City Manager

NOTES

1. Henry Jones Ford, "Budget Making and the Work of Government," *Annals*, November 1915, pp. 4–5.

2. Norman Gill, *Municipal Research Bureaus* (Washington, D.C.: American Council on Public Affairs, 1944), p. 12.

3. Jesse Burkhead, *Government Budgeting* (New York: Wiley, 1956), p. 13.

4. Jane S. Dahlberg, *The New York Bureau of Municipal Research* (New York: New York University Press, 1966), p. 150.

5. Ibid., p. 161.

6. Burkhead, *Government Budgeting*, pp. 17–18.

7. James D. Thompson and Arthur Tuden, "Strategies, Structures and Processes in Organizational Decisions," in James D. Thompson et al., *Comparative Studies in Administration* (Pittsburgh: University of Pittsburgh Press, 1959).

8. A. E. Buck, *Public Budgeting* (New York: Harper & Row, 1929), pp. 170–71, 272–75, 460–63.

9. *The Nineteenth and Concluding Report of the Commission on Organization of the Executive Branch of Government* (Washington, D.C.: Government Printing Office, 1949), p. 15.

10. *Appendix to the Budget for Fiscal Year 1979* (Washington, D.C.: Government Printing Office, 1978).

11. Burkhead, *Government Budgeting*.

12. Ali Eghtedari and Frank Sherwood, "Performance Budgeting in Los Angeles," *Public Administration Review*, Spring 1960, pp. 63–85.

13. James Jernberg, "Information Change and Congressional Behavior: A Caveat for PPB Reformers," *Journal of Politics* 33, no. 3 (August 1969): 722–40.

BIBLIOGRAPHY

Burkhead, Jesse. *Government Budgeting*. New York: Wiley, 1956.

Dahlberg, Jane S. *The New York Bureau of Municipal Research*. New York: New York University Press, 1966.

Eghtedari, Ali, and Sherwood, Frank. "Performance Budgeting in Los Angeles." *Public Administration Review*, Spring 1960, pp. 63–85.

Fuchs, Victor R. *Production and Productivity in the Service Industries*. New York: National Bureau of Economic Research, 1969.

Kraines, Oscar. "The President Versus Congress: The Keep Commission, 1905–1909." *Western Political Quarterly* 23, no. 1 (March 1970): 5–54.

Lynch, Thomas D. *Public Budgeting in America*. New York: Prentice-Hall, 1979.

Mosher, Frederick. *Program Budgeting: Theory and Practice*. Chicago: Public Administration Service, 1954.

Ridley, Clarence E., and Simon, Herbert. *Measuring Municipal Activities*. Chicago: ICMA, 1943.

U. S. Bureau of the Budget. *A Work Measurement System: Development and Use*. Washington, D.C.: Government Printing Office, March 1950.

Chapter 5

Design of the Executive Budget: From PPB to ZBB

When Robert McNamara became Secretary of Defense in 1961, he found that he lacked the tools necessary to manage the huge military organization effectively. Previous secretaries had to resort to the use of a "budget ceiling" approach in which the President would indicate the general level of defense expenditures and the Secretary would then allocate this figure among the three military services. Each service (Army, Navy, Air Force) would in turn prepare its basic budget submission, allocating its ceiling among its own functions, units, and activities. In addition, each service would submit an addendum budget to include expenditures which could not be accommodated within the ceiling. Finally, all budget submissions would be reviewed by the Secretary in an attempt to achieve some balance among the three services.

As a result, in the words of Charles Hitch, McNamara's Comptroller, "each service tended to exercise its own priorities, favoring its own unique missions to the detriment of joint missions, striving to lay the groundwork for an increased share of the budget in future years by concentrating on alluring new weapon systems, and protecting the overall size of its own forces even at the cost of readiness."[1] Since attention was focused on only the next fiscal year, the services were encouraged continually to propose new starts with little attention given to the long-range investment consequences of such actions.

Also the new Secretary found almost a complete separation between budgeting and military planning. The latter was performed in terms of missions, weapon systems, and military forces—the outputs of the department. Budgeting was based on intermediary products (such as construction, maintenance) and resources purchased (objects of expenditures). Thus the budget structure of each of the three services consisted of (1) Military Personnel, (2) Operation and Maintenance, (3) Procurement, (4) Research and Development, and (5) Military Construction. McNamara concluded that if the budget were to reflect the planning process, it would have to be restructured along lines employed for operational decision making by the three services. To accomplish this end, all combinations of activities contributing to a common goal were packaged together into a "program element." Close to 1000 of these elements were identified. Each element was classified under one of nine major programs or missions of the department:[2]

1 *Strategic Retaliatory Forces*: forces designed to carry out the long-range strategic mission and to carry the main burden of battle in general
2 *Continental Air and Missile Defense Forces*: weapons systems, warning and communication networks, and ancillary equipment required to detect, identify, track and destroy unfriendly forces approaching the North American continent
3 *General Purpose Forces*: forces relied upon to perform the entire range of combat operations short of general nuclear war
4 *Airlift and Sealift Forces*: forces required to move troops and cargo promptly to wherever they might be needed
5 *Reserve and National Guard Forces*: equipment, training, and administration of the Reserve and National Guard personnel
6 *Research and Development*: all research and development not directly identified with the elements of other programs
7 *General Support*: support activities of the several services and agencies that serve the entire department
8 *Military Assistance*: equipment, training, and related services provided for armed forces of allied and friendly nations
9 *Civil Defense*: federal assistance for fallout shelters, warning and radiological monitoring systems, training and education for emergency preparedness, and so on

McNamara had also found that past budgeting practices in the department, based on a one-year time line, had failed to consider all future cost consequences of budgeting decisions. In the development of weapons systems three different kinds of cost had to be considered: research and development (planning), investment (assembly), and operations and maintenance. The timing of each of these costs for the development of a particular weapon over a six-year period might look like this:

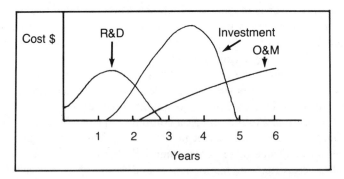

Making a first-year budget decision, then, strictly on the basis of the availability of funds for R&D, could create major problems in committing the department to investment expenditures for years 2 through 5 and O&M expenditures for subsequent years. To avoid such consequences, the new budget system required that the outputs of each program element be programmed for a nine-year period, with R&D, investment, and O&M costs shown for the first six years, as indicated in Figure 5.1.

Since each program package contained a number of elements contributing to a com-

PROGRAM ELEMENT SUMMARY DATA	IMPLEMENTING DOD COMPONENT: Dept. Of The Air Force	PROGRAM CHANGE NO. 3.88.77.01.4-2
PROGRAM ELEMENT: F-202		CODE 3.88.77.01.4

APPROVED PROGRAM - BY FISCAL YEAR

FORCES	CFY:63	FY64	FY65	FY66	FY67	FY68	FY69	FY70	FY71
U.E.									
Wings						1	2	6	6
Squadrons 20					1	3	6	18	18
Total U.E.					20	60	120	360	360
GAM. 99 (non-add)									
Squadron (ea.)25									
Total U.E					25	75	150	450	450

TOTAL OBLIGATIONAL AUTHORITY (In millions of dollars)

	CFY:63	FY64	FY65	FY66	FY67	FY68	FY69	FY70	FY71
RESEARCH AND DEVELOPMENT:									
RDT&E	100	200	300	200	50				
MILITARY CONSTRUCTION									
TOTAL RESEARCH & DEV.	100	200	300	200	50				
INVESTMENT:									
Aircraft Proc.			150	500	900	750			
Missile Proc.			15	20	25	25			
Other Proc.					1	1			
MILITARY CONSTRUCTION									
TOTAL INVESTMENT			165	520	926	776			
OPERATING:									
O&M									
Aircraft Proc.				1	2	3			
Missile Proc.			1	3	5	7			
Other Proc.					1	1			
MILITARY PERSONNEL					1	5			
TOTAL OPERATING			1	4	8	16			
TOTAL OBLIGATIONAL AUTH.	100	200	466	724	984	792			

MANPOWER (in thousands)

	CFY:63	FY64	FY65	FY66	FY67	FY68	FY69	FY70	FY71
MILITARY									
OFFICER					.1	.3			
ENLISTED					.3	1.5			
CIVILIAN									
DIRECT HIRE									
CONTRACT FOREIGN NAT'L									

NET CHANGE SINCE LAST SUBMISSION OF 1 April 1963 (date)

	CFY:63	FY64	FY65	FY66	FY67	FY68	FY69	FY70	FY71
FORCES (Squadrons)								+6	+6
TOTAL OBLIGATIONAL AUTH.					+450	+400			
MANPOWER MILITARY									
CIVILIAN									

BASIS FOR CHANGES: Authorized increase in forces - Program Change, 1 May 1963

DATE 15 May 1963	IMPLEMENTING DOD COMPONENT (signature)

FIGURE 5.1 Hypothetical Element. *(From Samuel A. Tucker,* A Modern Design for Defense Decision, *Washington, D.C.: Industrial College of the Armed Services, 1966, p. 87)*

mon department goal, the new system encouraged the use of system analysis to identify what combination of means (elements) would best accomplish the end sought. For example, what combination of tanks, foot soldiers, and air support would contribute most effectively and efficiently to accomplishing the General Purpose Forces Mission? The analytic talents of several RAND Corporation staffers, led by Charles Hitch, were employed to install and operate the system.

THE PPB BUDGET

By 1965 the system had attracted so much attention by interrelating the planning and budgetary operations of the three services in a common planning-programming-budgeting (PPB) process that President Johnson decided to extend the system to all federal agencies. He announced the decision at a press conference on August 25, 1965, by saying:

> This morning I have just concluded a breakfast meeting with the cabinet and with heads of Federal agencies and am asking each of them to immediately begin to introduce a very new and very revolutionary system of planning and programming the budgeting throughout the vast Federal Government, so that through the tools of modern management the full promise of a finer life can be brought to every American at the lowest possible cost.
>
> Under this new system each cabinet and agency head will set up a very special staff of experts who, using the most modern methods of program analysis will define the goals of their departments for the coming year. And once these goals are established this system will permit us to find the most effective and the least costly alternative to achieving American goals.
>
> This program is designed to achieve three major objectives: It will help us find new ways to do jobs faster, to do jobs better, and to do jobs less expensively. It will ensure a much sounder judgment through more accurate information, pinpointing those things that we ought to do more, spotlighting those things that we ought to do less. It will make our decision making process as up to date, I think, as our space-exploring programs.[3]

The Bureau of the Budget issued instructions on how to implement this directive on October 12, 1965:[4]

1 The program structure should be output-oriented and should present data on all of the operations and activities of the agency in categories which reflect the agency's end purpose or objectives.
2 It might be desirable to have the basic program categories cut across bureau lines to facilitate comparisons and suggest possible trade-offs among elements which are close substitutes. It is desirable to develop program formats which facilitate comparisons across agency lines.
3 To facilitate top level review, the number of program categories should be limited. For example, a cabinet department should normally have fewer than 15 program categories.
4 Program categories and subcategories should not be restricted by the present appropriations pattern or budget activity structure.

How does such an approach differ from performance budgeting? The bureau guidelines would seem to be consistent with what has been described as a performance budget in the previous chapter. If so, why not merely reinvigorate performance budgeting? Performance budgeting does indeed focus on the volume of work to be performed, but not necessarily on what difference such effort is expected to make in society. The activities of a city garbage program might be defined by performance budgeting as: the collection and disposal of garbage. Tons of garbage collected and disposed of might be the applicable output units for measuring these two activities. But why is garbage collected? To prevent the spread of infectious diseases? To protect property values? To maximize the utilization of land? If these are reasons for performing the activity (collection), does the collection of garbage actually result in lowering the rate of infectious diseases, maintaining property values, facilitating the use of land for purposes other than storage of garbage? It should be possible to measure these relationships. Thus the goals of the garbage department might be:

	Goal	*Measurement Criteria*
1	Prevent spread of infectious disease	Rate of infectious disease/frequency of collection
2	Protect property values	Change in property values/frequency of collection
3	Maximize utilization of land	Ratio of garbage collected to total space available

A PPB budget therefore attempts to identify the goals established through *planning*, relate them to the activities required for goal achievement (*programming*), and show the mix of resources required (*budgeting*). How is a budget structured to accomplish these ends? One must first define what differences one wants to make in society. These "differences" can then be restated as goals to be accomplished. Thus a city fire department will want to minimize the losses sustained by persons and property from fires. To do so, it will have to intervene either before the fire has been started or after it is in process. The department's goals therefore aimed at making some difference in the occurrence and magnitude of fires are: fire prevention and fire fighting. To prevent fires the department might educate the public about fire hazards, investigate arson possibilities, and the like. Public education and arson investigations may consequently be considered as objectives which, if accomplished, will lead to the attainment of the goal: fire prevention.

But some criterion must also be developed for measuring whether activities undertaken actually result in accomplishment of objectives. Thus, if one conducts educational demonstrations for groups in neighborhood areas, do hazard-induced fires decline, or do the losses sustained from such fires decline after the educational demonstrations? If one observes no improvement, perhaps door-to-door instruction should be substituted for the group education sessions. Note that in this example two phenomena—an objective and an activity—are being measured. From performance budgeting rationale, one identifies the appropriate output unit: number of persons contacted. The impact to be made by such output is: fires prevented. But how do we relate the volume of output generated to the magnitude of impact realized? If hazard-induced fires decline (impact) at an increasing rate after the neighborhood group meetings (activity) have been held, does this mean that the decline resulted from the knowledge people who attended the meetings acquired? Before drawing that conclusion, we must consider other circumstances that could have led to or contributed to the decline in hazard-induced fires. Perhaps the "before" months were during the winter when extensive use of space heaters increased the possibility of such fires occurring. And perhaps the "after" months were during the summer when such appliances are not used extensively. Such seasonal differences are, of course, easy to identify and take into consideration in interpreting data. But what if one is comparing hazard-induced fires occurring during the winter months after educational meetings have been conducted with those that occurred during the same winter months the previous year, and before the meetings were held? Even in this instance a decline in such fires may not necessarily be attributable to the information conveyed in the meetings. The first winter may have been cold, occasioning the use of many space heaters; the second winter was mild with less frequent use of such potentially hazardous equipment. Or perhaps the City Council had passed a law before the onset of the second winter requiring heavy-duty electrical outlets when space heaters were used. Any number of circumstances or events could have had some influence on the rate of hazard-induced fires. The intent here is not to discourage attempts to link activity outputs to societal impacts, but to urge that when such relationships are inferred, due consideration is given to other environmental factors that may be affecting the relationship.

Returning to the question of program structure, the PPB approach calls for:

- Definition of *goals* and *subgoals* in terms of some general differences to be made in society
- Definition of *objectives* required to accomplish each subgoal, and measurable in terms of a specific impact made in society
- Identification of the *activities* employed to accomplish each objective, measured in outputs

To make matters more confusing, PPB developed its own terms for describing each of these analytic stages:

			PPB
1	Goals	=	Programs
2	Subgoals	=	Categories
3	Objectives	=	Subcategories
4	Activities	=	Elements

Perhaps an illustration will clarify how such a structure would look. Figure 5.2 shows a sample program structure developed by Robert Mowitz for representing one of the major goals (programs) for Pennsylvania. The state goal (program) identified is: protection of persons and property. Subgoals (categories) established to accomplish this goal are: traffic safety, control and reduction of crime, and so forth. Three objectives (subcategories) are set forth to achieve the subgoal of control and reduction of crime: crime prevention, criminal law enforcement, and reintegration of adult offenders. Finally, ten activities (elements) are shown that contribute to the accomplishment of the latter objective: reintegration of adult offenders.

Table 5.1 illustrates how goals, subgoals, objectives, and activities used in this example are defined and measured. Note that several impact and output units are suggested for the measurement of a single objective (subcategory) and activity (element). This suggests that frequently no one single unit of measurement will be entirely satisfactory for measuring either output or impact. Nevertheless, a preferred measure for each will be selected for use in the actual calculation of unit costs.

Under federal PPB requirements each agency was required to submit its budget estimates in a Program and Financial Plans (PFP) document. Programs, categories, subcategories, and elements were set forth in terms of output and costs projected for a five-year period into the future. A second document, the Program Memorandum (PM), provided a verbal explanation of the rationale involved in the construction of each program category. Similarly, states adopting PPB were required to develop reporting forms that showed the relation of objectives to activities (outputs) and resources (inputs). Figure 5.3 shows how California instructed its departments to organize its budget submissions. This primary form was to be accompanied by a support document, "Program Distribution By Object for 19__ Fiscal Year," depicting an objects of expenditure breakdown for each program.[5]

Considerable effort was exerted by federal agencies between 1966 and 1971 to implement the PPB system. In the latter year the system was officially discontinued, but departments and agencies were encouraged by OMB to continue use of the process internally.

Resistance to the PPB system was substantial from the beginning. Few guidelines were provided by the Bureau of the Budget for developing program structures. What were goals? How were they to be distinguished from means? Did an agency really want to commit itself to quantitative goal accomplishment when it was uncertain how its means (activities) related to such goals?

By 1969, however, GAO found that 20 of 21 agencies surveyed had succeeded in developing PPB program frameworks.[6] And most departments did succeed in developing programs that crossed agency lines of responsibility, which was, it will be recalled, an early Bureau of the Budget recommendation. For example, HEW developed four major program categories. All five of the major operating agencies in HEW contributed to one category (health), three to a second (social and rehabilitation), and two to a third (education). Only one category, income maintenance, was to be accomplished solely within one agency (Social Security). How comprehensively such frameworks were developed, though, was open to question. According to a survey published four years later (1973) by the Joint Economic Committee, only four of eleven departments surveyed had developed ultimate goals or activity output measures for all or most of their programs.[7] Some departments expressed great interest, others very little.

At the state and local levels, many governments jumped on the PPB bandwagon shortly after the system was introduced in the federal government. Early in 1966 the State-Local Finances Project was organized at George Washington University to establish PPB pilot projects in five states, five counties, and five cities for demonstration purposes.[8] Funded by the Ford Foundation, this 5-5-5 Project made significant progress in all fifteen locations.[9] Furthermore, the State-Local Finances Project circulated a series of succinctly written PPB notes that provided guidance for hundreds of other local governments developing PPB systems. The influence of the illustrative program structure discussed in Note 3[10] and depicted in Table 5.2 can be seen in the perusal of almost any local government program budget in use in the country today.

Category	Subcategory	Element
General administration and support		
Traffic safety and supervision		
Control and reduction of crime	Crime prevention	
Maintenance of public order	Criminal law enforcement	
Provision of public services to local governments	Reintegration of adult offenders	Maintenance of inmate security
Water damage control and prevention		Maintenance of inmates' physical-mental health
Protection of the forest resource		Counseling of inmates for personal and social problems
Occupational health and safety		Education of inmates
Consumer protection		Occupational and vocational training of inmates
Community and housing hygiene and safety		Inspection of county and municipal institutions
		Social investigation
		Supervision for social and personal change
		Financial and professional assistance to county probation departments
		Screening to determine risk

FIGURE 5.2 Sample Program Structure: Commonwealth Program II — Protection of Persons and Property. *(From Robert J. Mowitz, The Design and Implementation of Pennsylvania's Planning, Programming, Budgeting System, University Park: Pennsylvania State University, Institute of Public Administration, p. 52)*

TABLE 5.1. Sample Program Structure Statements and Program Plan Plan Logic Robert J. Mourtz, *The Design and Implementation of Pennsylvania's Planning, Programming, Budgeting System*. (University Park: Pennsylvania State University, Institute of Public Administration, n.d.), p. 53.

Commonwealth program—protection of persons and property

Goal: To provide an environment and social system in which the lives of individuals, and the property of individuals and organizations are protected from natural and man-made disasters, and from illegal and unfair action.

Program category—control and reduction of crime

Subgoal: To provide a high degree of protection against bodily injury, loss of life, and loss of property resulting from unlawful or unfair actions by individuals or organizations; to provide a sufficiently secure setting for offenders in order to safeguard the community and provide for their health and well being; and to cure or alleviate the socially aberrant behavior of the offender and to assist the offender to function to the best of his potential upon release from an institution or while on probation.

Program subcategory—reintegration of offenders

Objective: To decrease the recurrence of crime by replacing criminal behavior with socially acceptable behavior

Impacts: Number and percent of persons released convicted for new crimes
Number and percent of evaluations of inmates reflecting gain in social skills and emotional controls
Number of releases under supervision of court parole or Pennsylvania Board of Parole
Number of admissions who are parole violators

Program element—counseling for personal and social problems

Outputs: Number of inmates receiving recommended individual counseling
Number of inmates receiving recommended group counseling
Number of inmates receiving recommended self improvement group counseling
Number of inmates receiving recommended psychiatric treatment

Need and/or demand: Number of inmates recommended for individual counseling   Program statement
Number of inmates recommended for group counseling
Number of inmates recommended for self improvement group counseling
Number of inmates recommended for psychiatric treatment

Funds required   Direct state activities   Financial statement
Payments to jurisdictions

Manpower required   Man years   Manpower statement
Funds required

SOURCE: Office of Management and Budget, *Bulletin No. 77–9*, February 14, 1977, p.53.

DEPARTMENT OF COMMERCE

Headquarters Office at Sacramento

Departmental Objectives

Describe departmental objectives clearly, and concisely and explain the contribution of each program to the accomplishment of departmental objectives and overall state-wide goals. Define in general terms the short and long-term results to be realized through carrying out the programs.

Authorized Programs [1]

SUMMARY OF PROGRAM REQUIREMENTS

Continuing Costs and Workload Adjustments

	ACTUAL 1965-66	ESTIMATED 1966-67	PROPOSED 1967-68
I. Program A [2]	$4,960,715	$5,215,407	$5,421,978
II. Program B	4,937,148	6,063,098	6,233,732
III. Program C	8,232,541	9,091,439	9,143,386
IV. Program D	1,203,077	1,341,995	1,344,385
V. Program E	349,359	400,128	455,421
VI. Program F	166,363	190,777	191,217
Subtotals	$19,849,203	$22,302,844	$22,790,119
VII. Departmental Administration, Undistributed	96,812	106,848	107,426
TOTALS, AUTHORIZED PROGRAMS	$19,946,015	$22,409,692	$22,897,545
Personnel man-years	1,971.7	2,145.6	2,160.1

I. PROGRAM A

Set forth information which would fulfill the needs of a department head or higher official to exercise effective program evaluation and management and provide an adequate basis for legislative review. This narrative will cover the objectives, authority, need and general description for the program (Management Memo 66-16). This statement should, where possible, indicate the program's relationship to statewide needs and to other programs of a similar, parallel or related nature, in and outside of state government. Include a statement of specific program objectives to be accomplished in the budget year and the allocation of resources required to achieve the objective including workload adjustments. State relationship of program to departmental organizational structure, fixing responsibility for achievement of objectives.

Discuss program output data and workload plans (Management Memo 66-17). Report program input data (personnel man-year requirements and program costs) under the "Program Requirements" header below. Man-year requirements are to be reported in net amounts; i.e., authorized positions after workload and administration adjustments, proposed new positions and estimated salary savings have been applied. The total of man-year requirements in all programs in the department should equal the "Net Totals, Salaries and Wages" figure in the summary by object table. Present all the factual and analytical detail which is the basis for the program statement.

Program Output Data

Units Processed:	Past year	Current year	Budget year
Cases closed	–	–	–
Applications processed	–	–	–

PROGRAM REQUIREMENTS	PERSONNEL MAN-YEARS			ACTUAL 1965–66	ESTIMATED 1966–67	PROPOSED 1967–68	
	65–66	66–67	67–68				
Continuing program costs	493.9	504	504	$4,960,715	$4,784,407	$4,970,978	
Workload adjustments	–	26.5	31.3	–	431,000	451,000	
Totals, Program A	493.9	530.5	535.3	$4,960,715	$5,215,407	$5,421,978	
General Fund				*3,533,248*	*3,572,349*	*3,717,487*	
Department of Commerce Fund				*1,427,467*	*1,643,058*	*1,704,491*	

Program Elements, Components and Tasks of Program A

Discuss program elements and associated components and tasks to the extent needed to properly set forth key objectives to be obtained to support a system of management by objectives within the program.

Such discussion should give specific objectives to be accomplished in budget year; specific operations to be conducted in current year and list accomplishments in past year.

Program Element I	Actual 1965–66	Estimated 1966–67	Proposed 1967–68
Component A	---	---	---
Component B	---	---	---
Totals	$---	$---	$---
Personnel man-years	---	---	---

Workload Adjustments

State the impact of anticipated workload. Workload adjustments to be presented are those which are mandatory to support continuing programs. Indicate sufficient detail to justify workload adjustments.

[1] Include programs to which the Legislature has given approval in session or which have been reported to the Legislature under the provisions of Sections 28 or 32 of the current budget act.
[2] Departmental program titles should be used. Letter designations have been used for illustrative purposes only.

FIGURE 5.3 Departmental Objectives. (*From State of California, Department of Finance, Management Memo No. 66-31, Exhibit, p. 1, July 25, 1966*)

TABLE 5.2. Illustrative Program Structure Summary Page

I.	Personal Safety
II.	Health (physical and mental well-being)
III.	Intellectual Development and Personal Enrichment
IV.	Satisfactory Home and Community Environment
V.	Economic Satisfaction and Satisfactory Work Opportunities for the Individual
VI.	Satisfactory Leisure-Time Opportunities
VII.	Transportation-Communication-Location
VIII.	General Administration and Support

SOURCE: State-Local Finances Project, *Planning Programming Budgeting for City State County Objectives*, Washington, D.C.: George Washington University, June 1968, p. 10.

THE ZBB BUDGET

The excitement and controversy over PPB had hardly died down before another budget reform, zero base budgeting (ZBB), came along. This analytical technique was developed in a private organization, Texas Instruments, in 1969. It was first applied to government by Governor Jimmy Carter of Georgia in the preparation of his fiscal year 1973 budget. Since then, eleven states and dozens of local governments have adopted ZBB,[11] and in 1977 President Carter mandated its use in the federal government.[12] Although not a reporting requirement under President Reagan, many agencies continue to employ the rationale found in ZBB.

The term "zero base" tends to be confusing. It would seem that an agency using ZBB must start from scratch in developing its whole budget every year. As the U.S. Department of Agriculture found in 1962 when they attempted to employ the zero base concept in this way, it does not work. The budget is a political document based on the political, legal, and social constraints existing in society.[13] Any budget exercise that ignores this fact is doomed to failure. By requesting their operating officials to develop budget estimates without reference to legislative mandates, past commitments, or existing political alignments, Agriculture found that it was asking the impossible. To make sense, a budget must be constructed in the context of a real legal and political environment.

But ZBB, as the term is used today, is not meant to convey such an artificial construction of the budget document. Rather, ZBB is viewed as a means of systematically deciding how activities and resources should be allocated to accomplish agreed-upon goals. And the word "systematically" means giving purposive consideration to alternate ways of accomplishing each goal.

ZBB accomplishes this end by identifying *decision units*, alternative *program packages* for each unit, and *ranking* the importance of each package in relation to all other packages. First, one begins by identifying the originating units of the process, called the decision units. These are the locations in the organization where operating officials "make significant decisions on the amount of spending and the scope and quality of work to be performed."[14] In other words, the starting point of ZBB is lodged with those operating managers who bear major program responsibilities. If the budget is organized on a PPB basis,

e.g., Category (goal)
　　Subcategory (objective)
　　　Element (activity)

the ZBB process will typically begin at the Element (activity) level. Where the budget is constructed on an objects of expenditure basis, responsibility centers, budget units, or other organizational units may be identified as the appropriate decision unit level.

Each decision unit prepares one or more sets of decision packages to reflect alternative efforts directed to the accomplishment of a single goal. The decision packages must provide management with the information needed to evaluate and rank each decision unit against all other units competing for funding and to decide whether to approve or disapprove the unit's request. To accomplish these ends information included in decision packages may consist of:

- Major goal to be accomplished
- Immediate objective to be accomplished
- Resources required
- Organization of activity effort
- Evaluation measures (efficiency and effectiveness)
- Different levels of effort possible

Two steps are involved in developing decision packages:

1　Identify alternative methods of accomplishing the goal or performing the operation. All meaningful (politically, economically,and organizationally feasible) alternatives should be developed and evaluated. If an alternative to the current method of performing the work is selected, both methods should be shown in the decision packages.
2　Set forth different levels of effort for performing the operations required for the method selected, arranging levels (packages) in hierarchical order according to how essential each is to the accomplishment of the objective.

The decision unit is requested to identify (typically) three different levels of effort possible to accomplish the major goal: a minimal level, the current level (required for continuance of effort at present standards), and an improvement level (an increase over the current level of expenditures). Since it is frequently difficult for a decision unit to arrive at a minimal level—and to prevent operating officials from resorting to the all-or-nothing strategy discussed in the next chapter—many agencies have found it necessary to suggest an arbitrary minimal level, such as 75 or 85 percent of the current spending level. The U.S. Department of Justice developed an even more flexible approach to this problem. Justice established a minimum funding level at 75 percent of *the organization's*, not the decision unit's, current level of funding. Hence the organization head could choose to vary the level of minimum spending among decision units, as long as no minimum decision package exceeded its estimated current level and the sum of all minimal level decision packages was less than, or equal to, 75 percent of the organization's total current level budget. Even this formula proved to be inadequate. Justice continued to employ this approach in developing their 1980 fiscal year budget, but raised the minimum funding level to 85 percent.[15]

Tables 5.3, 5.4, and 5.5 illustrate how the process of submitting multiple estimates has been operationalized in Georgia. Note that the decision unit is the Field Audits program. The major objective (goal) of this program is to examine every state-chartered bank and thrift institution in Georgia on an annual basis and to investigate promptly all requests for establishing new institutions. The current objective—that is, the operational objective at present employed by the organization—is to examine 95 percent of the banks and 100 percent of the thrifts during the year and to average two weeks investigation time per request for new or expanded banks and thrifts. Table 5.3 presents a program package designed to perform the major objective at the minimal level acceptable. Here the operational objective would be to examine 90 percent of the banks and 84 percent of thrifts during the year and average 4, rather than 2, weeks investigation time per request for new or expanded banks or thrifts. The total cost of this minimum package would be $241,492 instead of the $291,822 budgeted for the current year.

Table 5.4 sets forth a program package showing the effort and resources required to maintain the current program being carried on by the unit. The cost of bringing the minimum objective level (Table 5.3) program up to the current level is $89,772. This amount, combined with the $241,492 required to perform at the minimum level, brings the total cost of the program up to $331,264.

If one hopes to improve on the performance level of the unit over the present year—by examining 98 percent of the banks and 100 percent of the thrifts and cutting new investigation time to one week—the decision package in Table 5.5 shows that an additional $33,257 would be required. The total budget request for performing at this level would therefore be: package 1 plus package 2 plus package 3, or $364,521.

Following this procedure, all the program packages of each decision unit are ranked according to priority of importance. Minimum-level packages necessarily receive the highest priority ratings, since each represents performance at the lowest level possible. Thus if the manager of an Air Quality Control program developed decision packages for Air Quality Laboratory, Reviews and Permits, Source Evaluation, Registration, and Research, he might rank them as follows:[16]

Rank	Decision Package	Incremental Cost	Cumulative Cost
1	Reviews and Permits (1 of 2)	$116,000	$116,000
2	Source Evaluation (1 of 4)	103,000	219,000
3	Air Quality Lab. (1 or 3)	140,000	359,000
4	Registration (1 of 3)	273,000	639,000
5	Source Evaluation (2 of 4)	53,000	685,000
6	Air Quality Lab. (2 of 3)	61,000	746,000
7	Source Evaluation (3 of 4)	45,000	791,000
8	Air Quality Lab. (3 of 3)	45,000	836,000
9	Reviews and Permits (2 of 2)	50,000	886,000
10	Research (1 of 2)	85,000	971,000

When the program packages have been prepared and ranked, they are sent to higher authorities for review. The next higher level of authority reviews the program packages

TABLE 5.3. Decision Package—Minimum Objective Level OPB-Budget-30

BANKING Department **Examination** Activity **Field Audits** Program

Positions This Package 14	Program F.Y. 77	This Pkg. F.Y. 78	Cum. Amount
A. TOTAL PERSONAL SERVICES	196,912	165,712	
1. M. V. Expenses and Repairs	2,900	2,300	
2. Supplies and Materials	3,900	3,300	
3. Repairs and Maintenance	500	500	
4. Communications	16,000	14,000	
5. Power, Water, Natural Gas	2,406	2,406	
6. Rents	12,916	13,208	
7. Insurance and Bonding			
8. Workmen's Comp. and Indemn.			
9. Direct Benefits			
10. Tuition and Scholarships			
11. Grants to Counties or Cities			
12. Assessments by Merit System	864	756	
13. Other Operating Expenses	1,000	750	
14. Extraordinary Expenses			
B. REG. OPER. EXP. (Add 1-14)	40,486	37,220	
C. TRAVEL	26,912	20,880	
D. MOTOR VEH. EQUIP. PURCH.	10,962	4,880	
E. PUBLICATIONS AND PRINTING	9,450	8,800	
F. EQUIPMENT PURCHASES	5,000	4,000	
G. PER DIEM AND FEES	2,000	2,000	
H. COMPUTER CHARGES	18,500	16,400	
I. OTHER CONTRACT. EXP.	1,600	1,600	
J. AUTHORITY LEASE RENTALS			
K. GENERAL OBLIGATION BONDS			
L. CAPITAL OUTLAY			
M. LIST OTHER OBJECTS:			
TOTAL EXPEND. (Add A - M)	311,822	261,492	
FEDERAL FUNDS	16,000	16,000	
OTHER FUNDS	4,000	4,000	
STATE GENERAL FUNDS	291,822	241,492	

Describe the Program in terms of its Major Objective
To examine every State Chartered Bank and Thrift Institution in Georgia on an annual basis and to investigate promptly all requests for establishing new institutions.

Describe the Program in terms of the Current Objective in F. Y. 1977
To examine 95% of all Banks and 100% of all Thrift Institutions during F. Y. 1977 and to average two weeks investigation time for new or expanded Banks or Thrift Institutions.

Explain the Minimum Level Limited Objective this Package provides
To examine 90% of all Banks and 84% of all Thrift Institutions during F. Y. 1978 and to average four weeks investigating time per request for new or expanded Banks or Thrift Institutions. Ten Examiners and four Secretaries will be employed.

Explain the service now provided that this Minimum Objective Level excludes
5% of the State Chartered Banks and 15% of the Thrift Institutions examined in F. Y. 1977 will not be examined in F. Y. 1978. New Banks and Thrift Institutions will be investigated over a four-week period rather than two weeks. Delete 2 Bank Examiners and related operating expenses.

Evaluation Measures (Effectiveness and Efficiency) Program Workload	F. Y. 1977 Current Objective	F. Y. 1978 Minimum Object.
% of Banks examined	95%	90%
% of Thrift Institutions examined	100%	84%
Average time to investigate new institutions	2 weeks	4 weeks
Average cost per Bank examination	$2,745	$2,890
Average cost per Thrift Institution examination	$348	$362
Average cost per new institution	$600	$550

Package Name: Field Audits   Package 1 of 3
Prepared By: John Doe   Activity Rank 4

SOURCE: Office of Planning and Budget, State of Georgia, *Zero-Base Budget Procedures & Instructions*, 1977.

TABLE 5.4. Decision Package—Current Objective Level OPB-Budget-31

BANKING	Examination	Field Audits	
Department	Activity	Program	

Describe the Program in terms of its Major Objective

To examine every State Chartered Bank and Thrift Institution in Georgia on an annual basis and to investigate promptly all requests for establishing new institutions.

Describe the Program in terms of the Current Objective in F.Y. 1977

To examine 95% of all Banks and 100% of all Thrift Institutions during F.Y. 1977 and to average two weeks investigation time for new or expanded Banks or Thrift Institutions.

Explain any cost change in the Current Level over the Minimum Level

Add 2 Financial Examiner I's and related operating expenses to find the Current Objective Level not including workload of additional Banks and Thrift Institutions described below.

Explain any Workload change in the Current Level over F.Y. 1977

Four new Banks and one new Thrift Institution were created in the State during F.Y. 1977. In order to maintain examination of 95% of the Banks and 100% of the Thrift Institutions, 1 new Financial Examiner I and 1 new Clerk-Typist I and related operating expenses are requested to maintain the Current Objective.

Positions This Package 4 **	Program F.Y.77	This Pkg. F.Y.78	Cum. Amount
A. TOTAL PERSONAL SERVICES	196,912	72,000	237,712
1. M.V. Expenses and Repairs	2,900	800	3,100
2. Supplies and Materials	3,900	1,300	4,600
3. Repairs and Maintenance	500		500
4. Communications	16,000	3,000	17,000
5. Power, Water, Natural Gas	2,406	594	3,000
6. Rents *	12,916	1,292	14,500
7. Insurance and Bonding			
8. Workmen's Comp. and Indemn.			
9. Direct Benefits			
10. Tuition and Scholarships			
11. Grants to Counties or Cities			
12. Assessments by Merit System	864	216	972
13. Other Operating Expenses	1,000	250	1,000
14. Extraordinary Expenses			
B. REG. OPER. EXP. (Add 1-14)	40,486	7,452	44,672
C. TRAVEL	26,912	7,120	28,000
D. MOTOR VEH. EQUIP. PURCH. *	10,962		4,880
E. PUBLICATIONS AND PRINTING	9,450	200	9,000
F. EQUIPMENT PURCHASES *	5,000		4,000
G. PER DIEM AND FEES *	2,000		2,000
H. COMPUTER CHARGES *	18,500	3,000	19,400
I. OTHER CONTRACT. EXP. *	1,600		1,600
J. AUTHORITY LEASE RENTALS			
K. GENERAL OBLIGATION BONDS			
L. CAPITAL OUTLAY			
M. LIST OTHER OBJECTS:			
TOTAL EXPEND. (Add A - M)	311,822	89,772	351,264
FEDERAL FUNDS **	16,000		16,000
OTHER FUNDS **			
STATE GENERAL FUNDS	291,822	89,772	331,264

*Attach detailed schedule for F.Y. 1978 Current Objective Level (including Minimum Objective Level funds requested)
**Detailed schedule for the Current Objective Level is to be developed at the Activity Level.

Program Evaluation Measures (Effectiveness and Efficiency) Workload	F.Y. 1977 Current Objective	F.Y. 1978 Current Objective
% of Banks examined	95%	95%
% of Thrift Institutions examined	100%	100%
Average time to investigate new institutions	2 weeks	2 weeks
Average cost per Bank examination	$2,745	$2,910
Average cost per Thrift Institution examination	$348	$376
Average cost per new institution	$600	$620

Package Name: Field Audits   Package 2 of 3

Prepared By: John Doe   Activity Rank 7

SOURCE: Office of Planning and Budget, State of Georgia, *Zero-Base Budget Procedures & Instructions*, 1977.

TABLE 5.5. Decision Package—Improvement Objective Level OPB-Budget-32

BANKING Department	Examination Activity	Field Audits Program		
	Positions This Package 2	Program F.Y. 77	This Pkg. F.Y. 78	Cum. Amount
Describe the Program in terms of its Major Objective To examine every State Chartered Bank and Thrift Institution in Georgia on an annual basis and to investigate promptly all requests for establishing new institutions.	A. TOTAL PERSONAL SERVICES *	196,912	24,499	262,211
	1. M. V. Expenses and Repairs	2,900	300	3,400
	2. Supplies and Materials	3,900	400	5,000
	3. Repairs and Maintenance	500		500
	4. Communications	16,000	800	17,800
Describe the Program in terms of the Current Objective in F.Y. 1977 To examine 95% of all Banks and 100% of all Thrift Institutions during F.Y. 1977 and to average two weeks investigation time for new or expanded Banks or Thrift Institutions.	5. Power, Water, Natural Gas	2,406		3,000
	6. Rents *	12,916	150	14,650
	7. Insurance and Bonding			
	8. Workmen's Comp. and Indemn.			
	9. Direct Benefits			
	10. Tuition and Scholarships			
	11. Grants to Counties or Cities			
Explain the Improvement Level Limited Objective this package provides To examine 98% of all Banks and 100% of all Thrift Institutions during F.Y. 1978 and to average one week investigation time for new or expanded Banks or Thrift Institutions.	12. Assessments by Merit System	864	108	1,080
	13. Other Operating Expenses	1,000		1,000
	14. Extraordinary Expenses			
	B. REG. OPER. EXP. (Add 1:14)	40,486	1,758	46,430
	C. TRAVEL	26,912	3,600	31,600
Explain this Package in terms of cost To examine an additional 3% of the Banks will require 2 new Financial Examiner I's and related operating expenses.	D. MOTOR VEH. EQUIP. PURCH. *	10,962		4,880
	E. PUBLICATIONS AND PRINTING	9,450	500	9,500
	F. EQUIPMENT PURCHASES *	5,000	900	4,900
	G. PER DIEM AND FEES *	2,000		2,000
	H. COMPUTER CHARGES *	18,500		19,400

Evaluation Measures Program Workload (Effectiveness and Efficiency)	F.Y. 1977 Current Objective	F.Y. 1978 Improve. Obj.		
			I. OTHER CONTRACT. EXP. *	1,600	1,600
% of Banks examined	95%	98%	J. AUTHORITY LEASE RENTALS		
% of Thrift Institutions examined	100%	100%	K. GENERAL OBLIGATION BONDS		
Average time to investigate new institutions	2 weeks	2 weeks	L. CAPITAL OUTLAY *	2,000	2,000
			M. LIST OTHER OBJECTS:		
Average cost per Bank examination	$2,745	$2,900	TOTAL EXPEND. (Add A-M)	311,822	33,257	364,521
Average cost per Thrift Institution examination	$348	$372	FEDERAL FUNDS *	16,000		16,000
Average cost per new institution	$600	$620	OTHER FUNDS *	4,000		4,000
			STATE GENERAL FUNDS	291,822	33,257	364,521

Package Name: Field Audits   Package 3 of 3

Prepared By: John Doe   Activity Rank 10

SOURCE: Office of Planning and Budget, State of Georgia, *Zero-Base Budget Procedures & Instructions*, 1977.

from each of the decision units reporting to him. Figure 5.4 illustrates the review process. Here we see that the higher authority, Manager X, evaluates the packages submitted by Decision Units A, B, and C. For Decision Unit A he disagrees with the way that manager has ranked his packages, concluding that package A2 is less important than packages A3 and A4. He therefore reorders the priorities assigned to these packages.

When he has completed his review of the program packages submitted by Decision Units A, B, and C, he proceeds to rank each package against all others, thereby establishing a composite rank ordering of all packages. He now sends this prioritized list to his superior, Manager R, who goes through the same analytical steps for the submissions he receives from his subordinates, Manager X and Manager Y. By this time the prioritized list of packages is getting long and unwieldly. So Manager R has the additional task of deciding how program packages can be consolidated before submitting them to the next higher level of authority. The assumption is that this rather complex procedure gives the decision maker at each level some control over the substantive mix of programs that eventually comes to make up the agency's budget proposal.

There are programs where the program manager has no control over the level of expenditures required by law. In such cases a single program package is prepared and submitted. Some governments utilizing ZBB also have simplified the process described above by limiting analysis to the lower-ranked, more discretionary program packages.[17] While one may protest that this revision reintroduces the budget base concept of incrementalism and thus seems to negate the zero base rationale of ZBB, the fact is that ZBB is basically a technique for encouraging systematic analysis, not for propounding idealistic reforms. Thus most ZBB proponents encourage agencies to tailor the technique to meet their own localized needs and not worry over theoretical inconsistencies that may result therefrom.

A recent survey by Anne DeBeer on the implementation of ZBB in three federal departments—Agriculture, Commerce, and Labor—concludes that ZBB in practice does not yield the comprehensive rationale decision-making process envisioned by the theory.[18] The ninety budget and program managers and analysts interviewed indicated that the greatest weaknesses of ZBB were (1) the amount of paperwork it generated, (2) unrealistic and arbitrary minimum-level decision packages, (3) lack of criteria for ranking packages, (4) failure to integrate other management and budget processes (such as Management by Objectives) with ZBB and (5) failure of OMB to bring its own reviewing techniques into accord with ZBB requirements. Despite these criticisms, the majority of the respondents felt that ZBB *should* become a permanent part of the federal budget process—if the perceived weaknesses could be eliminated.

They observed that ZBB had encouraged more concentration on objectives in their agency, more serious consideration given to effecting decreases in current spending levels, and increased use of quantitative data to support budget requests. They did recommend, though, that PPB be limited to those programs over which management has discretionary control at the budget level.

DeBeer concludes that ZBB cannot be implemented in totality in government agencies because ZBB rests on the assumption that decisions can be based solely on the rational calculus of choice. In fact, however, she finds that budget requests of program managers are determined by a variety of factors: what they think they need to do their

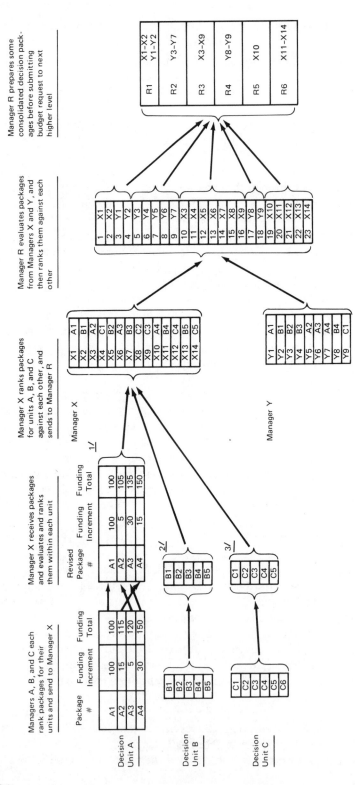

FIGURE 5.4 Decision Package Ranking and Consolidation Process Illustrated. (*From Office of Management and Budget*, Bulletin No. 77-9, *Washington, D.C.: The White House, February 14, 1977*)

[a] Higher level manager reorders the proposed priorities of the subordinate decision unit managers. The packages may be revised by either the initial decision unit manager or the higher level manager.

[b] Higher level manager accepts proposed priorities of the subordinate manager.

[c] Higher level manager accepts proposed priorities of the subordinate manager, but chooses not to propose funding of lowest priority package.

job, what they think they are likely to get in light of political realities, and how much support they can expect from legislators. In short, ZBB is regarded as a good tool to assist in decision making but a poor sole criterion for decision making.

CURRENT PROGRAM BUDGET DEVELOPMENTS

One finds continued interest in the use of the program-type budget in states, local governments, and other nonprofit organizations across the land. In the federal government the formal reporting requirements of the PPB system have disappeared, but many federal agencies continue to refine their program structures. Congress also continues to express interest in encouraging the use of program terminology in the budget document. The Congressional Budget Act of 1974 requires that the budget "shall contain a presentation of budget authority, proposed budget authority, outlays, proposed outlays, and descriptive information in terms of—(1) a detailed structure of national needs which shall be used to reference all agency missions and programs; (2) agency missions; and (3) basic programs."[19] Figure 5.5 and Table 5.6 illustrate how these provisions are now being incorporated into the budget document.

The General Accounting Office (GAO) has also recommended that Congress begin to experiment with a new concept called "mission budgeting" in carrying out its budgetary review, authorization and appropriation functions.[20] Mission budgeting, to be fully adopted, would require that budget authorizations and appropriations be predicated on a definitive statement of agency missions and the needs underlying each of these missions. Where this has not been done, it would be up to Congress to clarify what agency missions are or should be in relation to current national policy. Congress would also require budget justifications to show clearly the relationship of the requested funding to mission needs, beginning at the individual program level and aggregating into the composite presidential budget.[21] The philosophy underlying mission budgeting is, of course, closely related to the concepts upon which PPB and ZBB are based. Mission budgeting, though, would give the legislature a more focal role in the development of the goal-setting process upon which program budgets are based. The legislature would, in effect, enact specific, measurable program goals into law; and GAO would have the responsibility for auditing agency performance for compliance.

The *Appendix to the Federal Budget* still includes budget requests for all responsible agencies in terms of appropriation language; program activities; verbal explanations of program activities, including workload statistics; and objects of expenditures. In short the federal budget today includes presentations based on all the major formats discussed in the last two chapters—objects of expenditure, performance, PPB, and ZBB. Why is it necessary to have so many different ways of depicting proposed expenditures in this document?

SUMMARY

This chapter can probably best be summarized by showing how budget formats discussed in this and the previous chapter contribute to the understanding of the whole

TRANSPORTATION

National Needs Statement:

- Assure development of the Nation's transportation system to meet the needs of commerce and the public.
- Promote safe, reliable, and efficient operation of that system.
- Ensure that transportation programs help meet the Nation's energy, environmental, and social goals.

The objective of Federal transportation policy is to promote a safe, efficient, and responsive system wherein the user pays, to the extent possible, for the benefits received. Of equal importance is the administration's goal of reducing and, where possible, eliminating unneeded government regulations that maintain high fares and stifle competition, creative management, and efficiency in the private sector. The thrust of the new legislative proposals will be to simplify many transportation programs and provide State and local governments greater flexibility in setting priorities and carrying out programs.

To address national needs in transportation in 1979, the Federal Government will spend an estimated $17.4 billion in support of the following missions:

- Ground transportation: $12.0 billion.
- Air transportation: $3.4 billion.
- Water transportation: $1.9 billion.
- Other transportation: $0.1 billion.

The budget reflects policies designed to serve these missions. The major proposals include:

- new highway-transit legislation that consolidates 42 narrow categorical programs and gives State and local governments greater flexibility in using Federal ground transportation funds;
- development of rail passenger service in the Northeast corridor to emphasize increases in ridership and economic viability;
- reduced fares and improved carrier efficiency in the regulated transportation industries with special focus on airlines and trucks;
- increased general aviation safety through an automated aviation weather and navigation information system;
- upgraded marine safety, environmental, and enforcement activities by the Coast Guard; and
- waterway user charge legislation.

FIGURE 5.5 Transportation. (*From* United States Budget in Brief, 1979, *p. 143*)

TABLE 5.6. National Need: Transportation Systems (Functional code 400: in millions of dollars)

Major missions and programs	Recommended budget authority for 1979	Outlays			
		1977 actual	1978 estimate	1979 estimate	1980 estimate
Ground transportation:					
Highway improvement and construction.....	55	5,719	6,461	349	301
Proposed legislation....................	6,850	-------	-------	[1] 6,545	6,763
Highway and traffic safety...............	258	583	638	246	257
Proposed legislation....................	950	-------	-------	645	837
Mass transit...........................	19	2,000	2,180	61	25
Proposed legislation....................	2,865	-------	-------	2,250	2,525
Railroads..............................	2,015	1,676	1,796	1,825	1,916
Proposed legislation....................	−279	-------	-------	-------	-------
Regulation.............................	69	59	64	69	69
Subtotal, ground transportation........	12,803	10,037	11,140	11,990	12,693
Air transportation:					
Airways and airports...................	3,094	2,369	2,753	2,877	3,072
Proposed legislation....................	−3	-------	-------	−3	−4
Aeronautical research and technology......	522	344	415	466	509
Air carrier subsidies....................	69	80	77	69	63
Regulation.............................	27	23	24	27	27
Subtotal, air transportation...........	3,709	2,816	3,269	3,436	3,667
Water transportation:					
Marine safety and transportation.........	1,494	1,149	1,350	1,403	1,465
Ocean shipping........................	537	591	546	532	604
Regulation.............................	11	8	10	10	11
Subtotal, water transportation........	2,042	1,749	1,906	1,946	2,080
Other transportation.................	86	76	82	93	86
Deductions for offsetting receipts...........	−66	−42	−86	−66	−67
Total.................	18,573	14,636	16,310	17,399	18,459
ADDENDUM					
Off-budget Federal entity:					
U.S. Railway Association................	23	219	97	23	−50

SOURCE: *The Budget in Brief, 1979*, p. 144.

[1] Excludes $950 million in highway safety programs, which accounted for in the "Highway and traffic safety" category.

budget process. A budget organizes the information needed to make decisions about what, where, when, and how to undertake government or governmentally sponsored actions. A budget should be designed, therefore, in such a manner as to guide the collection of information required to make these decisions. But such decisions are not all made from the same perspective. In an earlier chapter the steps involved in two stages of the budget cycle—budget preparation and budget authorization—were set forth. The first centers on the actions of the Executive; the second, the actions of the legislature. Each performs a different role in the budget cycle; the Executive proposes action, the legislature deliberates and decides which actions should be undertaken. Each requires information organized in a different way. The Executive needs information arranged in such a manner that he or she can decide strategically how much of what different governmental efforts (security, health, welfare, education, transportation, etc.) should be undertaken. He or she is thus concerned with the optimal distribution of scarce resources among competing functions to obtain the maximum impact on society. A PPB or impact-based budget comes closest to meeting the needs. Legislators, on the other hand, prefer budgets that allow them to respond to the immediate and changing needs of their constituents. An objects of expenditure budget that identifies goods and services to be purchased but not outcomes to be produced undoubtedly provides the greatest flexibility for the legislative bargaining process.

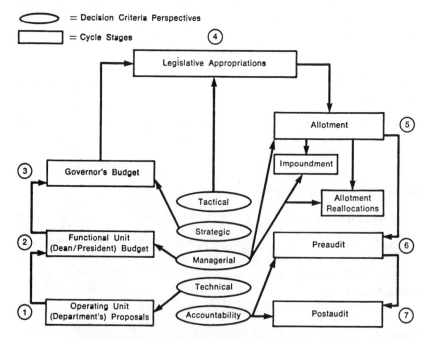

FIGURE 5.6 Decision-Making Criteria for Different Stages of the Budget Cycle. (From Fremont J. Lyden, "The Budget Cycle as a Basis for Decision-Making," Planning for Higher Education 4, no. 5, October 1975)

TABLE 5.7. Decision Criteria Perspectives

Perspective	Definition	Basis for development of criteria	Measures of accomplishment	Budget form
1. Tactical =	maximal responsiveness to immediate needs of constituents (Leg. appropriations)	Satiate immediate needs of constituents	Enactment of laws Get elected	Object expend. (input) budget
2. Strategic =	optimal dist. of scarce resources among competing functions (education, welfare, law enforcement, etc.) to obtain maximal impact on society (Gov. Budget)	Effect societal changes	Literacy rate Poverty rate Crime rate	PPB (impact) budget
3. Managerial =	allocations of scarce resource combinations in terms of competing client needs (Deans' & Pres. budget allocations to depts.)	Balance client & taxpayer needs against requirements of prof. providers	Unit cost per: career success resp. citizen research finding	Performance (input-output) budget
4. Technical =	determinants of work process by profs. (teachers determining content of courses, sequence of courses)	Knowledge acquisition	Academic performance Degrees granted	Process (curriculum or thruput based) budget
5. Accountability =	spending in accordance with law	Financial responsibility	Disallowance rate.	Object expend (input) budget Perf. budget

SOURCE: Fremont J. Lyden, "The Budget Cycle as a Basis for Decision-Making," *Planning for Higher Education* 4, no. 5 (October 1975).

Each of the other stages of the budget cycle depicted in Figure 5.6 also has its own peculiar informational requirements. In this instance the process is applied to a public university, but the same stages can be observed in any governmental agency. Table 5.7 sets forth the decisional criteria needed for each perspective: bases for developing criteria, resulting measures of accomplishment, and the budget format most appropriate. At the operating level, stage 1, academic departments propose the performance of activities intended to result in the acquisition of knowledge by students. Such decisions will be based upon what kinds of instruction to offer, delivered in what developmental order of instruction (lower division courses, upper division courses, etc.). Department proposals are submitted to academic deans and to the university president (stage 2), who will attempt to allocate the scarce resources they control in terms of balancing client (student) and taxpayer needs against the requirements of the professional provider (teacher). The dean and president's perspective is therefore managerial, and their decisions will be facilitated by information assembled on a performance basis. In stage 3 of the cycle, the governor must balance the university's budget requests against those of other departments—a strategic decision, as explained earlier. The legislature in stage 4 will probably prefer to make its tactical decisions using an objects of expenditure assembled budget.

Then, in administration of the budget appropriated, funds will be allotted to the spending units from a managerial perspective, where again the performance budget becomes most useful. The last two stages of the cycle—preaudit by the spending unit before funds are actually obligated and postaudit by an independent agency after the fact—both center on an accountability perspective, and consequently the objects of expenditure is most appropriate for both.

In a sense, of course, the actors in each of these seven stages of the budget cycle are interested in how their decisions will contribute to the whole budget process. Con-

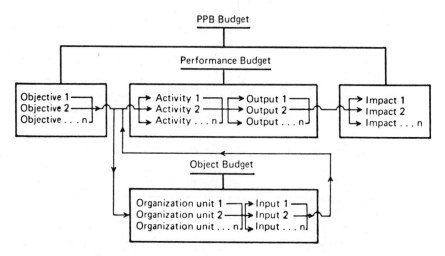

FIGURE 5.7 Informational Orientations Emphasized by PPB Performance, and Object Budget Formats. (*From Fremont J. Lyden and Ernest G. Miller,* Public Budgeting: Program Planning & Implementation, *New York: Prentice Hall, 1982, p.4*)

sequently each actor will also tend to keep in mind how his particular informational requirements are related to the informational needs of others, not because of any particular concern for the needs of other actors but to ensure that one's own needs are not sabotaged. Figure 5.7 depicts the relationships that exist between PPB, performance, and objects of expenditure ordered budgets. As will be noted, the performance budget is premised on the identification of governmental objectives. The PPB budget begins with the consideration of such objectives but can be evaluated only through an understanding about (1) what activities (2) producing which outputs (3) achieve what impacts in society. Finally, activities can be evaluated only in terms of how resources (inputs) are used to accomplish outputs.

Thus we can see that the information provided by the budget formats discussed in the past two chapters is essential for decision making in the budget process. The question is no longer which budget format to use, but how to present the information yielded by all formats in such a way as to facilitate rather than frustrate or impede decision making.

CASE STUDY

The reader is now invited to try his or her hand at constructing a budget using the tools described in the past two chapters. In the toxulemia case that follows, the reader is asked to design a performance budget for the state department of health. The information and data presented in the case simulate the amount and variety of information that would likely be available to most agencies contemplating the introduction of a new budget format. The reader should also consider whether a PPB or a ZBB budget would be more appropriate than a performance budget or whether the new budget should reflect some combination of all three. As a basis for making such a decision, the reader should show how the toxulemia program could be depicted in performance, PPB and ZBB formats and then compare the information resulting from each. Which format (or combination of formats) best provides the department with the information it needs to monitor and evaluate the recently modified Toxulemia program? What complications could the department anticipate if it were to change its existing budget system to reflect the requirements of a performance, PPB or ZBB budget? Finally, then, what advice would you give to the department about modifying its present budget format?

CASE STUDY

Performance Budgeting For Toxulemia

David Paulsen

Toxulemia is an imaginary disease. It was invented especially to demonstrate the process and problems in designing a performance budgeting system. Toxulemia, a fairly dread disease, requires an isolation hospital program (like tuberculosis), a treatment program for patients discharged from the isolation hospitals, and an analysis activity in the State Department of Health. Treatment procedures are changing rapidly: both medical and management decisions will have to be made in the next two to three years to accommodate changes in circumstances. The case problem for the student is built around such questions as these: How could a performance budget system be used to guide future decisions? How should elements of the program be linked together to provide an over-all view of progress? How should different types of operating performances be measured, compared, and used to control work?

Read the case carefully, noting especially Tables I - III at the end. Then answer the questions listed in Part V from the standpoint of a consultant called in to advise the Department of Health on the development of a performance budget for the program.

I. STABILITY AND CHANGE IN TOXULEMIA

Historically, toxulemia has been a minor public health problem. Although the disease is extremely contagious, its easy detection has nearly eliminated the possibility of epidemics. In the early, and most infectious stages of the disease, patients turn a vivid blue. Over the course of treatment, patients' color changes to a delicate mauve, and then returns to normal. Toxulemia has remained a minor health problem, too, because of prompt public agency action and a major commitment to extended treatment. As soon as diagnosis is confirmed, patients are sent to the nearest isolation hospital. There are four in this state, all some distance from settled communities, and all maintained at public expense.

Over the years, isolation hospitals have been the exclusive source of treatment, consisting largely of rest, fresh air and a special diet. Since toxulemia is a debilitating disease, patients have often remained for two years or more. Obviously, maintenance of these institutions has been a major source of health expense for the State. After appropriate terms at isolation hospitals, patients are returned to homes and jobs. Although required, by administrative regulation, to report to their local health department for physical examinations every three months, patients seldom complied.

Reprinted by permission of the author.

The pressure of re-establishing homes and incomes usually precluded them from reporting. In fact, the renewed pressures of community life often caused a return of the disease: almost 18% of all discharged patients were returned to hospitals sooner or later with new attacks.

About three years ago, treatment for toxulemia changed radically. Researchers developed a new drug which countered the effects of the disease within a few months. Fortunately, the drug changed the color of patients almost as rapidly. About the same time, other scientists discovered that whirlpool baths, when combined with radium treatments, combatted the debilitating effects of toxulemia. The drug and the baths were quickly introduced into the treatment programs of all toxulemia hospitals, including those in this State. Despite the rapid increase in costs of the medical program, total program costs have declined because the new therapy has reduced the average hospital stay from about two years to just over one year, with further decreases expected.

Although patients could be discharged as cured many months sooner than under the old program, health experts soon found that both drugs and whirlpool baths were needed for an extended period after discharge to prevent a relapse. The first group of patients discharged under the new program had the same relapse rate as under the old program: over 18%. With the reintroduction of therapy for a second, small group of dischargees, the relapse rate fell to an acceptable 3%–5%. Very little is now known about the conditions which make termination of post-discharge treatment appropriate, just as little is known about the best point to release patients from isolation hospitals. Clearly, much needs to be done to fully capitalize on new medical advances and yet assure safety of the community with reasonable effectiveness in the management of program funds.

II. MOVING TOWARD A NEW TOXULEMIA PROGRAM

Earlier this year, the State Department of Health carefully reassessed current treatment practices for toxulemia. They concluded that major improvements in the program were necessary. First, and most obvious, the Department of Health needed to establish an effective medical treatment process for patients after they were discharged from the State's isolation hospitals. Only in this way could the benefits of recent medical advances be realized. An effective post-discharge program could reduce the relapse rate and thereby reduce the medical, personal and public financial costs of the disease. Second, public health officials had to develop an effective system of control over the discharged patients to ensure effective care for them and to protect the safety of the community. Third, the Department had to establish the appropriate administrative mechanisms to operate the post-discharge program: none now existed. And finally, the Department had to work toward a new balance in the isolation hospital part of the hospital. Stable and consistent patient treatment processes and terms of residence were needed to operate those hospitals needed in the future.

To meet these needs, the State Department of Health made two basic policy decisions. As the first, they made private physicians responsible for examination, prescription of drugs, and for general oversight of treatment in the post-discharge program. The state chapter of the American Medical Association, the Anti-Toxulemia Society and medical specialists in the field gave enthusiastic support for this, essentially permanent, policy decision. To help overcome current problems with the disease, all cooperating medical groups and specialists agreed to prepare detailed records of examinations and of case progress for analysis by the State Health Office statistical group. As the second major policy decision for the Department, Health officials made a decision to provide post-discharge medical treatment at public expense in the eight county health department offices in the State. At least in the short run, public health officials were forced into this decision: private and public hospitals refused to undertake whirlpool bath treatment programs because of high capital and operating costs, uncertain workloads, and possible early obsolescence of the equipment now used. The State Department, itself, was uncertain about the level or distribution of workloads, and consequently, they were uncertain about the best arrangements for treatment. Past records were so uncertain and incomplete that they provided no guide to current needs. Too, no one knew now many former patients, discharged up to several years ago, might be interested in participating in the new post-discharge program as a preventive. Given these uncertainties, selection of the local public health offices appeared to be the best possible short-run decision. Public Health officials hoped to be able to use this relatively controlled experience to gather the time, workload and cost data needed to guide them to appropriate selection of public and private clinics, mobile units, subsidized baths operated by individual physicians, or the like.

The Department of Health then made several complementary policy decisions. First, they decided to use a conditional discharge system, giving them at least some legal control over ex-patients. To reduce the possibility of legal problems arising from the arrangement, they decided to utilize a "credit-card" device which would permit patients on the post-discharge program to receive drugs and treatment anywhere in the State with minimum difficulty. In this way, Department leaders hoped to adjust to the needs of former patients, who tended to move frequently during the first years after discharge from isolation hospitals. As a second collateral decision, the Department's leaders concluded that they should develop an integrated medical and administrative workload information system. In it, county offices would act as collectors of information, and the State Office Statistical Section would summarize and analyze the data. Health officials hoped, with this system, to institute the checks and controls necessary for present administrative management and for future program decisions. As a third decision, the Department decided to close one of the four isolation hospitals—Lachrymose Point—but to operate the others for at least three more years. At that time, they hoped that the medical, administrative and cost information would be available to tell them how many, and which, hospitals to shut down. Finally, the State Office decided to move toward a performance budget system for the toxulemia program. They wanted the system developed so as to interrelate program and administrative information and controls for present management guidance and for analysis of future program choices.

III. NEW OPERATING PROCEDURES FOR THE TOXULEMIA PROGRAM

The State Department of Health has established a series of operating procedures to carry out its policy decisions in toxulemia, as in all other programs. For some of the toxulemia program procedures, enormously detailed manuals have been prepared, or revised from past instructions. For other procedures, the State Office has issued only the most general guidelines. Here, only a summary flow of events and actions are described as background for the proposed performance budgeting system.

The patient entering a toxulemia isolation hospital today would find, at least superficially, little difference from the medical procedures of several years ago. Rest, special diet and fresh air are still the basic ingredients of rehabilitation. However, intensive whirlpool bath therapy and regular use of the newly-developed drugs have been added to create substantial reductions in the time patients must stay in isolation hospitals. Medical records, reflecting the increased emphasis on clinical work, have been revised and significantly improved. Isolation hospitals now prepare extensive medical records for each patient. At the completion of the patient's stay, these hospitals summarize important clinical data on a *Patient Case* History Record (form #11). They send the original of Form #11 to the county health department nearest the dischargee's home, and then forward the duplicate to the statistical group in the State Department office.

When the patient reports to his local health department, the Toxulemia Section clerk set in motion the medical and administrative post-discharge program process. From the Form #11, she has already prepared a *County Master Control Record* (Form #9). After verifying the patient's address, she sends the Form #11 to the physician of his choice. The Section clerk then issues a master credit card, which can be used anywhere in the State for treatment and anti-toxulemia drugs. Using the card to actuate the system, the clerk then makes an appointment for a first whirlpool bath treatment and a first month's supply of drugs. These transactions are entered on the *Master Control* (Form #9).

Each month, the patient is required to receive a thorough medical examination from his physician. After the examination, the doctor completes a Monthly Record Examination Form (Form #12), and forwards it to the local health office. The physician retains the *Case History Record* (Form #11), using it as the basis for his permanent record, and his final case report. There, the Toxulemia Section clerk sends a reminder form to the patient for his monthly treatment. When he appears, the Section nurse conducts his bath and issues his next month's supply of drugs. Appropriate notations are made on the Form #12, which is forwarded to the State Office, and on the local *Master Control* (Form #9). Each month the local Section clerk, aided by the Section nurse, prepares a summary of patient workload, treatments given, and time spent by public health personnel. Medical data are also summarized from Form #9.

At the State Health Department Toxulemia Section, a clerk posts data from the Form #12 to the state *Master Control* record for each patient. Medical statisticians analyze the records and prepare resumes of trends in treatment and complete summaries of progress of various classes of post-discharge patients. These data are compared with patient trend data from the isolation hospitals. State statisticians also summarize work activity for all departments in the isolation hospitals and for all local health offices.

IV. STAFFING AND BUDGETING FOR THE NEW TOXULEMIA PROGRAM

The organization for the toxulemia program is composed of a small staff in each of the eight county health departments and the Statistical Section in the State Office. Each county health officer provides immediate supervision of local operations; the State Program Director, general technical supervision of the whole program. As shown in Table I, twenty-six professional and clerical personnel are distributed among the eight county offices, and nine employees are assigned to the program in the State Office. All positions in the counties are included in regular county budgets, but wholly funded by the State.

Table II, following, shows the Department's budget estimate to the state legislature for the toxulemia program for FY 1971. As a new program, and as a new concept of budgeting, both the Department and the state legislature regard the format and content as only tentative. All expect that some items will be added, and others dropped, as experience accumulates. For example, now all the salaries of nurses and clerks in the local health offices are charged in total to toxulemia, although as much as 50% of their time might be used in other programs. A different method of costing might well be indicated here. Too, the current budget assumes that county health officers will devote time to general direction of the program. Following standard practice, an arbitrary, and standard, portion of their salaries is charged to the program. This procedure might also be improved. Finally, the budget presentation assumes that the present practice of renting the whirlpool baths will continue. Rentals are quite high, since manufacturers try to recover costs, plus a return on their investment, in three years. Obviously, if the Department wished to purchase the equipment and run the risks of obsolescence, then costs in the operating budget would be much lower.

Table III displays available data which might be used in developing a performance system. The Department's leaders sent the data—in somewhat revised form—to the legislature as indicative of some of the potential information which could be derived from a performance budget. Department budget personnel assembled the data and worked out the ratios shown just before the State Department Director appeared to defend his budgets. Because of the limited time spent in prepar-

TABLE 1. Personnel Assignments Toxulemia Program (FY 1970)

Location	Clerk Stenos	Jr. Program Nurse	Sr. Program Nurse	Equipment Repairman	Junior Statistician	Senior Statistician	Program Director	Total
A. Metropolitan Counties								
Ableton	3	1	1	1	1			7
Baker	2	1	1	1				5
Subtotal	5	2	2	2	1			12
B. Urban Counties								
Charleston	1	1	1					3
Dalton	1		1					2
Eagleton	1		1	1				3
Foxgrove	1	1						2
Subtotal	4	2	3	1				10
C. Rural Counties								
Howerton Office[a]	1	1						2
Kingston Office[b]	1	1						2
Subtotal	2	2						4
All Counties Subtotal	11	6	5	3	1			26
D. State Office								
Toxulemia Section	4		1		2	1	1	9
TOTAL TOXULEMIA PROGRAM	15	6	6	3	3	1	1	35

[a] Includes service to Georgetown, Howertown and Islip Counties.
[b] Includes service to Johnstone and Kingston Counties.

ing the material, Budget office personnel say privately that the data could be considerably improved. For example, one problem found in preparing and presenting the data is demonstrated by items I.C. and I.D. on Table III. Despite closing one major hospital, Lachrymose Point, and a more rapid discharge rate, the average annual cost declines only slightly in total, and increases at the level of the individual hospital. The Budget Office of the Department believes that this circumstance can be explained by the sharp increase in medical program costs and by the fact that hospital overhead—buildings and grounds maintenance, laundry, etc.—must be distributed over fewer patients.

V. STATEMENT OF THE PROBLEM

You have been appointed as a consultant to the Director of the State Department of Health to review arrangements in the toxulemia program and to recommend a performance budget system.

TABLE 2. Program Costs for Toxulemia (FY 1969–FY 1970)

	Actual[a] FY 1969	Estimated[b] FY 1970	Estimated FY 1971
I. Isolation Hospital Program			
A. Medical Program	$ 400,000	$ 900,000	$1,225,000
B. "Hotel" Costs (room & board, utilities, grounds, etc.)	9,000,000	7,000,000	4,975,000
Hospital subtotal	$9,400,000	$7,900,000	$6,200,000
II. Discharge Program			
A. Local Medical Program			
Drug therapy		90,000	$ 150,000
Whirlpool baths		120,000	200,000
Nurse-therapist		41,000	79,000
Subtotal		$ 251,000	$ 429,000
B. Local Department Administration			
Clerical salaries		23,000	46,000
Supplies & materials		2,000	4,000
Prorated overhead[b]		4,000	6,000
Subtotal		$ 29,000	$ 56,000
C. State Office Administration			
Toxulemia section salaries[c]		32,000	62,000
Supplies & Materials[c]		6,000	10,000
Travel		2,000	5,000
Prorated overhead[b]		4,000	6,500
Subtotal		$ 44,000	$ 83,800
Post-Discharge Subtotal	$	$ 324,000	$ 568,800
TOTAL PROGRAM COSTS	$9,400,000	$8,224,000	$7,143,800

[a] Based on 6 mo. actual experience, plus 6 month estimates.

[b] Local and state overhead based on an estimate of the time spent by local and state health officers and major assistants.

[c] Includes the 50% total expense proration to be paid by the Anti-Toxulemia Society.

The State Director has asked you to prepare a memorandum for the use of the Departmental leadership group. Since no public distribution of your report is planned, you should be completely candid. In your discussions with the Director, you have agreed to attempt to answer questions in these two areas:

A. General

1. To what extent can performance budget data be used to guide program choices in the toxulemia program? Where—and why—will it be more, or less, useful?

2. How can performance budget data be used here, and by whom, to control and adjust performances and costs?

B. Specific

1. What sort of overall performance units would you suggest for toxulemia?

2. What items of cost now shown on the program budget should be excluded? What other items added?

3. What sort of a report should be used in the performance budget system? (Here, you may wish to sketch a form, or a report, to help the Director in visualizing the process.) Who should prepare the report and for whom?

4. Can the performance reporting system be developed so as to provide automatic signals for major policy changes, as the closing of an isolation hospital?

5. What steps, and goals, would you recommend for the installation of a performance budgeting system? (i.e., how will the Department know when they have an effective system?)

TABLE 3. Statistical Data—Toxulemia Program (FY 1970–FY 1971)

	Estimated FY 1970	Estimated FY 1971
I. *Isolation Hospital Program*		
A. Hospital Capacity (persons)		
Lachrymose Point	600	—
Sharon Lake	300	300
Harms Valley	500	500
Edenville	600	600
Program Total	2,000	1,400
B. Average Patient Population		
Lachrymose Point	480	—
Sharon Lake	240	270
Harms Valley	400	450
Edenville	480	540
Program Average	1,600	1,260
C. Average Annual Cost Per Patient, By Hospital		
Lachrymose Point	$5,824	$ —
Sharon Lake	4,650	5,001

TABLE 3. Statistical Data—Toxulemia Program (FY 1970–FY 1971)

	Estimated FY 1970	Estimated FY 1971
I. Isolation Hospital Program		
C. Average Annual Cost Per Patient		
Harms Valley	4.560	4,950
Edenville	4,509	4,856
Program Average	$4,938	$4,920
D. Average Annual Cost Per Patient, By Program		
Medical Program	$ 563	$ 972
"Hotel" Costs	4,375	3,948
Total	$4,938	$4,920
E. Average Stay Per Patient	14 mo.	10 mo.
F. Average Total Cost Per Patient	$5,350	$4,100
II. Post-Discharge Program		
A. Average Patient Population		
Current workload	1,100	2,000
Inactive	11,000	11,000
Total	12,100	13,000
B. No. of Monthly Treatments, by County		
Ableton	4,300	8,500
Baker	3,900	6,000
Charleston	1,800	3,000
Dalton	900	1,750
Eagleton	973	1,750
Foxgrove	850	1,500
Howerton (& Gordontown, Islip)	687	1,050
Kingston (& Johnstone)	180	450
Total	13,590	24,000
C. Average Cost Per Patient Treatment		
Anti-Toxulemia Drugs	$ 6.62	$ 6.25
Whirlpool baths	11.85	11.62
	$18.47	$17.87
D. Average Annual Cost Per Patient		
Local Medical	$228.18	$214.44
Local Admin. Direction	26.36	28.00
State Section Administration	40.00	41.90
	$294.54	$284.34
III. Total Toxulemia Program		
A. Average Total Patient Population	2,710	2,260
B. Average Total Annual Cost Per Patient	$5,232.54	$5,204.34

TABLE 4. State Population by County

	1970 Census Population
A. *Metropolitan Counties*	
Abelton	1,000,000
Baker	783,000
Subtotal	1,783,000
B. *Urban Counties*	
Charleston	355,000
Dalton	200,000
Eagleton	163,000
Foxgrove	120,000
Subtotal	838,000
C. *Rural Counties*	
Howerton Office[a]	73,000
Kingston Office[b]	46,000
Subtotal	119,000
TOTAL ALL COUNTIES	2,740,000

[a] Includes Georgetown, Howerton and Islip Counties

[b] Includes Johnstone and Kingston Counties

NOTES

1. Charles Hitch, *Decision-Making for Defense* (Berkeley: University of California Press, 1965), p. 24.

2. David Novick, "The Department of Defense," in his *Program Budgeting* (Washington, D.C., Government Printing Office, 1964), pp. 59–60.

3. *New York Times*, August 26, 1965.

4. Bulletin 66–3, Executive Office of the President, Bureau of the Budget, October 12, 1965.

5. Department of Finance, State of California, "*Programming and Budgeting* System—Program Format," *Management Memo* No. 66–31, July 25, 1966, Exhibit 1, p. 1; Exhibit 3.

6. Comptroller General of the United States, *Survey of Progress in Implementing the Planning-Programming-Budgeting System in Executive Agencies*, B-15398, July 27, 1969, p. 1.

7. Subcommittee on Priorities and Economy in Government, Joint Economic Committee, *Benefit-Cost Analysis of Federal Programs* (Washington, D.C.: Government Printing Office, January 2, 1973), p. 61.

8. The five states were California, Michigan, New York, Wisconsin, and Vermont; the five counties were Dade (Florida), Nashville-Davidson (Tennessee), Los Angeles (California), Nassau (New York), and Wayne (Michigan); the five cities were Dayton, Denver, Detroit, New Haven, and San Diego.

9. Subcommittee on Economy in Government, Joint Economic Committee, *Innovations in Planning, Programming, and Budgeting in State and Local Government* (Washington, D.C.: Government Printing Office, 1969); State-Local Finances Project, *PPB Pilot Project Reports* (Washington, D.C.: George Washington University, February 1969).

10. *Planning Programming Budgeting for City State County Objectives*, Note 3 (Washington, D.C.: State-Local Finances Project, George Washington University, 1967), p. 10.

11. Perry Moore, "Zero Base Budgeting in American Cities," *Public Administration Review* 40, no. 3 (May/June 1980): 253.

12. Office of Management and Budget, Bulletin No. 77–9, April 19, 1977.

13. Aaron Wildavsky and Arthur Hammann, "Comprehensive vs. Incremental Budgeting in the Department of Agriculture," *Administrative Science Quarterly* 10, no. 3 (December 1965).

14. Office of Management and Budget, Bulletin No. 77–9.

15. James Hoobler, "ZBB and Evaluation in the U.S. Department of Justice," *GAO Review* 14, no. 4 (Fall 1979): 52.

16. This example is drawn from Peter A. Pyhrr, "The Zero Base Approach to Government Budgeting," *Public Administration Review* 37, no. 1 (January/February 1977): 262.

17. Joseph Wholey, *Zero-Base Budgeting and Program Evaluation* (Lexington, Mass.: Lexington, 1978).

18. Anne M. DeBeer, "The Attitudes, Opinions and Practices of Federal Government Workers on the Zero Base Budgeting Process," *Government Accountants Journal* 29, no. 1 (September 1980): 13–23.

19. *The Budget of the United States Government, Fiscal Year 1979*, p. 278.

20. Comptroller General of the United States, *Mission Budgeting: Discussion and Illustration of the Concept in Research and Development Programs*, PSAD-77-124, July 27, 1977.

21. Barry Holman, "Mission Analysis: A Response to the Taxpayer Revolt," *GAO Review*, Spring 1979, pp. 26–29.

BIBLIOGRAPHY

Hartley, Harry. *Educational Planning-Programming-Budgeting: A Systems Approach*. Englewood Cliffs, N.J.: Prentice-Hall, 1968.

Hebert, Joseph L., ed., *Experiences in Zero Base Budgeting*. New York: PBI, 1977.

Hitch, Charles J. *Decision-Making for Defense*. Berkeley: University of California Press, 1965.

Lyden, Fremont J., and Miller, Ernest G. *Planning Programming Budgeting: A Systems Approach to Management*. Chicago: Markham, 1968, 1972.

———. *Public Budgeting*. 3rd ed. Chicago: Rand McNally, 1978. 4th ed. Englewood Cliffs, N.J.: Prentice-Hall, 1982.

Novick, David, ed. *Program Budgeting: Program Analysis and the Federal Budget*. Cambridge: Harvard University Press, 1967.

Sarant, Peter C. *Zero-Base Budgeting in the Public Sector*. Reading: Addison-Wesley, 1978.

State—Local Finances Project. *Planning Programming Budgeting for City State County Objectives, PPB Notes 1–11*. Washington, D.C.: George Washington University, 1967–69.

Tucker, Samuel A. *A Modern Design for Defense Decision: A McNamara-Hitch-Enthovan Anthology*. Washington, D.C.: Industrial College of the Armed Services, 1966.

Turnbull, Augustus B. *Government Budgeting and PPBS: A Programmed Introduction*. Reading: Addison-Wesley, 1970.

Chapter 6

Decision Making in the Formulation and Administration of the Budget

Chapter 5 dealt with the different ways one may develop the form and structure of a budget. In this chapter we turn to a consideration of the decision-making process that determines the content of budget categories and their respective places in the total budget structure. Everyone makes decisions using some analytic frame of reference or set of value assumptions. When such a frame of reference has been developed according to rigorous rules of logic, it is referred to as a theory or a theory-based frame of reference. When it consists of a more loosely connected set of interrelated ideas, it may be regarded as an analytic model or a heuristic frame of reference. The theory of gravity would be an example of the former, compensatory spending an example of the latter. The traditional analytic perspectives developed for this purpose in budgeting tend to be rule-of-thumb methods for controlling the relative size and scope of the budget.

BUDGET CONTROL TECHNIQUES

Since budgets are characteristically assembled piece by piece at the operating level and then aggregated at higher review levels, analytic techniques focus on different ways of allocating the use of discretion in the making and reviewing of budgetary decisions. Verne Lewis[1] has identified six major techniques commonly employed:

- Open-end budgeting
- Fixed ceiling budgeting
- Workload measurement and unit costing
- Increase-decrease analysis
- Priority listing
- Item-by-item control

The *open-ended method* allows the operating program official to submit a budget estimate for whatever he decides to recommend. Typically such an estimate represents the official's judgment as to the optimum program for his agency for the coming year, tempered by the realities of the economic and political environment within which his request will be considered. The rationale for this approach is that budgets, being work programs aimed at accomplishing change, should be developed initially to reflect the changes to be accomplished rather than the resources to be saved in the performance of work. The problem with using this approach, of course, is that resources are never unlimited; consequently, some constraints must inevitably be employed.

The *fixed ceiling method* of budgeting is one way of exercising control. The agency centrally establishes ceilings within which each operating official must construct his budget estimate. This approach has the advantage of allowing operating officials freedom in selecting the mix of resources they deem most appropriate, as long as they stay within their ceiling. By restricting in advance the total amount available to the operating official, however, one following this approach takes the chance of judging a case before the evidence is heard. It may not be possible, for example, for an operating official to carry out all the programs for which he is responsible within the budget ceiling assigned to him. Using the fixed ceiling approach, the operating official may be forced to propose estimates that may be politically questionable or programmatically undesirable.

The *workload measurement and unit costing technique* requires that estimates be constructed in terms of the quantitative units of resources needed to accomplish specified volumes of work output. Performance budgeting utilizes this approach; Figure 4.1 in Chapter 4 describes the mechanics involved in the analytic process. By employing this method, a reviewing official can, theoretically, ascertain immediately how any proposed reduction (or increase) in resources will affect the volume of work produced. But how does the reviewing officer decide the amount of work that "should" be produced? Workload measurement and unit costing provide no answer.

Increase-decrease analysis is based on the assumption that budgets are incremental in nature; therefore, one need only determine what should be added to last year's budget to carry out the agency's missions. It is argued that this is a practical approach to budget analysis. The sheer volume of work involved in reviewing estimates necessitates that one concentrate attention on "what is new." By assuming that last year's expenditures provide an agreed-upon starting base, one can direct attention to the new directions of effort. This approach may be criticized on the grounds that it fails to compare the relative importance of new programs with the agency's existing programs, those that make up the base. There is consequently no consideration given to the possibility of reducing existing programs in exchange for undertaking new ones. Although operating officers may be thankful they do not have to make such decisions, the realities of inflation no longer allow such questions to be ignored.

One method of budget analysis that does allow budgets to be formulated with due consideration given to new programs in terms of existing programs is *priority listing*. All existing and new programs are ranked according to their perceived order of importance on the basis of some criterion such as relative need. For example, one might rank programs in a capital budget in terms of the following classification:[2]

AAA—Hazard to safety

AA—Required for present operations

A—Required to fully utilize present facilities

B—Required for present program expansion

C—Required for future program expansion

The triple-A programs are the most essential to undertake first because they are aimed at protecting the public from some perceived danger, such as the collapse of a condemned building or bridge. Double-A programs come next in importance, since they are required to keep present operations going. Stopping or interrupting the construction of a project already underway may result in the loss and/or deterioration of the facility thus far completed. Once these two priorities have been considered, one may direct attention to the more complete utilization of present facilities, the expansion of present facilities, and the development of future programs. The hierarchy of need upon which this classification is based is thus clearly apparent.

Another example of this form of control is found in the instructions issued by the Bureau of the Budget for the implementation of PPB.[3] By these instructions all agencies were required to classify all their budget estimates according to a commitment rationale:

1   Programs controlled by *statutory formulae* (class 1). Included are all programs where recipients and the amounts to be provided are specified by law (e.g., social security payments, veterans' pensions).
2   Programs controlled by *workload level* (class 2). Included are programs that must be performed to meet specified needs and the volume of the work in fact sets the requirements (e.g., delivery of mail).
3   *Market related* programs (class 3). These are programs in which the government is committed to respond to market conditions (e.g., interest on the public debt, agricultural price supports).
4   New programs *requiring legislation* (class 4).
5   *Administrative commitments* (class 5). The class consists of programs to which the President has publicly and specifically committed the administration to changes but do not require new legislation or have not been included in the budget-year legislative program.
6   Programs controlled by *level of appropriations* (class 6). Where the level of activity effort to be undertaken is limited only by the amount of money appropriated—in other words, no line item specification of expenditures.

Expenditure requirements for classes 1, 2, and 3 programs are, of course, least subject to control. The Social Security Administration must send checks out to all eligible beneficiaries; the Postal Service must deliver all the mail; interest on the public debt must be paid when it comes due. The programs involved in classes 4, 5 and 6 are more amenable to change. Newly proposed legislation and administrative commitments may be canceled, changed in scope or character, or delayed. Existing programs controlled only by the level of existing appropriations may be reordered and revised, within recognized legal constraints, to reflect changing needs. Although this commitment classification provides only a rough prioritization of programs, it does distinguish between programs that are most and least controllable in the short range. It also suggests that the seeds for the development of ZBB were planted in the elaboration of the PPB system.

Line item control is the oldest and perhaps still the most frequently used technique for guiding the direction of budget decisions. This approach requires that each individual item of expenditure be approved by higher authority. The items may be objects of expenditures, activities, or some mixture of the two. Some line item budgets require that a separate line be used to list the wage or salary of every employee on the payroll. Where activities are listed on a line item basis, the list may be long and detailed, such as "replacement of valve in water pump" or "generator overhaul for six fleet automobiles." The difficulty of effecting systematic changes in a line item controlled budget is obvious. A governmental agency, for example, may require top-level authorization for the initiation of all new construction activities. An operating-level unit may thus have to nurse a proposal for a relatively small and standardized construction proposal through several levels of review before gaining permission to proceed. Organizations using this kind of review tend to be sluggish in responding to the need for change.

Many organizations employ combinations of these methods in an effort to obtain a balance between the delegation of decisions and the maintenance of control. Furthermore, budget decisions are not made in a vacuum. Decision makers are human beings who exhibit the same emotional needs as the rest of us. Therefore, to understand these tools of budget analysis we must view them in their behavioral context. Take, for example, the strategies an operating program official may utilize to discourage cuts in his budget. He will develop strategies to deal with (1) which programs to cut, (2) the consequences of a cut, and (3) whose decision the cut should be. A popular strategy addressed to the first question is the ploy of suggesting that your most popular program be cut. Thus the National Park Service, threatened with a budget cut, might counter by proposing the closure of the Washington Monument or the Statute of Liberty in order to reduce its maintenance budget. As a counterstrategy, the higher authority requesting the cut may require an across-the-board cut on the less visible expenditures (such as travel allowances) that cannot be easily attributable to service reductions. The across-the-board strategy may backfire, of course, as many state legislatures have found in using ratable reductions (i.e., single rate percentage cuts across the board) to curb the costs of welfare programs. Some programs may have more options for recouping their losses (e.g., availability of grant funds) than others. Consequently, across-the-board cuts can have unequal effects upon the different clienteles served by the agency. No wonder legislatures seem unduly preoccupied with the examination of travel allowances, administrative services, and other such expenditures that can usually be related only indirectly to program outputs.

What different kinds of behavioral strategies, then, are available to the program official that will enable him or her to prevent budget controls from emasculating programs?[4]

BEHAVIORAL STRATEGIES

The budget originating official may adopt the *all-or-nothing strategy*; that is, it is better to eliminate the whole program than to emasculate it. If used as a bluff, this strategy could be dangerous. Higher authorities might call the operating official's bluff if political support for the program is not too evident. And, since political support and clientele needs may be quite different, a whole program may be endangered. To guard against this possibility, many operating-level officials review their budget proposals with local clientele groups so that if any budgetary threats are forthcoming, they may be countered by political pressures exerted by the clientele groups.

One alternative to the all-or-nothing strategy is the *production sacrifice* approach. The budget originating official may argue that the requested budget cut could not be absorbed solely through the more efficient use of resources. Consequently the level of service output (number of interviews conducted, counseling sessions held, etc.) must be reduced. One might then go on to argue that the reduced level of output can be produced only at a higher unit cost. That is to say, some of the resources involved—buildings, heat, light—cannot be represented by variable costs. Such fixed or step-function costs would not decrease as output was cut back, and consequently the unit cost per output unit would increase. In other words, the agency would be forced to use its resources less efficiently than if present output levels were maintained.

A variation of this strategy is the argument that a budget cut may represent a *short-term saving* but would actually cost the agency more in the long run. A budget cut might be effected by decreasing expenditures on preventive maintenance (i.e., replacing a part before it breaks). In the long run such economies could lead to expensive breakdown maintenance expenditures.

There is also the question of who is going to take the responsibility for deciding on the budget cut. Legislatures and top-level policy officials will prefer to attribute budget cuts to "circumstances": the rising rate of inflation, decreasing sources of revenue, and so on. The operating official, on the other hand, is left to explain to clients why circumstances have resulted in a budget cut for his agency but not for a sister agency, or for one of his programs but not for others. To forestall such an eventuality the temptation is great for the operating official to maintain sufficient contingency funds (known as *"squirreling away"*) to tide him over short-term budget crunches. The availability of such funds may only delay the eventual day of reckoning, but it may also facilitate a less painful gradual reduction in the long run.

So far we have discussed strategies used to deal with budget cuts. What about justifications for budget increases? One strategy is the *foot-in-the-door approach*. That is, begin by requesting exploratory funds. Such requests may be minimal at first, but as the investigation proceeds, more funds are requested for the more promising possibilities. Soon, so much has been invested in developing the feasibility of undertaking a program that the authorization for operating funds is almost inevitable.

A variation of this strategy is the *temporary adjustment approach*. There is a temporary shortfall in revenues for a particular program, so assistance is requested from the General Fund. When revenues begin flowing back into the program's fund again, it may be argued that these "new funds" should now be used to improve service or decrease backlogs in the program. In other words, short-term assistance from the General Fund has now become institutionalized into the program's spending rituals; so the program manager may argue that the temporary assistance should be made permanent.

Another attractive strategy by the budget originating official is *the crisis*. A completely unanticipated circumstance has occasioned the need for expanding a program. Some circumstances—floods, earthquakes, nuclear meltdowns—are perhaps crises in terms of the above definition. Other emergencies, though, like a rash of maintenance breakdowns or power failures, may be due more to inadequate preventive maintenance than the acts of God. An agency therefore cannot afford to gain a reputation for continually "crying wolf," or the credibility of its whole management style may come into question.

One final example of strategies employed to justify budget increases that might be mentioned is the *spending to save approach*. This strategy argues that an increase in expenditures now may pay off in economies in the future. For example, if you don't build a new maintenance shop now, your insurance rates will go up on the existing building and inflation will raise the cost of future construction. This strategy can, of course, be attacked for having its own inflationary effects.

These are just a few examples of strategies employed by budget decision makers to respond to the budget controls discussed earlier. One should not draw the inference that the use of such strategies implies insincerity on the part of the decision maker. On the contrary, each decision maker undoubtedly really believes he or she is acting objectively in the evaluation of programs. But, like the operating program official, the perspectives of actors located in different parts of and at different levels of the agency are influenced by their own immediate environments. One must therefore expect differences of perception to occur and for each actor involved to employ strategies of behavior to reflect his or her own perceptions of reality.

The discussion thus far would seem to give substance to the assertion made many years ago by V. O. Key that we lack a real theory of budgeting.[5] Decision making in budgeting seems to be an ad hoc process based upon the programmatic use of mechanical controls and behavioral strategies. None of these techniques tell us, in Key's words: "On what basis shall it be decided to allocate x dollars to activity A instead of activity B?"[6] Or, to carry the question farther, when should funds not be spent on either A or B but left to the taxpayer to spend according to his or her personal preferences?

BUDGETARY THEORY: BENEFIT-COST ANALYSIS

An early attempt to provide a rationale for answering such questions may be observed in the development of benefit-cost analysis in water resource administration. Both the Bureau of Reclamation and the Corps of Engineers have employed this kind of analysis for many years. In fact, Congress first mandated the use of benefit-cost analysis by the corps in the Flood Control Act of 1936. By the late 1930s the corps, the bureau, and the Soil Conservation Service were all using benefit-cost analysis, each according to its own set of rules. All three recognized the need for the development of uniform evaluation practices. Consequently, the three agencies joined together with the Federal Power Commission in 1946 to form the Federal Interagency River Basin Agreement. Out of this association uniform standards emerged, known in their published form as the Green Book.

An illustration might clarify how federal agencies applied benefit-cost analysis in these early years.[7] Table 6.1 shows a benefit-cost presentation for a municipal-water and irrigation multiple-use project proposed by the Bureau of Reclamation. In examining this table item by item we note that the municipal and industrial loan supply benefit was determined by estimating the value of constructing, operating, and maintaining a single-purpose, privately financed project—$5,304,000. A further benefit of $1,400,000 was estimated as the value of ground water formerly used for domestic water purposes that would be replaced by surface water, thereby releasing the ground water for irrigation use. The total benefit—$5,304,000 + $1,400,000—is thus $6,704,000.

Flood-control benefits estimated by the Corps of Engineers include $124,500 for loss prevention and $7,500 for land enhancement, a total of $132,000. The former relates to the prevention of possible losses to bridges and pipeline crossings, interruptions in traffic, and damage from grading and scoring of the flood plain. Land enhancement refers to prevention of the caving in of banks, destroying useful land.

Fish and wildlife benefits of $70,000 annually are based on the value of the storage reservoir for fish and wildlife facilities. The recreation benefit is computed by amortizing* over 50 years at 3 percent interest an allocation of $2,454,000 of capital cost recommended by the National Park Service as a program expenditure for recreational facilities. This armortization would require $57,800 annually. Operation and maintenance costs would add another $32,000 annually. The two together would yield a total annual benefit of $89,800.

TABLE 6.1. Municipal-Water and Irrigation Multiple-Purpose Project

Annual Benefits		
Municipal and industrial water supply		$6,704,000
Flood control		132,000
Fish and wildlife		70,000
Recreation		89,000
Irrigation		532,000
	Total benefits	$7,527,000
Annual Costs		
Total construction costs		$85,383,000
Interest during construction		8,538,000
	Total investment	$93,921,000
Annual cost of amortizing the investment at 2.5% over 50 years		$3,312,000
Annual operation and maintenance cost		1,005,000
	Total costs	$4,317,000

SOURCE: Alfred R. Golze, *Reclamation in the United States* (New York: McGraw-Hill, 1952), p. 128.

*To amortize is to liquidate an indebtedness or charge, usually by periodic payments made to a sinking fund.

The calculation of irrigation benefits is a bit more complicated, since both direct and indirect benefits are calculated. Direct benefits representing increased income to farmers and increased interest payments on farm loans are estimated to constitute $283,000 annually. Indirect benefits from sales due to increased crop values brought about by irrigation add another $195,000 annually. Finally, indirect benefits from increased purchasing power of farmers resulting from increased income attributable to irrigation add another $54,000 annually—a total of $532,000 for irrigation benefits.

Turning to the costs, the total for the project is estimated to be $85,383,000 spread over a six-year construction period. Interest during construction adds another $8,538,000. Thus a total investment of $93,921,000 is amortized at 2.5 percent over 50 years, yielding an annual amortization cost of $3,312,000. Annual operations and maintenance costs are estimated to run $1,005,000.

Comparing annual benefits to costs we get a ratio of 1:7. Since no intangible benefits, such as contributions to the national defense (this was during World War II) and added national income, were calculated, the bureau considered the 1:7 ratio to be conservative. They concluded that since benefits outweighed costs, the project should be undertaken.

But just how are these estimated costs and benefits arrived at? Some costs and benefits are correctly registered in markets by prices, and may be appropriately used in benefit-cost analysis. Other prices prevailing in the market reflect monopolistic or subsidy practices and do not convey the true market value of the goods or services involved. In some instances there is no market price for a commodity or service, but one can estimate what the public would pay for the commodity or service if it were privately provided. Such an estimate is called a "shadow price." In the illustration just discussed the bureau used a shadow price to determine the municipal and industrial water supply benefit of the proposed project. This was based, it will be recalled, on the estimated cost of constructing, operating, and maintaining a single-purpose, privately financed project.

Some benefits and costs are nearly impossible to derive from any kind of market valuation process. How does one, for example, estimate the value of a beautiful landscape? In such cases costs and benefits are arrived at subjectively. If the decision on whether or not to undertake the project turns on the benefit-cost ratio, the temptation is to weight the subjective benefits high enough to more than balance costs. Arthur Maass illustrates this practice in a study of the controversy between the Bureau of Reclamation and the Corps of Engineers over who should build the King's River Dam.[8] The bureau could justify building the dam if the single largest benefit accrued to irrigation; the corps if the single largest benefit accrued to flood control. The differences in their respective allocations of benefits to irrigation and flood control are dramatically revealed in the 1940 reports of each agency:

Annual Benefits from	Corps of Engineers 1940 Report	Bureau of Reclamation 1940 Report
Irrigation	$995,000	$1,255,000
Flood Control	1,185,000	1,185,000
Power	none	683,000

As can be seen, there is no disagreement about the benefits accruing from flood control. So the bureau had to demonstrate that irrigation benefits exceeded this amount if they hoped to build the dam. The corps, on the other hand, had to show the opposite if they were to justify building the project. Congress accepted the corps' rationale and commissioned them to build the dam. In 1948, with construction well under way, though, the corps recalculated prospective benefits as follows: $2,126,000 for flood control; $3,382,000 for irrigation. In other words, the corps now admitted that the project was primarily an irrigation, not a flood-control, facility. But by this time it was too late for the Bureau of Reclamation to take over.

In spite of the difficulties of listing and quantifying project benefits and costs, benefit-cost analyses have been extremely useful. Analysts have been forced to specify their assumptions about projects. Managers have been provided with a framework for allocating scarce resources. In Chapter 7 on capital budgeting, cost-benefit techniques and their assumptions are presented in detail.

PROGRAM ANALYSIS: COST EFFECTIVENESS

There are areas in government where benefit-cost analysis is not feasible, usually because of the difficulties involved in measuring the value of benefits. This is true of many projects in defense, regulatory activities, crime prevention, and social welfare.[9]

In such cases one can sometimes estimate the costs of different ways of producing similar outputs and determine which is the most cost effective. This can be done by conducting constant-cost and least-cost studies. Constant-cost analysis tells us what varying amounts of different outputs can be achieved for a given, fixed level of expenditure. For example, if the Air Force identifies on output as number of planes shot down in defense of American air bases and another output as number of hits scored in bombing enemy installations, a constant-cost analysis will indicate what different combinations of planes shot down and targets hit can be accomplished with a fixed budget. This allows decision makers to visualize what different output combinations are possible with a fixed set of constraints.

Least-cost studies focus on identifying the least expensive way of producing a given quantity of a particular output. If an agency's desired output, say, is 1000 residential housing units with a public work force, one may consider: contracting for construction by private companies, providing incentives for private companies to themselves initiate construction, and perhaps several other alternatives. Each alternative will be costed out, and the least-cost alternative will be chosen. Of course cost may not be the only consideration. The first two alternatives obviously ensure greater control over the quality of the work product, but the third alternative may have a more positive effect on a depressed construction industry. Thus the least-cost approach implies an equivalent product and effect whichever alternative is chosen. If this assumption cannot be made, the relative cost of each alternative must be viewed in terms of the differential effects produced by each alternative. The alternative selected will then be the one which has the *most acceptable* least cost.

Cost effectiveness is a method associated with systems analysis. But what is systems analysis? Quade says:

It is not a method or a technique; nor is it a fixed set of techniques; but rather a concept, or a way of looking at problems. In other words, a philosophy for carrying out decision oriented interdisciplinary research, a perspective on the proper use of the available tools.[10]

The "way of looking at problems" is identified by Alain Enthoven as

. . . a cycle of definition of objectives, design of alternative systems to achieve these objectives, evaluation of the alternatives in terms of their effectiveness and costs, a questioning of other assumptions underlying the analysis, the opening of new alternatives, the establishment of new objectives, etc.[11]

Cost effectiveness, then, is an analytic technique used in systems analysis to evaluate costs in relation to outputs (resources). It is typically used by systems analysts within the framework that Quade and Enthoven define that rather nebulous but influential approach to analysis. It first played a prominent part in budget decision making in the early 1960s when the Defense Department was developing the PPB system. Hitch and McKean's *The Economics of Defense in a Nuclear Age* became the first authoritative source for analysts interested in the employment of this analytical technique.[12]

In its budgetary application, cost effectiveness is usually employed in connection with special studies that are undertaken whenever new programs or major revisions of existing programs are being considered. In the federal PPB system, for example, issue papers were required whenever such changes were anticipated. Such papers were expected to include:[13]

• Background data about the issue
• Definition and magnitude of the problem
• Probable causes
• Program objectives and related evaluation criteria
• Current activities relative to the problem
• Types of alternative solutions
• Analysis of alternatives
• Program proposal

Increasingly, city and county councils are requiring the submission of such disciplined presentations when new program directions are being proposed by departments and agencies.

In using cost-effectiveness and benefit-cost analytic methods it should be borne in mind that the primary criterion for measuring each is efficiency. Other criteria, such as equity or political feasibility, may be as important or more important in making program decisions, even if such criteria are less quantifiable in dollar terms. Consequently, attention should be drawn explicitly to such criteria when presenting the results of cost-effectiveness and benefit-cost studies so that undue weight is not given to economic efficiency.

The benefit-cost and cost-effectiveness movements described above brought the program analyst into contact with the budget process but rarely made him a part of the process. The budget process follows a highly routinized procedure in which deadlines are critical. Decisions must be made on schedule whether all the facts are in or not. But the program or policy analyst is trained to make rigorous investigations into the causal circumstances underlying problems and to make systematic recommendations for the solution of such problems. As a result, the program-policy analyst has experienced difficulty in plugging his or her analytical skills into the budget process. Schick and Wildavsky have both argued that the role of the policy analyst should be separated from the ongoing budgetary process. This kind of analyst should rather concentrate on new legislative proposals and major developments in existing programs.[14] Yet the budget process is where agency priorities are largely determined, so the program-policy analyst cannot afford to become too isolated from its workings.

DECISION MAKING IN THE ADMINISTRATION OF BUDGETS

The Executive Authorization Process.   Thus far we have indicated the kinds of controls employed in the formulation of the budget. But decision making does not end when funds have been appropriated; on the contrary, a whole new series of controls comes into effect.[15] At the federal level, the Antideficiency Act of 1906 was passed in an attempt to discipline the spending of authorized funds over the course of the budget year. Department and agency heads were made responsible for apportioning the spending of funds, on a monthly or quarterly basis, over the budget year. But such officials were also authorized to waive or modify these apportionment requirements when they deemed it necessary. It was not until the apportionment authority was transferred to the Director of the Bureau of the Budget in 1933 that this mechanism became an effective tool in preventing deficiencies. Under this new procedure drawing funds were not set up in the Treasury for a department or agency until apportionment schedules had been filed with and approved by the bureau. Revisions during the year could also be made only after thorough justifications were made with the bureau.

While they no longer controlled the apportionment process, department and agency heads continued to exercise the authority for allocating funds to their subordinates in terms of programs, projects, or some other classification scheme that could be used to hold subordinates responsible for the funds budgeted to them. In effect, the use of such an allotment system serves as a major means of delegating responsibility to subordinates for the spending of public funds. Figure 6.1 depicts the budget execution process.

Many state and local governments do not have such formalized machinery for allocating the expenditure of funds, but most of them do require departments to file a work plan with the budget office after the passage of a statute or ordinance. Such a document becomes the basis for monitoring expenditures as they occur or in terms of periodic reports from each department.

Monitoring of expenditures must follow the progress of the budget from the obligation of funds to the disbursement of monies. In purchasing goods, for example, one first identifies the work program (*allotment*) for which the goods are to be used. Next a purchase order is drawn up, representing the agency's commitment to buy the goods (*obligation*). When the goods are received, as evidenced by the accompanying invoice,

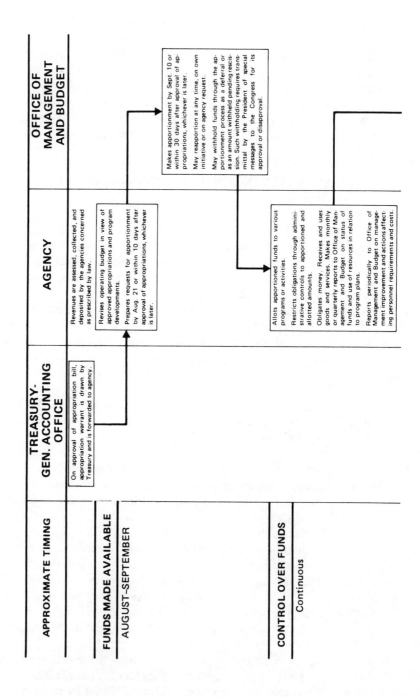

APPROXIMATE TIMING	TREASURY-GEN. ACCOUNTING OFFICE	AGENCY	OFFICE OF MANAGEMENT AND BUDGET
FUNDS MADE AVAILABLE AUGUST–SEPTEMBER	On approval of appropriation bill, appropriation warrant is drawn by Treasury and is forwarded to agency.	Revenues are assessed, collected, and deposited by the agencies concerned as prescribed by law. Revises operating budget in view of approved appropriations and program developments. Prepares requests for apportionment by Aug 21 or within 10 days after approval of appropriations, whichever is later.	Makes apportionment by Sept. 10 or within 30 days after approval of appropriations, whichever is later. May reapportion at any time, on own initiative or on agency request. May withhold funds through the apportionment process as a deferral or as an amount withheld pending rescission. Such withholding requires transmittal by the President of special messages to the Congress for its approval or disapproval.
CONTROL OVER FUNDS Continuous		Allots apportioned funds to various programs or activities. Restricts obligations through administrative controls to apportioned and allotted amounts. Obligates money. Receives and uses goods and services. Makes monthly or quarterly reports to Office of Management and Budget on status of funds and use of resources in relation to program plans. Reports periodically to Office of Management and Budget on management improvement and actions affecting personnel requirements and costs.	

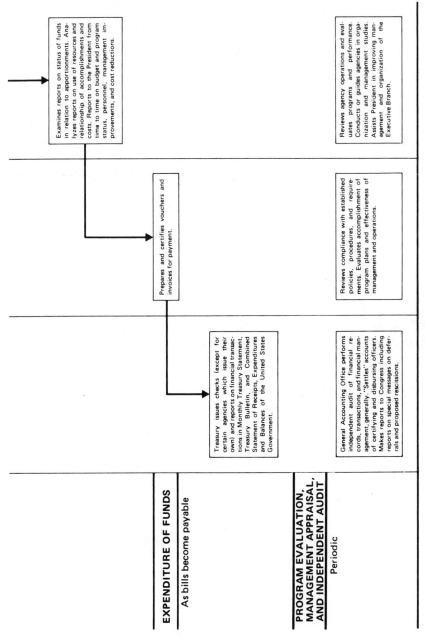

FIGURE 6.1   Execution of Enacted Budget. (*From Office of Management and Budget, 1977*)

135

TABLE 6.2. Allotment Ledger

Activity: _____ Annual Allotment: $ _____ Apportionment: _____

1st quarter $ _____
2nd quarter $ _____
3rd quarter $ _____
4th quarter $ _____

Account	Description	Applied Cost	Accrued Expenditure	Obligations	Allotments	Unobligated Balance

y ↓ MINUS ↑ x

the obligation becomes an *accrued expenditure*. Next the issuance of goods, as reflected by a work order, turns the accrued expenditure into an *applied cost*. Finally, when a voucher is prepared for paying the bill, the applied cost becomes a *disbursement*. Use of an allotment ledger such as that indicated in Table 6.2 allows one to see the status of every item at every moment in time. Also by subtracting obligations (Y) as they are incurred from the allotments remaining (X), one has a running record of the unobligated balance remaining.

The Expenditure Control Process.   In 1793 Alexander Hamilton set off a controversy in Congress over the exercise of *transfer authority*, or the taking of funds from one appropriation account and placing them in another. In justification he gave an example where the conditions of roads were worse than anticipated and, as a result, exhausted the specific funds appropriated for wagon repairs. Concurrently the consumption of forage by animals turned out to be less than expected. So why not, he asked, have the public agent transfer the surplus of the latter to the repair of the wagons? If such were not allowed, " 'the motions of the army might, in this way, be suspended, and in the event, famine and ruin produced.' "[16]

William Giles of Virginia presented a number of resolutions to the House charging Hamilton with improper use of funds. Giles asserted that Hamilton had illegally transferred funds and utilized them for purposes not specified by appropriation. In defense of Hamilton, William Smith of South Carolina argued that the administration ought to be free to depart from congressional appropriations whenever the public safety or credit would be improved. Instead of construing such transfers automatically as a crime, Congress should examine the wisdom of the Executive's exercise of discretion and act accordingly. The Giles resolutions were voted down, and transfer authority became an acknowledged reality. In most cases, of course, the Executive seeks specific legislative authority to effect transfers. When granted by Congress, restrictions are usually placed on the exercise of such authority to ensure that legislative intent is not affected by the transfer. Over the years many congressmen and senators have been uneasy over the use of the transfer authority, but the alternative of tying the Executive's hands in the face of emergencies or changes in circumstances has been viewed as even more objectionable.[17]

Another form of executive control can be exercised through *reprogramming* funds, that is, shifting funds *within* an appropriation account, moving them from one program to another. Appropriations typically identify a lump sum to be expended. Yet there are voluminous backup materials—departmental justifications, legislative reports, hearing testimony—that commit the department to spend the money appropriated in terms of the policy references established during the legislative authorization process. The very integrity of the budget process depends upon the Executive's willingness to adhere to these nonstatutory policy commitments. On the other hand, Congress recognizes that a budget proposal is put together many months, indeed in some instances, years, before expenditures will be made. Thus the Executive must be allowed to reprogram funds to accommodate unforseen developments, changing requirements, incorrect price estimates, wage-rate adjustments, and legislation enacted after appropriations have been made.[18] The term "reprogramming" was not used until the mid-1950s, but the practice has long been carried out under such names as "adjustments," "interchangeability," or "transfers," even though the latter term should refer strictly to the moving of funds from one appropriation account to another. Typically, Congress has attempted to control the process by (1) not allowing the amount reprogrammed to exceed 15 percent of the original amount available, (2) requesting that the appropriate congressional committee be advised of all reprogrammings over a stated dollar amount, and (3) prohibiting the reprogramming of funds to projects not included in the agency's original budget justification. Such controls do not always work. Agencies may be hesitant to call attention to reprogramming, for whenever they request that funds be transferred they are admitting that (1) the original program was overfunded, (2) there has been slippage in the original program, or (3) the original program has been downgraded in priority.[19] Nevertheless, the majority of reprogramming actions occasion little discussion. As Louis Fisher points out, though, reprogramming in the Defense Department alone amounts to billions of dollars a year, a fact that underscores the highly tentative nature of original budget estimates.

The President may also control the use of appropriated funds by impounding them, or placing them in reserve, thereby making them unavailable for expenditure by the authorized government agency. This practice originated in 1803 when President Jefferson informed Congress of his refusal to spend $50,000 appropriated for gunboats to patrol the Mississippi River. It did not become a major budget tool, though, until 1941 when President Franklin Roosevelt impounded funds in order to prevent the construction of flood-control projects that would have diverted scarce resources away from the war effort. Since that time, Presidents have continued to impound funds on occasion. When this has been done to prevent deficiencies, effect savings, or take into consideration other developments that have emerged since the appropriation was passed, the practice has seemed defensible. Yet what are "other developments that have emerged?" In 1966 President Johnson concluded that funds needed to be impounded because government expenditures were contributing to the expansion of inflation. Under President Nixon this rationale was extended until literally billions of dollars—17 to 20 percent of all controllable expenditures from 1969 to 1971—were being impounded to support the President's anti-inflation policy.[20]

Carried to this extreme, the impoundment authority threatened to wipe out congressional control over the appropriation process. Consequently, in the Congressional Budget and Impoundment Control Act of 1974 the President's authority to impound funds is limited in two ways, through recissions and deferrals. When the President has no expectation that appropriated funds will be spent in the future, he may request a recission. When he merely wishes to delay the expenditure until some time in the future, he requests a deferral. Funds proposed for recission must be made available for obligation if Congress does not adopt a recission bill within 45 days after receipt of the President's request. Funds proposed for deferral must be released if either house adopts a resolution of disapproval. It remains to be seen how these provisions will be interpreted by different Presidents. Some will undoubtedly see the provisions as giving the President, in effect, a limited item veto over congressional appropriations. Other Presidents will probably be more constrained, limiting the use of recissions and deferrals to preventing deficiencies and effecting efficiencies.

Expenditure Control in State and Local Government.   States, cities, and counties also have developed controls for monitoring the expenditure process, although they tend to be less elaborate than those found in the federal government. Not all jurisdictions use formal allotment controls, but if not, they normally require departments to submit work programs that may be used by budget analysts to monitor expenditures. The budget analyst does so by reviewing such things as:

- Personnel requests (requests for personnel action)
- Quarterly progress reports on program completion
- Appropriation requests for supplemental funds
- The cash flow relation between expenditures made and revenues available.

By requiring that departments get at least informal approval by the budget office in terms of these ongoing review criteria, the chief executive of the state can exercise control over the spending activities of the departments under his direction in much the same way as his or her counterpart in the federal government.

Postaudit Controls.   The independent postaudit ensures that funds are expended in accordance with all legal requirements. Such audits occur after the fact, in order to ensure that the spending agency will be held responsible for its actions. In fact, of course, the auditor's views have an impact before funds are expended as well. In the federal government, for example, each spending agency has its certifying officer, bonded under law, to authorize the issuance of vouchers. The precedents established by past decisions made by the Comptroller General, head of the General Accounting Office, exercises controlling influence over the decisions of the certifying officer.

At one time all transactions were audited, but as government has become larger and more complex such a procedure has become impractical. The individual transaction audit has been replaced by the systems audit. Here a sampling of transactions are audited to test the integrity of the system as a whole. Where errors are found the accounting system is redesigned to rectify the problem.

Another change in auditing procedure that has emerged in the past twenty years or so is the advent of the management audit. Originally all audits were fiscal audits, aimed at determining whether funds were being expended in accordance with law. In recent years, though, legislatures have become increasingly interested in monitoring the managerial efficiency with which funds are expended. Consequently, the General Accounting Office and its counterparts at state and local levels now spend a considerable portion of their time auditing how well funds have been spent in accomplishing agency missions. GAO publishes "blue books" at the completion of each management audit, which are available to Congress and the public generally. Typical titles of such reports are:

The Swine Flu Program: An Unprecedented Venture in Preventive Medicine, HRD-77-115, June 17, 1977.

Food Stamp Receipts—Who's Watching the Money?, CED-77-76, June 15, 1977

Reducing Federal Judicial Sentencing and Prosecuting Disparities: A Systemwide Approach Needed, GGD-78-112, March 19, 1979.

Should the Appalachian Regional Commission Be Used as a Model for the Nation?, CED-79-50, April 27, 1979.

Several hundred such volumes are issued each year. The findings of a few even make the headlines of the major metropolitan daily newspapers. Responsible directly to Congress, the GAO can through these reports contribute managerial advice that agencies are unlikely to receive within the executive branch. And the advent of the managerial audit certainly underscores the extent to which the Executive Budget has become a major instrument for reflecting public policy in governments today.

TABLE 6.3. Supplemental Appropriations Authorized by Congress, 1964–80[a] (in billions of dollars)

Fiscal Year	Total Supplemental Appropriations
1964	$0.3
1965	4.9
1966	8.8
1967	7.2
1968	4.5
1969	4.6
1970	6.3
1971	10.0
1972	11.6
1973	11.4
1974	13.7
1975	29.6
1976	22.3
1977	36.3[b]
1978	16.1
1979	14.0
1980	16.9

SOURCE: Adapted from two tables in Dennis Ippolito, *Congressional Spending* (Ithaca: Cornell University Press, 1981), pp. 162 and 164.

[a] Vietnam war appropriations have been omitted.

[b] In addition to this figure, $13.1 billion in supplemental funding was required by a technical change in the handling of the long-term costs associated with housing contracts; actual funding was not increased.

Administrative Controls in Practice. The controls discussed for the administration of the budget, like the budget formulation controls discussed earlier, operate in a behavioral setting. One would, perhaps, expect a sizable decrease to have occurred in the number of supplemental budget requests after the enactment of the Congressional Budget and Impoundment Control Act of 1974. Such has not been the case. For fiscal years 1975–80, more than two dozen supplemental bills have been passed, resulting in budgetary increases that averaged more than $20 billion annually.[21] As can be seen in Table 6.3, this certainly represents no decrease over the practices occurring before 1975. The budget committees in Congress routinely provide a cushion in the second budget resolution to accommodate anticipated supplements. In 1975, 1976, and 1978 shortfalls in spending and a sufficient cushion for supplementals enabled Congress to enact supplementals without raising the spending ceiling. In 1977, 1979, and 1980, however, Congress had to raise its budget ceilings to make room for supplemental appropriations. In 1977 a third budget resolution and an accompanying $20 billion supplemental were justified on grounds of fiscal policy. In 1979 and 1980, though, unanticipated increases in uncontrollable spending, particularly in the indexed entitlement programs, forced Congress to raise its budget ceilings to make room for supplemental appropriations. If such occurrences continue to force Congress to increase its second budget resolution ceiling to accommodate for supplemental requests, the discipline of the budget control process will be badly compromised.[22]

The use of reprogramming and fund transfers in the expenditure of appropriated funds also provide control mechanisms; but when the use of such techniques involves the shifting of several billions of dollars a year within a budget, as in the case of the Defense Department, the effectiveness of such instruments in the control over the exercise of discretion may be questioned. In short, all controls operate within a dynamic political environment and must be flexible enough to be responsive to the changing needs of the environment. On the other hand, they must structure discretionary decision making sufficiently to ensure that decision makers reflect the needs of their political environments, not their own rationalizations of such needs. Striking a balance between these two requirements becomes the objective of every effective budget control.

SUMMARY

This chapter has dealt with the frames of reference or value orientations employed in budgetary decision making. Previous chapters have considered how budgets may be structured. In this chapter we have discussed the analytic tools used to make decisions once a budget structure has been established. Kinds of budget controls and behavioral strategies for enforcing or avoiding such controls have been examined in the contexts of budget formulation and budget administration. The nature of the analytic techniques stemming out of program management and systems analysis, that is, benefit-cost analysis and cost effectiveness analysis, have been considered in terms of their application to the budget process. It was concluded that budgetary decision making must be viewed as the intermixture of rational and behavioral perspectives centered on specific public policy issues as they became incorporated into the budget structure.

CASE STUDIES

Two cases follow, one illustrating program analysis and the other how budget controls operate in real-world contexts.

The swimming pools case is intended to give the reader a feel for the dynamics involved in the analysis of programs. Although the case is brief, it should be read with great care. Sufficient information is provided to allow one to utilize benefit-cost and cost-effectiveness principles in determining which alternative should be selected. Therefore, calculate the cost of each alternative, set forth the benefits associated with each alternative, and recommend which course of action should be taken. Remember that the construction of a swimming pool is not an end in itself but merely a means to the accomplishment of some other end(s) in the community.

The clean-water impoundment case demonstrates how budget controls affect the exercise of discretion in decision making. Is impoundment a legitimate mechanism for the Chief Executive to use to effect savings or encourage the more economical use of resources? Can impoundment for these reasons be distinguished from impoundment for policy reasons? What, then, is the legitimate use of the impoundment procedure? What other nonstatutory means of control does the President have at his command? Why may he prefer to employ impoundment rather than such other controls? What do you see as the likely use of impoundment procedures in the future? Is it likely to become a control device used by chief executives at the state or local level of government? Why or why not?

CASE STUDY A

Provision on Swimming Opportunities in the Dade County Model Neighborhood

Graeme M. Taylor

In July, 1968, a team of three analysts representing the Dade County (Florida) Park and Recreation Department, the Department of Housing and Urban Development, and the Dade County Community Relations Board were conducting an analytic study to determine the best method of providing swimming opportunities for residents of Dade County's Model Neighborhood. The decision to undertake this analysis had been made following a request by residents of Brownsville (a community within the Model Neighborhood) for construction of a swimming pool in Brownsville.

Data Gathered For the Study:

Admission fees for pools operated by Dade County were $ .15
per day. The team had gathered the following information on the use
of three County pools:

Neighborhood pool	Average daily attendance (summer)	Population living within 1½ mile radius of pool	Type of neighborhood
Bunche Park	150	18,000	poor; black
Richmond Park	200	5,750	upper-middle; black
Cutler Ridge	350	10,000	upper-middle; white

The population of the Model Neighborhood, as determined by a 1964
study, was 75,000; it was expected that this would rise to 80,000 by
1985. The area of the rectangularly-shaped Model Neighborhood was 9
square miles, consisting primarily of single-family dwellings on small
lots. The population was predominantly black; average family income
was $3,000.

National recreational organizations had issued "rules of thumb"
concerning the percentage of the population living near a pool that would
use the pool on an average day; these estimates ranged from 1% to 5%.
Various standards had been established for the minimum acceptable
surface area of water per swimmer per day, ranging from 15 square
feet to 30 square feet, with 19 square feet approximating Dade County's
own experience. It was estimated that 1½ miles was the maximum
practical distance that any potential swimmer would walk to use a pool.

The analytic team had gathered cost information on two sizes of
swimming pools - "standard" and "olympic."
Standard: A standard pool had 5,000 square feet of water surface, and
would require a total of two acres of land. Construction costs were
estimated at $127,900, including equipment. Operating expenses, in-
cluding lifeguards' wages, were estimated at $20,800 per year.

Graeme M. Taylor is with Management Analysis Center, Inc., a general management
consulting firm. Formerly Senior Vice President in charge of the firm's Washington
office, he is now a member of MAC's corporate staff in Cambridge, Massachusetts.
This case was prepared with the cooperation of Dade County, Florida, on behalf of
the Ford Foundation and the State-Local Finances Project, George Washington
University. It is intended for class discussion only, and certain names and facts may
have been changed which, while avoiding the disclosure of confidential information,
do not materially lessen the value of the case for educational purposes. This case is
not intended to represent either effective or ineffective handling of an adminstrative
situation, nor does it purport to be a statement of policy by the County involved.
    The author wishes to acknowledge his debt to Gloria Grizzle, Budget and Analysis
Division, Dade County, and J. Robert Perkins, Chief, Planning and Research, Park
and Recreation Department, Dade County, for their cooperation and assistance in
the preparation of this case.

Olympic: An olympic pool would be 11,700 square feet, and would require five acres of land. Construction and equipment costs were estimated at $278,900, and annual operating expenses at $39,100.

Land costs in the Model Neighborhood area were estimated at $120,000 per acre, including acquisition, demolition, and relocation. Each acre of land, on average, contained property returning $656 per year in property taxes to Dade County. The "life" of a pool was estimated to be 17 years.

It was possible to construct a pool at each of three locations in the Model Neighborhood area, selected such that all residents would be within a $1\frac{1}{2}$ mile radius of a pool. Several other sites were available. Six pools, for example, could be located so that all residents of the Model Neighborhood would be no more than 2/3 mile from a pool. County-operated swimming pools were normally open from March 15 to November 15.

Bus Swimmers to Crandon Park: Another possibility considered by the analytic team was to bus swimmers to Crandon Park, a Dade County beach park located approximately an hour's bus ride from the Model Neighborhood area. This would operate each day during the four summer months, and on 20 weekends during the remainder of the year, for a total of 162 days of operation. Crandon Park contained a zoo, various amusement rides, and other attractions such as miniature golf and skating. Buses and drivers could be hired for $44 per bus per day; each bus could carry 72 passengers. It was considered desirable to have one adult recreation leader for every 30 children; the leader's wages would be $18.25 per day. Admission to the beach and all amusement attractions was free. The beach was supervised by lifeguards employed by the County: it was anticipated that no additional lifeguards would be necessary if children were bused from the Model Neighborhood.   Public transportation operated between the Model Neighborhood area and Crandon Park; however, service was limited and several changes were necessary.

Questions:

1.   Analyze the alternatives presented in the case.

2.   Which method of providing swimming opportunities to the residents of the Model Neighborhood would you recommend based on the information in the case?

3.   What additional information would you want before making a final decision if you were the responsible Dade County official?

CASE STUDY B

Impoundment of Clean-Water Funds

The Limits of Discretion

Louis Fisher

In recent decades Congress has acquired the reputation of being an unequal partner in the legislative process, losing much of the initiative to the president. Any number of cases could be assembled, however, to show that such a view is oversimplified. Often we give credit to the president when the impetus, innovation, and leadership lay with legislative forces. Often it is the president who behaves in a negative fashion, trying to restrain an active and assertive Congress. Such was the situation in 1972–73 when President Nixon refused to spend $9 billion that Congress had provided for water pollution control.

A few weeks before the presidential election of 1972, amid recriminations between the executive and legislative branches regarding prerogatives and balance of power, President Nixon vetoed the Clean Water Bill. Although both houses quickly and decisively overrode the veto, President Nixon proceeded to impound exactly half of the $18 billion that Congress had provided for waste treatment plants. The impoundment crisis became a bitter element in the confrontation between the two branches, eventually giving rise to dozens of cases in the federal courts, a U.S. Supreme Court decision, and passage of the Impoundment Control Act of 1974.

LEGISLATION ENCOUNTERS A VETO

The purpose of the Clean Water Act (the Federal Water Pollution Control Act Amendments of 1972) was "to restore and maintain the chemical, physical, and biological integrity of the Nation's waters." To that end the act provided $18 billion in federal assistance to construct publicly owned waste treatment works. Deadlines were established to eliminate the discharge of pollutants into navigable waters and to provide for the protection and propagation of fish, shell-life, and wildlife. Major research efforts were required to develop the necessary technology.

The responsibility for administering this complex act, which runs to almost a hundred pages, fell to the Environmental Protection Agency (EPA). In addition to protecting the responsibilities and rights of the states to eliminate pollution, the act encouraged public participation in the development, revision, and enforcement of regulations established by EPA and the states.

The Clean Water Act was more than two years in the making. The Senate Subcommittee on Air and Water Pollution, part of the Committee on Public Works, held hearings during the spring of 1970. Because of action on the Clean Air Act of 1970 and the Resource Recovery Act of 1970, the subcommittee did not report legislation for water pollution control that year. But hearings were held the following year, at the start of the Ninety-second Congress, and on October 28, 1971, the Senate Public Works Committee reported a Clean Water Bill, S. 2770.

The committee found that the national effort to control water pollution "has been inadequate in every vital aspect." Rivers, lakes, and streams were being used as a waste treatment system to dispose of man's wastes, rather than to support life and health. The committee proposed a major change in the federal enforcement mechanism. Instead of relying on water quality standards (purity levels), the committee wanted pollutants controlled at their source (effluent limitations for "point sources"). After a day's debate, the bill was adopted unanimously on November 2, 1971, by a Senate vote of 86 to 0.

The House Public Works Committee conducted its own set of hearings over a seven-month period and reported legislation on March 11, 1972. Three days of debate ended with a vote of 380 to 14 in favor of the bill.

At that point the House and Senate bills went to conference committee to resolve the many differences between the two bills. After thirty-nine different meetings, many of them starting early in the morning and running late into the evening, the bill emerged from conference on September 28, 1972. Senator Edmund Muskie, floor manager of the bill, told his colleagues that during his thirteen years in the Senate he had never participated in a conference "which has consumed so many hours, been so arduous in its deliberations, or demanded so much attention to detail from the members." On October 4 the Senate agreed to the conference report by the unanimous vote of 74 to 0. On the very same day the House of Representatives adopted the conference report, 366–11.

Despite the top-heavy majorities by which the two houses had passed the bill, it was vetoed on October 17. President Nixon told Congress that the attack on water pollution could not ignore "other very real threats to the quality of life, such as spiraling prices and increasingly onerous taxes." The "laudable intent" of the legislation, he said, was outweighed by its "unconscionable" cost. The price tag seemed to him so high that it literally "broke the budget." He maintained that the highest national priority was the need to protect workers against tax increases and renewed inflation. The presidential rhetoric increased in tempo as Nixon declared his intention to veto any bill which would lead to higher prices and higher taxes: "I have nailed my colors to the mast on this issue; the political winds can blow where they may."

And indeed the political winds were blowing. The veto was handed down on the eve of the presidential election, just a few short weeks away. For a number of months President Nixon had berated Congress for excessive and irresponsible spending. On July 26 he claimed that the budget crisis of deficits and inflation was the result of "hoary and traditional" congressional procedures. A nationwide radio address on October 7 warned that excessive spending by Congress might cause a "congressional tax increase" in 1973.

The issue reached fever pitch when President Nixon asked Congress to establish a spending ceiling of $250 billion for fiscal year 1973. Whenever outlays threatened to go above the statutory ceiling, Nixon wanted complete discretion to decide which programs to curtail or eliminate. To delegate such authority to the president was offensive to many members, and yet they were under heavy pressure to support the president's stance on economy. Wilbur Mills, a ranking Democrat and chairman of the House Ways and Means Committee, warned his colleagues that a vote against the spending ceiling would put an end to their political careers.

It was in the midst of this intense "Battle of the Budget" that Nixon vetoed the Clean Water Bill. Conscious though they were of the economy motif and the risk to their own careers, the Congress voted overwhelmingly to override the veto. Republicans deserted the president in droves. The final tally in the Senate was 52–12, far in excess of the two-thirds needed. The override vote in the House was even more lopsided: 247–23.

$9 BILLION IMPOUNDED

In vetoing the bill, President Nixon had called attention to the existence of of a certain amount of discretionary spending authority. Some of the provisions, he said, "confer a measure of spending discretion and flexibility upon the president, and if forced to administer this legislation I mean to use those provisions to put the brakes on budget-wrecking expenditures as much as possible."

A month later, on November 22, President Nixon instructed EPA administrator William Ruckelshaus to withhold from the states more than half of the waste treatment allotments. Instead of the statutory schedule of $5 billion for fiscal 1973 and $6 billion for fiscal 1974, $3 billion was held back from each year. Later President Nixon released only $4 billion of the $7 billion scheduled for fiscal 1975. In short, exactly half of the $18 billion provided for the three years was impounded.

The response from Congress was swift and critical. Senator Muskie, in a joint statement with the chairman of the House Public Works Committee, John Blatnik, denounced the president for acting in "flagrant disregard" of the intent of Congress. In a separate address, on December 12, Muskie said that the president had apparently "defied constitutional limitations of his powers in an area where the public and the Congress have left no doubt as to their desires and their determinations to pay the costs of restoring water quality." Anti-impoundment legislation was introduced in both houses. States and private parties filed suit in federal courts to have the clean-water funds released. To comprehend the issue, and its final settlement in the courts, the reader must grasp the essential language of the statute and its legislative history.

Statutory Language

In most cases, when Congress funds a program, it passes an appropriation act. Agencies then obligate and spend the money. The Clean Water Act relied on a different financing method called "contract authority," which allows agencies to enter into obligations in advance of appropriations. To pay for those obligations ("liquidate" the contract authority), Congress must appropriate funds at some later date. In other words, contract authority reverses the usual chain of events. Instead of first appropriating funds, followed by obligations and expenditures, obligations *precede* appropriations.

The act directed the EPA administrator to allot contract authority to the states on the basis of ratios established by Congress. The states would then submit to the administrator, for his approval, proposed projects for the construction of waste treatment works. His approval would represent a contractual obligation of the United States to pay 75 percent of the cost. The states would pay the remaining amount (a 75–25 matching grant program).

If the administration wanted to limit the level of spending for waste treatment plants, there were two potential means of control: withholding the initial allotments of contract authority from the states, or withholding the obligation and expenditure of funds at a later date. Whether discretion existed at either stage requires a close reading of the statute.

On its face, the Clean Water Act appeared to make the allotment step mandatory. Section 205 directed that sums authorized to be appropriated "shall" be allotted by the EPA administrator not later than the January 1 immediately preceding the beginning of the fiscal year for which they were authorized, except that the allotment for fiscal year 1973 was to be made not later than thirty days after the act (which became law October 18, 1972). The amounts authorized to be appropriated were governed by Section 207, which provided $5 billion for fiscal 1973, $6 billion for fiscal 1974, and $7 billion for fiscal 1975—a total of $18 billion.

However, the mandatory nature of Section 205 was weakened by two changes made in the bill while in conference. The original language of the House bill had directed that "all sums" shall be allotted. The word "all" was eliminated by the conferees. Moreover, the conferees appeared to enhance administrative flexibility by inserting the phrase "not to exceed" before the dollar amounts authorized in Section 207. That made it appear that the amounts were mere ceilings rather than mandatory levels.

Statements abound throughout the legislative history, demonstrating without question that the president was granted a measure of spending flexibility. Crucial issues were left hanging. First, did the president enjoy any flexibility at the *allotment* stage, or was he required to allot the full amount to the states? And second, if he had discretion at the obligation and expenditure stages, what was the *extent* of that discretion? On neither point was the legislative history unambiguous. Normally we could turn to the conference report for guidance as to legislative intent; but the report was silent. It merely indicated that the word "all" had been deleted from Section 205 and that the phrase "not to exceed" had been added to Section 207. There is nothing in it to explain the purpose or motivation behind those two changes.

The next place to look are the floor debates that took place when the House and Senate acted on the conference report. Edmund Muskie, leading Senate sponsor of the bill, explained that the two changes had been made in conference to reduce the possibility of a veto. Clearly a concession had been made by Congress, since President Nixon had "gone public" on the need to control spending. But what was the concession? What had Congress given away? Muskie explained that all of the sums authorized "need not be committed, though they must be allocated [i.e., allotted]." The two provisions had been added to give the administration "some flexibility concerning the obligation of construction grant funds."

According to Muskie, then, the allotment step was mandatory, while some flexibility existed for obligations and expenditures. The scope of the latter discretion appeared to be modest. Muskie stressed that the two changes made in conference were not to be used "as an excuse in not making the commitments necessary to achieve the goals set forth in the act." Only in cases where the obligation of funds might be contrary to other congressional policies (such as expressed in the National Environmental Policy Act) would the EPA administrator be expected to refuse to enter into contracts for construction.

When the House took up the conference report, additional qualifications were added. William Harsha of Ohio, ranking Republican on the conference committee, said that elimination of the word "all" and insertion of the phrase "not to exceed" were intended to "emphasize the president's flexibility to control the rate of spending." What was meant by "flexibility" and "rate"? Could the president dictate the scope of the program? What was the relationship between "rate of spending" and the specific statutory step of allotting contract authority to the states? Some legislative history was developed by a dialogue between Harsha, Robert Jones (D–Ala., and chairman of the House conferees), and minority leader Gerald Ford:

> Mr. Ford: Mr. Speaker, the gentleman from Ohio [Harsha] has made a very excellent presentation and as I listened I thought he answered the major question that I have in my mind. I am for the conference report, but I think it is vitally important that the intent and purpose of Section 207 is spelled out in the legislative history here in the discussion on this conference report.
>
> As I understand the comments of the gentleman from Ohio, the inclusion of the words in Section 207 in three instances of "not to exceed" indicates that is a limitation. More importantly that it is not a mandatory requirement that in 1 year ending June 30, 1973, there would be $5 billion and the next year ending June 30, 1974, $6 billion and a third year ending June 30, 1975, $7 billion obligation or expenditure?
>
> Mr. Harsha: I do not see how reasonable minds could come to any other conclusion than that the language means we can obligate or expend up to that sum—anything up to that sum but not to exceed that amount. Surely, if the Executive can impound moneys under the contract authority provision in the highway trust fund, which does not have the flexible language in this bill, they could obviously do it in this instance.

Ford then asked Jones whether he agreed with the statement by Harsha.

> Mr. Jones: Mr. Speaker, if the gentleman will yield. My answer is "yes." Not only do I agree with him but the gentleman from Ohio

offered this amendment which we have now under discussion in the committee of conference, so there is no doubt in anybody's mind of the intent of the language. It is reflected in the language just explained by the gentleman from Ohio (Mr. Harsha).

Mr. Ford: Mr. Speaker, this clarifies and certainly ought to wipe away any doubts anyone has. The language is not a mandatory requirement for full obligation and expenditure up to the authorization figure in each of the 3 fiscal years. Therefore, without any reservations Mr. Speaker, I support the conference report.

Of course that did not resolve all of the doubts about the bill's intent. The only point acknowledged was that there was some discretion at the obligation and expenditure stages, which Muskie himself had conceded. The extent of that discretion was still in the air. Nor was it clear whether the president had any discretion over allotments. Neither issue was clarified when the two houses overrode the veto. Muskie continued to say that the president had some flexibility concerning obligation. Harsha spoke of the president's flexibility to control the "rate of spending" and the "rate of expenditures."

Harsha's reference to highway impoundments did not do much to advance the administration's cause. On August 7, 1972, a U.S. district court had decided that the secretary of transportation could not withhold obligational authority from Missouri. Chief Judge Becker described the attempt to impound highway funds—part of the administration's anti-inflation policy—as "unauthorized by law, illegal in excess of lawful discretion and in violation of the Federal-Aid Highway Act." His decision was upheld the following April by the U.S. Court of Appeals for the Eighth Circuit. Subsequently the administration lost seven more highway impoundment cases, the decisions being handed down in Iowa, South Carolina, Montana, California, and Nebraska (all in 1974), and in Alabama, Kansas, and the District of Columbia (in 1975). The latter was a class action suit involving twelve states: Louisiana, Nevada, Oklahoma, Pennsylvania, Texas, Washington, Alaska, Idaho, Wisconsin, Arizona, Utah, and Michigan.

Commitment and Timetable

The issue of presidential spending discretion in the Clean Water Act cannot be decided simply by examining the language and legislative history of Sections 205 and 207. They must be read in concert with another central feature of the act: the commitment on the part of Congress to combat water pollution within a scheduled period of time. Section 101, which set forth the declaration of goals and policy, established a national goal of eliminating the discharge of pollutants into navigable waters by

1985. It was also a national goal that, wherever attainable, an interim goal of water quality—providing for the protection and propagation of fish, shell-life, and wildlife, and providing for recreation in and on the water—be achieved by July 1, 1983. Section 301 defined additional goals for effluent limitations.

The nature of the commitment was the subject of conflicting interpretations. During action on the conference report, Muskie admitted that $18 billion was "a great deal of money," but insisted it would cost that much to "begin to achieve the requirements set forth in the legislation." That was the "minimum amount needed to finance the construction of waste treatment facilities which will meet the standards imposed by this legislation." But Robert Jones, manager of the bill on the House side, characterized the 1985 target date as a "goal, not a national policy." While he hoped that the date could be met, he said that the conference report recognized that "too many imponderables exist, some still beyond our horizons, to prescribe this goal today as a legal requirement." The chairman of the full House Committee on Public Works, John Blatnik, offered this answer to those who called the bill too costly: "We must act now, and must be willing to pay the bill now—or face the task of paying later when, perhaps, no amount of money will be enough." Harsha, while agreeing that the committee had accurately assessed the need for a large sum of money, argued that spending flexibility had been added because of the many competing national priorities.

Those statements were made in the hope of averting a veto. But after Nixon's disapproval the congressional tone switched more firmly to the concept of a commitment. Jones was now to say that everyone knew the program was a costly undertaking, but "we know also that the people who are the greatest Nation on earth are prepared to pay the price of this undertaking." Harsha added that Congress had "an overriding environmental commitment to the people of this Nation. We must keep it." Would overturning the veto, Harsha asked, mean a vote for higher taxes? He gave this counsel: "So be it, the public is prepared to pay for it. To say we can't afford·this sum of money is to say we can't afford to support life on earth."

On the Senate side, during the vote to override the veto, Muskie stressed that the "whole intent of this bill is to make a national commitment." The legislation imposed requirements on industry, on the states, and on local governments. The commitment on those sectors required a commitment by the federal government. As Muskie concluded, "What we were asking of the Congress was a commitment that these people in other levels of government and the private sector could rely upon. Of course there is a commitment."

Spokesmen for President Nixon claimed that it was administratively impossible to use the full amount of contract authority provided by Congress. John Ehrlichman, as director of the Domestic Council, said that there are "only so many contractors who can build sewer plants. There is only a certain amount of sewer equipment that can be purchased. It becomes obvious that there is no point in going out and tacking dollar bills to the trees. That isn't going to get the water clean."

Why did the administration assume that the environmental industry lacked the ability to respond and to increase its capacity? A more realistic assumption would have been to expect industry to gear up to meet the clean-water commitment—provided that the government committed itself financially to the goal and expressed a determination to adhere to the target dates. When President Eisenhower and Congress joined in a commitment to build 41,000 miles of interstate highways, or when President Kennedy announced the goal of putting a man on the moon by the end of the 1960s, no one argued that those commitments could not be met because of a lack of contractor capability. The commitment came first; the capability followed.

After the president's veto, EPA administrator Ruckelshaus appeared before Senator Ervin's hearings on impoundment to argue that it was economically unwise to allot the full amounts authorized by Congress: "The fastest way to increase inflation is to pour more money into the community than the construction industry can absorb." Not only did that argument rest on the idea of an industry fixed in size, it contradicted what Ruckelshaus had written to Office of Management and Budget director Caspar Weinberger *prior* to the veto. At that time Ruckelshaus strongly recommended that the president sign the bill. With regard to near-term construction costs, he said that they would correspond closely to what would have been initiated under the administration bill. Thus, the "potential inflationary impact upon the entire construction sector would be minimized."

As to the total costs resulting from the $18-billion figure, Ruckelshaus pointed out that the additional spending authority provided by Congress was "largely the result of the Congress adopting a later EPA needs survey than the one that provided the basis for the administration's request." Moreover, the EPA estimate did not allow for inflation, nor did it include funds for combined, storm, and collection sewers, or for recycled water supplies. Those were some of the responsibilities under the bill that passed Congress. During Senate debate on the override, Muskie offered several other reasons to justify the $18-billion figure. The EPA estimate was based on existing standards and requirements. The clean-water act, in making those standards more stringent, would make it more expensive to meet them. Also, the older estimates did not take into account the statutory deadlines, which accelerated the construction timetables and required spending more money in less time.

During the 1973 Government Operations hearings on impoundment, under the chairmanship of Senator Ervin (D–N.C.), Senator Muskie and EPA administrator Ruckelshaus jostled on the question of whether Congress had voted an unreasonable and impractical sum of money to combat water pollution. After Ruckelshaus had defended the record of the administration, pointing out how much had been spent in the past few years, this exchange occurred:

> *Senator Muskie:* Have you heard Senator [Eugene] McCarthy's definition of a liberal Republican? He is a fellow who would throw a rope ten feet long to a fellow drowning twenty feet offshore. If you are spending $10 million and it is only 20 percent as much as the need, you are not doing enough.
>
> *Mr. Ruckelshaus:* You don't need to throw him a forty-foot rope either when he is twenty feet offshore.
>
> *Senator Muskie:* You look at your letter to Weinberger at the time of the first veto in which you don't describe this as a forty-foot rope, you describe the dollars in this as based upon your own statements of what is needed. So don't give me the forty-foot rope business.

SEARCH FOR JUDICIAL REMEDIES

How could the conflicting concepts of spending flexibility and goal commitment be reconciled? If a commitment existed, why would Congress give the president unbridled discretion in releasing the funds? Did the administration use its discretion to undermine the commitment? These were some of the complex issues injected into the federal courts.

The first decision handed down was by Judge Oliver Gasch of the U.S. District Court for the District of Columbia. He concluded that the discretion implied by "not to exceed" and the deletion of "all" referred to the obligation and expenditure stages, not to allotment. He held that the Clean Water Act required the administration to allot the full sums authorized to be appropriated by Section 207. Note that the court was not called upon to determine whether the EPA administrator should *spend* any given amount of money for sewage treatment works. Allotment, in the words of Judge Gasch, was not "tantamount to *expenditure* or even commitment of the funds."

His decision was affirmed by the U.S. Court of Appeals for the District of Columbia, which found in the legislative history an intent by Congress to specifically commit federal funds: "It did so in recognition of the necessity of assuring the states that federal aid would be available." The

goal by Congress guided the court in interpreting the funding mechanism, "for if discretion in allotment would make the achievement of this
goal more difficult, it must be assumed that Congress intended no such
authorization." With regard to Harsha's statement that the president had
discretion to "control the rate of spending," the court restricted that control to the obligation and expenditure stages.

A number of other district courts agreed that full allotment was mandatory. Judge Lord of the U.S. District Court in Minnesota emphasized
the commitment given by Congress to environmental protection:

> Any such exercise of discretion must be consistent with the policy
> and provisions included in the Act itself. Congress has clearly given
> the highest priority to the cleaning up of the nation's waters. Noth-
> ing in the Act grants the Administrator the authority to substitute
> his sense of national priorities for that of the Congress.

Similar decisions were handed down by district courts in Florida and
Texas. In each case the courts determined that the act required full allotment (though not necessarily full obligation and expenditure). The
purpose of Congress in adopting the contract authority and allotment
approach was to permit long-range planning against water pollution. It
was a method of ensuring an unequivocal financial commitment by the
federal government, enabling state and local governments to enter into
long-term contracts and to finance long-term bonds. It would be illogical,
said Judge Roberts of Texas, to think that Congress would inject uncertainty back into the funding system by giving the administration discretion to choose how much to allot. Evaluation of the act as a whole evinced
"an unmistakable congressional intent to marshal the requisite federal
funds to achieve the water quality goals set forth in the Act." In the
Florida decision, Judge Middlebrooks also stressed Congress' concern
with the ability of states to effect long-range plans in combating inflation:
"Indeed the planning problem was the reason for the implementation of
the allotment procedure rather than the normal appropriation procedure
in the Act."

District courts in Illinois, Ohio, and Maine also decided against the
administration. Although newspaper accounts typically reported that
federal courts had directed the administration to "spend" the clean-water
funds, the courts were careful to limit its holding to the allotment stage,
not to obligation and expenditure.

In a Los Angeles decision—the nearest the administration came to a
"victory" on these lower court decisions—Judge Hauk dismissed the case
for reasons of standing. He said that the plaintiffs had failed to show that
they had been injured or impaired by EPA's refusal to allot the full
amount. They had not produced affidavits indicating that proposals had

been rejected by EPA because of impoundment. But having disposed of the case on procedural grounds, he later maintained in dicta that even if the case did proceed to the merits, the plaintiffs could not compel the EPA administrator to allot the funds. The legislative history of the act demonstrated to Judge Hauk that the statute did not require full allotment. The two changes in conference, as proposed by Congressman Harsha, pointed to a desire to limit funds, not maximize them: "The passage 'sums authorized to be appropriated . . . shall be allotted' hardly means that the entire amount must be disgorged, and the phrase 'not to exceed' connotes limitation, not disbursement." Furthermore:

> No one has convinced us that when a legislature removes the word "all" from the phrase "All sums authorized to be appropriated shall be allotted," they mean that every penny must be spent. Nor has anybody argued successfully that adding the phrase "not to exceed" before a sum means anything more than that an upper limit must be imposed.

Of course the issue before Judge Hauk was not whether "every penny must be spent" but whether the entire sum had to be allotted. He attempted to buttress his argument by quoting a long passage from President Franklin D. Roosevelt, who wrote to Senator Richard Russell in 1942: "While our statutory system of fund apportionment is not a substitute for item or blanket veto power, and should not be used to set aside or nullify the expressed will of Congress, I cannot believe that you or Congress as a whole would take exception to either of these purposes which are common to sound business management everywhere." But when we turn to the full text of Roosevelt's letter, we find that it does not reinforce the argument of Judge Hauk. Quite the opposite, in fact. What did Roosevelt mean by "either of these purposes"? He was referring to two types of routine withholding actions: setting aside budgetary reserves either to prevent deficiencies or to effect savings. In contrast, the clean-water funds were impounded for policy reasons. The administration believed that Congress had appropriated too much, that it had paid insufficient regard to combating inflation. Moreover, the impoundment of clean-water funds *was* a substitute for "item or blanket veto power." As to whether impoundment was used to "set aside or nullify the expressed will of Congress," that was the precise issue before the courts.

A wholly different type of interpretation was handed down by Judge Robert Merhige of the U.S. District Court for the Eastern District of Virginia. Although he ruled that the impoundment of 55 percent ($6 billion out of $11 billion for the first two years) constituted a violation of the Clean Water Act, he concluded that Congress *did* intend for the executive branch to exercise some discretion with respect to allotment.

Judge Merhige found the deletion of "all" in Section 205 to be "highly significant." Even the plaintiffs, Campaign Clean Water, conceded some discretion at the allotment stage.

Nevertheless, the withholding of $6 billion conflicted with Congress' commitment to environmental protection and its willingness to incur "vast expenses in achieving that commitment." While Congress had purposefully incorporated provisions in the act to give the president some discretion, motivated in part by a desire to avoid a veto, the large margins by which Congress overrode the veto reaffirmed the "massive national commitment to environmental protection." Judge Merhige was satisfied that the impoundment of 55 percent of the funds was a "violation of the spirit, intent and letter of the Act and a flagrant abuse of executive discretion." Instead of issuing an injunction against the administration, to compel the release of funds, he simply declared that the impoundment policy was null and void.

This opinion was not sustained at the circuit court level. The U.S. Court of Appeals for the Fourth Circuit returned the decision to Merhige for further proceedings. It wanted to know whether the exercise of discretion at the allotment could be reviewed by the courts and, if so, what standards or criteria should be used to assess the validity of its exercise. The circuit court questioned the right of a district court to find an executive action arbitrary, on its face, without any other evidentiary support. The administration had made a number of claims. The EPA administrator denied that he was evading any responsibilities given him under the act. The withholding of allotments was justified on the ground that greater amounts could not be spent in a "wise or expeditious manner" in achieving the goals of the act. Moreover, it was argued that there was insufficient technical capacity to carry out a more extensive program. The administrator also asserted that a more rapid rate of spending would inflate the cost of the program without appreciably accelerating the program.

The court of appeals concluded that there was "no way for us at this juncture to venture an opinion whether the administrator had been 'dragging his feet' in approving projects or whether these figures indicate that the allotments made represented reasonable goals for the two fiscal years in controversy." The issue could not be resolved by a per se rule. It required an inquiry into the basis for the administrator's action. The district court had to develop a record which would support its decision. Why was the withholding of 55 percent a "flagrant abuse"? What if the administrator had withheld 40 percent? Thirty percent? At what point would withholding no longer conflict with the policy and provisions of the Clean Water Act?

Enter the Supreme Court

The State of Georgia tried to resolve such questions by taking the issue directly to the U.S. Supreme Court. On May 10, 1973, Georgia brought action against the Nixon administration for withholding funds from three federal programs: Federal-Aid Highways, National Defense Education Act, and the Clean Water Act. The action requested the Court to exercise its original jurisdiction, granted under Article III of the Constitution, and thereby dispense with the initial review by lower courts. In view of the controversy and acrimony swirling around the impoundment dispute, Georgia felt it would be in the national interest to put to rest, at the earliest possible time, the constitutional question of who was entitled to terminate or curtail a federal program.

The administration urged the Court to accept the case and refer it to a "special master" who would conduct a full evidentiary hearing and make an initial determination of the legal issues. The brief by the government, contending that the matter lay within the Court's original jurisdiction, claimed that the controversy constituted "one of those extraordinary and important cases which ought to be taken directly by this Court." Unless there was a final determination by the highest court, Congress could not know the full effect of its legislative efforts. The brief also argued that the state of uncertainty made it difficult for the president to know whether to veto an appropriation bill he regarded as inflationary. Could he sign the measure and withhold the excess funds? If not, veto might be his sole recourse.

Ten states filed a brief asking the Court to deny Georgia's petition. Each of the states—Connecticut, Louisiana, Massachusetts, Missouri, Minnesota, Oklahoma, Pennsylvania, Texas, Vermont, and Washington— was a party in one or more impoundment cases pending in the lower courts. A number of private organizations joined the ten states in the brief, pointing out that the exercise of original jurisdiction would probably retard the progress of impoundment cases through the lower courts "since those courts would be reluctant to rule on issues pending before this Court." And whereas the government took the position that only at the Supreme Court level (with the assistance of a special master) could impoundment issues be decided on a fully developed record, the brief for the ten states contended that the Court would be better able to decide the issues after they had first been considered and resolved by lower courts.

The brief also expressed doubt that the exercise of original jurisdiction would have any appreciable effect in expediting the Court's ultimate resolution. The investigation contemplated by the government "would surely require months of discovery, let alone trial, as dozens of depositions would have to be taken, documents requested and produced, interrogatories filed and answered, and, of course, objections raised and ruled on." The brief, noting that any delay would serve the interests of the government, added that there was an understandable desire by the government to "rush headlong into this Court with an impoundment case before they and other federal officials receive any further judicial rebuffs at the hands of the district courts and, especially, the courts of appeal."

In a separate brief, the City of New York also opposed the granting of the Georgia petition. The brief said that the Supreme Court should not permit its original jurisdiction to be used as a litigating tactic to circumvent lower-court decisions "with which the Government is unhappy." Furthermore, unless the Court decided that presidential discretion to withhold funds was unreviewable by the courts, a decision by the Court would not put an end to litigation. There would always be questions of statutory construction and interpretation, unique to each law, giving rise to new action in the courts. On October 9, 1973, the Supreme Court declined to hear the Georgia case.

Meanwhile, as the clean-water cases progressed through the federal courts, the Supreme Court was faced with a new demand—not of original jurisdiction but of appellate jurisdiction. After decisions had been handed down at the circuit court level on the District of Columbia and Virginia clean-water cases, the Court agreed, on April 29, 1974, to hear the two cases.

In its brief before the Supreme Court, the government maintained that the case was not one in which the president asserted a power to control the rate of spending in opposition to the wishes of Congress. Rather, it was a case "in which courts have improperly cut into and endangered a discretion Congress intended the president to have." It was the president's job to estimate the level and timing of spending that would ensue from a commitment; the income resources likely to be available to the government; the nature of competing program needs and demands; the state of the economy; and the impact of spending on the economy. "The very nature of those judgments," said the government, "makes it inappropriate for the courts to attempt to review the Administrator's judgment."

Oral argument was held on the afternoon of November 12, 1974. The exchange between the justices and the attorneys lasted slightly more than an hour. Robert Bork, solicitor general for the government, told the Court that the full amount of $18 billion would be allotted to the states at some time. According to Bork, the issue was therefore solely one of timing, not of scope. To many in the room, including the author, this marked the first time that the administration had promised full allotment. Chief Justice Burger asked the attorney for Campaign Clean Water,

W. Thomas Jacks, if this announcement by the government did not weaken the plaintiff's case. Jacks replied that it gave him no comfort to hear that the government would release all of the funds "at some time." The Clean Water Act had established specific deadlines for the achievement of various standards of water purity.

One could also add that the distinction between "timing" and "scope" was imaginary. To the extent that the government could dictate timing, stretching out the program for a number of years, the scope of the program would be very much affected. Each year of delay meant that inflation was consuming the potential value of the $18 billion that Congress had provided. The cost of constructing waste treatment plants was increasing by hundreds of millions of dollars each year.

The Court handed down its decision on February 18, 1975. It was unanimous, all nine justices deciding against the administration. The thirteen-page opinion, delivered by Justice White, was rather brief considering the complexity of the case. Most of the opinion consisted of a review of the legislative history, the administration's action, and lower court decisions. Justice White rejected the argument that the addition of "not to exceed" in conference implied administrative discretion to allot less than the full amounts. The language merely reflected the possibility that approved applications for grants might not total the maximum amount authorized to be appropriated. As for striking the word "all" from Section 205, White said that the word "sums" had no different meaning in the context of that section than the words "all sums." In either case the action was mandatory upon the government to allot the full amount. Here the concept of a legislative commitment came into play:

> We cannot accept the addition of the few words to §207 and the deletion of the one word from §205 as altering the entire complexion and thrust of the Act. As conceived and passed in both Houses, the legislation was intended to provide a firm commitment of substantial sums within a relatively limited period of time in the effort to achieve an early solution of what was deemed an urgent problem. We cannot believe that Congress at the last minute scuttled the entire effort by providing the Executive with the seemingly limitless power to withhold funds from allotment and obligation.

The decision was a convenient one for the Court. Not much was at stake, in the sense of having the administration defy the Court's order. Two weeks before the decision was handed down, the administration's budget for fiscal 1976 had announced the release of $4 billion in clean-water funds. That left $5 billion impounded. The solicitor general had promised full allotment in his oral argument. Thus, release of the funds had already been settled before the Court reached its decision.

To read the legislative history differently, as surely was possible, would have placed the Court in an awkward position. If it adopted the argument of Judge Merhige, and maintained that the EPA administrator possessed some discretion at the allotment stage but not as much as actually exercised, where would the Court draw the line? At 20 percent withholding? Ten percent? To justify a given percentage would require a needs survey by the Court of the environmental problems facing the nation's water supply, a task for which the Court was ill equipped. The simplest thing was to come down on the side of full allotment.

As for the administration, one could say that it lost the battle but won the war. Despite numerous setbacks in the lower courts, and a resounding defeat at the hands of a unanimous Supreme Court, it had succeeded in delaying the program for several years. From the time of President Nixon's directive to EPA administrator Ruckelshaus on November 22, 1972, to the decision by the Supreme Court, almost twenty-seven months had elapsed. It was now impossible for the administration, even with full allotment, to meet the deadlines established by Congress. When EPA administrator Russell Train appeared before the Senate Public Works Committee on March 1, 1974, Senator Muskie asked whether because of underfunding by the administration "we have abandoned any hopes that we can meet the deadlines established in the act, the performance deadlines established in the act, 1977–78 and 1983." Train replied that the reduction in the levels of funding "certainly are resulting in slowing down the program and deferring the accomplishments of these targets."

Besides the slowing down of the program because of impoundment, progress was also delayed because of administrative difficulties in using even the funds that had been allotted. Here we enter the world of "quasi-impoundments."

QUASI-IMPOUNDMENTS

As one court after another delivered blows to the administration, some members of Congress began to conclude that the impoundment dispute might be resolved once and for all by the courts. Let the litigation continue, they reasoned—a convenient proposition, since it eliminated the need for congressional action.

This strategy assumed that a single decision, announced from on high by the Supreme Court, would dispose of all the problems. But in case after case the courts avoided the larger constitutional questions, preferring to treat each dispute as one of statutory construction. Typically the central question was: Did the statute confer the discretionary authority claimed by the executive branch? Disposition of one case, therefore, had little bearing on other impoundments arising from different statutes. It was highly unlikely that the Supreme Court could (or would want to) devise a general remedy for the whole area, issuing a sweeping declaration either for or against that kind of executive power. In the absence of a general remedy, there would always be new statutory language, new questions of construction and congressional intent, and thus fresh opportunities for continued litigation.

Moreover, the courts were not in a position to administer the government. Federal judges cannot be expected to sit within the confines of an agency to supervise its operations. At some point, after Congress has passed its laws and the courts have handed down their judgments, a program needs implementation. That requires thousands of agency officials to draw up regulations, promulgate them, receive and process applications, and disburse funds to qualified recipients. In cases where the courts have ordered agencies to process applications and implement a program, judges necessarily relied on good-faith administrative efforts to carry out the program in accordance with statutory criteria and judicial directives.

The manner in which the Nixon administration impounded funds allowed courts to play a large role. Funds were withheld in an overt and public manner, with presidential documents at hand and administration justifications finely honed. But "quasi-impoundments" are more difficult to detect and to litigate. Programs can be delayed because of slow processing of applications, frequent change of agency regulations, rejection of applications for minor technical deficiencies, and many other administrative actions (or inactions). How does one know whether the resulting delays are inherent in the legislation, a deliberate effort by the administration to sabotage a program it did not want, or merely the by-product of normal bureaucratic problems? It is difficult for plaintiffs to contest actions that are so deeply imbedded in the administrative process.

The framers of the Clean Water Act had anticipated some of this problem. Section 101(f) of the legislation set the national policy that to the "maximum extent possible the procedures utilized for implementing this Act shall encourage the drastic minimization of paperwork and . . . prevent needless duplication and unnecessary delays at all levels of government." Still, the complexity of the legislation and its subsequent implementation by EPA produced the very paperwork and delay that the act had sought to avoid.

The procedures of the act necessitated a considerable amount of paperwork. For the purpose of encouraging the development of area-wide waste treatment management plans, the EPA administrator was required to publish guidelines in order to identify areas that had substantial water quality control problems. Those guidelines were to be published within ninety days after enactment of the Clean Water Bill. After publication of the guidelines, the governors of each state would have sixty days to identify problem areas. Within another 120 days the governors were to designate the boundaries of each area and the organization capable of developing effective waste treatment management plans. In the case of areas that involved more than one state, governors would have 180 days to designate the boundaries and select the organization.

Not later than one year after their designation, the organizations were to have in operation a planning process. Among other features, the plans would identify the treatment works needed to meet the requirements of the area over a twenty-year period, updating the list each year. The initial plan was to be certified by the governor (or governors where interstate areas were involved) and forwarded to EPA within two years from the time the planning process was in operation.

Administrative complications began to surface during the early months of 1973. Members of Congress, waiting for EPA to write regulations and begin the process of approving applications, became concerned that the clean-water program was being truncated not only by presidential impoundment but by agency delays. A subcommittee of the House Public Works Committee held a hearing on June 14, 1973, to determine the extent of the bureaucratic problem and what could be done to relieve it. James Cleveland, Republican of New Hampshire and ranking minority member on the subcommittee, protested that the president's impoundment had been augmented by "another little wrinkle in the program now which for all intents and purposes has brought this thing to a screeching halt."

Among those invited to testify at the hearing was Clarence Metcalf, director of municipal services for the New Hampshire Water Supply and Pollution Control Commission. He vigorously rejected the claim of the administration that there was a shortage of contractor capability in the country to carry out the clean-water legislation, even at the reduced pace contemplated by the administration. He anticipated no shortage of qualified construction services. On a recent small project, about three-quarters of a million dollars, sixteen contractors picked up bid documents. In the past two years New Hampshire had never had a job where there were fewer than five to six contractors bidding on a project. Metcalf predicted that if the clean-water program were fully funded, at the $18-billion level established by Congress, there would be sufficient contractual services in the building field in his state to take care of any additional work.

Another member of the subcommittee, Kenneth Gray (D–Ill.), said that many communities found themselves "between a rock and a hard place." The EPA would issue a cease-and-desist order to force a community to stop polluting the waters, but when local officials applied to

EPA for money to construct waste treatment plants they were told that federal funds were not available.

The same House Public Works subcommittee held hearings in 1974, meeting on ten separate days between February 5 and July 16. Jim Wright of Texas, the chairman, announced that the subcommittee staff had informed him that "a proliferating array of galloping guidelines and changing directives from EPA has badly impeded the flow of even those funds which the president has released." One city had to rewrite its application nine times over a period of two years.

One official from Pennsylvania noted that under the 1965 water pollution control act, there were ten federal guidelines; under the 1972 legislation the number of guidelines and regulations leaped to 132. Another state official, from New York, told the subcommittee that he had planned to bring the rules and regulations to the hearings in a wheelbarrow, "but I just lost my courage when I saw them. I have a back problem, and after I lift so much, it throws it out." An official from the New England area computed that EPA had produced regulations, guidelines, and support reference material at a rate of approximately two pages per minute, or about double the average person's reading speed. EPA was churning out material faster than it could be read.

Congress relied on its watchdog agency, the General Accounting Office, but even there the results were uneven. Dr. Robert Sansom, an environmental consultant, told the Senate Public Works Committee on February 28, 1975: "The problem now is that the intervention of the Congress in the process has been largely by sending the GAO out to second-guess some bureaucrat who has made a decision about a grant, and to ask him why he did it that way, and most of these kinds of investigations have had the effect of scaring the people more than . . . of getting them to commit themselves to getting more money out." Senator Muskie added that Congress had tried to "prod every way we can, but words don't always seem to move bureaucracy."

IMPOUNDMENT CONTROL ACT OF 1974

Impoundment has been an executive practice from the earliest administrations. There is no difficulty in discovering early precedents. However, in an effort to lend respectability to its own actions, the Nixon administration misapplied those precedents. For example, officials in the administration took great delight in pointing out that President Jefferson had impounded $50,000 for gunboats. But that was a routine impoundment, not in the least bit threatening to the prerogatives of Congress. Jefferson explained that the "favorable and peaceable turn of affairs on the Mississippi rendered an immediate execution of that law unnecessary." Since the emergency contemplated by Congress failed to materialize, because of the Louisiana Purchase, Jefferson saw no reason to spend the money. Nor did any member of Congress. A year later, having taken the time to study the most recent models of gunboats, Jefferson informed Congress that he was proceeding with the program.

In what possible way does this episode relate to the Nixon impoundments? Jefferson's action was temporary, in contrast to decisions by President Nixon to terminate such programs as the Rural Environmental Assistance Program (REAP) and subsidized housing. Jefferson did not damage or curtail a program; Nixon used impoundment to cut in half the Clean Water Act. The routine action by Jefferson did not challenge the right of Congress to make policy and decide priorities; Nixon's behavior was a distinct threat. And lastly, Jefferson acted in response to a genuine change in events, a change which made unnecessary the immediate release of funds. The critical issues facing the country during the Nixon years—such as housing shortages and polluted water—did not disappear.

Faced with the unprecedented scope of impoundment under President Nixon, Congress enacted an impoundment reporting bill on October 27, 1972. The bill directed the president to report the following: the amount of funds impounded, the date the funds were ordered to be impounded, the date the funds were actually impounded, the departments involved, the period of time during which the funds were to be impounded, the reasons for impoundment, and the estimated fiscal, economic, and budgetary effects of impoundment.

The first report in response to this act announced $8.7 billion in "budgetary reserves." The report managed to leave out approximately $9 billion in other funds that had been impounded: $6 billion in clean-water funds (for fiscal 1973 and 1974), $441 million held back because of the housing moratorium, $382 million in proposed rescissions (requests to cancel budget authority), $1.9 billion withheld from the departments of Labor and Health, Education and Welfare, and $300 million for the farm disaster loan program.

How could the administration impound $6 billion in clean-water funds and not include that action in the impoundment report? The answer lies in the definition of contract authority, for in the context of the Clean Water Act it is "budget authority" that allows states to enter into obligations. But the states could not enter into obligations until the EPA administrator allotted the authority. From the standpoint of the Office of Management and Budget (OMB), the unallotted portion of $6 billion did not satisfy the technical definition either of contract authority or budget authority. By that reasoning, nothing existed to impound or place in reserve. The problem with this kind of reasoning is that Congress called for reports on *impoundment*, not "budgetary reserves," and no amount of technical distinctions could obscure the fact that clean-water funds had been impounded. To believe otherwise would be to assume that the courts were entertaining themselves with imaginary issues.

The coequal status of Congress as a branch of government was severely tested by the Nixon impoundments. In response, legislation was introduced in both houses to curb the president's power to withhold funds. On June 25, 1973, the House of Representatives passed legislation which allowed either house of Congress to disapprove an impoundment within sixty days. This was one of many examples of recent decades in which Congress turned the constitutional tables, allowing the president to initiate a policy but subjecting it to a "legislative veto."

The Senate adopted a different tack. It felt strongly that once Congress had passed an appropriation, and perhaps had to act again to override a veto, it should not have to act a third time to disapprove an impoundment. The Senate bill therefore required the funds to be released unless both houses supported the impoundment within sixty days. Thus, where the House of Representatives placed upon either the House or the Senate the responsibility for overturning an impoundment action, the Senate put the burden on the administration to enlist the support of both houses. In other words, the presumption of the House bill was in favor of impoundment, unless disapproved by one house. The presumption of the Senate bill was *against* impoundment, unless supported by both houses within a specified number of days. The conceptual and philosophical differences between the two bills were so substantial, with neither house willing to make concessions, that the legislation remained in a dormant state in conference committee.

During this suspended state of affairs Congress made progress with budget reform legislation. At the height of the furor over the $250 billion ceiling proposal, in the fall of 1972, Congress established a Joint Study Committee on Budget Control. The committee was directed to propose procedures for "improving congressional control over budgetary outlay and receipt totals" and to assure full coordination of an "overall view of each year's budgetary outlays" with an "overall view of the anticipated revenues for that year." An interim report of February 7, 1973, promised recommendations on impoundment, but the final report of April 18, 1973, was silent on that subject.

The general idea of congressional budget reform was to establish budget committees in each house and make them responsible for reporting a budget resolution in the spring. The resolution would establish tentative targets for outlays, budget authority, and revenues, including an appropriate surplus or deficit in light of economic conditions. The spring resolution would also divide the budget totals into large functional categories, such as National Defense, Commerce and Transportation, and Income Security. The purpose was to permit Congress to establish control not only over budget totals but also over budget priorities.

After passage of the initial budget resolution, Congress would proceed to act on individual appropriation bills and other legislation that affected budget authority and revenues. In the final month prior to the start of the new fiscal year (now changed to begin October 1, rather than July 1, to give Congress additional time), members would pass a second budget resolution, this time fixing binding totals. If a discrepancy existed between the second budget resolution and action on other bills involving appropriations and revenues, Congress would complete a reconciliation process.

At the heart of this process was a desire by members of Congress to reassert legislative control over budget priorities. Members from both houses began to realize that what had been done at budget resolution time could be undone later by impoundment. To preserve the shape of the budget, as passed by Congress, an impoundment title would have to be added to the budget reform legislation. But how could the House and Senate approaches, seemingly incompatible, be reconciled?

The impasse was broken by devising two types of impoundment: "deferral" (to be governed by the one-house veto) and "rescission" (requiring the support of both houses within forty-five days). A deferral was meant to be a temporary kind of impoundment; the administration intended to spend the money but not now. Rescission was a step which canceled budget authority; it was thus a permanent action.

The comptroller general of the General Accounting Office received major new responsibilities. As the auditing and investigative body of Congress, GAO was directed to monitor the impoundment actions of the president. If the comptroller general found that the president, the OMB director, or any other executive official impounded funds and failed to report the matter to Congress, the comptroller general would notify Congress. The report of the comptroller general would be received just as though it had come from the president. Thus, Congress would be free to disapprove it (in the case of a deferral) or let the forty-five-day period run out (in the case of a proposed rescission). Another responsibility of the comptroller general was to examine impoundment reports to see that they are correctly classified. If he determined that the president submitted an impoundment as a deferral, which was actually a proposed rescission, or vice versa, he could reclassify the action. Furthermore, if the administration failed to release funds in accordance with the procedures of the act, the comptroller general was authorized to bring suit in the U.S. District Court for the District of Columbia. Those were the main provisions of the Impoundment Control Act of 1974 (P.L. 93-344).

President Ford presented the first packet of proposed rescissions and deferrals, transmitting the messages to Congress on September 20, 1974. He notified the lawmakers that, in the opinion of the attorney general, the Impoundment Control Act applied "only to determinations to withhold budget authority which have been made since the law was approved" (July 12, 1974). Some of the impounded items were listed merely for the information of Congress, not for congressional ratification or disapproval. Those items, marked with an asterisk, included the deferral of $9 billion in clear-water funds—$3 billion withheld from each of the fiscal years 1973, 1974, and 1975.

This raised an issue that Congress had not anticipated. Did the Impoundment Control Act apply only to new impoundments, or was it retroactive? In an October 15 letter to Congress, Comptroller General Elmer B. Staats disagreed with the attorney general's interpretation. Staats maintained that the act *did* apply to deferrals made prior to the statute's enactment. He based his conclusion on two factors: a disclaimer in the act (nothing in the act was to be construed as ratifying or approving any prior impoundment) and the definition of deferral (which included executive action or inaction). The decision not to release the clean-water funds after July 12, 1974, represented an inaction by the administration.

But now that the issue was joined, who would resolve it? Administration officials said they would follow the interpretation of the attorney general. Congress, of course, sided with the comptroller general. But it is in the nature of coequal branches that the comptroller general could not force his decision upon the executive branch when the attorney general held to a different interpretation. The matter was ripe for the courts.

A number of legislators treated the deferral of clean-water funds as an action subject to congressional disapproval. Resolutions were introduced to disapprove the impoundment, but none was ever acted on. In fact, the administration received a measure of support from the GAO and the House Appropriations Committee. On October 15, 1974, the comptroller general advised Congress that the "inability to expend the [clean-water] funds effectively is a possibility." This was a practical judgment regarding the effect of releasing $9 billion, raising doubts as to the capability of EPA and the states to use the money, but it duplicated the misconception of Judge Hauk in the Los Angeles case. Expenditure (or even obligation) was not at issue. What was at stake was the *allotment* of contract authority so that states could enter into long-range planning and be confident of federal assistance.

The House Appropriations Committee also acted in a way to support the administration's deferral of clean-water funds. During hearings on November 21, 1974, Congressman Jamie Whitten, chairman of the appropriations subcommittee on Agriculture-Environmental and Consumer

Protection, criticized the Clean Water Act as "probably the prime example of how far and wide of the mark an authorizing committee will go and what the Appropriations Committee is willing to match in dollars and cents." His protest was directed at the back-door method (contract authority) by which Congress had circumvented the Appropriations Committee. When funds had to be appropriated later to liquidate the obligations, the committee's role was perfunctory. It was denied an opportunity to control the level of the program. Whitten said that the authorization committees (in this case the Public Works Committees) "had no doggoned relationship to what we could appropriate with the resources available."

The House Appropriations Committee reported a rescission bill on November 26, 1974, accepting some of the proposed rescissions by President Ford but rejecting the major items. The report also chose to comment on deferrals, even though no impoundment resolution—the vehicle for disapproving deferrals—was before the House of Representatives. The comments could be described as a form of legislative dicta in the sense that they were not necessary for the rescission bill.

Nevertheless, the report listed eight deferrals "accepted" by the committee, including $9 billion in clean-water funds. A footnote to the table explained: "Committee has been assured of *immediate* release of such funds as can be effectively utilized to increase employment and protect the environment and accepts the deferral only because of such assurances." The Clean Water Act was now characterized as a type of antirecession measure, with funds released to stimulate the economy. That was never part of the original intent. Moreover, the language in the report overlooked the need for full allotment of clean-water funds as a necessary step for long-range planning by states. The issue of full allotment, at least, was laid to rest by the Supreme Court's decision of February 18, 1975.

CONCLUSION

A large factor at stake in the impoundment controversy was the ability of Congress to delegate power. If Congress can delegate broad grants of discretionary authority, without having the discretion abused, administrators are able to adapt to changing circumstances and carry out the purposes of legislation more effectively. But when flexibility in a statute is used to frustrate congressional policy, the lesson for members of Congress is to confine executive action, to restrict administrators to narrow statutory details.

That point was brought home forcefully in 1973 when EPA administrator Ruckelshaus appeared before the Ervin impoundment hearings. Senator Muskie complained that Congress had given EPA some flexibility in carrying out a difficult piece of legislation, only to have that flexibility used to cut in half a legislative commitment. The administration's action, Muskie warned, was "just a temptation to Congress to be more inflexible, not more flexible in the future." Then he added:

> Having in mind the devious motives that you pursued to undercut the purposes of the Congress, I could now write better language and believe me, I will. Believe me, I will.
>
> The clear language and debate was what we were giving you, is what we understood to be legitimate administrative discretion to spend the money, not defeat the purposes. Then to have you twist it as you have, is a temptation to this Senator to really handcuff you the next time.

The extraordinary and unprecedented use of impoundment by the Nixon administration left Congress with the choice of fighting back or having its power over the purse impaired, perhaps permanently. Congress could not allow the president to justify impoundment on the grounds of combating inflation and higher taxes. Those policy objectives, attractive though they may be, do not stand alone. Constitutional government depends on more than the pursuit of desirable goals. More fundamental than goals are the means employed. Who sets the goals? What standards and procedures shall be devised to ensure that public policy is built upon the law rather than administrative convenience? The response to those questions was the Impoundment Control Act of 1974.

For all its trappings of conservatism and "strict constructionism," the Nixon administration never demonstrated an understanding of what lies at the heart of the political system: a respect for procedure, a sense of comity and trust between the branches, an appreciation of limits and boundaries. Used with restraint and circumspection, impoundment was a viable instrument, capable of being used on occasion without precipitating a crisis. But restraint was replaced by abandon, precedent stretched past the breaking point, and statutory authority pushed beyond legislative intent.

Without good-faith efforts and integrity on the part of executive officials, the custom of delegation, discretion, and nonstatutory controls must be abandoned. The consequences for public policy, implementation, and program effectiveness are profound. Long after the impeachment proceedings and the resignation of Richard Nixon, the practical need for good-faith efforts on the part of administrative officials was being felt.

Case Study Bibliography

Fisher, Louis. *Presidential Spending Power*. Princeton, N.J.: Princeton University Press, 1975. Covers the growth of presidential budgeting and the various types of discretionary spending powers available to executive officials. In both cloth and paperback editions.

Schick, Allen. "Budget Reform Legislation: Reorganizing Congressional Centers of Fiscal Power," *Harvard Journal on Legislation* (February 1974): 303–50. Analysis of the executive-legislative conflicts that led to enactment of the Congressional Budget and Impoundment Control Act of 1974.

U.S. Congress. *Impoundment of Appropriated Funds by the President*, Joint Hearings before the Senate Committees on Government Operations and on the Judiciary, 93d Cong., 1st sess. (1973). Provides essential background material and documents from executive agencies.

———. *A Legislative History of the Water Pollution Control Act Amendments of 1972*, a committee print prepared for the use of the Senate Committee on Public Works, 93d Cong., 1st sess. (1973). A two-volume collection of committee reports, floor debate, and other parts of the legislative history.

———. *Court Challenges to Executive Branch Impoundments of Appropriated Funds*, cumulative to March 15, 1974. Special report of the Joint Committee on Congressional Operations, 93d Cong. 2d sess. (1974). Reprints forty-five court decisions involving impoundment of agriculture, education, health, water pollution control, and other funds.

———. *Analysis of Executive Impoundment Reports*, a committee print prepared by the Senate Committee on the Budget, 94th Cong., 1st sess. (1975). Includes the impoundment proposals of President Ford and a committee critique.

Wildavsky, Aaron. *The Politics of the Budgetary Process*, 2d ed. Boston: Little, Brown, 1975. Standard study on the strategies employed by agencies as they seek funds from Congress. In paperback.

NOTES

1. Verne B. Lewis, "Toward A Theory of Budgeting," *Public Administration Review* 12, no. 1 (Winter 1952).

2. A. M. Hillhouse and S. K. Howard, *State Capital Budgeting* (Chicago: Council of State Governments, 1963), p. 64.

3. U.S. Bureau of the Budget, Bulletin No. 68–9, April 2, 1968.

4. Aaron Wildavsky, *The Politics of the Budgetary Process* (Boston: Little, Brown, 1979).

5. V.O. Key, Jr., "The Lack of a Budgetary Theory," *American Political Science Review* 34 (December 1940).

6. Ibid.

7. Alfred R. Golze, *Reclamation in the United States* (New York: McGraw-Hill, 1952), pp. 127–29.

8. Arthur Maass, *Muddy Rivers: The Army Engineers and the Nation's Rivers* (Cambridge: Harvard University Press, 1951).

9. Neil M. Singer, *Public Microeconomics* (Boston: Little, Brown, 1972), p. 219.

10. E. S. Quade, "Systems Analysis for Public Administration," in *New Techniques in Public Administration*, ed. R. Martin Lees, vol. 1 (Bruges, Belgium: College of Europe, 1971), p. 133.

11. Ibid., p. 135.

12. Charles J. Hitch and Roland McKean, *The Economics of Defense in the Nuclear Age* (Cambridge: Harvard University Press, 1960).

13. *Planning Programming Budgeting for City State County Objectives*, PPB Note 11 (Washington, D.C.: State-Local Finances Project, George Washington University, July 1968), pp. 11–20.

14. H. Glennerster, *Social Service Budgets and Social Policy* (New York: Barnes & Noble, 1975), p. 95.

15. Frank D. Draper and Bernard T. Pitsvada, "Limitations in Federal Budget Execution," *Government Accountants Journal* 30, no. 3 (Fall 1981): 15–25.

16. Louis Fisher, *Presidential Spending Power* (Princeton: Princeton University Press, 1975), p. 99.

17. Ibid., pp. 99–122.

18. Ibid., p. 76.

19. Ibid., p. 92.

20. James P. Pfiffner, *The President, the Budget and Congress: Impoundment and the 1974 Budget Act* (Boulder, Colo: Westview Press, 1979), p. 41.

21. Dennis S. Ippolito, *Congressional Spending* (Ithaca: Cornell University Press, 1981), Chap. 7.

22. Ibid., p. 164.

BIBLIOGRAPHY

Fisher, Louis. *Presidential Spending Power*. Princeton: Princeton University Press, 1975.

Gramlich, Edward M. *Benefit-Cost Analysis of Government Programs*. Englewood Cliffs, N.J. Prentice-Hall, 1981.

Hatry, Harry, et al. *Program Analysis for State and Local Governments*. Washington, D.C.: Urban Institute, 1976.

Howe, Charles W. *Benefit-Cost Analysis for Water System Planning*. Washington, D.C.: American Geophysical Union, 1971.

Ippolito, Dennis S. *Congressional Spending*. Ithaca: Cornell University Press, 1981.

LeLoup, Lance T. *Budgetary Politics*. Brunswick, Ohio: King's Court Communications, 1977.

Marcus, William B. *Note on Benefit-Cost Analysis*. Boston: Intercollegiate Clearing House, 1976.

Mishan, E. J. *Economics for Social Decisions*. New York: Praeger, 1972.

Patton, Michael Q. *Utilization-Focused Evaluation*. Beverly Hills, Sage, n.d.

Pfiffner, James P. *The President, the Budget and Congress: Impoundment and the 1974 Budget Act*. Boulder, Colo: Westview Press, 1979.

Quade, E. S. "Systems Analysis for Public Administration." In R. Martin Lees, ed., *New Techniques in Public Administration*. vol. 1. Bruges, Belgium: College of Europe, 1971.

Wildavsky, Aaron. *The Politics of the Budgetary Process*. Boston: Little, Brown, 1979.

Chapter 7

The Capital Budgeting Process

In the early 1980s the City Council of a typical American municipality decided to develop a downtown beautification program. The program included widening streets and improving the storm sewer system, developing a park, remodeling city buildings, and constructing a new stadium. When the city fathers tried to discuss the project as part of the operating budgetary process, they encountered immediate difficulties. The operating budgetary process enabled them to plan projects and allocate funds annually. Yet the downtown beautification project required careful planning and the allotment of funds for six years. They obviously could not undertake such an ambitious endeavor unless they were assured of multiyear funding. In addition, their typical annual budget included only the costs of operating services in existing facilities, such as the costs of running the municipal swimming pool during the summer. In contrast, the downtown beautification project required a budget for the construction of recreation facilities such as the new stadium, which later would need an operating budget to manage sport activities. After considering the special characteristics of the new project, the city fathers decided to develop a municipal capital budget that included the downtown beautification project, rather than place it in the existing operating budget.

Public organizations frequently use *capital budgeting* to tie plans for the development of capital facilities together with the multiyear programs necessary to provide them. Whereas in the federal government operating and capital budgets are merged, the overwhelming number of state and local governments provide separate capital and operating budgets. McClain defines this process as

> . . . a unified series of steps for the development of a documented work program for priority-based building (and equipment purchase) projects, covering a five or six year period; for linking the program with a formal plan of financing; and the carrying out of the program according to a definite work schedule. Capital budgeting includes (*a*) preparation of revenue and expenditure estimates in view of the work to be done in a formal program and fiscal plan, (*b*) submission of the plan for approval, (*c*) legislative approval, and (*d*) execution. The capital budget is not a one-shot plan to solve . . . [public organizations'] physical facilities problems, but a continuous program with a new year added as the current budget year is completed.[1]

The purpose of this chapter is twofold. First, it describes the rationale, process, actors, and practices currently associated with capital budgeting. Second, it reviews in more detail some techniques that underlie the preparation and analysis of capital budgets. Although capital budgeting, like all budgeting, is as much a political[2] as a technical activity, this chapter is limited to the technical dimensions of the process.

AN OVERVIEW OF CAPITAL BUDGETING

Rationale

Public-sector capital projects have at least three distinct features that make them different from activities normally included in operating budgets.[3] First, project construction and financing is multiyear in nature. Second, once facilities and equipment are constructed, purchased, or leased, they have a relatively long life. Third, the end products of such projects may be thought of in relatively simplistic terms as a form of capital goods, which, when combined with operating expenses such as labor or materials, help produce actual services. For example, the investment in construction of the municipal stadium provided a basic facility from which annual sports events could be run. The authors of the International City Management Association text *Municipal Finance Administration*[4] argue that these distinct features create special problems that justify separate capital and operating budgets. For example, they assert that the multiyear nature of capital facilities construction and financing requires the collection of more detailed information about future revenues and expenditures than is necessary when budgeting for operating expenditures.[5] These trend data are supposed to reveal what proportion of capital expenditures could be financed with future revenues and what will have to be borrowed. At the same time, because capital projects take so long to complete, they do not fit into the annual operating budget cycle easily. It is also argued that the long life of capital facilities ensures that future generations will benefit from their use. Thus, financing strategies that pass some of the costs on to future generations can be justified more easily for capital as opposed to annual operating expenditures.

Moreover, the location of facilities and capital projects have longer-range impacts on the community than operating expenditures do. Highway construction may provide the conditions necessary to stimulate the location of new business, or the failure to locate a large municipal facility in an area may result in the relocation of businesses out of the jurisdiction and changes in residential housing patterns. Furthermore, some sources (e.g., Bierman and Smidt) argue that expenditures should be treated differently from operating expenditures because they are nonrecurrent. The construction of a municipal stadium might be thought of as a "one time only" expenditure, whereas the operation of the facility will require recurring operating expenses. Finally, the separation of capital from operating expenses helps provide a basis for analyzing whether future revenues will be sufficient (from the project or the general community) to repay the capital costs of the facility.

While the separation of operating and capital budgets leads to a clearer analysis of capital project cost and benefits and to better monitoring of long-term capital improvement programs, it is not without its pitfalls. Although some capital facilities expenses (e.g., those used to build a municipal stadium) are nonrecurrent, others (e.g., the periodic replacement of machinery in a public water authority) must take place on a recurrent, although not annual, basis. Moreover, captial expenses in most larger organizations take place on an annual basis even if the specific expenditure items are not always the same. Failure to inform voters, funders, and clientele groups about the recurrent nature of certain capital expenses may lead to future resistance to vital projects. Lack of recognition of the recurrent nature of some capital expenses may result in the need to approve more costly future capital projects than necessary. The failure to maintain buildings periodically, or to renovate them at appropriate times, may force an organization into costly new building projects in future years.

But probably more important, the conceptual separation of capital and operation budgets has contributed to the separate design, negotiation, implementation, and monitoring of capital and operating activities that are vitally interrelated. Since public capital project decisions structure the volume and kind of services to be delivered in the future, they set the parameters for future operating expenses. The decision to construct a municipal swimming pool implies the acceptance of future operating expenses for lifeguards, custodians, and supplies. If revenue and expenditure projections show that the municipality will not be able to afford these operating expenses in the future (even when user fees are charged), it will have overextended itself. Treating operating and capital budgeting decisions separately may result in the failure to consider the implications that one set of decisions has for the other. Thus an analysis of the effectiveness of any organization's capital budgeting process should include assessment of the way capital and operating budget activities are linked together.

Process

Private-sector capital budgeting provides an arena where future corporate survival is determined. The process generates investment decisions that dictate what new courses of action will be pursued. Corporate capital budgeting

> . . . is a many-sided activity that includes searching for new and more profitable investment proposals, investigating engineering and marketing considerations to predict the consequences of accepting the investment, and making economic analysis to determine the profit potential of each investment proposal.[6]

Capital budgeting within the public sector also attempts to link strategic future organizational plans with a concrete policy of capital investment. However, the activities of most public organizations, particularly units of government, are so complex and diverse that it is difficult to design overall plans and prioritize alternative projects. Although techniques of benefit-cost analysis have been used with increasing success, the simple standard of profitability used in private-sector investment decisions is lost when comparing widely different public projects. Furthermore, the political merits of project choices must be weighed carefully. It is not easy to incorporate such factors into the analysis. Under the worst circumstances, capital budgeting in many public organizations is nothing more than a series of disconnected steps where no decision maker analyzes the whole capital development program.

In an effort to ensure that the capital budgeting process in public organizations results in coherent choices, the International City Management Association recommends a sequential process with five basic components:

1 *The Public Services Program.* This is a long-range plan for all public services and represents a projection of the annual operating budget. In formulating such a program, the city determines . . . [the magnitude and kinds of services it wants to deliver in the future]. It is based on the measurement of objectives and needs of each city department, the standards of municipal services desired, and the principal cost factors for each kind of service.
2 *The Capital Improvement Program.* This consists of a comprehensive list of projects and facilities that are or will be needed by the community in order to carry out the program of public services agreed upon . . . The capital improvements program . . . is closely related to the public services program and both are based on the comprehensive plan of the community.
3 *The Long-Term Revenue Program.* Some means must be found to finance these programs. This can be accomplished by developing a tentative revenue policy with a judicious balance of current revenues, reserve funds, various means of borrowing, and debt-incurring capacity.
4 *The Capital Budget.* The capital budget relates, on the basis of a five- or six-year time period, the more generalized capital improvements and long-term revenue programs defined above. It represents a listing in priority order of those expenditures which involve additional investments in community facilities. . . . The capital budget includes a balanced presentation of the revenues to finance the various projects. The first year of the capital budget is incorporated with the annual operating budget to show capital outlay items for one fiscal year.
5 *The Operating Budget.* This is the annual projection of revenues and expenditures for regular and recurring operations of the city government and serves as a primary instrument of planning and financial control.[7]

A more detailed operational plan, based on many factors of the ICMA process, is followed by public organizations. For example, the Audit Division of King County, in the State of Washington, describes more detailed activities: master planning, program planning, capital budgeting, operational planning and scheduling, property acquisition, design, and construction.[8] (See Table 7.1 for a listing of activities and subactivities and Figure 7.1 for a presentation of the activity sequence.)

Analytical techniques can improve the quality of decisions made in the capital budgeting process. For example, during the master planning and program planning stages, it is important to perform an *inventory* of existing facilities and those proposed to accomplish future objectives. This is often done informally, or according to some useful, highly detailed formats. (see Figures 7.2 and 7.3). Before the actual capital budget is prepared, a process for *setting project priorities* must be developed. While often no systematic methods are used, some organizations use *ranking techniques* of varying levels of complexity.[9] At the same time, decision-making techniques based on *benefit-cost analysis* are used to help officials make choices among project alternatives.[10] Within the capital budgeting stage, financial planning requires careful *revenue and expenditure projections*.

TABLE 7.1. The Capital Improvement Development Process

Principal Activities

1 *Master* *Planning*	—Identifies legitimate needs and establishes capital project standards and policies in coordination with Comprehensive and Community Planning. —Projects anticipated capital development needs based on policy and standards.
2 *Program* *Planning*	—Define individual projects to meet needs identified during Master Planning. —Identify and evaluate alternative approaches to meeting needs. —Define specific project requirements, scope and general location. —Develop specific program proposal and justification.
3 *Budgeting*	—Develop specific budget request. —Develop financial plans and policies. —Review project proposals for justification in master and program plans, ability to efficiently meet needs, appropriate consideration of alternatives, accuracy of cost estimates. —Appropriate project budgets. —Coordinate budgets with scheduling (i.e., stage 4). —Monitor allocations and expenditures.
4 *Operational* *Planning and* *Scheduling*	—Develop specific budget request. —Develop financial plans and policies. —Review project proposals for justification in master and program plans, ability to efficiently meet needs, appropriate consideration of alternatives, accuracy of cost estimates. —Appropriate projects budgets. —Coordinate budgets with scheduling (i.e., stage 4). —Monitor allocations and expenditures.
5 *Property* *Acquisition*	—Schedule acquisition in accord with stage 4. —Locate specific site appropriate to needs. —Identify property owners and negotiable acquisition. —Carry out condemnation as necessary.
6 *Design*	—Define design work needed per program plan and budget —Select designer(s) and define fees. —Negotiate contract and schedule design in accord with stage 4 and develop project cost model. —Monitor and approve design work including cost estimates in accord with project budget, program plan, and schedule. —Prepare, review, and approve final plans and specifications.
7 *Construction*	—Select contractor and define costs. —Schedule construction in accord with stage 4. —Monitor construction and change orders. —Final acceptance and close out.

SOURCE: King County Auditor, *Management Audit of the Parks Capital Improvement Program Report*, King County, Washington, August 1979.

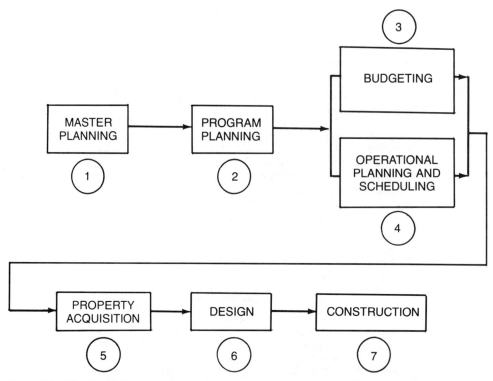

FIGURE 7.1   The Capital Improvement Development Process. (*From King County Auditor*, Management Audit of the Parks and Facilities Capital Improvement Program Report, *No. 72, August 1979, p. xxiii, King County, Washington*)

Sometimes the projections do nothing more than extrapolate from existing trends. Occasionally more sophisticated modeling techniques are used.[11] Presentation of the actual capital budget itself requires careful consideration of appropriate format (see Figure 7.4). Finally, within operational planning, property acquisition, design, and construction, *scheduling techniques* such as PERT/CPM help ensure that an orderly sequence of activities is performed. Later sections of this chapter explore the use of some of these techniques in greater detail.

Actors and Organization

Public agencies organize to implement capital budgeting in many different ways. Some centralize all activities within a single department or several departments; others create an executive legislative commission to supervise the process.[12] Let's review these organizational styles in more detail.

With *the departmental approach*, a single unit such as the budget bureau, finance committee, or building or planning department has primary responsibility for putting together the capital budget. It usually transmits the executive's requests for projects to the departments, and serves as a conduit for coordinating information and performing financial analysis. It produces a completed budget in consultation with the executive,

FORM A

City of _____

Summary Sheet of _____ Dept. _____

Division of _____ Date Submitted _____

Page _____ of _____

Recommended Financing

GR Gen. Revenue FA Fed. Aid
SC Service Chgs. SA State Aid
UR Utility Rev. RB Rev. Bonds
GOB Gen.Obl.Bonds SR Spec.Reserves for Cap.Exp.

Status of Plans

0 Plans not needed	4 Work on plans sched.
1 Nothing done except this rept.	5 Sketch plans in prep. 6 Sketch plans compltd.
2 Prelim. est. rec'd.	7 Detail plans in prep.
3 Surveys completed	8 Detail plans and specifications

Proj. No.	Name & Location of Project	Total Est. Cost	Total for 5 years	Year in Which Expenditure Is Needed						Addit. Annual Opr. Costs After Compl.	Status of Plans	Remarks (benefits) & Ref. to Master Plan
				1962–63	1963–64	1964–65	1966–67	Prior	Later			

FIGURE 7.2 Estimates for Five-Year Program of Capital Improvements 1962–67. (*From International City Management Association, Municipal Finance Administration, Chicago: ICMA, 1962, p. 354.*)

179

City of _____ Project No. _____ Date _____ 19 _____

1. Department _____ 2. Division of _____

3. Description of Project —
   a. Name, physical descript., location —
   b. Purpose —
   c. Shown on map attached _____
     (Yes or No)

4. Need for project (use sep. sheet if necessary)
   a. Why requested —
   b. In Master Plan? _____ Page _____

5. Relation to other projects, where applicable —

6. Estimated cost —
   A. Planning (totals a,b,c) _____
     (a) Architects
       services _____
     (b) Engineering _____
     (c) Inspection _____
   B. Land _____
     (a) Site is secured _____
     (b) To be secured _____
   C. Construction (totals a,b) _____
     (a) Labor _____
     (b) Non-labor _____
   D. Miscellaneous equipment _____
     (totals a,b) _____
     (a) Equip. _____
     (b) Furniture _____
   E. Other _____
     TOTAL ESTIMATED COST _____
   F. Cost prior to July 1, 1962
     (included above) _____
     ESTIMATED ADDITIONAL COST __

7. Future burden resulting from
   Project — _____
   (a) Annual cost: maintenance,
     repair cost operation _____
   (b) Annual estim. cost of
     new staff required _____
   (c) Future exped. for
     addit. equip. not
     included in proj. cost _____

8. Income from project (Estimated annual direct and indirect)

9. Estimated construction period —

10. Status of plans and specifications —
    (Place check mark opp. proper status)
   _____ 0 Plans not needed
   _____ 1 Nothing done except this report
   _____ 2 Preliminary estimate received
   _____ 3 Surveys completed
   _____ 4 Work on plans scheduled
   _____ 5 Sketch plans in preparation
   _____ 6 Sketch plans completed
   _____ 7 Detail plans in preparation
   _____ 8 Detail plans and specifications
       completed

11. Proposed maner of construction —
    (contract or day labor)

12. Project expenditures by year —
   1962–63 _____ 1964–65 _____
   1963–64 _____ 1965–66 _____
       1966–67 _____

ENDORSEMENT (Questions 13, 14, 15 to be filled in by department Heads)

13. Priority rating —

14. Year recommended
   for construction —

15. Recommended financing:

General Revenue	GR	
Service Charges	SC	
Utility Revenues	UR	
Gen. Oblign. Bonds	GOB	
Federal Aid	FA	
State Aid	SA	
Revenue Bonds	RB	
Special Reserves for	SR	
Capital Expenditures		
Working Capital or	WC	
Revolving Fund		

Total

FIGURE 7.3 Individual Project Estimate. (*From International City Management Association*, Municipal Finance Administration, *Chicago: ICMA, 1962, p. 355*)

FORM C

City of _____

Page ___ of ___ pages

Projects	Total Est. Cost	Cost to Agencies Other Than City			Cost to City						
		State	Fed. Govt.	Other	New Bonds					Other	Total
					1962–63	1963–64	1964–65	1965–66	1966–67		

FIGURE 7.4 Summary of Five-Year Capital Improvement Program Showing Methods of Financing.

who sends it to legislative decision makers. The capital budgeting process used by California most clearly exemplifies this approach.

> Policy guides for capital budgeting are established by the Governor. These guides are translated into instructions by the Budget Division and transmitted to program agencies. . . . The program agencies obtain information from the Office of Architecture and Construction in estimating costs. This information is transmitted to the line department and its decisions are in turn transmitted to the Budget Division. The budget staff prepares the final program and through the Governor transmits it formally to the legislature.[13]

There are obvious strengths in California's departmental approach. Since one agency is responsible for the entire process, a breakdown resulting from coordination problems is less likely than under some of the other models. At the same time, clear executive responsibility for the process increases the chance that decisions about the organization's future will be in line with other organizational actions. Furthermore, the linkage between operating and capital budgeting is more assured because the budget bureau coordinates both processes. Finally, both operating and capital budgets follow the same executive and legislative review sequences.

In contrast, the *multidepartmental approach* maintains executive control but divides capital budget preparation responsibilities among a series of agencies like the budget bureau, the planning department, or the building department. Maryland's capital budgeting process most clearly demonstrates this format and its problems.[14] In Maryland the State Planning Department and the Budget Bureau share budget preparation responsibilities. The Planning Department receives the Governor's instructions and passes them on to the agencies. Agencies rely on the Department of Public Improvements for help with cost and technical data. They then pass information about their projects on to both the Planning Department and the Bureau of the Budget. The Budget Bureau assists the Planning Department in developing the final capital budget, which is submitted for the Governor's approval and then to legislative review.

The system provides a substantial opportunity for capital budgets to be linked to long-range plans, but it is not without deficiencies. Since it does not parallel the operating budgetary process, it is difficult to coordinate the priorities within the two documents. At the agency level, ambiguity exists about whether to pass information on to both the Planning Department and the Budget Bureau. There are potential problems in the overlapping roles of the Budget Bureau and the Planning Department in the final preparation of the document.

The *executive commission approach* separates the capital budgeting process from the operating budget process even more substantially. Using this approach, a separate appointed commission in Wisconsin is responsible for preparation of the capital budget and its submission to the Governor.[15] The Governor is the chairperson of the commission and retains executive control. Staff work is performed by multiple agencies and departments. The commission reviews the proposals and makes decisions that result in the final budget, which is submitted to the legislature.

While this approach provides for more outside review than some of the others, commission members are frequently lay people without substantial knowledge of the technical aspects of project design and selection. They are asked to coordinate the process and make a series of complicated technical decisions often made at lower organizational levels in the other organizational formats. Furthermore, with small personal staffs, such commissions have difficulty coordinating a detailed process and gaining agency cooperation.

A final model, the *legislative commission approach*, takes responsibility for preparation of the capital budget out of the hands of the executive entirely. Using this approach, Minnesota has a legislative commission that consists of five state senators, five state representatives, and the Commissioner of Administration (the executive of the major administrative support agency to the Governor).[16] The commission is responsible for continuing review of capital priorities and has the authority to obtain information from agencies to prepare a capital budget. Its staff work is carried out by the Department of Administration.

This organizational format is rather unusual and was developed because of difficulties with the previous organizational model. Initially, the responsibility for capital budgeting in Minnesota was centralized in the hands of the Department of Administration. In the 1950s, however, the state went through a period where it was necessary to improve highways and buildings. State officials felt that the department had not exercised its responsibilities sufficiently. They created the permanent legislative building commission with the functions mentioned above. While the use of a legislative commision helps provide strong legislative control, and separates operating and capital budgetary processes substantially, one can predict certain problems. For example, there might be role conflicts for Department of Administration staff, who must work for both legislators and the executive. Finally, commission members might not have the technical expertise necessary to make good judgments about many features of the capital budgeting process.

Current Practice

Although many sources have recommended long-term financial planning and capital budgeting since the early 1900s, its widespread use in public organizations has occurred only in recent years:

> Prior to 1920 only one city had any experience with the preparation of a long term capital budget. By 1937 the National Resources Committee was able to publish a list of 56 cities which had experience with comprehensive long range plans. . . . In 1959, according to the *Municipal Yearbook* for that year, 198 cities over 10,000 population had a capital improvement program with most of these programs covering a period of five or six years.[17]

By the end of the 1960s most cities over 10,000 population[18] and most states had adopted many features of the capital budgeting process. However, highly systematic use of the process is still the exception rather than the rule. Selected conclusions from the following audit report are not an atypical description of capital budgeting practices in many units of government.

> *Master Planning.* Some agencies requesting capital projects do not perform master planning. Standards and policies useful in identifying and planning capital facility needs have not been fully developed.

Program Planning. Program planning requirements are inadequate because guidelines are not sufficiently detailed and approved plans are not a prerequisite to project funding.

Economic criteria used for valuing capital projects are not formalized and standardized, and include inappropriately low discount rates.

Program guidelines are lacking for facilities because no county-wide space standards exist, project scope is not consistently reviewed, and program criteria selected are not substantiated.

Analysis of program alternatives is often deficient because total program costs of alternatives is often incomplete and inaccurate.

Review and supervision of program planning is inadequate because the project program and economic criteria are often established by the client agency or consultants and not adequately reviewed by AD and Budget Division staff.

Budgeting. The CIP budget development process is inadequate because often budgets are prepared prior to development of program plans, the basis for cost estimates is not detailed, and project operating costs are not generated.

Analysis of project budget requests is unsatisfactory because frequently project scope is not analyzed, review of construction and development costs is lacking, and associated project costs are not adequately justified.

Monitoring of budget and program changes is deficient because changes in project elements, scope and cost are not documented and justified. . . .[19]

More comprehensive studies of public-sector capital budgeting practices identify the same kinds of problems.[20] For example, McClain's study of capital budgeting in four states concludes:

> This study results in but one principal conclusion. The concepts, activities, and procedures for the capital budgeting process have not thus far measured up to the potential of the standard definition of capital budgeting. In none of these states is there a documented program of priority-based building projects covering a five or six year period. Rather, tentative programs of capital improvements exist. In none of the four states is such a program linked with a formal plan of financing, and there is no system of fiscal or management control to assure that execution is an extension of the preparation phase and that the program is executed as it was planned according to a definite work schedule. However, these states have recognized that the orderly provision of buildings and equipment to satisfy program demands is a serious problem. They also have taken the first steps necessary to solve the problem.[21]

In addition to the reorganization of capital budgeting in order to link it more effectively to the operating budgetary process, capital budgeting can be improved through the use of analytical techniques presently used by some public organizations. Although the number of available techniques is rather large, we limit our discussion to methods of setting priorities and methods of cost-benefit analysis. Let us look at each of these areas in more detail.

ANALYTICAL APPROACHES TO CAPITAL BUDGETING

Setting Priorities

If the capital facilities planning sequence described in Table 7.1 was followed, organization-wide master and program plans might be developed. Once departments were asked to submit inventories of physical facilities, and project proposals (see Figures 7.1 through 7.4), some method would need to be employed to set priorities and relate them to the overall master plan. Let's review some of the methods currently in use to select priority projects. Steiss makes the useful distinction between *intangible* and *point system* approaches.[22]

Intangible Approaches. Intangible approaches attempt to rate project priorities on the basis of rough rules of thumb. They assume that projects are too widely different for rigid ranking and that informal political criteria are important as well. Some of the more frequently used informal criteria for project ranking are (1) whether the project is essential to community health and safety, (2) whether it fills a gap in existing service provision, (3) whether it conserves upon or maintains existing service levels, and (4) whether it meets emergency needs. Other considerations, such as the strength of community or interest group support, also play a vital role in such decisions. Each decision maker may value some of these factors more highly than others, and final consensus is usually reached through a bargaining process.

For example, one politician may place a high value on emergency housing, while his colleague believes that all funds should be allocated to the city beautification project. Yet one may be willing to allocate funds for his colleague's pet housing project if his colleague votes to provide funds for city beautification in return.

Steiss suggests that even the intangible process can be made more systematic through the use of a simple six-way breakdown to rate projects as (1) urgent (highest priority), (2) essential, (3) necessary, (4) desirable, (5) acceptable, and (6) deferrable (lowest priority).[23] Such a system does not reveal why decision makers might have made the choices they did, but it at least provides an ordering technique. The ordering techniques used in zero base budgeting, described in earlier chapters, may be equally applicable in capital budgeting.

Point Systems. Some organizations go beyond a simple ranking of projects on a six-point scale such as the one presented by Steiss. They attempt to evaluate intangible factors and then develop point scores based on preferences. For example, emergency projects might have an automatic point score of 200, while necessary maintenance projects might receive a weight of 50. Once projects are ranked according to a point score, a cutoff point can be established based on available dollars compared with project costs. This might be done to establish the parameters of the five- to six-year capital budget as well as the current year portion of that budget. Rhode Island uses this approach.[24]

The intangible and point system methods were particularly useful in comparing large numbers of projects with different objectives. They provided useful systems for setting priorities for final inclusion in the capital budget. The methods were loose enough to include not only cost factors but project urgency (i.e., emergency responses), degree of relationship to the master plan, and degree of client support.

A series of more highly developed analytical techniques is used in some public organizations to compare similar kinds of projects, such as water resource projects or large-scale agricultural development projects. The techniques can be used when it is relatively easy to specify primary and secondary costs and benefits in dollar terms. Based on such data it is possible to see, for example, which projects generate more benefits for a given level of costs. The literature on cost-benefit techniques is an extensive one.[24] Our purpose is not to provide a comprehensive treatment of the subject; rather, we expand upon the discussion of the basic logic and limitations of the approach described in an earlier chapter and explore in detail some of the methods most frequently used in analysis of public-sector projects.

Project Analysis with Undiscounted Measures

Deciding whether one project is preferable to another would be relatively easy if the projects' costs and benefits all took place in less than one year.[25] For example, we might imagine two simple pumps for water treatment systems with a one-year operating life. Each pump might have different dollar costs, but might produce the same dollar value of benefits. Under these circumstances, we might simply see which system cost less for the given level of benefits and select that system.

Capital facilities projects rarely can be constructed within one year, however. Nor are their additional costs or benefits limited to a single year. As soon as projects have multiyear costs and benefits, the choice becomes more difficult. For example, Table 7.2 shows data for three projects. Each project has a different stream of capital and operating costs and benefits during its three-year life. Let's look at a few very simple ways to compare projects.

Payback Period. One method used in project analysis is the study of a project's payback period—the number of years that elapse before capital costs are repaid. For example, in project 1 in Table 7.2, $10,000 of capital costs are paid out in year one, and 2.0 years elapse before these costs are recovered. In project 3, it takes 2.3 years to recover costs. Analysts use the payback period to make choices when projects are risky and they wish to recover capital costs quickly, or when they want projects that for political reasons need to generate political and economic benefits quickly.

It is relatively easy to notice, however, that although the payback period for project 1 is quicker than its alternatives, the other projects continue to generate benefits in future years, whereas project 1 does not. The payback criteria is not sensitive to overall project benefits or streams of costs and benefits that occur after the payback period is complete. Thus, other measures are used.

Net Proceeds per Dollars of Capital Outlay and Other Undiscounted Measures. One criterion that takes the overall return generated by the project into account is the *ratio of net proceeds to dollars of capital outlay*. It is a form of capital output ratio that looks at undiscounted dollars of net benefits divided by undiscounted capital costs.

TABLE 7.2. Comparison of Three Projects with Undiscounted Measures

Project	Year	A Capital Costs	B Operating Maint. Costs	C Total Costs (A+B)	D General Benefits	E Net Benefits (D−B)	Payback[a] (No. of Yrs.)	Net Benefits per Capital Outlay (E/A)	Undiscounted Gen. Benefit Cost Ratio (D/C)	Undiscounted Value of Gen. Benefit Minus Cost (D−C)
1	1	10,000	4,000	14,000	9,000	5,000				
	2	—	4,000	4,000	9,000	5,000				
	3	—	—	—	—	—				
	T	10,000	8,000	18,000	18,000	10,000	2	1	1.0	0
2	1	3,000	4,000	7,000	9,000	5,000				
	2	7,000	4,000	11,000	7,000	3,000				
	3	—	3,000	3,000	10,000	7,000				
	T	10,000	11,000	21,000	26,000	15,000	2.28	1.5	1.23	+5,000
3	1	15,000	6,000	21,000	11,000	5,000				
	2	—	4,000	4,000	10,000	6,000				
	3	—	4,000	4,000	16,000	12,000				
	T	15,000	14,000	29,000	37,000	23,000	2.33	1.53	1.27	+8,000

[a] Years of net benefits to payback initial capital investment. Where remaining capital costs are paid off in a portion of a year, the remaining amount of capital costs to be repaid is treated as the % of net benefits accrued during that year. In project 3 at the beginning of year 3, $4,000 of capital costs are outstanding. They represent 1/3 of net benefits in that year, so it is assumed that they are recovered in the first third year; thus, the payback period for project 3 is 2.33 years.

187

Using this criteria, project 3 in Table 7.2 appears to be the most advantageous. This project also appears to generate more *undiscounted gross benefits for total undiscounted gross costs* incurred (1.27 B/C ratio for project 3 as opposed to 1.23 for project 2 and 1.0 for project 1). Finally, in overall dollar terms project 3 generates a larger *magnitude of net benefits* ($8000) than the other projects as well.

The measures give different results, and they allow the analyst to make judgments based on different criteria. For example, payback period looks at how fast capital costs can be covered, whereas undiscounted *benefit/cost* or *magnitude of net benefits* measures look at the productivity of the investment as a whole. None of these preliminary measures, however, takes into account the sequence of costs and benefits in different years. The critical limitation underlying this failure is the failure to consider the time value of money. Let's examine this concept in more detail.

Discount Cost-Benefit Analysis: The Foundations

The Time Value of Money. It should be obvious that a dollar given to someone today is worth more to that person than that dollar given a year from now. With the dollar in hand today, the individual can invest it at, for example, an interest rate of 5 percent and have $1.05 a year from now. Furthermore, a dollar today is worth considerably more than that same dollar three years from now because of a process known as *compounding*. Through the compounding process, a dollar from this year and its interest create a larger sum which can be invested at the same rate of interest to produce an even larger sum in the future. For example, in the calculations below the dollar becomes $1.1576 by the end of three years.

Year	Principal		Interest		Sum of Principal + Interest
1	1.00	×	1.05	=	1.05
2	1.05	×	1.05	=	1.1025
3	1.1025	×	1.05	=	1.1576

Just as a dollar today becomes worth substantially more in the future because of compounding, the value of a dollar promised five years from now is worth less today when we *discount* its value back to the present. The discounting process, which is just the opposite of compounding, helps us to take into account the compounded principal and interest lost because we were not able to have the full dollar today to invest. For example, if we decide that we lose the ability to make 5 percent interest on our dollar during each of the three years, our calculations show that a dollar three years from now, discounted at 5 percent per year, is worth only .864 cents.

Year	Principal		Discount Rate		Sum of Principal + Interest
3	1.00	−	1.05	=	.95
2	.95	−	1.05	=	.907
1	.907	−	1.05	=	.864

Since it becomes tedious to multiply all the numbers when we borrow or lend money on a long-term basis, we simplify matters by using compounding and discounting tables. The discount tables of Figure 7.5 list project years down the left side and discount rates across the top. If we want to find out the present discounted value of a dollar someone plans to give us in three years with a discount rate of 5 percent, we look at those coordinates on the table and find a discount factor of .864. If we multiply this factor times the number of dollars (in this case, 1) promised in the future, we discover that the present discounted value of this money is .864 cents (.864 × $1 = .864).

Discounted Streams of Costs and Benefits. We can use the ideas of discounting to adjust for the fact that costs and benefits in projects occur at different times. For example, if we want to know the present discounted value of general benefits that might come from project 1 (Table 7.2), which we discussed earlier, we might select a discount rate (for example, 10 percent) and multiply each year's gross benefits by the factor shown on the discounting table for that year at a 10 percent discount. We then add up these sums and know the present discounted value of that benefit stream. For example, for project 1 (Table 7.2) the discounted value of general benefits is $15,615.

Project 1 General Benefits Discounted at 10%

Year	Total Benefit		Discount Factor		Discounted Value
1	$9000	×	.909	=	$8181
2	9000	×	.826	=	7434
3	0	×	.751	=	0
	$18,000				$15,615

Notice that when we take into account the time value of money, dollars we receive in the future are worth less than those we receive earlier. Thus, $9000 at the end of the first year is worth only $8181; but another $9000 two years from now is only worth $7434. The $18,000 of undiscounted benefits for the three-year period are only worth $15,615 when discounted at 10 percent.

It should be obvious that through discounting the streams of project costs and benefits, we will get a more realistic assessment of their present value. In a moment, we will do this and see which of our three projects fares best with some of the ratios already introduced using discounted dollars. But first we need to pay more attention to the discount rate.

Selecting a Discount Rate. In previous discussion we have treated the discount rate as a given when we made our calculations. But how do we really decide what discount rate to use? Two basic criteria are used: The *opportunity cost of capital*[26] and the *social rate of time preference*.[27]

The *opportunity cost of capital* approach assumes that no funds will stand idle in a society. They will be used to generate the best rates of return their owners can find. When the government raises funds for an investment project, it must bid them away from the private sector (or from other government activities) where they would have been invested at the most profitable rate of return. The cost of diverting these funds to a government project is called the opportunity cost (or the rate of return that would have been received within the private sector for those funds if they had not been diverted). Some analysts argue that since the government is bidding away funds from the private

A-1. DISCOUNT FACTOR—How much 1 at a future date is worth today.

Year	1%	3%	5%	6%	8%	10%	12%	14%	15%	16%	18%
1	0.990	0.971	0.952	0.943	0.926	0.909	0.893	0.877	0.870	0.862	0.847
2	0.980	0.943	0.907	0.890	0.857	0.826	0.797	0.769	0.756	0.743	0.718
3	0.971	0.915	0.864	0.840	0.794	0.751	0.712	0.675	0.658	0.641	0.609
4	0.961	0.888	0.823	0.792	0.735	0.683	0.636	0.592	0.572	0.552	0.516
5	0.951	0.863	0.784	0.747	0.681	0.621	0.567	0.519	0.497	0.476	0.437
6	0.942	0.837	0.746	0.705	0.630	0.564	0.507	0.456	0.432	0.410	0.370
7	0.933	0.813	0.711	0.665	0.583	0.513	0.452	0.400	0.376	0.354	0.314
8	0.923	0.789	0.677	0.627	0.540	0.467	0.404	0.351	0.327	0.305	0.266
9	0.914	0.766	0.645	0.592	0.500	0.424	0.361	0.308	0.284	0.263	0.225
10	0.905	0.744	0.614	0.588	0.463	0.386	0.322	0.270	0.247	0.227	0.191
11	0.896	0.722	0.585	0.527	0.429	0.350	0.287	0.237	0.215	0.195	0.162
12	0.887	0.701	0.557	0.497	0.397	0.319	0.257	0.208	0.187	0.168	0.137
13	0.879	0.681	0.530	0.469	0.368	0.290	0.229	0.182	0.163	0.145	0.116
14	0.870	0.661	0.505	0.442	0.340	0.263	0.205	0.160	0.141	0.125	0.099
15	0.861	0.642	0.481	0.417	0.315	0.239	0.183	0.140	0.123	0.108	0.084
16	0.853	0.623	0.458	0.394	0.292	0.218	0.163	0.123	0.107	0.093	0.071
17	0.844	0.605	0.436	0.371	0.270	0.198	0.146	0.108	0.093	0.080	0.060
18	0.836	0.587	0.416	0.350	0.250	0.180	0.130	0.095	0.081	0.069	0.051
19	0.828	0.570	0.396	0.331	0.232	0.164	0.116	0.083	0.070	0.060	0.043
20	0.820	0.554	0.377	0.312	0.215	0.149	0.104	0.073	0.061	0.051	0.037
21	0.811	0.538	0.359	0.294	0.199	0.135	0.093	0.064	0.053	0.044	0.031
22	0.803	0.522	0.342	0.278	0.184	0.123	0.083	0.056	0.046	0.038	0.026
23	0.795	0.507	0.326	0.262	0.170	0.112	0.074	0.049	0.040	0.033	0.022
24	0.788	0.492	0.310	0.247	0.158	0.102	0.066	0.043	0.035	0.028	0.019
25	0.780	0.478	0.295	0.233	0.146	0.092	0.059	0.038	0.030	0.024	0.016
26	0.722	0.464	0.281	0.220	0.135	0.084	0.053	0.033	0.026	0.021	0.014
27	0.764	0.450	0.268	0.207	0.125	0.076	0.047	0.029	0.023	0.018	0.011
28	0.757	0.437	0.255	0.196	0.116	0.069	0.042	0.026	0.020	0.016	0.010
29	0.749	0.424	0.243	0.185	0.107	0.063	0.037	0.022	0.017	0.014	0.008
30	0.742	0.412	0.231	0.174	0.099	0.057	0.033	0.020	0.015	0.012	0.007
35	0.706	0.355	0.181	0.130	0.068	0.036	0.019	0.010	0.008	0.006	0.003
40	0.672	0.307	0.142	0.097	0.046	0.022	0.011	0.005	0.004	0.003	0.001
45	0.639	0.264	0.111	0.073	0.031	0.014	0.006	0.003	0.002	0.001	0.001
50	0.608	0.228	0.087	0.054	0.021	0.009	0.003	0.001	0.001	0.001	0.000

20%	22%	24%	25%	26%	28%	30%	35%	40%	45%	50%
0.833	0.820	0.806	0.800	0.794	0.781	0.769	0.741	0.714	0.690	0.667
0.694	0.672	0.650	0.640	0.630	0.610	0.592	0.549	0.510	0.476	0.444
0.579	0.551	0.524	0.512	0.500	0.477	0.455	0.406	0.364	0.328	0.296
0.482	0.451	0.423	0.410	0.397	0.373	0.350	0.301	0.260	0.226	0.198
0.402	0.370	0.341	0.328	0.315	0.291	0.269	0.223	0.186	0.156	0.132
0.335	0.303	0.275	0.262	0.250	0.227	0.207	0.165	0.133	0.108	0.088
0.279	0.249	0.222	0.210	0.198	0.178	0.159	0.122	0.095	0.074	0.059
0.233	0.204	0.179	0.168	0.157	0.139	0.123	0.091	0.068	0.051	0.039
0.194	0.167	0.144	0.134	0.125	0.108	0.094	0.067	0.048	0.035	0.026
0.162	0.137	0.116	0.107	0.099	0.085	0.073	0.050	0.035	0.024	0.017
0.135	0.112	0.094	0.086	0.079	0.066	0.056	0.037	0.025	0.017	0.012
0.112	0.092	0.076	0.069	0.062	0.052	0.043	0.027	0.018	0.012	0.008
0.093	0.075	0.061	0.055	0.050	0.040	0.033	0.020	0.013	0.008	0.005
0.078	0.062	0.049	0.044	0.039	0.032	0.025	0.015	0.009	0.006	0.003
0.065	0.051	0.040	0.035	0.031	0.025	0.020	0.011	0.006	0.004	0.002
0.054	0.042	0.032	0.028	0.025	0.019	0.015	0.008	0.005	0.003	0.002
0.045	0.034	0.026	0.023	0.020	0.015	0.012	0.006	0.003	0.002	0.001
0.038	0.028	0.021	0.018	0.016	0.012	0.009	0.005	0.002	0.001	0.001
0.031	0.023	0.017	0.014	0.012	0.009	0.007	0.003	0.002	0.001	0.000
0.026	0.019	0.014	0.012	0.010	0.007	0.005	0.002	0.001	0.001	0.000
0.022	0.015	0.011	0.009	0.008	0.006	0.004	0.002	0.001	0.000	0.000
0.018	0.013	0.009	0.007	0.006	0.004	0.003	0.001	0.001	0.000	0.000
0.015	0.010	0.007	0.006	0.005	0.003	0.002	0.001	0.000	0.000	0.000
0.013	0.008	0.006	0.005	0.004	0.003	0.002	0.001	0.000	0.000	0.000
0.010	0.007	0.005	0.004	0.003	0.002	0.001	0.001	0.000	0.000	0.000
0.009	0.006	0.004	0.003	0.002	0.002	0.009	0.000	0.000	0.000	0.000
0.007	0.005	0.003	0.002	0.002	0.001	0.001	0.000	0.000	0.000	0.000
0.006	0.004	0.002	0.002	0.002	0.001	0.001	0.000	0.000	0.000	0.000
0.005	0.003	0.002	0.002	0.001	0.001	0.000	0.000	0.000	0.000	0.000
0.004	0.003	0.002	0.001	0.001	0.001	0.000	0.000	0.000	0.000	0.000
0.002	0.001	0.001	0.000	0.000	0.000	0.000	0.000	0.000	0.000	0.000
0.001	0.000	0.000	0.000	0.000	0.000	0.000	0.000	0.000	0.000	0.000
0.000	0.000	0.000	0.000	0.000	0.000	0.000	0.000	0.000	0.000	0.000
0.000	0.000	0.000	0.000	0.000	0.000	0.000	0.000	0.000	0.000	0.000

FIGURE 7.5 Discount Tables. (*From J. Price Gittinger*, Economic Analysis of Agricultural Projects. *Baltimore: Johns Hopkins University Press, 1972, pp. 212–13*)

sector for its own investment purposes, the appropriate discount rate for projects is the *opportunity cost of capital*.

However, not all students of the subject accept the *opportunity cost of capital* approach. Some analysts argue that the use of the opportunity cost of capital sets the discount rate too high. This rate ensures high profitability, but does not take into account the welfare of future generations. Instead, they recommend that the discount rate be set according to the *social rate of time preference* (the premium society requires to defer a dollar's worth of consumption until next year). They argue that since concern for the future is not reflected in high market rates of interest, public projects discount rates should be considerably lower than market rates of interest.

The selection of low vs. higher discount rates makes a substantial difference in decisions about which projects are ultimately judged as preferable. For example, the use of a lower discount rate often makes capital improvement projects with heavy initial capital investments and later benefits look more favorable than they would if a higher discount rate was used. Table 7.3 shows a simple analysis of a project using two different discount rates to calculate the present value of costs and benefits. In each case a machine with a 30-year life, which will save $25,000 in workers' salaries annually, is purchased at the beginning of the project. Heavy project costs are incurred initially, and the benefit stream stretches out for a long period of time. If we used the *social rate of time preference criteria* and selected a 1 percent discount rate, the project generates substantial savings (+$290,400). However, if we used a 10 percent discount rate, the project shows a loss of −$528,650.

At different times, the U.S. government has leaned in the direction of each of the two theories for selection of a discount rate. During the early 1960s the Kennedy administration favored the social rate of time preference theory and set discount rates for federal projects at 2.5 percent, while the equivalent rate in the private sector was at greater than 6 percent.[28] By the late 1960s the federal government favored the opportunity cost of capital approach and set the discount rate at 10 percent.[29] This latter approach is still in

TABLE 7.3. **Program Planning Discount Rate: Hypothetical Illustration**

	Alternative I *Discount Rate at 1%*	*Alternative II* *Discount Rate at 10%*
Present value of manpower savings	$1,290,400[a]	$471,350[b]
Present cost of investment	(1,000,000)	(1,000,000)
Impact	$290,400 − Savings	$(528,650) − Loss

SOURCE: King County Auditor, *Management Audit of the Parks and Facilities Capital Improvement Program* (King County, Washington, Report No. 79, August 1979), Appendix II-A, p. 4.

[a] This is calculated as $50,000 times the present value factor (P/A present value of an annuity) of 25.808 for a 1% discount rate for 30 years. This is comparable to saying that the present (i.e., current) value of $1 per year for 30 years would be $25.81.

[b] P/A factor at 10% discount rate is 9.427.

use at the federal level. (See Figure 7.5 for example of a standard discount table used in cost-benefit projections.)

Cost-Benefit Analysis: Discounted Measures for Project Comparison

In an effort to take the time value of money into account, we need to use measures that discount the present value of costs and benefits in project analysis. Some of the measures most commonly used in public-sector analysis, particularly with water resource projects, are benefit-cost analysis, net present value analysis, and the internal rate of return. Let's look at each of these measures more carefully.

Benefit-Cost Analysis. Benefit-cost analysis attempts to relate the present discounted value of (gross or net) benefits associated with a project with its present discounted costs.[30] Projects that have a benefit-cost ratio of greater than one are considered economically viable. Assuming scarce resources resulting in budget constraints, projects with a greater ratio of benefits to costs are usually given priority over those with smaller ratios. For projects with a benefit-cost ratio of less than one, it is advisable to reject them and use scarce resources for other activities.

To demonstrate how to compute benefit-cost ratios based on discounted present values of costs and benefits, we will do an analysis of the three projects we studied earlier, using a discount rate of 10 percent (see Table 7.4). In order to compute a general benefit-cost ratio for each project we need to follow these steps:

1 List the total undiscounted project costs for each project (columns A and D).
2 Select a discount rate (in this case 10 percent) and list the discount factor for each year (columns B and E).
3 Multiply each project's yearly cost times its discount factor to get a present value for that year (column C). For example, for project 1, year one, multiply $14,000 times .909 = $12,726.
4 Multiply each project's yearly benefits times the discount factor for that year to get the present value for that year (column F).
5 Sum up the present value of annual costs to get a total present value of costs. For example, for project 1, $12,726 + $3304 = $16,030.
6 Sum up the present value of annual benefits.
7 Compute the ratio of benefits to costs (column F total divided by column C total). For example, for project 1 the benefit-cost ratio is $15,615 ÷ $16,030 = .97.

If we follow this procedure for all projects in Table 7.4, we get some rather interesting results.

One of the projects (project 1) that previously had an undiscounted benefit-cost ratio of 1.00 (see Table 7.2) now has a discounted benefit cost ratio of .97. Because we have taken into account the time value of money, a project that was acceptable with undiscounted measures has greater costs than benefits.

This is because its capital costs are heavy in initial periods, whereas benefits are spread more evenly throughout the project. Since the benefits and the costs that occur further in the project's future are discounted more heavily and since a greater proportion

TABLE 7.4. Comparison of Three Projects Using Discounted Measures

Project	Year	Total Costs (A)	Discount 10% (B)	Total Costs (C) (A×C)=C	Total Benefits (D)	Discount 10% (E)	Gen. Benefit (F) (D×E)=F	Discounted Total Benefit/ Cost Ratio (F/C)	Net Present Worth (Value) (F-C)
I	1	14,000	.909	12,726	9,000	.909	8,181		
	2	4,000	.826	3,304	9,000	.826	7,434	$\frac{15,615}{16,030}$ = .97	−415
	3	—	.751	—	—	.751	—		
	T	18,000		16,030			15,615		
II	1	7,000	.909	6,363	9,000	.909	8,185		
	2	11,000	.826	9,086	7,000	.836	5,782	$\frac{21,473}{17,702}$ = 1.213	+3,771
	3	3,000	.751	2,253	10,000	.751	7,510		
	T	21,000		17,702	26,000		21,473		
III	1	21,000	.909	19,089	11,000	.909	9,999		
	2	4,000	.825	3,304	10,000	.826	8,260	$\frac{30,375}{25,397}$ = 1.197	+4,978
	3	4,000	.751	3,004	16,000	.751	12,016		
	T	29,000		25,397	37,000		30,375		

of benefits occur in the future (year two) than costs, the project's costs end up outweighing its benefits.

Table 7.4 reveals some other interesting results as well. In our previous analysis the undiscounted benefit-cost (B/C) ratios made project 3 our most desirable project (project 3 had B/C = 1.27 while project 2 B/C = 1.23 and project 1 B/C = 1.00). When we discount the streams of costs and benefits for all projects, project 2 ends up with the most desirable benefit-cost ratio (project 2 B/C = 1.213, project 3 B/C = 1.197 and project 1 B/C = .97). Once again the undiscounted data did not reflect the shape of the cost and benefit streams for the projects over time. Because project 2's costs come later, whereas benefits are relatively even during the three year period, its benefit-cost ratio is higher than that of project 3, which incurs its costs early while its benefits are spread more evenly.

Net Present Value. While benefit-cost analysis provides a ratio useful in project selection, at times we want to know the dollar value of *net present value (or worth)* of a project. To compute the dollar value of net present benefits, we would follow the same steps we used to compute the benefit-cost ratio. However, instead of computing the benefit-cost ratio (step 7), we subtract the present value of costs from the present value of benefits for each project. For example, for project 1 (Table 7.4), we could subtract the present value of total costs, $16,030 (column C), from total benefits, $15,615 (Column F), to get a net present value −$415 (column F total − column C total). The net present value approach is useful where we are concerned with the actual size of the returns from the project.

The computation of the net present value for each of the three projects in Table 7.4 creates some new dilemmas. Project 3 has a less favorable ratio of benefits to costs but a greater net present value than project 2. If we select only the project with the greatest net present value, we must reverse our choice and say that project 3 is now the most favorable. Our difficulties are due to the fact that the net present value method favors projects of larger size, whereas the benefit-cost method favors projects with better benefit to cost ratios. It is possible that use of the net present value criteria, particularly in overseas projects, might result in the choice of large capital-intensive projects which did not accomplish some additional objectives, such as the use of intermediate technology and large amounts of labor. Additional methods have been devised to take project scale into account. Where budget resources are limited, most sources recommend selecting projects with the highest benefit to cost ratios. Within a political context, however, the examination of the project's net present value and benefit to cost ratios might take place simultaneously with decisions based on political and other criteria, such as those we mentioned in the discussion of priority ranking (emergency, health and safety, new service provided, or maintenance and replacement of existing services).

Internal Rate of Return. A final method used in the assessment of projects is the *internal rate of return*. By this method the discount rate for the project is selected that makes the net present value of benefits equal to the net present value of costs. At this discount rate, the net value of the project is 0 and the benefit to cost ratio is 1. To decide which projects were worth selecting using this criteria, we would invest in all projects whose internal rate of return was above the opportunity cost of capital. For instance, if

TABLE 7.5. Comparison of Three Projects Using Discounted Cash Flow Techniques to Compute The Net Present Value and Internal Rate of Return for Each Project

| | | | | | Net Present Value Calculation | | |
Project	Project Year	Total (A) Costs	Total (B) Benefits	Incremental (C) Benefits (B-A)	(D) Discount Rate For Market Based on Opportunity Cost 10%	(E) Incremental Net Present Value	(F) Net Present Value of Project at 10% Discount Rate
	Test Discount Rate						
I	1	10,000	9,000	−9,000	.909	−8181	
	2	4,000	8,500	+4,500	.826	+3717	−709
	3	2,000	7,000	+5,000	.571	+3755	
	T	16,000	16,500	+ 500		− 709	
II	1	10,000	2,000	−8,000	.909	−7272	
	2	4,000	6,000	+2,000	.826	+1652	+388
	3	2,000	10,000	+8,000	.751	+6008	
	T	16,000	18,000	+2,000		+ 388	
III	1	10,000	2,000	−8,000	.909	−7272	
	2	4,000	8,000	+4,000	.826	+3304	+1,289
	3	2,000	10,000	+7,000	.751	+5257	
		16,000	20,000	+3,000		+1289	

| Project | Project Year | Internal Rate of Return | | | | Discount Rate that Represents Internal Rate of Return |
		(G) Discount Factor	(H) Incremental Net Present Value	(I) Discount Factor	(J) Incremental Net Present Value	
	Test Discount Rate	5%		6%		
I	1	.952	−8,568	.943	−8,478	Between
	2	.907	+4,458	.890	+4,005	5 and
	3	.864	+4,320	.840	+4,200	6%
	T		+ 210		− 282	
		13%		14%		
II	1	.885	−7,072	.887	−7,096	Between
	2	.783	+1,566	.769	+1,538	13 and
	3	.693	+5,544	.675	+5,400	14%
	T		+ 38		− 158	
		21%		22%		
III	1	.826	−6,608	.820	−6,560	Between
	2	.683	+2,732	.672	+2,688	21 and
	3	.565	+3,955	.551	+1,857	22%
			+ 79		− 15	

we decided that the opportunity cost of capital was 10 percent and the internal rate of return for the project was 14 percent, we would consider it worth accepting.

To use the internal rate of return method, we must develop figures based on something called a *discounted cash flow approach* (which subtracts each year's project costs from benefits and then discounts each year's net figure by the appropriate discount figure). We can use this approach to get some data for both *net present value* and *internal rate of return* for three new projects in Table 7.5. To make our calculations, we will perform the following steps:

1   List the total undiscounted costs and benefits for each project (columns A and B).
2   Compute undiscounted incremental benefits by subtracting total costs each year from total benefits each year (column B − A). For example, in project 1, incremental benefits for year one are 10,000 − 1000 = 9000.
3   Now to get net present value at our selected opportunity cost of capital, 10 percent, multiply each incremental benefit for each year by the appropriate discount factor (column C × D), to get the incremental net present value for each year (column E). For example, for project 1, year one, − 9000 × .909 = −8181).
4   Sum each project's incremental net present value for each year (column E), and the totals (column F) are the net present values of each project.
5   To use the net present value criteria, select those projects with the largest positive net present value (column F).
6   Now to find the *internal rate of return*, perform steps 3 and 4 with a variety of discount rates until one is found that yields an internal rate of return closest to zero for each project. For example, for project 2, discount rates between 13 and 14 percent yield an internal rate of return to close to 0 (see columns G through K).

Using the discounted cash flow approach to calculate net present value of our three new projects at a discount rate of 10 percent revealed that project 1 was unacceptable. Project 3 had a net present value of $1289; and project 2, $388. Each of the projects had a different internal rate of return. Project 1 was unacceptable because its internal rate of return was between 5 and 6 percent. This was lower than the opportunity cost of capital, which we set at 10 percent. Both projects 2 and 3 had internal rates of return higher than the opportunity cost of capital (project 2 between 13 and 14 percent, and project 3 between 21 and 22 percent). If resources were not scarce, we might select them both. If resources were scarce, we would select the project with the highest internal rate of return.

The internal rate of return method has certain benefits because it helps establish the break-even point for various projects through showing that rate of discount at which costs and benefits are equal. By comparing this discount rate to the opportunity cost of capital, an analyst can see how large a difference exists between the opportunity cost of capital and the internal rate of return. Where the ranges are narrow, the project might be more subject to difficulties if there are greater than anticipated costs or smaller than anticipated benefits.

However, the internal rate of return method is subject to certain limitations as well. Like the other methods, it does not take project scale and size into account. Thus it must be used with caution when comparing mutually exclusive projects. Furthermore, under certain circumstances, there are multiple discount rates that might generate a 0 internal rate of return. This latter condition most frequently happens when large negative discounted cash flows in later project years cancel out positive discounted cash flows in earlier years. When time streams of costs and benefits make this problem likely, it is advisable to use other techniques.

SUMMARY

This chapter provided a definition of capital budgeting and a description of the capital budgeting process, rationale, actors, and organization. An attempt was made to contrast the theory of capital budgeting with its actual practice in organizations. A detailed explanation of a series of analytical approaches to steps in the capital budgeting process was provided. Among the techniques reviewed were ranking techniques for setting priorities among capital projects and discounted and undiscounted benefit-cost measures. Some of the analytical techniques, such as ranking, are equally useful in operating and capital budgets. Discounted and undiscounted cost-benefit measures, however, are specifically useful where multiyear high-cost investments in physical facilities are involved.

EXERCISES AND CASE STUDY

1. Annex A contains economic data prepared for two sewage treatment projects, each with a ten-year life. Assuming that only narrow economic criteria were involved, which project would you select and why? (Assume a 10 percent discount rate and develop benefit-cost ratios as well as data on net present value and rate of internal rate of return.) What components of the cost and benefit streams contributed to the kinds of benefit-cost ratios each project had?

2. Analyze the same two projects using a 2 percent discount rate. Would you still make the same project choice? Why?

ANNEX A

Benefit-Cost Analysis Exercise: Comparison of Two Proposed Sewage Treatment Facilities

Project	Year	Capital Costs	Operating and Maintenance Costs	Total Costs	Total Benefits
	1	$1,000,000	—	$1,000,000	—
	2	600,000	50,000	650,000	200,000
	3	400,000	80,000	480,000	250,000
	4		100,000	100,000	300,000
	5		100,000	100,000	350,000
A	6		100,000	100,000	400,000
	7		100,000	100,000	500,000
	8		100,000	100,000	500,000
	9		100,000	100,000	500,000
	10		100,000	100,000	500,000
Total	10	$2,000,000	$830,000	$2,830,000	$3,500,000

ANNEX A *(cont.)*

Benefit-Cost Analysis Exercise: Comparison of Two Proposed Sewage Treatment Facilities

Project	Year	Capital Costs	Operating and Maintenance Costs	Total Costs	Total Benefits
	1	$1,500,000	—	$1,500,000	—
	2	$1,000,000	100,000	$1,100,000	500,000
	3		120,000	120,000	600,000
	4		120,000	120,000	700,000
B	5		110,000	110,000	700,000
	6		110,000	110,000	600,000
	7		110,000	110,000	600,000
	8		110,000	110,000	500,000
	9		110,000	110,000	400,000
	10		110,000	110,000	400,000
Total	10	$2,500,000	$1,000,000	$3,500,000	$5,000,000

PREPARING FOR THE CASE

In the following case study you have been put in the role of technical assistant to a parking authority administrator in a medium-sized city. You have prepared preliminary data on the feasibility of building a new municipal parking facility. Look at the data carefully. Consider alternatives to the proposed facility and then answer the following questions:

1 Should the city construct the proposed garage?
2 What rates should be charged?
3 What additional information should be obtained before a final decision is made?

CASE STUDY

Downtown Parking Authority

Proposed Municipal Parking Facility

Graeme M. Taylor

In January, 1968 a meeting was held in the office of the Mayor of Oakmont to discuss a proposed municipal parking facility. The participants included the mayor, the traffic commissioner, the administrator of Oakmont's Downtown Parking Authority, the city planner, and the finance director. The purpose of the meeting was to consider a report by Richard Stockton, executive assistant to the Parking Authority's administrator, concerning estimated costs and revenues for the proposed facility.

Mr. Stockton's opening statement was as follows:

As you know, the Mayor proposed two months ago that we construct a multi-level parking garage on the Elm Street site. At that time, he asked the Parking Authority to assemble all pertinent information for consideration at our meeting today. I would like to summarize our findings briefly for you.

The Elm Street site is owned by the city. It is presently occupied by the remains of the old Embassy Cinema, which was gutted by fire last June. The proprietors of the cinema have since used the insurance proceeds to open a new theatre in the suburbs; their lease of the city-owned land on which the Embassy was built expired on December 31st.

We estimate that it would cost approximately $40,000 to demolish the old Embassy. A building contractor has estimated that a multi-level structure, with space for 800 cars, could be built on the site at a cost of about $2 million. The useful life of the garage would probably be around forty years.

The city could finance construction of the garage through the sale of bonds. The Finance Director has informed me that we could probably float an issue of 20-year tax-exempts at 5% interest. Redemption would commence after three years, with one seventeenth of the original number of bonds being recalled in each succeeding year.

A parking management firm has al-

This case was prepared by Graeme M. Taylor under the supervision of Richard F. Vancil, Associate Professor of Business Administration, Harvard University, on behalf of the U.S. Bureau of the Budget. The case is intended for class discussion only, and certain names and facts may have been changed which, while avoiding the disclosure of confidential information, do not materially lessen the value of the case for educational purposes. This case is not intended to represent either effective or ineffective handling of an administrative situation, nor does it purport to be a statement of policy by the agency involved.

Graeme M. Taylor is with Management Analysis Center, Inc., a general management consulting firm. Formerly Senior Vice President in charge of the firm's Washington office, he is now a member of MAC's corporate staff in Cambridge, Massachusetts. Reprinted by permission of the author.

ready contacted us with a proposal to operate the garage for the city. They would require a management fee of $30,-000 per year. Their proposal involves attendant parking, and they estimate that their costs, exclusive of the fee, would amount to $240,000 per year. Of this amount, $175,000 would be personnel costs; the remainder would include utilities, mechanical maintenance, insurance, etc. Any gross revenues in excess of $270,000 per year would be shared 90% by the city and 10% by the management firm. If total annual revenues are *less* than $270,000, the city would have to pay the difference.

I suggest we offer a management contract for bid, with renegotiations every three years.

The city would derive additional income of around $50,000 per year by renting the ground floor of the structure as retail space.

It's rather difficult for the Parking Authority to estimate revenues from the garage for, as you know, our operations to date have been confined to fringe-area parking-lots. However, we conducted a survey at a private parking garage only three blocks from the Elm Street site; perhaps that information will be helpful.

This private garage is open every day from 7 a.m. until midnight. Their rate schedule is as follows: 75¢ for the first hour; 50¢ for the second hour; and 25¢ for each subsequent hour, with a maximum rate of $2.00. Their capacity is 400 spaces. Our survey indicated that, during business hours, 75% of their spaces were occupied by "all-day parkers"—cars whose drivers and passengers work downtown. In addition, roughly 400 cars use the garage each weekday with an average stay of three hours. We did not take a survey on Saturday or Sunday, but the proprietor indicated that the garage is usually about 75% utilized by short-term parkers on Saturdays until 6 p.m., when the department stores close; the average

stay is about two hours. There's a lull until about 7 p.m., when the moviegoers start coming in; he says the garage is almost full from 8 p.m. until closing time at midnight. Sundays are usually very quiet until the evening, when he estimates that his garage is 60% utilized from 6 p.m. until midnight.

In addition to this survey, we studied a report issued by the City College Economics Department last year. This report estimated that we now have approximately 50,000 cars entering the central business district (CBD) every day from Monday through Saturday. Based on correlations with other cities of comparable size, the economists calculated that we need 30,000 parking spaces in the CBD. This agrees quite well with a block-by-block estimate made by the Traffic Commissioner's office last year, which indicated a total parking need in the CBD of 29,000 spaces. Right now we have 22,000 spaces in the CBD. Of these, 5% are curb spaces (half of which are metered, with a 2-hour maximum limit for 20 cents), 65% are in open lots, and 30% are in privately owned and operated garages.

Another study indicated that 60% of all auto passengers entering the CBD on a week-day were on their way to work; 20% were shoppers, and 20% were businessmen making calls. The average number of people per car was 1.75.

Unfortunately, we have not yet had time to use the data mentioned thus far to work up estimates of the revenues to be expected from the proposed garage.

The Elm Street site is strategically located in the heart of the CBD, near the major department stores and office buildings. It is five blocks from one of the access ramps to the new crosstown freeway which we expect will be open to traffic next year, and only three blocks from the Music Center which the Mayor dedicated last week.

As we all know, the parking situation

in that section of town has steadily worsened over the last few years, with no immediate prospect of improvement. The demand for parking is clearly there, and the Parking Authority therefore recommends that we go ahead and build the garage.

The Mayor thanked Mr. Stockton for his report and asked for comments. The following discussion took place:

Finance Director: I'm all in favor of relieving parking congestion downtown, but I think we have to consider alternative uses of the Elm Street site. For example, the city could sell that site to a private developer for at least $1 million. The site could support an office building from which the city would derive property taxes of around $200,000 per year at present rates. The office building would almost certainly incorporate an underground parking garage for the use of the tenants, and therefore we would not only improve our tax base and increase revenues but also increase the availability of parking at no cost to the city. Besides, an office building on that site would serve to improve the amenity of downtown. A multi-level garage built above ground, on the other hand, would reduce the amenity of the area.

Planning Director: I'm not sure I agree completely with the Finance Director. Within a certain range we can increase the value of downtown land by judicious provision of parking. Adequate, efficient parking facilities will encourage more intensive use of downtown traffic generators such as shops, offices, and places of entertainment, thus enhancing land values. A garage contained within an office building might, as the Finance Director suggests, provide more spaces, but I suspect these would be occupied almost exclusively by workers in the building and thus would not increase the total available supply.

I think long-term parking downtown should be discouraged by the city. We should attempt to encourage short-term parking—particularly among shoppers—in an effort to counteract the growth of business in the suburbs and the consequent stagnation of retail outlets downtown. The rate structure in effect at the privately operated garage quoted by Mr. Stockton clearly favors the long-term parker. I believe that, if the city constructs a garage on the Elm Street site, we should devise a rate structure which favors the short-term parker. People who work downtown should be encouraged to use our mass transit system.

Finance Director: I'm glad you mentioned mass transit, because this raises another issue. As you know, our subways are presently not used to capacity and are running at a substantial annual deficit which is borne by the city. We have just spent millions of dollars on the new subway station under the Music Center. Why build a city garage only three blocks away which will still farther increase the subway system's deficit? Each person who drives downtown instead of taking the subway represents a loss of 50 cents (the average round trip fare) to the subway system. I have read a report stating that approximately two-thirds of all persons entering the CBD by car would still have made the trip *by subway* if they had *not* been able to use their cars.

Mayor: On the other hand, I think shoppers prefer to drive rather than take the subway, particularly if they intend to make substantial purchases. No one likes to take the subway burdened down by packages and shopping bags. You know, the Downtown Merchants Association has informed me that they estimate that each new parking space in the CBD generates on average an additional $10,000 in annual retail sales. That represents substantial extra profit to retailers; I think retailing after-tax profits average about 3% of gross sales. Besides, the city treasury benefits directly from our 3% sales tax.

Traffic Commissioner: But what about some of the other costs of increasing parking downtown and therefore, presumably, the number of cars entering the CBD? I'm thinking of such costs as the increased wear and tear on city streets, the additional congestion produced with consequent delays and frustration for the drivers, the impeding of the movement of city vehicles, noise, air pollution, and so on. How do we weigh these costs in coming to a decision?

Parking Administrator: I don't think we can make a decision at this meeting. I suggest that Dick Stockton be asked to prepare an analysis of the proposed ga-

rage along the lines of the following questions:

(1) Using the information presented at this discussion, should the city of Oakton construct the proposed garage?

(2) What rates should be charged?

(3) What additional information, if any, should be obtained before we make a final decision?

Mayor: I agree. Dick, can you let us have your answers to these questions in time for consideration at our meeting next month?

QUESTION

As Mr. Stockton, prepare your response to the Mayor's request.

NOTES

1. Jackson M. McClain, *Capital Budgeting in Selected States* (Lexington, Ky.: Bureau of Business Research, College of Commerce, University of Kentucy, 1966), p. 10. Some authors, like Alan Walter Steiss in *Local Government Finance* (Lexington, Mass.: Lexington Books, 1975), Chap. 1, call the overall process the capital facilities planning process. They see the capital budget as the document with a one-year life span of allotments for capital projects which is published along with the regular operating budget. We call the entire long-range planning process the capital budgeting process since the outcome of concern to us is the capital budget—the five- to six-year document described by McClain. We refer to the one-year portion of this budget that appears with the operating budget as the annual portion of the capital budget.

2. See, for example, Aaron Wildavsky, *The Politics of the Budgetary Process* (Boston: Little, Brown, 1964).

3. Harold Bierman, Jr., and Seymour Smidt, *The Capital Budgeting Decision*, 4th ed. (New York: Macmillan, 1975).

4. The International City Management Association, *Municipal Finance Administration* (Chicago: International City Management Association, 1962).

5. See, for example, Daniel Lynch, *Kentucky's Debt—Something to Think About* (Lexington, Ky.: Bureau of Business Research, 1963), pp. 2–3. Also A. M. Hillhouse and S. Kenneth Howard, *State Capital Budgeting* (Chicago: Council of State Governments, 1963), pp. 82–83.

6. Bierman and Smidt, *The Capital Budgeting Decision*, p. 4.

7. International City Management Association, *Municipal Finance Administration*, pp. 338–39.

8. King County Auditor, *Management Audit of the Parks and Facilities Capital Improvement Program*, Report No. 79 (King County, Wash.: August 1979).

9. See, for example, Special Assistant to the President for Public Works Planning, *Planning for Public Works* (Washington, D.C.: Government Printing Office, 1957), p. 14.

10. William B. Marcus, *Note on Benefit-Cost Analysis* (Cambridge, Mass.: Kennedy School of Government, 1976).

11. Claudia DeVita Scott, *Forecasting Local Government Spending* (Washington, D.C.: Urban Institute, 1972).

12. For an excellent discussion of organizational formats, see McClain, *Capital Budgeting in Selected States*.

13. Ibid., pp. 48, 49.

14. George A. Bell, *State Budget Administration in Maryland* (College Park, Md.: Bureau of Governmental Research, 1977).

15. McClain, *Capital Budgeting in Selected States*, Chap. 5.

16. Ibid., Chap. 4.

17. International City Management Association, *Municipal Finance Administration*, pp. 337–38.

18. Lennox L. Moak, *Administration of Local Government Debt* (Chicago: Municipal Finance Officers' Association of the United States and Canada, 1970), p. 8.

19. King County Auditor, *Management Audit of the Parks and Facilities Capital Improvements Program*, pp. 1–3.

20. McClain, *Capital Budgeting in Selected States*, p. 212. Also see Hillhouse and Howard, *State Capital Budgeting*.

21. Steiss, *Local Government Finance*, Chap. 2.

22. Ibid., p. 38.

23. Ibid., p. 24.

24. See, for example, E. J. Mishan, *Cost Benefit Analysis*, rev. ed. (New York: Praeger, 1976): E. Price Gittinger, *Economic Analysis of Agricultural Projects* (Baltimore: Johns Hopkins University Press, 1972); A. R. Prest and R. Turvey, "Cost Benefit Analysis: A Survey," in *Surveys of Economic Theory*, Vol. 3, *Resource Allocation*, ed. American Economics Association and the Royal Economic Society (New York: St. Martin's Press, 1966).

Gittinger and others like to distinguish between economic vs. financial analysis of public-sector projects. Economic analysis used primarily in public-sector benefit-cost studies looks at the social and economic return to the whole society. Financial analysis looks at the costs and benefits contributed and received by specific individuals, groups, or organizations. This discussion looks at benefit-cost analysis from the standpoint of economic analysis.

25. See Gittinger's discussion of undiscounted measures for more detail.

26. For more detail, see William Marcus, *Note on the Use of Discount Rates in the Federal Government* (Cambridge, Mass.: Kennedy School of Government, 1977); and Stephen A. Marglin, "The Opportunity Cost of Public Investment," *Quarterly Journal of Economics*, May 1963, pp. 274–89.

27. See E. J. Mishan, *Economics for Social Decisions: Elements of Cost Benefit Analysis* (New York: Praeger, 1972); and William J. Baumol, "On the Social Rate of Discount," *American Economic Review*, 1968, pp. 788–802.

28. Marcus, "Note on the Use of Discount Rates in the Federal Government," p. 2.

29. Ibid., pp. 2–7.

30. See Gittinger, *Economic Analysis of Agricultural Projects*, pp. 80–90 and 110–29.

BIBLIOGRAPHY

Bell, George A. *State Budget Administration in Maryland*. College Park: Bureau of Governmental Research, 1977.

Baumol, William J. "On the Social Rate of Discount." *American Economic Review*, September 1968, pp. 788–802.

Bierman, Harold, Jr., and Smidt, Seymour. *The Capital Budgeting Decision*. New York: Macmillan, 1975.

Gittinger, E. Price. *Economic Analysis of Agricultural Projects*. Baltimore: Johns Hopkins University Press, 1972.

Hillhouse, A. M., and Howard, S. Kenneth. *State Capital Budgeting*. Chicago: Council of State Governments, 1963.

International City Managers' Association. *Municipal Finance Administration*. Chicago: International City Management Association, 1962.

Lynch, Daniel. *Kentucky's Debt—Something to Think About*. Lexington, Ky.: Bureau of Business Research, 1963.

McClain, Jackson M. *Capital Budgeting in Selected States*. Lexington, Ky.: Bureau of Business Research, 1966.

Marcus, William B. *Note on Cost Benefit Analysis*. Cambridge, Mass.: Kennedy School of Government, 1976.

Mishan, E. J. *Cost Benefit Analysis*. New York: Praeger, 1976.

————. *Economics for Social Decisions: Elements of Cost Benefit Analysis*. New York: Praeger, 1972.

Moak, Lennox. *Administration of Local Government Debt*. Chicago: Municipal Finance Officers' Association of the United States and Canada, 1970.

Scott, Claudia DeVita. *Forecasting Local Government Spending*. Washington, D.C.: Urban Institute, 1972.

Steiss, Alan Walter. *Local Government Finance*. Lexington, Mass.: Lexington Books, 1975.

Chapter 8

Revenue Systems

State Planners Overestimate Revenues by a Billion Dollars

SEATTLE POST INTELLINGENCER, 1982

Governor Looking for Millions in New Taxes

SEATTLE POST INTELLINGENCER, 1982

Arlington County Voters Reject School Tax Levy Increase

WASHINGTON POST, 1982

In earlier chapters we treated government revenues as a given and examined the concepts, techniques, and problems inherent in the design and analysis of the economic, fiscal, and executive budgets. As the above quotes indicate, however, government revenues can hardly be taken for granted. In fact every budget director needs to consider three basic questions when analyzing the revenue system in his jurisdiction. First, how much money will be available? Second, where will it come from? Third, who will provide the money and at what level of sacrifice? In small governmental jurisdictions all three questions are very important because the chief financial officer may be responsible not simply for preparing the budget but also for making revenue projections and suggesting to his city council what new taxes might be levied in order to balance the budget. The same financial officer may be asked to comment on which members of the community will be most negatively affected by the proposed new taxes. In larger jurisdictions, like the State of New York, revenue-estimating functions are separated from the budget preparation and analysis function. Nevertheless, budget officers must know how much money is going to be available and be ready to comment on which new taxes might be used to raise more funds, should legislators or the Governor want their testimony.

The purpose of this chapter is to describe the concepts and techniques most frequently used to answer three critical questions:

1 How much money is available for government spending?
2 Where will revenues for government spending come from?
3 Who will provide government revenues and at what level of sacrifice?

HOW MUCH MONEY IS AVAILABLE FOR GOVERNMENT SPENDING?

Simple Extrapolation of Past Trends

Many organizations decide whether they have sufficient revenues to meet new needs by extrapolating from past trends in revenue growth. To make such projections, an analyst reviews the revenue statistics for past years and establishes what the previous rate of annual revenue growth has been. For example, if city revenues grew at 5 percent per year during each of the past three years and if economic conditions, population growth, and other factors that helped generate such revenues are expected to stay the same, an analyst using this method would assume that the same rate of revenues growth (5 percent) would continue in the new fiscal year.

If an increase of 5 percent in city revenues is sufficient to pay for operating expenses (e.g., salaries of city garbage collectors) and for necessary capital expenses (e.g., putting in a new sewer system), then city officials can prepare their budgets without major changes in their strategy. If, however, a 5 percent increase in revenues will not be sufficient to balance the operating and capital budgets, officials will have to decide whether to borrow money, raise new taxes, or cut their budgets.

Projecting future revenues from past trends has the same dangers as driving a car forward while looking only through the rear-view mirror. Is it safe, for example, to assume that factors which affect the size of the city's tax base, such as population growth and economic conditions, will stay the same from year to year? In an effort to overcome some of the difficulties of this approach, more complex modeling techniques are occasionally used.

Modeling

Modeling is a technique that attempts to build a mathematical approximation of the way that key variables, such as population growth, affect revenue and expenditure growth. For example, to build a model to project income tax revenues, an analyst might assume that income tax growth is determined by the number of newly employed people in different income groups who live in, as well as move into, the jurisdiction during the fiscal year. He will then ask what factors cause these people to move into or stay in the tax jurisdiction. The list of factors might include general economic growth prospects of the area, resultant new employment possibilities, and the availability of housing that will enable new job seekers to live in the jurisdiction. After the analyst has considered all the factors, he will analyze studies of the relationships between these factors and income tax generation. He will then try to specify mathematically the effect, for example, that changes in economic growth rates will have on new job creation and resultant growth of income tax revenues. He often makes preliminary projections using his model and compares his projections with historical data where there are large variations between his projections and what actually happened. He corrects the model and tries to make it more reliable.

One of the most sophisticated expenditure models constructed at this time is Claudia DeVita Scott's *New Haven Expenditure Model*.[1] Projections in the model are based on different assumptions about rates of change for population, salary, and service variables. The model is used to produce separate estimates for future expenditures in the areas of (1) education, (2) library services, (3) police and public safety, (4) fire protection, (5) health, (6) welfare, (7) public works, (8) parks and recreation, and (9) administration and development. According to Steiss:

> Debt service requirements are projected through the use of an accounting model which employs information on the amount of debt outstanding, plans for new capital expenditures, and expectation regarding future interest rates (an exogenous factor) to derive forecasts of the principal and interest payments on public debt. Policy variables are specified concerning the mix of financing techniques for long term capital expenditures.[2]

Both simple extrapolation and complex modeling projections are made within the constraints of the organization's debt policy, its policy on raising additional taxes and cutting its budget and services. Three kinds of debt policies are normally discussed: *pay as you go, reserve funds,* or *borrowing*. The *pay as you go* strategy implies that the organization will make capital improvements only through current revenue surpluses associated with the operating budget. Within such an approach, analysts would assume no future debt was allowable when making future revenue projections. The analysts would then establish the gap between future revenues and program expenditures. Capital project resources would be available only if future budget surpluses were projected.

In contrast, some organizations would attempt to set up *reserve funds* from projected budget surpluses or from projected allowable debt to pay for capital projects. Reserve funds would be expected to pay for future projects due to compound interest received from investments.

Finally, some organizations build assumptions about *allowable borrowing* into their projections. If no future revenues are available from projected current operations to permit capital expenditures without borrowing, then a series of borrowing strategies is proposed.

In the event that an organization can afford to incur no further debt and it is not possible to cut the budget, then officials must decide to raise more taxes. The moment they make this decision, they must answer the next key question: Where will the money for additional government revenues come from?

WHERE WILL THE MONEY COME FROM?

Governments finance themselves through a combination of taxes and fees, intergovernmental transfers, and borrowing. Within each method there are a variety of options, each of which has its particular strengths and weaknesses. Let us examine each method and its options in more detail.

Taxes and Fees

Individual and Corporate Income Taxes.[3]   The individual and corporate income taxes are the most important sources of government revenue. They comprised 39 percent of all government revenues in 1980—fifty-five percent of federal revenues and 24 percent of state revenues. More than forty states used some form of individual or corporate income tax to generate funds. The income tax became widely used in the United States after 1913 when the Sixteenth Amendment to the Constitution provided a legal justification for its implementation. Its principal feature is the ability to combine all sources of individual and corporate income under a single taxable source, called *gross and adjusted income*. The concept of gross adjusted income combines income from wages, rent, interest, royalties, profits, and other items. Taxable income is gross adjusted income minus exemptions, deductions, credits, and other special items. Tax rates for individual income earners range from 14 percent paid on income above $3400 and $5500 to more than 70 percent on income above $215,000. Corporate income tax rates include 17 percent on the first $25,000, 20 percent on the second $25,000, 30 percent on the third $25,000, 40 percent on the fourth $25,000, and 46 percent above $100,000.

Some of the principal advantages of the income tax are (1) its ability to combine all income sources under a single source; (2) the connection of tax liabilities with the ability of an individual to pay; (3) its broad coverage, which does not conform to any small jurisdictions; and (4) the ability to administer the tax efficiently through a national system of employer withholding.

The income tax is not without its negative features. For example, in inflationary periods individuals are often thrust into higher tax brackets long before the tax structure can be performed. The consequence, particularly for individuals with lower income, is to cut their disposable income drastically. Another difficulty is that nonwage income, for example in-kind services, is often not reported. Economic downturns and unemployment cut income tax revenues and result in unstable collections and difficulties in main-

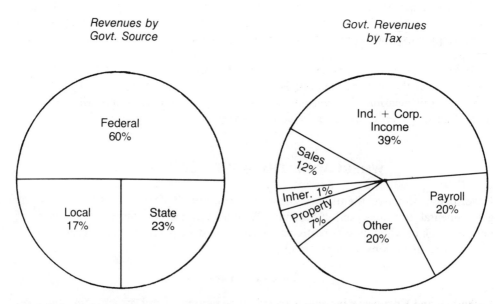

FIGURE 8.1 Government Revenues by Source and Tax in 1980. (*From U.S. Bureau of the Census, Government Finances 1979–80, p. 4, Table B*)

taining government expenditures. The withholding system puts a special burden on employers, who have to collect these taxes for the government. Finally, as a special feature of the U.S. system, the capital gains legislation helps to flatten out the progressive nature of the income tax. According to Musgrave and others, the effective rate above $210,000 is not 70 percent but rather around 30 percent due to the prudent use of capital gains benefits by large-income earners.[4]

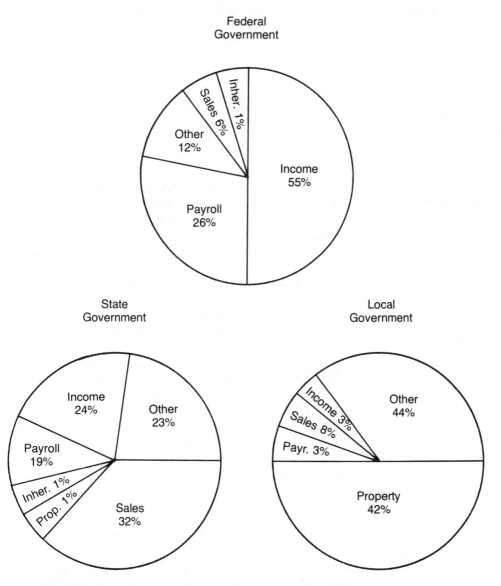

FIGURE 8.2   Tax Revenues by Level of Government, 1980. (*From U.S. Bureau of the Census*, Government Finances 1979–80, p. 817, Table 4)

Sales Tax.[5]   The sales tax accounted for more than 12 percent of the revenues of all units of government in 1980. Although it contributed less than 6 percent of federal and 8 percent of local revenues, it was the principal tax collection device for state governments (32 percent of state revenues). The use of the sales tax, particularly at the state level, is a relatively recent development. Before 1900 the principal tax for state government was the property tax. With the advent of motor vehicles, the sales tax came into use at the state level. In 1919 four states, Colorado, New Mexico, North Dakota and Oregon, pioneered the use of the gasoline tax. In the 1930s, with the wholesale collapse of mortgage repayments during the Great Depression, the property tax lost its viability as a source of state revenues because many Americans defaulted on their home and property loans. As a result, the states began to switch to the use of sales taxes. In the 1980s all but four states use the sales tax rather extensively. State taxes are used largely on consumer goods, and rates generally vary between 2 and 6 percent. At the federal level, sales taxes are used for special goods, such as alcohol and gasoline. At the local level, governments usually apply a surcharge to the state sales tax and use the same tax base.

Some of the critical characteristics of the sales tax are that it is imposed on the seller's side; it usually applies to consumer goods, such as gasoline; and unlike the income tax, it treats all consumers equally. It permits no special treatment (at least directly) for differences in income level, family size, or status. Sales taxes can be imposed at various stages of the production process or at a single stage. For example, a sales tax could be collected when manufacturers sell to wholesalers, when wholesalers sell to retailers, or when retailers sell to consumers. *Single-stage taxes* collect at only one point in the exchange process. Most state sales taxes, for example, collect at the point when retailers sell to consumers. However, it is possible to collect taxes at various stages in the process. Some typical examples of *multistage taxes* are *turnover taxes* and *value added taxes*.

A *turnover tax* is one that is collected at every stage in a production process and sale. For example, in the production of automobiles turnover taxes would be collected not only on the sale of all raw materials to the manufacturer but at every point up to the ultimate sale to the consumer. *Value added taxes* are also collected at every stage in the production cycle but only on the difference between income and expenses. Thus, they provide little income on production stages, which produce little value added.

The sales tax has a number of principal advantages. It has a relatively large tax base in the economy and has produced substantial government revenues, particularly during the post-World War II period. Furthermore, single-stage sales taxes are relatively easy to administer. They are managed by the merchant. In general, however, lower-income taxpayers must pay the same tax rates for the purchase of goods as higher-income taxpayers. As a result, lower-income taxpayers are said to be penalized because they must use a higher percentage of their income to purchase necessities. Some of the remedies to this problem have been to exempt food purchases from the sales tax (thus cutting between 20 and 25 percent of the sales tax base in typical states), to provide tax credits to low-income families when they file their state and federal income tax returns, and to propose an expenditure tax with rates based on individual income.

In addition to the problems of the general single-stage tax, turnover and value added taxes have special problems. With turnover taxes, the difficulty of administration increases because the tax must be collected at every stage. At the same time, it has been argued that companies try to gain control of every stage of production and distribution to eliminate the need to pay turnover taxes. With the value added tax, there are some special advantages. Relatively few producers need to be monitored because significant value added occurs at relatively few stages in the production process. The value added tax, used widely in Western Europe, is of increasing interest to U.S. policy makers as a potential new revenue source.

Property Taxes.[6] Property taxes accounted for about 7 percent of all government revenues in 1980. However, they were the most important source of local government revenues, accounting for more than 42 percent of all local government taxes. Local governments collected 96 percent of all government property taxes in 1978. The property tax is one of the oldest taxes used in the United States. Its use extends back to the original thirteen colonies. The property tax is characteristic of a tax on wealth and assets. In the absence of other wealth taxes in the United States, the property tax concentrates on real estate with about half of the tax collected from business and half from individual real estate.

Property taxes account for anywhere from 10 to 25 percent of the cost of lodging, and as such are highly visible to taxpayers. Property tax administration is a complicated process that requires assessors, collectors, and administrators. Rates are usually set per $1000 of assessed valuation. Within local jurisdictions there are often differences between the assessed value of property and the market value. Within some communities the policy is to reassess property frequently to assure that market and assessed value remain the same. In other communities, the policy is to assess at a percentage of the market value.

The property tax has few true advocates. It is difficult to administer. It requires a group of assessors and a constant process of property reassessment. It is highly visible and since it represents a substantial percentage of the cost of lodging, homeowners do not like it. It is often used to pay for services such as schools, from which some property owners without school-age children believe they gain few direct benefits. In times of inflation assessed property value may be increased to a point where older people living on fixed incomes are forced to move to cheaper lodging. In spite of all of its difficulties, it is difficult to find an alternative tax source for local government.

Payroll Tax.[7] Payroll taxes in 1980 accounted for more than 20 percent of all government revenues. They accounted for more than 26 percent of federal and 19 percent of state revenues. Their principal function is to pay for a series of social insurance programs such as old age survivor's insurance, disability insurance, Medicaid, and unemployment insurance. In principle, such programs were expected to be self-financing. Old age survivor's insurance and unemployment insurance were developed in 1935. The former program was a federal program and the latter a state program to be administered at the state level. Disability insurance was added at the federal level in 1956 and Medicaid in the 1960s.

With the major social insurance items, employers pay one-half of the amount and employees the other half. However, the employer alone pays for unemployment insurance at a rate of roughly 3.2 percent, which covers the first $4200 in earnings. The rates paid in 1980 for old age and disability were 5.8 percent by both employer and employee (up to $30,000) and 1.2 percent for Medicaid.

Like the income tax, payroll taxes are relatively easy to administer. They can be managed by the employer and taken out on a monthly basis. They have the advantage of ensuring a set of basic benefits for the population based on a revenue collection method that can be easily administered. Nevertheless, some critics believe that individuals could make more effective investments and develop individual retirement plans that would provide a better benefits package than the federal system. Furthermore, the self-financing nature of the Social Security System has been called into question due to a combination of rates that are too low to guarantee the benefits at present provided for by the law and factors such as inflation.

Estate, Inheritance, and Gift Taxes.   Estate, inheritance, and gift taxes represent one of the most neglected areas in government financing. They comprise 1 percent of all government taxes, 1 percent of federal taxes, and 1 percent of state revenues. *Federal estate taxes* are levied against the total market value of an estate after debts are subtracted. An exemption of $60,000 is provided as well as one-half of the value of the estate if one's spouse is to receive an exemption. In addition the first $120,000 of an estate is tax exempt. Once exemptions are taken, rates vary from 3 percent on the first $5000 to 77 percent on amounts above $10 million. *Inheritance taxes* are levied on those individuals receiving that privilege to inherit property. Each individual is treated as a separate taxpayer and after exemptions is subject to tax rates between 5 and 30 percent. Inheritance taxes are more frequently used by state governments than by the federal government. *Gift taxes* are paid upon transfers of resources before death in an effort to limit avoidance of both estate and inheritance taxes.

Other Revenues—User Fees.[8]   User fees, licences, and related items provide for a surprisingly large proportion of government revenues (20 percent in 1980). Forty-four percent of local government financing, 23 percent of state, and 12 percent of federal revenues came from this mix of sources. The rationale for such charges is that the user who is directly benefiting from such a service as garbage collection, water, transportation, or postal service should pay all or part of the cost of delivering the service. Such charges are most frequently used where a tangible service can be directly consumed by a specific individual.

Grants-in-Aid[9]

Types of Grants.   In addition to taxes and fees for service, a second major way of gaining government income is through grants-in-aid. In 1980, for example, 23 percent of state income came from federal and local grants, and 40 percent of local government income came from state and federal grants. Such resource transfers may be thought of in two categories: conditional grants and unconditional grants. *Conditional grants* are provided for a specific purpose with certain highly specific requirements. Such grants are often justified on the basis of a principle called the *benefit spillover principle*, which assumes that some services, for example, education provided by a local government, have a series of benefits that accrue to other jurisdictions that are not paying directly for the service. Thus, there can be a justified reason to transfer money from other jurisdictions that benefit from the service to the jurisdiction where such a service is being provided. *Unconditional grants*, in contrast, can be used for any purpose a jurisdiction desires. They are often used to equalize access to revenues in jurisdictions that have fewer resources than others. The idea of transfers among units of government is hardly a new one. For example, in 1803 the Congress earmarked 5 percent of the proceeds from the sale of federal lands for distribution to the states where such lands were located in

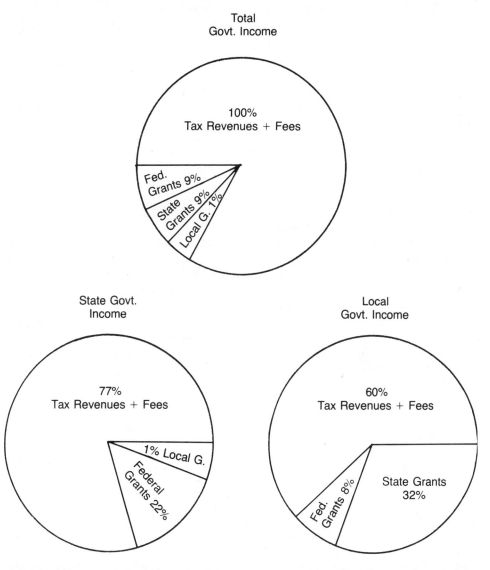

FIGURE 8.3   Grants-in-Aid as a Percent of Government Income in 1980. (*From U.S. Bureau of the Census*, Government Finances 1979 – 80, p. 14, Table 4)

order to finance transportation and educational expenses.[10] In the 1940s additional federal programs were designed to pass back general revenues to the states. Federal interest in such programs remained dormant until the 1960s. Since the turn of the century, however, state governments have provided grants for specific purposes to local government jurisdictions, primarily for education. In fact, state grants to local government have remained between 35 to 40 percent of state government spending for the past thirty years.

In the 1960s renewed interest in sharing federal resources resulted in a wide variety of proposals, such as the Heller Peckman Plan and President Nixon's plan for revenue sharing.[11] Depending upon the party and President in power, proposals for sharing by the federal government have vacillated between a preference for categorical grants, which restrict funds for specific purposes (by, for example, the Johnson administration), and general unrestricted revenue sharing.

The Nixon and, more recently, the Reagan administration have favored the use of revenue sharing or more general unconditional grants. The policies are based on the philosophy that "everything that can be run more effectively by state and local government we shall turn over to state and local governments—along with the funding sources to pay for it."[12] Concurrent with this policy idea, the Reagan administration has discussed three methods for turning back resources:

1 *Revenues Sharing on a Formula Basis*. Funds would be distributed by formulas that would take account of differences in fiscal capacity and need, as well as the magnitude of returned responsibilities.
2 *Tax Sharing on an Origin Basis*. Congress could provide a permanent state-local entitlement to specific portions of tax receipts, with shares of the same proportion as tax revenues generated. For instance, if California taxpayers account for 12 percent of all federal income tax receipts, California would receive 12 percent of the portion of the income tax revenue shared with the states.
3 *Conditional Relinquishment of a Federal Tax*. Congress could give up a portion of a tax or vacate an entire tax field without the requirement for a state or local pick up. Thus, if a state does not move into the area, the taxpayer benefits with a new tax reduction, for example, the phase-out of federal tax on amusement tickets during the 1960s.[13]

Problems with Grants-in-Aid.   Intergovernmental fiscal relations are not without problems. Whenever resources are to be redistributed, there will be disagreement about which definition of equity to use. Revenue sharing on a formula basis implies that states with less fiscal capacity may receive greater proportions of returned funds. In contrast, tax sharing on an origin basis would provide for proportional redistribution without giving special treatment to states and local jurisdictions with less fiscal capacity. A second problem is *tax competition*. For example, under tax relinquishment state and local jurisdictions will undoubtedly compete for the use of a new tax. Such competition already exists among states that attempt to attract new enterprises through changes in their tax laws. Finally, use of the same taxes by two or more levels of government present threats to the efficient operation of all units of government. Furthermore, when more than one unit of government is involved in collection of taxes for another jurisdiction, problems of *coordination* result. In spite of the difficulties, the advantages of inter-governmental resource sharing have made this an area of avid interest.

Borrowing: Rationale and Methods[14]

In addition to raising revenues through taxation and fees for service and through grants-in-aid, government also resorts to borrowing as a way of covering its expenditures. In fact, state and local governments borrow more than $15 billion dollars annually. In principle, borrowing is considered appropriate for capital expenditures. In practice, however, government also borrows small amounts for short periods of time to cover deficits in its operating budgets. For example, *tax anticipation borrowing* is used to cover cash flow deficits that will be made up by tax revenues to be collected during the same budget year. Under more questionable circumstances, during the early 1970s, New York City used tax revenues collected for the next budget year to cover its previous operating deficits.

The principal mechanisms for debt financing are *full faith and credit obligations* and *revenue bond financing*. *Full faith and credit obligations* through *general obligation bonds* have the full backing of all of the revenues and resources of that particular jurisdiction of government. In contrast, *revenue bonds* are tied specifically to the resources and revenues received in a particular project, such as a new toll bridge or highway. Bondholders will be repaid through revenues generated in the new project. In the event of difficulties, the governmental jurisdiction does not provide full backing beyond that of the specific project.

Bonds are generally issued in two forms: *term bonds* (bonds paid off in a lump sum after a period of years) and *serial bonds* (bonds with periodic interest and principal payments made from the time of sale until they are completely repaid). To repay bond-holders, the unit of government generally makes contributions to a debt service fund, which is invested. Bonds are repaid on their due date through contributions from the fund and its compound interest on invested contribution.

Problems of Borrowing: How Much Debt Is Appropriate? Because governmental units rely extensively on external financing to pay for the development of physical facilities, investors rely increasingly on credit ratings provided by organizations such as Moody's Investor's Services Inc., Standard and Poor's Corporation, and Fitch Investor's Service. The ratings provided by these firms provide their assessment of the jurisdiction's capacity to repay its obligations. Underlying the concept of *capacity* to pay is the assertion that methods must be used to judge the relationship between "the amount and quality of a community's resources and its legal and practical ability to draw upon these requirements for payment."[15]

The credit analysis organizations are said to rely about 50 percent on ratio analysis of solvency (the ability of government to meet its long term obligations) and 50 percent on subjective factors. Some of the most frequently used ratio measures are these:

1 *Debt Margins* (the percent of the legal debt limit still underutilized by the unit of government). Almost every governmental jurisdiction has a legally established debt limit—usually some percentage of the assessed valuation of the jurisdiction's property. For example, Seattle permits general-purpose indebtedness of 2.5 percent of the assessed value of property. While it is useful to know how close a jurisdiction is to its legal debt limit, the measure is misleading in establishing capacity to pay. For example, if a high debt limit is established, the jurisdiction may have little capacity to repay its obligations long before it reaches its debt limits.

2 *Net Direct Debt as a Percentage of the Market Value of Real Estate.* Since a large proportion of municipal debt is serviced through property tax revenues, these measures attempt to link debt size to property tax base. Bond rating companies often use this rating with an upper limit of 10 percent as the danger point.

3 *Annual Debt Service Payments as a Percent of General Operating Expenses.* For this measure the International City Management's rule of thumb for the danger point for municipalities is 25 percent. Bond raters provide an excellent rating if the ratio is about 10 percent.

4 *Payout Ratings.* It is often suggested that debt not take more than twenty-five years to repay and that the payout ratio (debt servicing as a proportion of total jurisdiction debt) stay at 25 percent in five years and 50 percent in ten. This implies a twenty-year payout period to cover existing debt and even repayment in roughly equal five-year increments.

In addition to measures of overall solvency and financial health, bond rates use more indirect measures such as percent of population growth, percent increase in assessed valuation, percent of increase in the issuance of building permits, per capita income, levels of unemployment, growth of jurisdictional GDP, and debt per capita. (The ratings used by Moody's Investor's Service and their interpretations appear in Table 8.1.)

The rating a municipal bond issue receives is of vital importance because the lower the rating, the higher the borrowing costs are for the jurisdiction.

> A few years ago the difference between a single A and a double A would have meant perhaps 25 basis points of borrowing costs (100 basis points representing a full percentage point). For a borrower with a $100 million bond issue, an extra 25 points basis works out to an extra five million dollars over twenty years. . . .
> During 1974–75 a decision by the bond rating agencies that a bond was not worth even an A meant that it could find no market at all. . . . Thus, the rating agencies were in effect determining which companies could raise money and which could not.[16]

The importance of higher vs. lower bond ratings to the investor as well as the jurisdiction is also demonstrated by Table 8.2, which shows the yield averages for bonds of different ratings. Bonds with higher ratings paid less of a return to investors than bonds with lower ratings. Investors had to balance the risk of bond default of the lower-rated issues vs. the potential higher rate of return.

Problems of Borrowing: How Good Are the Bond Raters?   Government officials can help avert default by continuous analysis of the measures suggested here. Unfortunately, neither the jurisdictions themselves nor the outside monitors (like the rating agencies)

TABLE 8.1. Municipal Bond Ratings

Aaa

Bonds rated *Aaa* are judged to be of the best quality. They carry the smallest degree of investment risk and are generally referred to as "gilt edge." Interest payments are protected by a large or an exceptionally stable margin, and principal is secure. While the various protective elements are likely to change, such changes as can be visualized are most unlikely to impair the fundamentally strong position of such issues.

Aa

Bonds rated *Aa* are judged to be of high quality by all standards. Together with the *Aaa* groups they comprise what are generally known as high grade. They are rated lower than the best bonds because the margin of protection may not be as large as in *Aaa* securities, or fluctuation of protective elements may be of greater amplitude, or there may be other elements present that make long-term risks seem somewhat larger than in *Aaa* securities.

A

Bonds rated *A* possess many favorable investment attributes and are to be considered as upper-medium-grade obligations. Factors giving security to principal and interest are considered adequate, but elements may be present which suggest a susceptibility to impairment sometime in the future.

Baa

Bonds rated *Baa* are considered as medium-grade obligations (i.e., they are neither highly protected nor poorly secured). Interest payments and principal security seem adequate, but elements of protection may be lacking or may be characteristically unreliable over any great length of time. Such bonds lack outstanding investment characteristics and in fact have speculative characteristics as well.

Ba

Bonds rated *Ba* are judged to have speculative elements; their future cannot be considered well assured. Often the protective elements of principal and interest payments may be very moderate and thereby not well safeguarded during good times and bad times over the future. Uncertainty of position characterizes bonds in this class.

B

Bonds rated *B* generally lack characteristics of the desirable investment. Assurance of interest and principal payments or of maintenance of other terms of the contract over any long period of time may be small.

Caa

Bonds rated *Caa* are of poor standing. Such issues may be in default, or there may be present elements of danger with respect to principal or interest.

Source: Moody's Investor's Service, Inc.

perform timely detailed analysis. Some critics charge, for example, that the record of bond raters has been poor. For example: ". . . during the depression 78% of the municipal bonds that defaulted were rated triple A or double A at the time. The rating agencies have been favoured in the post war period of course by the favourable circumstance that their ratings have not had to survive a prolonged and devastating economic downturn. . . ."[17] However, in the case of the largest municipal financial crisis in recent years: "1.6 billion in New York City notes which had recently been rated investment grade by

TABLE 8.2. Moody's Municipal Bond
Yield Averages

	Aaa	Aa	A	Baa
1953	2.31	2.54	3.01	3.41
1954	2.04	2.16	2.56	3.09
1955	2.18	2.32	2.66	3.14
1956	2.51	2.72	3.02	3.50
1957	3.10	3.33	3.62	4.20
1958	2.92	3.17	3.39	3.95
1959	3.35	3.55	3.83	4.24
1960	3.26	3.51	3.77	4.22
1961	3.27	3.46	3.66	4.01
1962	3.03	3.17	3.32	3.67
1963	3.06	3.16	3.30	3.58
1964	3.09	3.19	3.32	3.54
1965	3.16	3.25	3.38	3.57
1966	3.67	3.76	3.95	4.21
1967	3.74	3.86	4.08	4.30
1968	4.20	4.31	4.54	4.88
1969	5.45	5.58	5.82	6.07
1970	6.12	6.28	6.49	6.75
1971	5.22	5.36	5.61	5.89
1972	5.04	5.19	5.38	5.60
1973	4.95	5.09	5.29	5.47
1974	5.89	6.04	6.27	6.34
1975	6.42	6.77	7.37	7.62
1976	5.65	6.12	7.17	7.49
1977	5.20	5.39	5.86	6.12
1978	5.52	5.68	5.99	6.27
1979	5.89	6.12	6.34	6.72
1980	7.85	8.06	8.44	9.01
1981	10.42	10.89	11.31	11.75

SOURCE: Moody's Investor's Service, Inc.
Reading Room and Moody's Municipal Government Manual, 1982.

Moody's faced a de facto default when the state posed a moratorium on their redemption."[18]

Insufficient defaults have occurred in recent years to analyze the relationship between default and poor performance on the traditional rating measures.

WHO WILL BEAR THE BURDEN AND HOW WILL THEY RESPOND?

In the previous section we reviewed the major sources of government financing. In this section we need to analyze who pays for government and how it affects them.

Basic Concepts

A series of basic concepts, such as tax burden, forms the foundations for such analysis. Although many alternative definitions have been used, we define *tax burden* as the effective tax rate, or actual tax payments as a percentage of income. In order to answer the question of who pays for government we need to study the *incidence* of various taxes, or the way in which the burden is shared among different income groups. When we talk of *income groups* we usually mean mutually exclusive groups organized according to levels or ranges of income they receive. For example, let us look at three income groups: $20,001 to $30,000, $10,001 to $20,000, and $1 to $10,000.

In order to study the incidence of a particular tax, we want to discover whether such groups share equally in the tax burden or whether some groups pay more than others. However, the concept of equity is a troublesome one. For example, with our three income groups each could pay an equal dollar amount in taxes, or an equal percentage of their income, or one could argue that to provide more equal distribution of income among the three groups the upper-income groups should pay a greater percentage of their income in taxes than the lower-income groups. Which approach is more equal? While the answer to this question depends entirely on one's values, economists have devised ways of describing these three definitions of equity (see Figure 8.4).

As Figure 8.4 shows, when each income group pays an equal dollar amount in taxes, upper-income groups end up paying a smaller percentage of their income than lower-income groups pay. These situations are known as *regressive* because when equal dollar amounts in taxes are paid by all income groups, as income goes up, taxes as a percentage of income goes down. Since we know that lower-income groups must use a larger

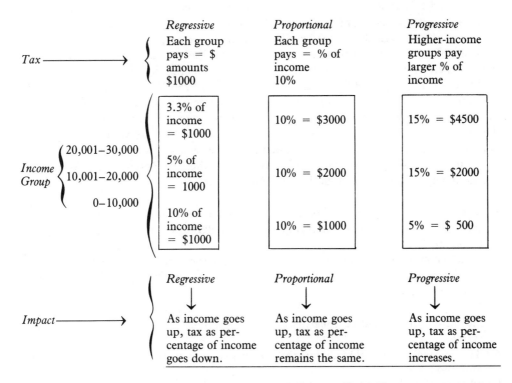

FIGURE 8.4 Examples of Regressive, Proportional, and Progressive Taxes. Tax percentage taxed on highest income of the income group.

proportion of their income for necessities, some people argue that lower-income groups are more negatively affected by regressive taxes than upper-income groups.

In contrast, some taxes are said to have a *proportional impact* on income groups. In such a situation each group would pay the same percentage of their income in taxes (for example, 10 percent, as in Figure 8.4). In absolute terms, upper-income groups end up paying more dollars, while the percentages remain the same. With *proportional taxes*, as income goes up, the tax as a percentage of income remains the same. Finally, some taxes are said to have a *progressive impact*. In this situation, as income levels go up, the percentage that each group pays in taxes goes up as well. This means that the absolute dollar amounts for each higher-income group go up as well.

Criteria for Design of Tax Systems

While we cannot decide which of the three systems—regressive, proportional, or progressive—provides greater equity, we can note that there are certain principles that tax systems design follows. One tradition for the design of tax systems is the *ability to pay principle*. Advocates of this principle argue that regardless of who receives the benefit from a particular service, such as medical care, those with higher levels of income have a greater ability to pay and should therefore bear a greater tax burden. They would argue for proportional or progressive taxes.

In contrast, another set of advocates would argue for something called the *benefit principle*. Using the benefit principle, those who receive more benefits should bear more of the tax burden regardless of their income level. For example, those people who use highways more or have school-age children should pay more of the costs for those services than people who do not drive or who have no children.

In designing a tax system for a unit of government, citizens must simply decide which principle of equity is most appropriate and then base their choices of taxes on principles that result in regressive, proportional, or progressive systems.[19] Equity, however, is not the only consideration in the design of a revenue system. A wide variety of theorists, philosophers, and economists has attempted to list the criteria appropriate for the design of revenue systems. Some of the more interesting are those of Rosvold[20] and Musgrave. For example, Musgrave suggests the following principles:

1   The distribution of the tax burden should be equitable. Everyone should be made to pay his or her "fair share" (depending upon the definition of equity selected by the community).
2   Taxes should be chosen so as to minimize interference with economic decisions in otherwise efficient markets. Such interferences impose "excess burdens" which should be minimized.
3   Where tax policy is used to achieve other objectives, such as to grant investment incentives, this should be done so as to minimize interference with the equity of the system.
4   The tax structure should facilitate the use of fiscal policy for stabilization and growth objectives.
5   The tax system should permit fair and nonarbitrary administration and it should be understandable to the taxpayer.

6 Administration and compliance cost should be as low as is compatible with other objectives.[21]

The Study of Tax Incidence

On the surface, the study of the tax burdens borne by various income groups seems straightforward enough. First, we need to estimate the effective tax actually paid by an income group and then estimate which income group particular taxpayers fit into. Finally, we need to estimate taxes as a proportion of the income held by a particular group. In practice it is extremely difficult to establish how much of the final tax was actually paid by particular income groups because of a series of responses by taxpayers and economic effects that occur between when tax rates are actually set and when taxpayers finally pay. For example, although economists disagree about who pays commercial property taxes, some argue that commercial property owners simply pass the property tax burden to their renters by raising the rent.[22] Addition of new corporate income taxes might simply cause an enterprise to leave the jurisdiction and seek one in which there are no similar taxes. In other words, studies of the tax burdens borne by various income groups must take into account the final impacts of *shifting tax incidence* from one income group to another as taxpayers respond to existing and new tax legislation.

In reality, the study of tax incidence is a highly complicated area filled with both disagreements[23] and differing approaches. Studies attempt to analyze the final tax burden after all effects of *shifting incidence forward* to consumers and *backward* to owners have been taken into account. The effects of a tax on demand and supply, the structure of markets, prices for factors of production and products, and the time period in which the changes take place must all be considered. Studies must also attempt to take into account not only the impact of a tax on revenues but also on expenditures by government.

SPECIAL ISSUES

Tax Incidence in the United States

Some of the most interesting recent work on tax incidence in the United States has been done by Musgrave, Case, and Leonard (see Table 8.3). They conclude:

> The federal system as a whole [line 6 in Table 8.3] is mildly progressive over most of the range, flanked by sharper pro-progression at both ends of the scale. If payroll taxes are included [line 7] the pattern becomes progressive throughout.
>
> The state and local picture shows a less progressive pattern for the income tax, which in fact turns regressive at the upper end. The regressivity of the general sales tax [line 11] exceeds that of excises, and the property tax distribution [line 13] is mildly regressive under the assumptions used here.
>
> The combined pattern, including federal, state and local taxes [line 17], is the most interesting part of the picture. We find the overall burden distribution to be more or less proportional over a wide range—from, say $5000 to $30,000—which includes the great bulk of all familes.[24]

TABLE 8.3. Estimates U.S.A.

| | | Income Brackets[a] | | | | | | | | | |
Taxes	Under $4,000	$4,000-$5,700	$5,700-$7,900	$7,900-$10,400	$10,400-$12,500	$12,500-$17,500	$17,500-$22,600	$22,600-$35,500	$35,500-$92,000	$92,000 and Over	All Brackets
Federal Taxes											
1. Individual income tax	2.0	2.8	5.9	7.1	7.9	10.1	10.6	12.7	14.8	18.5	9.9
2. Estate and gift tax	—	—	—	—	—	—	—	0.6	2.0	2.7	0.4
3. Corporation income tax	5.1	6.1	5.0	4.0	4.3	4.6	4.8	5.1	5.3	6.6	5.0
4. Excises and customs	2.5	2.8	3.1	3.0	2.9	2.7	2.1	1.1	0.9	0.6	2.3
5. Payroll tax	5.5	6.3	7.0	6.9	6.7	6.1	5.2	4.2	1.5	0.6	5.2
6. Total	15.2	17.9	20.8	21.6	21.6	23.4	22.6	23.8	24.5	29.1	22.7
7. Total excl. line 5	9.7	11.6	13.9	14.7	14.9	17.3	17.4	19.6	23.0	28.5	17.5
State and Local Taxes											
8. Individual income tax	—	0.1	0.3	0.6	0.7	1.1	1.4	2.3	1.6	1.3	1.0
9. Inheritance tax	—	—	—	—	—	—	—	0.2	0.6	0.8	0.1
10. Corporation income tax	0.4	0.5	0.4	0.4	0.3	0.4	0.4	0.4	0.4	0.5	0.4
11. General excise tax	3.4	2.8	2.5	2.3	2.2	2.0	1.7	1.0	0.5	0.3	1.8
12. Excises[b]	2.7	3.0	3.3	3.0	2.9	2.5	1.9	1.0	0.8	0.6	2.1
13. Property tax	6.7	5.7	4.7	4.3	4.0	3.7	3.3	3.0	2.9	3.3	3.9
14. Payroll tax	0.2	0.5	0.8	1.0	1.0	1.0	1.1	1.2	0.2	0.1	0.8
15. Total	13.4	12.5	11.9	11.6	11.1	10.6	9.7	9.1	7.1	6.9	10.3
16. Total excl. line 14	13.2	12.1	11.1	10.6	10.1	9.6	8.6	7.9	6.9	6.8	9.5
All Levels											
17. Total	28.5	30.5	32.8	33.1	32.8	33.9	32.4	32.9	31.6	35.9	33.0
18. Total excl. lines 5, 14	22.9	23.7	25.0	25.3	25.0	26.9	26.0	27.5	29.9	35.3	27.0

NOTE: Items may not add to totals because of rounding.

SOURCE: Richard and Peggy Musgrave, *Public Finance in Theory and Practice* (New York: McGraw-Hill, 1980) p. 267.

[a] As noted in the text, these estimates pertain to 1968 levels of income and revenue. Since personal income (per capita, in nominal terms) has doubled since then, the current pattern of effective rates may be approximated by doubling the income brackets accordingly.

[b] Includes motor vehicles licenses, excises, and miscellaneous revenue.

Taxes and Taxpayers' Behavior—Supply-Side Economics and the Laffer Curve

One of the most recent arguments about taxpayer behavior comes from Laffer, who argues that reducing tax rates will result in increased investment, productivity, and growth on the part of individuals and corporations and subsequently increases in tax revenues.[25] Laffer's assertion is part of the wave of popular sentiment, as well as some professional analysis, connected with the U.S. tax revolt of the late 1970s. Laffer's argument, explained with the assistance of Figure 8.5, is as follows: If taxes are 100 percent of all new income, individuals lose all incentive to produce, and as a result no government revenues will be generated. If at the same time tax rates are set at 0, the government will gain no revenues either. If taxes are decreased from 100 percent to point A in Figure 8.5 some producer will develop sufficient economies of scale to begin production and tax revenues will rise to point A. At the same time, if tax rates are increased from 0 to point B, most firms will continue to produce, although some will lose their incentives. However, similar revenues will be generated. If tax rates are dropped from point A to C, more firms will enter the production process, and additional tax revenues will be generated up to point C. If at the same time tax rates are raised from point B to D, more revenues will be generated, but some firms will leave the market or develop less incentive to produce. Ultimately, revenues and production are maximized at point E. Laffer talks of the prohibitive area of government where tax rates create a disincentive to production and reduce output and tax revenues.

SUMMARY

In this chapter we have attempted to provide an analysis of three critical questions that officials involved in public budgeting must be capable of answering: How much money will be needed to finance government operations? Where will government revenues come

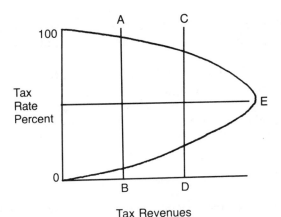

FIGURE 8.5 The Laffer Curve. (*From Jude Wanniski, "Taxes, Revenues and the 'Laffer Curve.'" In* The Public Interest, *Winter 1978, pp. 3–16*)

from? Who will bear the burden of financing government and how will they respond?

In order to answer the question *how much money will be needed to finance government operations*, we reviewed the major methods of revenue and expenditure projections. We paid special attention to simple extrapolation of past trends and modeling techniques such as those used in the New Haven model.

In an effort to provide answers to the question of *where government revenues come from*, we analyzed patterns of federal, state, and local revenue collection. We also examined the major characteristics, strengths, and weaknesses of individual and corporate income taxes; sales taxes; property taxes; payroll taxes; estate, inheritance, and gift taxes; user fees; and grants. We also explored the rationale and methods of government borrowing, and analysis of the debt capacity of various units of governnment.

Finally, in an effort to answer the question *who bears the burden of financing government*, we reviewed the basic concepts in the study of tax incidence, such as tax burden; regressive, proportional, and progressive taxes; and forward and backward incidence shifting. We reviewed criteria for the design of tax systems and explored recent studies of tax incidence at the federal level. We looked at some of the more recent theories of taxpayer behavior provided by supply-side economics.

The degree to which professionals in the budgeting field must work daily with the three basic questions about revenue systems depends greatly upon the size of the jurisdiction in which they work. Budget directors in small cities must not only design and analyze the expenditure side of their budgets but also make their own revenue projections, propose new taxes, and be aware of their impacts on the populace. In larger cities, states, and at the federal level, each of the critical questions about revenue systems may be handled by different people, departments, and in some cases totally different agencies. Regardless of where students of budgeting may work later, they need to be aware of the concepts and techniques used to provide answers to these critical questions.

PREPARING FOR THE CASE

The case which follows raises many of the critical issues about budgeting and revenue systems discussed in this book. Read it carefully with these questions in mind:

1 What are the major problems with New York's budgeting and revenue systems? What did the systems do or fail to do?
2 What changes should be made in existing systems?
3 What strategy should be employed for keeping the city liquid and solvent?
4 What should be done first and what later?

CASE STUDY

A case study of the financial crisis that occurred in 1975 in New York City follows. The reader is asked to consider him or her self as a decision maker in this situation. Using the analytic tools described in this chapter, attempt to identify the sources of the crisis. Were the borrowing techniques employed appropriate? The revenue and expenditure projections? The debt limits? Were income sources being applied correctly to the operating and capital budgets respectively? Which of the six ACIR "warning signs" discussed in Chapter three are observable in the New York case? Does the city have the data to construct a funds flow chart such as that depicted in Figure 3.1 of Chapter three? Would such an organization of the data provide the basis for an adequate control system? What recommendations would you make for solving New York's financial problem?

CASE STUDY

New York City's Financial Crisis 1965–1977

Maureen Malin

Introduction

In the fall of 1976, New York City was in the depths of a financial crisis. For many years, the city's costs for services of all kinds had outrun its income, and its ability to borrow funds was severely constrained. As a result of the city's sharp increase in borrowing and its simultaneous decline in revenues, New York had found itself unable to repay its outstanding loans. Thus, in 1975, the city had found itself on the brink of bankruptcy. It was spared the ignominy of insolvency by last minute state and federal intervention. However, the need to balance the city's budget had forced Mayor Beame to curtail expenditures, resulting in substantial cutbacks in services and in the layoff of large numbers of municipal workers.

Background

During the period from 1965 to 1973 the federal government channeled massive amounts of aid to urban areas, both directly and through the inter-mediation of the states. In the mid-sixties, the "Great Society" agenda of President Lyndon B. Johnson sought to bring new public services to poor and minority populations residing for the most part in the older central cities. The programs that were launched under its aegis ranged from early childhood education to neighborhood health care; from manpower training to legal aid. With a modest investment of local revenue, city officials were able to mount expensive new programs that offered numerous job opportunities and at least the prospect of making valuable services to the cities' poorer residents. General revenue sharing, initiated in 1972 by President Richard M. Nixon, differed fundamentally from the "Great Society." Instead of attempting to deliver specified services to specifically targeted recipients, revenue sharing moneys were given to state and local governments, virtually without strings, to be used as they saw fit.

For the older central cities, almost two-thirds of all additional revenue received during the years 1965-73 came from state and federal governments, or was borrowed. As such, taxpayers had to pay for only 35 cents of each dollar of new spending by their city governments, a reversal of the historical split between local and external funding. In view of the favorable terms on which federal assistance could be procured after 1965, it was not surprising that municipal spending climbed as rapidly as it did. Similarly, the failure of federal aid to grow since that time was responsible for much of the recent pressure on city budgets. Beginning in 1974, the rate of growth of federal assistance to the state and local sectors, which had averaged 17 percent per year for the previous decade, fell to 6.6 percent despite record inflation. Moreover, for some of the declining central cities, the showdown in federal aid actually began earlier. The cities that had been most successful in securing programmatic aid under the "Great Society" discovered that general revenue sharing, with its formula-determined aid allocation, treated them less generously than had their own skills at grantsmanship.

Between 1965 and 1973, New York, like other declining cities, relied on federal and state funding for most of its expenditure growth. Beginning in 1973, its traditional sources of external assistance failed. But, instead of balancing its budget through expenditure reductions or tax increases, New York City accelerated its net borrowings to meet its operating costs, treating the debt it accumulated as if it were merely transfer assistance which would never have to be repaid. From the beginning of fiscal 1973 through the end of fiscal 1975, the city's outstanding general purpose debt jumped from $9.0 billion to $12.4 billion, more than compensating for the lost growth in state and federal aid. By 1975, New York City accounted for almost 40 percent of all the outstanding short-term debt issued by local jurisdictions in the entire country.

New York City's financial difficulties were exacerbated by its general economic decline. Since 1969, New York had lost almost 660,000 jobs; in 1976 it had somewhat less than 3 million jobs to offer its 8 million residents. It was estimated that 3.5 million were required to sustain the city's population. In the late 1960s, the city responded to this decline in the private sector by creating 60,000 new municipal positions. However, most of these had been eliminated by 1976 in the government's efforts to balance its budget.

The most significant decline in jobs occurred in the manufacturing sector. Twenty years ago, New York City had more manufacturing than any metropolitian region in the United States. Its factories produced primarily consumer goods such as apparel, beer and printed products. The typical enterprise employed less than 500 people and was heavily dependent on a chain of other nearby enterprises. Over the years, however, the costs of manufacturing in the central city rose, and increasing numbers of employers moved their plants out of New York.

Large companies with headquarters in New York City were also leaving. Rising crime rates, deteriorating schools and neighborhoods, and high living costs made it increasingly difficult for corporations to attract managers to the city. As a result, although New York had been the headquarters for 140 of the country's 500 largest industrial companies in the 1960s, by 1976 only 94 remained. And, of those who stayed, many maintained sparcely staffed offices, preferring to house their central management operations elsewhere. This relocation of corporate headquarters further reduced jobs in the service and communications sectors.

One neighborhood especially affected by this decline in jobs was the South Bronx. By 1974, the South Bronx had lost 650 of the 2,000 manufacturing establishments which had been located there in 1959 and 17,688 of the 54,037 jobs they provided. Few businesses moved in, and those that did, among them the Hunts Point wholesale food market and the Coca-Cola warehouse, brought most of their employees with them from elsewhere in the city. Already one of the poorest neighborhoods in the city, the plight of the South Bronx and its 450,000 inhabitants worsened.

The South Bronx had once been a collection of predominantly white middle-income neighborhoods. However, in the two decades following World War II, increasing numbers of black and Spanish-speaking residents had moved in. By 1976, about half of the South Bronx's residents were Puerto Rican, a third were black and only 17 percent were white. Median family income averaged $5,200 in 1970, 46 percent below the citywide average of $9,682. Twenty-eight percent of the neighborhood's families were on welfare. About half of the sixteen to twenty-one year olds had dropped out of school, and of these 30 percent were unemployed. Housing stock had deteriorated, destroyed by neglect or by one of the neighborhood's 33 nightly fires; drug addiction and alcoholism abounded along with increases in reported assaults and robberies. The city responded to the neighborhood's needs by financing low-income housing projects and providing remedial, social and medical services to its inhabitants. For the most part, these efforts proved to be costly failures.

The Roots of the Financial Crisis

New York City's financial decline began at least a decade ago. Until the mid-1960s, the city had relatively small amounts of operating debt outstanding at year-end, but in 1965, the last year of Mayor Wagner's administration, the state legislature enabled the city to use a form of unadmitted deficit financing. Shortly before June 30, the end of the fiscal year, Wagner's 1964-1965 budget was in the red by about $100 million. Traditionally, the city government had closed budget gaps by drawing on reserves from a "rainy day" contingency fund and by issuing budget notes. Budget notes represented admitted deficit spending but under state law only very limited amounts could be sold in any year. Once the notes were issued, the mayor had to appropriate funds to cover them, usually in the next year's budget. Wagner's 1964-1965 budget gap exceeded by a wide margin the amount of budget notes he could legally issue. Moreover, he had dipped into the rainy-day fund so frequently that its reserves were insufficient, even when coupled with budget notes, to make up the revenue shortfall. The problem was resolved at the last minute on June 23, 1965, with new state legislation that increased the city's authority to issue "revenue anticipation notes," or RAN's.

The changes at first glance seemed to be minor, but the consequences were monumental. For years the city had been allowed to issue RAN's against forthcoming state and federal aid and certain uncollected fees and taxes, but they could not exceed the amount of such aid and fees actually collected during the prior year. In some years during the fifties and early 1960s, the city issued no RAN's at all, but when it did, this constraint assured that they were repaid by year-end. The new legislation made two substantial changes. First, it did away with the requirement that borrowings against aid be related to the prior year's collections. Instead, it allowed the city to borrow against the mayor's estimate of state and federal aid applicable to the current year's budget and left open the question of how the notes would be repaid if estimates turned out to be too optimistic. Secondly, the new law allowed the city to borrow, for the first time, against certain taxes and fees that, although owed, were not scheduled for payment during the year. Shortly after the legislation was passed, Mayor Wagner issued $56 million worth of RAN's to help close the budget deficit. All this led Moody's and Standard and Poor's to lower the city's "A" credit rating a notch.

In the fall of 1965, John Lindsay defeated Wagner's last comptroller, Abe Beame, in the mayoral election. He came into office publicly proclaiming his desire to restore fiscal integrity. However, Mayor Lindsay proved to better at raising revenues than at cutting back on spending. He installed an income tax, raised property taxes several times, and increased transit fares from 15 cents to 35 cents. In addition, Mayor Lindsay proved to be adept at attracting federal funds, and, despite his feuds with Governor Nelson Rockefeller, state aid flowed freely too, especially during his first term. In that period the share of the budget burden borne by the city revenues dropped from 67% to 58%.[1]

During Lindsay's first term, moreover, New York's fiscal affairs benefited from a flourishing local economy. The city's property tax base, which had expanded in the early 1960s with the apartment building boom, continued upward with office building expansion at the end of the decade. Between 1965 and 1969, the city's population was more or less stable and at the same time 220,000 additional jobs were created in the city. However, jobs in the municipal public sector accounted for 37% of that increase.[2] In addition, there was an ominous rise in the welfare rolls during this healthy economic period. When Mayor Lindsay came into office, about 500,000 New Yorkers were on welfare. By the end of 1969 the number had doubled.[3] In 1970, the nationwide recession adversely affected New York City. In that one year, there was a net loss of 53,000 jobs. Yet municipal employment continued to rise.[4] This played havoc with the 1969-1970 budget. But whatever the size of the true deficit, it was disguised by the sale of large amounts of revenue anticipation notes. During Lindsay's first term, the city almost always paid off borrowings against state and federal aid before the fiscal year was out. In 1970, however, year-end borrowings against these funds totaled some $420 million.[5] The comptroller at that time was again Abe Beame, who had won back his old job in 1969.

Once this borrowing began, it was difficult to halt. Revenues used to pay off the maturing notes had to be replaced with new borrowings. The only way to break the cycle would have been to make budget appropriations to pay off the debt. But this would have required cutting funds elsewhere, or raising additional revenues, or both. Another hefty layer of debt was added in 1971, when the economy deteriorated even further. Borrowings against state and federal receivables rose by 130% - to around $965 million.[6] Financial problems plagued Lindsay throughout his second term. The downturn in the city's economy that had begun in 1970 was not a cyclical dip but part of a persistent trend. Even with the city government's payroll expanding, New York City lost jobs in every succeeding year through 1975, a total of more than 500,000 jobs or 14% of the jobs that were available in 1969.[7] In the U.S. as a whole over this same period,

---

[1] Wyndham Robertson, "Going Broke the New York Way," Fortune, August 1975, p. 147.

[2] Ibid.

[3] The New York Times, August 17, 1975.

[4] Ibid.

[5] The Wall Street Journal (New York), May 28, 1975.

[6] Ibid.

[7] The New York Times, March 28, 1976.

nonfarm jobs increased by 7%.[1] Moreover, while the income tax base was
eroding, the city was losing the kicker provided earlier by state and federal
funds. Viewed as a percentage of the total budget, state aid peaked in 1968,
and then began to slope off. Mayor Lindsay responded to this changed environment by slowing the rise in spending. During his second term, the budget
rose by 40%, as compared to 60% during his first term.[2]

         Thus, the process by which New York City had been able to accumu-
late such large amounts of debt was a relatively simple one: the comptroller
issued both short-term notes (to be repaid in a year or less) and long-term
bonds. Both types of debt were then sold in the tax-free municipal market by
financial institutions. Once legal requirements had been met, there was no
formal limit to the amount of debt which these institutions could place. As
a result, the amount of the city's outstanding debt increased dramatically.
In 1974, for example, New York City sold $1.5 billion worth of bonds, three
times what it had sold in 1969. By the spring of 1975, the city had nearly
$8 billion in bonds outstanding.[3] In addition, its short-term borrowing had
climbed twelvefold in a decade. At the close of the 1975 fiscal year, New
York City had $6 billion in notes outstanding, about 40% of all the short-
term notes issued by all states, cities, counties and local authorities
in the nation.[4] In no other major city had the short-term borrowing grown
by such leaps and bounds. In no other city was the ratio of debt to the value
of taxable real estate so high.[5] Moreover, the cost of servicing the city's
debt had exploded from $644 million in 1969 to $1.2 billion in 1975. Debt
service, the cost of principal and interest on loans, amounted to nearly 17%
of its budget, almost twice the amount that the city spent on police and fire
protection.[6] And yet, as the city's borrowing had soared, it did so with
little real political opposition. Rather, the state legislature approved
one borrowing plan after another. Finally, the financial institutions,
marketers and purchasers of the city's debt, began to question the city's
fiscal soundness. (Exhibit 1 compares the changes in New York City's
operating budget expenditures for fiscal years 1966-67 and 1974-75.
Exhibit 2 presents the total city expense budgets and debt issued for the
fiscal years from 1965 through 1975. Exhibit 3 shows the growth in New
York's short-term debt, from FY 1968-69 through FY 1974-75.)

Lindsay's Legacies

         As borrowings increased, Lindsay began to court buyers of municipal
bonds, arranging tours of the city for big institutional investors from all
over the country. Underwriters began getting orders from new customers
around the U.S. and, by the end of 1973, both Moody's and Standard and Poor's,
apparently converted themselves, had restored the city's "A" credit rating.
The rating agencies and the new customers for the city's securities disre-

---

[1] Ibid.

[2] Robertson, op. cit., p. 148.

[3] The Wall Street Journal (New York), October 30, 1975.

[4] Ibid.

[5] The Wall Street Journal (New York), May 28, 1975.

[6] The New York Times, August 17, 1975.

garded not only the rapid buildup in borrowing but also two other fiscal innovations of the Lindsay administration. One was the practice of shifting operating costs out of the expense budget into the capital budget, and other accounting practices designed to obscure the deficit. The other was the expansion of pension benefits extracted by the various municipal employee unions during his administration.

In New York City, the capital budget is separate from the expense budget, and all the items in it (school construction, roads, etc.) are financed by issuing debt. Because the capital budget is not financed from normal revenues, Lindsay found it an attractive place to put a great variety of operating expenses. He began making these transfers as early as 1968, when the state legislature passed a law permitting cities in New York State to issue 30-year bonds for certain job-opportunity programs. Thus, for example, some manpower training programs came to be financed through the sale of bonds. The cumulative cost of these programs in 1976 was around $200 million, and the state comptroller's office estimated that for each dollar of direct costs incurred, the city would spend an additional 57 cents in interest over the life of the bonds. By the time the capital budget for the fiscal year 1974-75 was drawn up, Comptroller Harrison J. Goldin announced that it included $737 million worth of such expense items - or about 50% of the entire city-financed portion of the budget.[1] Since long-term borrowing was limited by law, this inevitably meant that brick-and-mortar projects suffered.

In addition to transferring operating expenses in to the capital budget, the Lindsay-Beame team also employed other accounting techniques to balance the city's budget, as required by state law. Utilizing the principle that "this year's costs are next year's costs," Comptroller Beame suggested in 1971, that Mayor Lindsay balance this budget by charging $25 million in end-of-the-year teachers' salaries to the following year by simply having the checks released on July 1 instead of June 30. Although Mayor Lindsay labeled the idea as "stopgap financial juggling," Mr. Beame issued the checks that way anyway, winning considerable praise for his legerdemain. Mayor Lindsay and Mr. Beame learned their lesson well. Good intentions went by the board and in 1975 $150 million worth of payrolls were pushed into July.[2] The trouble was that there was not enough cash coming into the city in July, thus forcing the city to borrow additional funds to meet the payrolls. Revenues were dealt with similarly. Here the rule that was applied read: "Next year's revenues are this year's revenues." For example, the city received large amounts of education aid in September, October and November of each year. Several years ago, New York City simply decided to count those payments as revenues to its fiscal year ending the previous June 30. It thus had the revenues but not the cash in hand. As a result, it had to borrow against future revenues to pay its bills. The city also borrowed against sales taxes and other revenues that came in as cash during the first quarter of the following year but that were generated in the fourth quarter of the current year.

---

[1] Robertson, op. cit., p. 149.

[2] The New York Times, August 17, 1975.

The above transfers of funds, however, did not prove sufficient to meet the city's financial needs. Consequently, as Mayor Wagner did before him, Mr. Lindsay won permission, in 1971, from the state legislature to borrow money to balance the budget at the end of the year, promising to pay it back within three years. He did not. In 1973, $308 million of the borrowing was still owed and Mr. Beame later increased that figure by $150 million to balance the budget for that year. In 1974, Mayor Beame borrowed another $62 million outright to balance his budget but proposed to liquidate the entire accumulated debt of $520 million with special 10-year bonds from a new corporation created by the state legislature.[1] Those bonds were never issued and the debt remained. However, New York City's borrowing was supposed to be repaid by revenues as they were received. But as soon as revenues were collected, there were other expenses that had to be met by borrowing. Further, in some cases, those revenues were dubious at best: in near desperation, the city had overestimated revenues and underestimated expenditures each year, thus insuring that it had to borrow more cash than it expected to receive. For years, the city had borrowed against the full value of real estate taxes to be collected, for example, even though tax delinquency in the 1970s had been the highest since the 1930s Depression. More specifically, real estate taxes of about $2.7 billion made up a quarter of New York City's total revenues in 1975. In the three-year period from fiscal 1973 through fiscal 1975, however, at least $400 million of this was in arrears. Total taxes in arrears, including taxes for the years prior to 1973 pushed this figure over $600 million.[2] In addition, an audit by the state comptroller found the city had been borrowing against federal and state aid which it had little chance of ever receiving. In several cases, the city had borrowed against aid that its books showed as still anticipated but which had actually been received and used to pay expenses.

The second legacy of the Lindsay years, the vastly enlarged pension costs, resulted from an increase in the numbers, salaries and benefits of municipal employees. By 1975, municipal workers in New York City numbered around 330,000 thus making them a significant voting bloc. In addition, the city's labor costs, which accounted for half of the expense budget, had risen by an average of more than 9% annually over the last two decades. As a reflection of their political potency, in mayoral election years average payroll increases had been closer to 14%.[3] Moreover, the public employee unions of New York City had been the first in the nation to develop clout at the bargaining table. They set an example for the rise of public unions in other cities as they aggressively led their members through a series of strikes that became landmarks of urban turmoil. But after a decade and a half of winning progressively richer contracts, the unions in New York found themselves, in 1976, battling to preserve what civil servants still cherish most: that certain paycheck in hard times.

Robert Wagner's relationship with the municipal unions was a clubby one which paid off in political support for him and rising salaries for the workers. In 1958, Mayor Wagner gave city employees the right to bargain collectively. However, he rarely showed much generosity with regard to pensions, although despite his objections, some pension benefits

---

[1] Ibid.

[2] The Wall Street Journal (New York), May 20, 1975.

[3] Robertson, op. cit., p. 145.

were liberalized by the state legislature. In the early sixties, the legislature passed a series of laws which changed the "base period" on which benefits were to be calculated. Traditionally, the basis had been the average of the employee's salary in the five-year period prior to retirement. The new legislation led to changing the base to the final year's salary. Because of earlier legislation enacted in the fifties, the base salary also included overtime, thus encouraging employees about to retire to accumulate sizable amounts of overtime in their last year.

When John Lindsay took office, he vowed to expel the union "power brokers" from City Hall. He tried to take the bargaining process out of politics by bringing in professionals to handle negotiations. It never worked. His dislike for hidden deals escalated wage disputes into moral confrontations, most notably the devastating sanitation workers' and teachers' strikes of 1968. To extract the city from these embroglios, the mayor ended up acquiescing to far heftier settlements than had his predecessors. Pension costs totaled $317 million when Lindsay entered office; it doubled in the next eight years and doubled again in the following two years. Experts predicted that the pension system would cost $1.7 billion by 1980.[1] In return, Mayor Lindsay failed, until the last two years of his tenure, to win any of the productivity improvements that might have softened the impact of skyrocketing costs. It took him years of negotiations, for instance, to switch the working schedules of garbage collectors so that more workers were on the job in the beginning of the week when more refuse was on the streets. Consequently, New York City's pension costs were considerably greater than those of private and most other government employers. The city paid more than 20% of payroll for employees covered by each of the major retirement programs. For nonmanufacturing corporations in the U.S., the average was estimated to be less than 10%.[2]

In the late 1960s, it was relatively easy for a city government to buy its way out of strikes: New York's bureaucracy was expanding; Congress was pumping money into urban programs; and the economy was exuberant. The atmosphere was conducive to the financing of collective-bargaining agreements through borrowing, especially when the city preferred not to expose in its budget the amount of money it was willing to pay to settle a contract. But the good times began to pall for the unions when Mayor Lindsay, trying to plug his own budget gaps, and cope with the recession moved to stunt the bureaucracy's growth by imposing a freeze on hiring. By the time Abe Beame moved into City Hall in 1974, the time was right to make a similar attempt to flag the growth of municipal pay increases. Similar in style to Robert Wagner, Mr. Beame benefited from a calmed social climate which had defanged the racial antagonism that had dominated union battles during the Lindsay administration, and his ace in the hole was the city's near financial collapse. At a time when the latest government figures showed major settlements around the country in the first quarter of 1975 averaging 12.5%, New York under Mayor Beame was able to offer no increases in salary or benefits.[3]

---

[1] The New York Times, August 17, 1975.

[2] Robertson, op. cit., p. 212.

[3] The Wall Street Journal (New York), June 30, 1975.

The Eleventh Hour

When Mr. Beame was elected mayor in 1973, he inherited a sizable deficit from Mayor Lindsay. After he was safely ensconced in City Hall, Mayor Beame acknowledged that the 1973-74 budget had a deficit of $150 million and that the revenue shortfall for fiscal 1974-75 would be about $370 million (most of which was accounted for by an appropriation to redeem budget notes issued under Mayor Lindsay).[1]

In the fall of 1974, the city's Comptroller Harrison J. Goldin, challenged Mr. Beame's estimates on the current budget. Mayor Beame had announced that shortfalls in revenues combined with anticipated expenditures had produced a $430 million deficit. Goldin claimed that the deficit was more like $650 million.[2] Many people were fascinated by the Beame-Goldin feud, but the city's bankers were not amused. In October 1974, a $475 million bond offering turned out to be what one banker called a "big red one." It was the largest tax-exempt bond offering in history and it had sold poorly. Many underwriters had suffered losses on the deal, and afterwards the interest charges which the city had to pay to borrow funds took a big step upward. In December and January, to the consternation of city officials, two large issues of notes were offered at a cost of around 9.5%, the highest in the city's history.

The largest banks in New York City held in their own portfolios about $1.25 billion of the $13 billion in city bonds and notes. However, it was not in the ownership of these notes and bonds that they had made their profits. Rather profits for the banks had come from trading. For years, the city's banks, along with banks and other financial institutions around the country, had been able to underwrite city notes and bonds and then resell them at what amounted to a substantial markup. In the autumn of 1974, however, banks around the country had become increasingly worried about the risk in holding and trading New York City notes and bonds. They had discovered, for instance, that they no longer needed tax-free municipal securities when they could purchase property through new leasing subsidiaries and then reap tax write-offs from the depreciation. As a result, the banks in New York had been finding that the market for the city's securities was shrinking at an alarming rate. To combat further erosion of confidence in New York City and its ability to meet its financial responsibilities, on December 17, 1974, top level municipal bond executives from Chase Manhattan, First National City, Chemical Bank, Morgan Guaranty Trust and others descended on Gracie Mansion for a hastily summoned emergency meeting. These bankers had requested an urgent meeting with Mayor Beame to complain about the spectacle of the city's top two political officers disagreeing over the size of the budget deficit. They also wanted to report that they had recently suffered their biggest losses in history in trying to support the city's debt. Mayor Beame's response was to blame the bankers for not trying hard enough to "sell" the city. Further, in subsequent speeches and press conferences, Mayor Beame accused the banks of "poisoning our well" with their "corrosive negativism," which, in his opinion, served to tarnish the city's image unfairly and to make it increasingly difficult to market its notes and bonds.[3]

---

[1] Robertson, op. cit., p. 212.

[2] The New York Times, August 17, 1975.

[3] Ibid.

Springtime saw the long, relentless slide of the city into fiscal incapacity. Mayor Beame continued to spar with leaders of the financial community as the city staggered from turning point to ominous turning point. There was the day, in February for instance, that a syndicate of banks headed by Bankers Trust and Chase Manhattan cancelled their purchase of $260 million in tax-anticipation notes because the city would not provide them with sufficient information about uncollected real estate taxes; the day that Standard and Poor's suspended its "A" rating on city securities because borrowing had gone out of control; the day that Mayor Beame travelled to Washington, hat in hand, with a vain plea to the Treasury Department for cash advances; and, finally, the day in May that Chase, Citibank and Morgan Guaranty closed the door in the city's face, refusing to buy $280 million in notes the city had to sell in order to pay its obligations. The mayor's staff, at the same time, tried to diminish the crisis by describing the city's financial situation as a cash-flow problem. The city was beginning to find it impossible to borrow the cash to pay its bills. In May and June, the city officials announced, New York was going to have to borrow $1.5 billion, most of it simply to pay off loans that were coming due. And, at the banks, meanwhile, grave concern was yielding to panic. One banker later remarked of this period: "We had a Million Dollar Club on Wall Street. You belonged to it if you had lost a million dollars underwriting city securities. Its membership was widespread."[1]

June brought further disturbing news from State Comptroller Arthur Levitt, who had undertaken an examination of the city's financial records. Although this study was by no means all-encompassing, Levitt found chaos in the city's record keeping for receivables in seven large agencies. His examiners looked only at receivables purportedly owed by the state and federal governments and only those still carried on the books as owing for fiscal years prior to July 1, 1974. They found that, whereas the city comptroller's records showed old receivables of $543.8 million and $373.3 million still owing on December 31, 1974 and March 31, 1975, proper accounting techniques would have put the figures at $110.9 million and $48.7 million.[2] The report's findings raised questions about the legality of the revenue anticipation notes (RAN's) issued against the nonexistent receivables. Beginning at least as early as 1973, when Beame was comptroller, RAN's had been issued against receivables that, even on the city's books, were insufficient to support these borrowings. Once Goldin had issued RAN's when there had been no supporting receivables on the books at the time of the issue. Six other issues had been sold when the book value of the receivables had either been insufficient or, in the judgment of the state examiners, overstated. In all, the dubious issues, over the course of 14 months (1973-1975), had amounted to $1.3 billion.[3] Goldin claimed that the city's method of processing fiscal information had made it impossible to obtain up-to-date figures.

Some wondered in retrospect why the bankers had waited until the market had virtually disappeared and the threat of litigation was upon them before they began questioning the city's fiscal policies and accounting procedures. When Thomas Labrecque, Executive Vice President at Chase Manhattan was asked why the banks had not moved sooner, he indicated that

---

[1] The New York Times, August 17, 1975.

[2] Robertson, op. cit., p. 214.

[3] Ibid.

bankers operate under a different set of rules when dealing with the credit problems of corporations on the one hand and a political entity such as New York City on the other. Referring to the "due diligence" meeting that precedes corporate underwritings, Labrecque noted:

> It clearly is not considered bad form, or wrong to rake a corporation over the coals. There was some question as to whether you had the right to rake the mayor over the coals... Could we have generated a confluence that would have brought this out earlier? I guess all I can say is I wish we had.[1]

It soon became apparent that the implementation of budgetary and accounting reforms alone would not be sufficient to alleviate New York City's financial woes. Rather what was needed was to balance the budget by decreasing municipal spending. However, although this solution seemed to be a sensible and businesslike approach to the city's troubles, New York was not a business. The recommended cost-cutting surgery proved to be a major operation, politically painful and socially tumultous.

Creation of the Municipal Assistance Corporation

Several people had been watching New York City's problems with unusual interest all spring, but few more than Governor Hugh L. Carey, Mayor Beame's long-time ally and comrade-in-arms from the political clubhouse world of Brooklyn. Mr. Carey had experienced default. In February of 1974, he had failed to prevent default on notes issued by the state Urban Development Corporation (U.D.C.) and then had to watch as interest rates on other state bonds climbed higher in response, bringing work on many state construction projects to a halt. In March, he had created a new state agency to issue bonds to help the U.D.C. As Governor Carey found himself being inexorably drawn into New York City's fiscal crisis, a crisis which offered little opportunity and many pitfalls, he pondered the advisability of creating a similar state agency to shore up the city's shaking financial obligations. His determination to intervene was clinched by an ill-fated visit to Washington with the mayor. In May, Governor Carey and Mayor Beame had sat in the Oval Office listening to Gerald Ford spin homilies about families living within their budgets. To make matters worse for the two New York officials, Nelson Rockefeller had been at the President's side, bringing up his favorite points about New York.

Although Governor Carey had been outraged by the reception he and Mr. Beame had received at the White House, he had been no less angered by the mayor and his staff. Carey had arranged the White House meeting in response to Beame's claims that the city needed to borrow $1.5 billion to meet its immediate financial obligations. However, shortly after the meeting with President Ford in Washington, Beame's staff announced abruptly that their needs were actually only $1 billion. A half-billion dollars had suddenly been "found" in a special segregated fund that, Deputy Mayor John Cavanagh explained, had been there all along, although there had been some legal question as to whether it could be used.

---

[1] Ibid.

About this same time, there had begun to be talk in New York
that the city should default. Proponents of default claimed that such a
strategy might give the city a chance to seize upon a court order from its
creditors to freeze wages, curtail its services and cut costs. In addition,
some politicians asserted that default would demonstrate to the banks that
they had to lend additional money to the city or suffer the consequences.
What these politicians failed to realize, however, was that a default would
not break the banks. The large New York banks themselves held $1.25
billion in the city's debt securities. That, plus whatever they held for
customers' trust accounts, could have brought the total in the banks'
holdings to $3.3 billion. Federal banking officials had estimated the
potential bank asset reduction from a drop in the market value of the bonds
at only $130 million to $140 million.[1] The banks, thus, were not likely to
feel compelled to offer new aid to protect their old investments.

Such thinking about default had alarmed Governor Carey. Unknown
to the Governor, however, one member in the city's financial community,
Felix G. Rohatyn, had been watching the same situation with even greater
fears than his. Mr. Rohatyn, an investment banker, was considered perhaps
the shrewdest and toughest merger-and-acquisition specialist in the business.
Known to some as the "Henry Kissinger of finance," his reputation had grown
as he had put together the deals that: bailed out Lockheed; called the
Justice Department off of its antitrust suit against International Telephone
and Telegraph; and staved off bankruptcy at shaky brokerage houses in 1970
and 1971. Default, in Mr. Rohatyn's view, would probably send the value of
$13 billion in city securities skidding, with enormous losses to their owners:
pension funds, charitable institutions and thousands of individuals and
businesses. Following the Urban Development Corporation default, a default
by New York might completely paralyze the borrowing ability of every other
city in the state. In addition to these economic factors, the city would
suffer vast humiliation as it became a national spectacle of insolvency.
And there was still another bleak vision, that of countless lawsuits brought
by the city's bondholders exercising their right to a first lien on the
city's tax revenues, a right that would probably be upheld in court with
the possible consequence that payment of municipal wages and salaries could
be held up for months. Under such a scenario, Mr. Rohatyn foresaw the workings
of the city grinding down, resulting in a series of violent social explosions.

In May 1975, Mr. Rohatyn expressed some of these thoughts over
breakfast in Washington with his friend Robert Strauss, national chairman
of the Democratic party. Within days, Mr. Strauss telephoned David Burke,
Carey's secretary. Mr. Rohatyn and Governor Carey met in New York City.
They were later joined by Mr. Rohatyn's friend, former Federal Judge Simon H.
Rifkind; Richard R. Shinn, head of Metropolitan Life Insurance; and
Donald B. Smiley, chairman of R.H. Macy. Within weeks their idea was born:
a new Municipal Assistance Corporation (MAC) would be created to undertake
$3 billion of the city's borrowing during the summer months by issuing
its own bonds. In the meantime the city would institute reforms, restoring
its own access to the marketplace. The MAC bonds would be protected by the
state's setting aside proceeds from the city's stock-transfer tax and sales
tax and transferring those proceeds to the corporation directly, bypassing
the city. This provision reflected the fact that the banks did not feel
the city was sufficiently responsible to handle these tax funds itself.

---

[1] The Wall Street Journal (New York), May 20, 1975.

It was a daring move. But the most serious final hurdle that faced "Big MAC," as Governor Carey called the new agency, was to sell the idea to a reluctant, suspicious mayor, City Council and Board of Estimate. Only if the city realized that it had no other choice would its leaders be willing to hand over to the corporation the broad authority to oversee the city's budget and institute a near revolutionary change in the city's accounting practices. There was something embarrassing about it to all city officials. The City Council and the Board of Estimate bridled; one borough president said it represented "a bailout for the banks, not the city."[1] The politicians stalled. Mr. Rohatyn told them their objections were thoughtful, perhaps, and possibly even relevant - to other circumstances in other days. But, said Mr. Rohatyn, the blunt truth was that if, by Monday, June 9, Big MAC was not in business, "you're finished."[2] Lawyers for the banks, the city and the state labored through the second weekend in June to come up with a Big MAC agreement that would save the city's face and yet rescue it from its plight. Monday arrived as the City Council and the state legislature deliberated through the night, coming up with a bill shortly before the sun came up. An aide took the bill to Carey's office at the Governor's Mansion in Albany; there, in his pajamas, Mr. Carey perused the papers and signed them. "There was great hope," he said.[3]

With MAC an accomplished fact, Beame moved to balance the 1975-76 budget, and he did so by threatening to lay off 50,000 employees unless the Republicans in Albany agreed to let him impose new taxes. It was the same old brinkmanship that had been guaranteed to work by years of experience. This year, however, Mayor Beame encountered more than the usual resistance from State Senate Majority Leader Warren M. Anderson, Republican attorney from Binghamton, who had been in the legislature for years but had never before had to deal so closely with the city's budgetary confusion. Pinning down numbers in the Beame administration, he and others were learning, was "as easy as holding down smoke with a hammer and a nail." Mayor Beame and Comptroller Goldin, for example, could not even agree on how many people actually worked for the City of New York.

To deal with Senator Anderson's cynicism, Mayor Beame had to do more than just talk about layoffs. Thus, on July 1, the first day of the fiscal year, Mr. Beame proclaimed that 40,000 persons were off the payroll and watched as chaos ensued. Of the 5,000 police officers who turned in their guns, several hundred angrily stormed Brooklyn Bridge, stopping traffic and even holding as hostage a New School professor who was on his way to Boston to lecture on the city's fiscal crisis. Firemen called in sick. And garbage collectors staged the most well-organized wildcat strike the city had ever seen, a 100% effective spontaneous walkout that left thousands of tons of garbage piling up for the nation to see. The strike lasted for several days, but it was long enough to force Anderson's hand. The city walked away with a hefty $330 million tax package, which in turn was enough to hire back thousands of employees.

---

[1] The New York Times, August 17, 1975.

[2] The Wall Street Journal (New York), May 20, 1975.

[3] The New York Times, June 10, 1975.

The nation watched Mayor Beame and the city struggle with its budget game, its layoffs, and its garbage strike. In July, in the midst of this chaos, the Municipal Assistance Corporation geared up for its sale of $2 billion in bonds at interest rates ranging to more than 9%, much higher than anyone had expected. Nevertheless, armed with good ratings from leading bond-rating agencies, the directors of Big MAC scoured the country for investors willing to buy their bonds. They found instead total confusion and total skepticism about any number published by the city, and an almost unbelievable hostility toward the city.

Although an entity of the state with guarantees for its revenues, MAC found itself too much associated with the city's fiscal predicament. Money lenders around the country shied away from the MAC bonds as they had from the city's bonds and notes. In late July, Big MAC's underwriters returned to the board of directors with the gloomy news that there was no market for its bonds until New York City did something "radical" to shed its fiscal image of both chicanery and profligacy. Throughout the summer, MAC urged the city to take the steps needed to restore investor confidence. The city's response was less than enthusiastic. According to Mr. Rohatyn, "We tried a series of actions that were embraced by the city with a fervor that could only be described as tepid."[1]

The primary need was a wage freeze. But because this was so distasteful to city unions, the mayor decided to hold off pressing for a wage freeze until the city was again on the verge of default and crisis leverage could be used. All spring long, the leaders of the city's big municipal labor unions had watched helplessly as Beame chipped away at their membership with his layoffs. No matter how much they cajoled and threatened, they knew there was nothing they could do to prevent the dismissals from taking place. But then, in July, MAC forced Mayor Beame to do something the unions thought they could prevent or at least make excruciatingly difficult, and that was the breaching of their contracts through the imposition of a wage freeze. Despite pressure from Big MAC, the wage freeze was not adopted until after days and nights of negotiations in bars, coffee shops and conference rooms at a scattering of midtown Manhattan hotels. At a news conference on July 31, the Mayor finally announced: that the majority of the city's workers had agreed to the freeze; that he would seek emergency legislation to impose it upon the policemen and firemen, who had not agreed; and he would seek a number of other austerity measures, such as increasing the transit fare to 50 cents, slashing the City University budget by so much that free tuition there seemed in peril, and abolishing a range of city programs and consolidating others. At the close of his announcement, Mayor Beame reflected: "There is nothing I have done in public life that has been more bitter."[2]

As the summer of 1975 wore on, more changes were made. The city's payroll was ultimately reduced by 10%. The budget was trimmed by about $1 billion. A management advisory board was installed to revamp city operations. As usual, however, these changes were made under pressure. According to Rohatyn, "Whatever reforms were adopted, they were adopted with such struggle and obvious reluctance that the impression around the country got worse and worse."[3]

---

[1] The Wall Street Journal (New York), October 30, 1975.

[2] The New York Times, August 1, 1975.

[3] The Wall Street Journal (New York), October 30, 1975.

By mid-August, it was clear that the MAC rescue had failed. This realization set in motion a fresh attempt to assuage bond investors by creating yet another agency to oversee the city's finances. In late August, Mayor Beame and Governor Carey agreed to establish a "panel" to supervise the city. At the announcement of that agreement, the mayor expressed his opinion that the new plan really would make no difference in the way the city was governed. Because of that statement, the banks, whose agreement was vital, rejected the plan the next day. Under redoubled pressure, the state legislature, in special session, rushed through a law establishing the Emergency Financial Control Board with tougher provisions for supervising the city and with a series of financing arrangements intended to meet the city's funds requirements until December.

The city lurched through September with its financing plan under a cloud of uncertainty. A teachers' strike compounded the city's problems further, and a costly settlement (which the control board rejected) did not enhance the bullet-biting image of the Board of Education. In October, amid seemingly endless confusion over the actual size of the city's operating deficit, the control board ordered the mayor to make $200 million more in economies. By mid-October, the seams split again on the financing plan when the teachers' pension fund balked at buying $150 million in MAC bonds. In the period from November through January, the city anticipated a cash shortage of about $1 billion, even if it made no payments on the debt coming due. In addition, by mid-November alone, the city needed $150 million to cover its expenses, with no visible source of funds as of the middle of October. In Mr. Rohatyn's opinion, federal assistance was desperately needed; without it, default by New York City was inevitable.

Federal Aid for New York City

Immediately after their meeting at the White House in May 1975, President Ford had denied Mayor Beame and Governor Carey's request for federal aid. To the President and his advisors, the mayor and the governor had been merely playing a game, the game of "crisis." Both the mayor and the governor saw the solution to their problems in a political formula that had worked in the past: Proclaim a "crisis" and use it to compel a rescue by external forces, in this case, Washington. In the White House, however, the counter strategy seemed equally obvious. This was to be the time, a White House official recalled, when New York "called a crisis and nobody came."[1]

Although Washington and New York tried to negotiate a solution behind closed doors, neither side abandoned its position. In August and September, Ford administration officials held meetings with state and city politicians to arrange a voluntary debt-restructuring plan that would have made federal involvement unnecessary. This plan was rejected by the New Yorkers who were holding out for federal loan guarantees. From mid-September through early November, New York politicians and bankers began a major lobbying effort to persuade Congress to enact legislation to aid the city, and the Ford administration counterattacked to kill the idea. Governor Carey, Mayor Beame and others took to the road, telling audiences around the country that default by New York would be an economic disaster for the nation. The city comptroller released lengthy lists of business firms around the country that were owed millions of dollars by the city, money that would become uncollectible after default. The city also provided the names of the Congressmen from the companies' districts. Warnings of financial doomsday, social chaos and diplomatic dangers issued from the stricken city.

---

[1] The Wall Street Journal (New York), November 11, 1975.

The Ford administration, meantime, was using every forum available –
Congressional testimony, press interviews, Presidential road trips – to
belittle the danger of default and to fuel the widespread antagonism to
federal help for the "profligate" New York. But their strategy started to
unravel in early October when both Vice President Nelson Rockefeller and
Federal Reserve Board Chairman Arthur Burns encouraged federal assistance
for New York. Ford's advisors were stunned and angry. Rockefeller's
comments blurred the administration's position, leading to speculation that
Mr. Ford was using his second-in-command to signal a U-turn in White House
policy, while Burns' warning of the dangers of default for the national
economy lent a new credibility to the dire predictions of the New Yorkers.
As the Senate and the House Banking Committee began writing loan-guarantee
bills to stave off default, administration officials concluded that their
position was in jeopardy. They urged the President to squash forcefully
the speculation that his position was softening.

The result was a major address delivered by President Ford before
the National Press Club in New York City on October 29, 1975. Blasting
New York's "scare tactics," President Ford vowed to veto any predefault
rescue plan for the city and urged court-controlled bankruptcy as the
proper solution for its problems. Bankruptcy thus became an almost certain
prospect. Mr. Ford's decision slammed the door on a Congressionally initiated
aid plan. Although New York City's champions in Congress continued their
efforts to pass some predefault rescue legislation, their task, never
easy, had become almost impossible with Mr. Ford's promise to veto any
assistance plan. In both the Senate and the House, proponents of predefault
rescue measures acknowledged the difficulty they faced in obtaining the
two-thirds majority votes in both Houses needed to override the President's
veto.

The President's Press Club speech was a pivotal point in the crisis.
It scotched federal assistance bills in Congress; it forced New York to begin
mapping a painful alternative solution involving higher taxes; it stunned
union leaders into realizing their labor contracts would be rewritten in a
bankruptcy court; and it painted President Ford into a rhetorical corner
from which there was no graceful escape. As a catalyst, however, the speech
worked. New York officials and Treasury Secretary William Simon began a new
set of negotiations to shape a new tax and debt-overhaul package. For the
first time in weeks, they began hinting that a solution was in sight. Meanwhile, political currents began to shift; a November Gallup poll found national
sentiment swinging slightly in favor of aid to New York City, in contrast to
earlier negative results. New York Republican officials thought a maneuver
of their own had influenced Mr. Ford. On November 8, GOP party officials
decided that they would send an uncommitted delegation to the 1976 Republican
National Convention, rather than one pledged to support Mr. Ford. State GOP
Chairman Richard Rosenbaum said the maneuver was not specifically aimed at
pressuring President Ford on federal aid, but the committee realized "that
could be a fallout benefit."[1] The ice started breaking November 11, when
House Republican Leader John Rhodes of Arizona came out in favor of federal
aid for New York. Rep. Rhodes claimed that he had acted on his own, without
White House prompting. But some colleagues suspected that he had received
a go-ahead from the administration. Indeed, White House aides soon began
telling the press that President Ford was impressed by New York's efforts
to solve its fiscal crisis and would consider some short-term help to cover
"seasonal" cash needs.

---

[1] The New York Times, October 30, 1975.

On November 26, less than a month after President Ford's Press Club speech and after a seven-month game of political brinkmanship, the President announced in a nationally televised news conference that, despite repeated declarations to the contrary, he now supported short-term loans to enable the city to meet its seasonal cash needs. According to Mr. Ford, the loans, not to exceed $2.3 billion outstanding at one time, would be made on a monthly basis until the program ceased on June 30, 1978. The city would have to pay back all outstanding loans by the end of each fiscal year to qualify for new loans for the next fiscal year.

President Ford's decision to lend New York City $2.3 billion raised a number of philosophical and practical issues pertaining to the relationship between the federal, state and local governments. However, although Deputy Treasury Secretary Gerard talked almost daily with Deputy Mayor Kenneth S. Axelson, and although the federal officials were outspoken in pointing up the areas in which reductions should be considered, they were adamant about leaving policy decisions up to the city. "There are enough pitfalls in being President without adding the woes of being Mayor of New York," a Treasury Department official exclaimed.[1] Nevertheless, the expectation was that the Federal Government would become increasingly involved with policy making in New York City.

Felix G. Rohatyn, Chairman of the Municipal Assistance Corporation, observed that "any time somebody lends money to somebody else, it implies a certain degree of involvement. It automatically means a new type of relationship, and one that involves a certain amount of intrusion."[2] Mr. Rohatyn noted when the creditor was a political entity, the intrusion would have political implications "because it is the political decisions that created the financial situation."[3] Nor did Mr. Rohatyn lament this change in traditional federal-state-city relations. "People are living in a dream world," he reflected. "We're living in an age of nuclear power and we think that archaic federal-state-city relations are sacrosanct. They're not."[4]

Impacts of Fiscal Crisis on New York City

The events of 1975 and the manner in which they were handled seriously damaged the city. For one thing, both the city and the State of New York were hit with millions of dollars of additional annual payments on bonds whose interest rates had soared to nearly 10% during the recent upheavals. New York City also lost about $2 million in revenue by having given a discount to property owners to induce them to pay $33 million in advance real estate taxes. Over the longer term, the city would be paying for its "crisis management" in ways that made New York City harder to govern and a more difficult place in which to do business. The mayor's power had been eroded in a city which enjoyed, nominally at least, a "strong mayor" form of government, and considerable controversy was likely to surround efforts to get his political house in order.

---

[1] The New York Times, April 11, 1976.

[2] Ibid.

[3] Ibid.

[4] Ibid.

Layoffs made under pressure to demonstrate overt improvements (and to dramatize the city's suffering) were mostly among line workers instead of back-office bureaucrats. Young, aggressive policemen on the department's "decoy squad," to cite a small example, were the first to go because of seniority considerations, despite their excellent conviction records. In the same vein, the freeze on wages for middle-level employees increased the "brain drain" of the city's best talents to private pursuits. Manhattan District Attorney, Robert Morgenthau, for example, reported that the resignation of many assistant district attorneys had made cases harder to try, had increased jail costs and, as such, would ultimately increase the crime rate. Further, Mr. Morgenthau pointed out that higher crime rates would adversely affect the city's economy, saying: "If we can't make people feel reasonably safe, a lot of them are going to move."[1]

In addition, as a result of its fiscal crisis, the city was forced to halt nearly $600 million in capital projects, which put additional people out of work and limited revenues. It shelved plans to build a big convention center designed to bring business into the city. It imposed a bond transfer tax and increased the stock transfer, which prompted several securities firms to plan moves to Jersey City. It increased the transit fare to 50 cents, a decision considered likely to reduce ridership on buses and subways and to make it harder for the poorest people to get to their jobs.

Not all of the impacts were negative, however. For instance, during the crisis an extraordinary working alliance of traditional adversaries – bankers, investment counsellors, corporation heads, union leaders, and city and state politicians – kept the city from going under. With regard to the city's banks, Steve Weisman, a New York Times reporter, observed:

> Of all the effects of the fiscal crisis on governmental operations, perhaps most remarkable is the new working relationship between the state and the banks. Not since the Depression has the private investment community had so critical a voice – and stake – in the daily workings of government.[2]

This shoulder-to-shoulder undertaking led to such once unimaginable examples of camaraderie as the comment by Victor Gotbaum, the head of the Municipal Labor Committee, which represents two hundred thousand city employees, that he had found David Rockefeller, chairman of the board of the Chase Manhattan Bank, "quite sensitive and quite understanding."[3] Of this alliance, Felix Rohatyn, the chairman of Big MAC, a member of the Emergency Financial Control Board, a senior partner in the investment house of Lazard Freres, and a devout capitalist, reflected: "We may be creating the first commune in the U.S. on such a large scale."[4]

---

[1] The Wall Street Journal (New York), October 30, 1975.

[2] The New York Times, March 28, 1976.

[3] Andy Logan, "Balancing Act," The New Yorker, March 14, 1977, p. 112.

[4] Ibid., p. 112.

Naturally, Mayor Beame turned to the city's banks and its municipal unions for help. For more than four months, city officials, bankers and union leaders struggled to work out terms for additional financing. However, as the court deadline rapidly approached, they were unable to reach an agreement. Instead, the city was rescued from default two days before the deadline by Mayor Beame's patching together sufficient funds from internal sources to meet the repayment schedule. The public squabbles between the key groups involved in the financial management of the city were not without cost, however. As the quarreling and name-calling went on, Felix Rohatyn sadly noted that the "fragile but workable coalition" that had once saved the city was "falling apart."[1] In an editorial, The New York Times commented:

Why then do serious leaders brawl in public over their respective prerogatives, making headlines that only add injury to appalling illness? Because they are stuck here, with their lives and investments, and because they know the politics of less must continue. They are struggling for votes about who gets how much less and when. . . .

The big commercial banks, which must market our debts, are into the city at least $1 billion, probably much more. They want such stringent controls over City Hall budgeting that our paper becomes surer than gold. In a fluid market, the banks could escape from under the clouds and take their business elsewhere.

The big unions, through their pension funds, are into the city for more than $3 billion. They can't get out but they are struggling against being thrown out of the rooms where it will be decided who loses more jobs and pension benefits and whose loans get paid off first, second and last in the tight times still to come.

And the major officeholders are struggling to get re-elected to jobs worth having. They know they cannot do more for the people, but even the politics of less is politics, which is their livelihood and patriotism.

As long as they are all in hock to each other, there is hope. They have come this far in hostile alliance because their participation in the fateful decisions of New York City, no matter how unpleasant, is preferable to having those decisions made by a Federal receiver or judge in formal bankruptcy. They still believe that, as long as they do, they dare not tip over the lifeboat in which they are jointly adrift.[2]

---

[1] Ibid., p. 123.

[2] The New York Times, March 6, 1977.

Regional Impacts of the City's Fiscal Crisis

The fiscal crisis showed that New York City's economic problems could not be contained within the borders of its five boroughs. Its credit crisis had grave budgetary consequences for every level of government in the region. For example, the city's financial difficulties drove up the cost of public borrowing for state and local governments throughout the region. Connecticut officials estimated that higher interest rates cost the state an extra $27.8 million in 1976.[1] The Patchogue School district in Long Island's Suffolk County found itself paying 12.5% interest on short-term notes.[2]

Moreover, with New York State's credit weakened by its save-the-city efforts, counties throughout the state saw their own spending projects stymied. Albert DelBello, county executive of Westchester County, explained: "We depend on state aid. If the state's credit is hurt and it can't make its commitment on a capital project, construction has to stop."[3] Before the fiscal crisis erupted, Nassau County on Long Island had been planning to tap into New York City's water supply, which was brought down from upstate reservoirs. Nassau County pumped its water from underground wells, and the water table there was low. The city had been building a new water tunnel that could have accommodated the county's demand, but budget cuts forced the project to be shelved. Nassau County was left high and dry.

Such incidents dramatized what economists and urbanologists have known for years: Seemingly isolated decisions by a city government could affect millions of people who never set foot inside its limits. A good example was how ballooning public employment in New York affected the labor market in the entire region. Since 1960, the number of people employed by the city increased nearly 60%.[4] Even as the economy cooled in the early '70s and private employment dropped 10%, the city kept hiring. Its work force grew 6% since 1970.[5] As businesses in and around New York City tried to compete with city salaries, they found their labor costs rising. At the same time, labor costs elsewhere were declining because of the slowing economy. As a result, this reduced the competitiveness of the regional economy. Economic activity in the region subsequently declined and unemployment rose. Unemployment in the suburbs increased until it was as great as in the city. And indeed, many suburban problems mirrored those in the city. Nassau and Westchester counties, long the wunderkinder of suburban growth, stopped growing. Businesses were no longer moving in: their populations were getting older and poorer. Because natural expansion no longer paid for increased costs, the only recourse was to raise taxes and cut services, something both counties began in 1976. This remedy, however, had merely driven the middle class into more distant havens.

---

[1] The Wall Street Journal (New York), December 29, 1975.

[2] Ibid.

[3] Ibid.

[4] Ibid.

[5] Ibid.

But even as the sense of shared urgency dawned on New York's neighbors, resistance to regional cost-sharing stiffened. One thing became clear: If the state and suburbs pitched in to bear more of the responsibility of city government, they would do so only out of an instinct for self-preservation. Indeed, neither upstate nor the urban refugees living in the bedroom communities of New Jersey, Long Island and Connecticut demonstrated an inclination to aid the city. State legislators in Albany refused to appropriate additional funds when Mayor Abraham Beame came calling. In passing the tax package that satisfied President Ford's final conditions for federal assistance, they merely authorized the city to tax itself another $200 million. A push to increase the tax on commuters was stopped dead, and great care was taken to avoid the impression that the state was raising taxes on the city's behalf. As the state became embroiled in a fiscal crisis of its own, sympathy for the city in the legislature was lower than ever.

But while few politicians were saying so explicitly, New York City's crisis resulted in a parcelling out of responsibility for the city's future financing. There was sure to be continued talk of a state take-over of the city university and a federal take-over of welfare. Most importantly, the city had already hocked its financial independence; the state's Emergency Financial Control Board, set up in the thick of the crisis, continued to wield a powerful influence over budget decisions. Such state supervision represented New York's first hesitant step on the path to regional government, an approach being tried in a number of other major cities around the nation as they experimented with a variety of techniques to redistribute the cost of municipal services.

New York and its suburbs long resisted regional plans. While other cities forged ahead with such plans, New York remained mired in the debate over the mechanics of cooperation. After the city's recent financial crisis, however, some of that resistance began to fade. The city and its adjacent counties joined in asking the state to assume the cost of education and to press for a federal takeover of welfare. But a financially weakened state was not eager to take on additional responsibilities, and the Federal Government, as President Ford has made clear, did not consider New York City a national problem. Short of state and federal intervention, the most natural way for the suburbs to aid the city would be to pay its taxes. This was the whole point of regionalism and also the point of greatest resistance in the suburbs. Even when they agreed in principle, suburban officials argued that the fiscal and political hurdles were too high. Albert DelBello, county executive for Westchester County, acknowledged his community's responsibilities but also asserted their inability to pay: "The city should expect the area to pay some of its exceptional costs. But we can't take money out of our pockets and put it into the pockets of New York. We can't afford it."[1] A top aide to Mayor Beame provided additional insight into the political problem involved: "Everybody admits it's in their interest to keep us alive, but then they all say, 'Give us a break, fellas, we've got primaries this year'."[2]

---

[1] The Wall Street Journal (New York), December 29, 1975.

[2] Ibid.

A major obstacle to the implementation of some form of regionalism was the attitude of the middle class toward the poor. In the 1960s, New York began pouring large amounts of its revenues into poverty programs in the hopes of putting a lid on the riots and violence that had flared there and in cities elsewhere. As it did so, other municipal services deteriorated, prompting more of the middle class to move to the suburbs. In all, 51 corporations left Manhattan between 1968 and 1972. As the tax base continued to shrink, suburban resentment towards the city's free spending poverty policies swelled. Those who fled the city wanted nothing to do with its problems. Further complicating plans for a regional realignment in New York was the necessary involvement of three separate state governments. For the people of New Jersey and Connecticut, New York City was in another state entirely, emotionally and geographically. To quote Bernard Schwartz, chairman of the Planning Board in Bergen County, New Jersey, home for many New York commuters: "There is no such thing as accomplishing things across state boundaries in this century. If I told people in New Jersey we ought to do something in respect to New York, they'd say, 'Hey, let's solve our own problems'."[1]

---

[1] The Wall Street Journal (New York), December 29, 1975.

Exhibit 1

NEW YORK CITY'S FINANCIAL CRISIS: 1965-1977

Comparison of New York City Operating Budget Expenditures
for Fiscal Years 1966-1967 and 1974-1975

	FY 1966-1967		FY 1974-1975	
	Dollar Amount (millions of $)	Percent of Total Budget	Dollar Amount (millions of $)	Per Cent of Total Budget
Education and Libraries	$ 901.6	23.7	$2,234.3	21.8
Health Services	471.7	12.4	871.2	8.5
Social Services	711.4	18.7	2,951.7	28.8
Debt Interest	76.1	2.0	461.2	4.5
Debt Redemption	475.5	12.5	717.4	7.0
Pension Contributions	216.8	5.7	963.4	9.4
Public Safety	433.7	11.4	963.4	9.4
Other	517.4	13.6	1,291.4	12.6
TOTAL	$3,804.	100.0	$10,249.	100.0

Source: Wyndham Robertson, "Going Broke the New York Way," FORTUNE, (August 1975), p. 146.

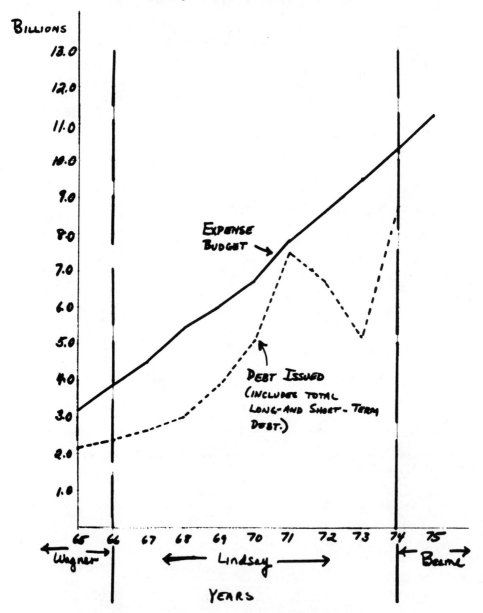

EXHIBIT #2: NEW YORK CITY EXPENSE BUDGETS AND DEBT ISSUED, FISCAL YEARS, 1965-1975.

SOURCE: NEW YORK COMPTROLLER'S OFFICE.

Exhibit 3

NEW YORK CITY'S FINANCIAL CRISIS: 1965–1977

Growth in New York City Short-Term Debt

(millions of dollars)

Fiscal Year	Debt Outstanding				Budget Notes	Total
	TANS	RANS	URNS	BANS		
1968–1969	155.5	128.8	58.3	404.6	–	747.3
1969–1970	170.0	536.7	113.8	457.6	–	1,288.1
1970–1971	206.0	1,096.3	122.2	586.5	308.3	2,319.3
1971–1972	232.0	1,180.0	89.7	687.6	460.8	2,650.2
1972–1973	265.0	887.1	100.0	957.1	308.3	2,517.5
1973–1974	317.0	1,798.3	83.6	908.7	308.3	3,415.9
1974–1975	390.0	2,990.8	62.6	1,817.6	520.0	5,781.0

TANS = Tax Anticipation notes (real estate)
RANS = Revenue Anticipation Notes
URNS = Urban Renewal notes
BANS = Bond Anticipation notes
Budget notes = Budget Anticipation notes

Source: Comptroller's reports, 1969–1974; 1975 figures estimated using tentative debt schedules contained in "Note on Essential Facts," issued to investory by the comptroller's office in conjunction with March debt sales; as compiled by the State Charter Revision Commissioner for New York City, in "Preliminary Recommendations of the State Charter Revision Commission for New York City," New York, 1975.

NOTES

1. Claudia DeVita Scott, *Forecasting Local Government Spending* (Washington, D.C.: Urban Institute, 1972).

2. Alan Walter Steiss, *Local Government Finance* (Lexington, Mass. Lexington Books, 1975), pp. 88–90.

3. For good source material on the income tax, see Richard Good. *The Individual Income Tax* (Washington, D.C.: Brookings Institution, 1976); Tom Obehofer, "The Redistributive Effect of the Federal Income Tax," *National Tax Journal* 29, no. 2 (June 1976); and A. C. Harberger and N. J. Baily, eds., *The Taxation of Income and Capital* (Washington, D.C.: Brookings Institution, 1969).

4. Richard and Peggy Musgrave, *Public Finance in Theory and Practice* (New York: McGraw-Hill, 1980), pp. 350–55.

5. For interesting source material on the sales tax, see John F. Due, *State and Local Sales Taxation* (Chicago: Public Administration Service, 1971): LL Ecker-Rac, *The Politics and Economics of State-Local Finance* (Englewood Cliffs, N.J.: Prentice-Hall, 1970); and John J. Minarik, ed., *What to Tax: Income or Expenditure?* (Washington: Brookings Institution, 1979).

6. For additional material, see Richard W. Lindholm, ed., *Property Taxation USA* (Madison: University of Wisconsin Press, 1969); and George E. Peterson, ed., *Property Tax Reform* (Washington, D.C.: Urban Institute, 1973).

7. For additional information, see John Brittain, *The Payroll Tax for Social Security* (Washington, D.C.: Brookings Institution, 1972).

8. See Wayland D. Gardner, *Government Finance: National, State and Local* (Englewood Cliffs, N.J.: Prentice-Hall, 1978); and John Brittain: *Inheritance and the Inequality of Wealth* (Washington, D.C.: Brookings Institution, 1978).

9. See Frederick D. Stocker. "Diversification of the Local Revenue System: Income and Sales Taxes, User Charges, Federal Grants," *National Tax Journal* 29 (September 1976): 313–22.

10. For a good historical analysis of revenue-sharing proposals, see Richard Nathan, Allen Manvel, and Susannah Calkins, *Monitoring Revenue Sharing* (Washington, D.C.: Brookings Institution, 1975), Appendix C.

11. For a good treatment of the major plans for intergovernmental fiscal relations, see George Break, *Intergovernmental Fiscal Relations in the United States* (Washington, D.C.: Brookings Institution, 1966).

12. Selma Mushkin and John Cotton, *Sharing Federal Funds for State and Local Needs* (New York: Praeger, 1969); and Robert Ingram, Martin McGuire, Wallace Oates, Jeffrey Pressman, and Robert Reischauer, *Financing the New Federalism* (Baltimore: Johns Hopkins University Press, 1975).

13. Ibid.

14. International City Management Association. *Management Policies in Local Government Finance* (Washington, D.C.: The Association, 1975), part 4; Investment Banker's Association of America, *Fundamentals of Municipal Bonds* (Washington, D.C.: Association, 1959); and Irving Ross, "Higher Stakes in the Bond Rating Game," *Fortune*, April 1976, pp. 135–45.

15. International City Management Association, *Municipal Finance Administration* (Chicago: The Association, 1962), p. 307.

16. Ross, "Higher Stakes in the Bond Rating Game," p. 140.

17. International City Management Association, *Municipal Finance Administration*, pp. 308–09.

18. Ross, "Higher Stakes in the Bond Rating Game," p. 135.

19. Musgrave and Musgrave, *Public Finance in Theory and Practice*, pp. 229–37.

20. Gerhard Rostvold, *Financing California Government* (Belmont, Calif.: Dickinson, 1967).

21. Musgrave and Musgrave, *op. cit.*, p. 235.

22. For literature on the controversy surrounding analyses of property tax incidence, see Dick Netzer, *The Economics of the Property Tax* (Washington, D.C.: Brookings Institution, 1966); and idem, "The Incidence of the Property Tax Revisited," *National Tax Journal* 26 (December 1973): 515–35. Or Charles McClure, "The New View of the Property Tax: A Caveat," *National Tax Journal* 30 (March 1977): 69–75.

23. See, for example, Peter Mieszkowski, "On the Theory of Tax Incidence" *Journal of Political Economy* 75 (June 1967): 250–62; and idem, "Tax Incidence Theory: The Effects of Taxes on the Distribution of Income," *Journal of Economic Literature* 7 (December 1969): 1103–24.

24. Musgrave and Musgrave, *op. cit.*, pp. 268.

25. For a good summary review of Laffer's argument, see Jude Wanniski, "Tax Revenues and the 'Laffer Curve,' " *The Public Interest*, Winter 1978, pp. 3–16.

BIBLIOGRAPHY

Aronson, Richard J., and Schwartz, Eli. "Forecasting Future Expenditures." Management Information Service 2, No. S-7. Washington, D.C.: International City Management Association, July 1970.

Break, George. *Intergovernmental Fiscal Relations in the United States*. Washington, D.C.: Brookings Institution, 1966.

Brownlee, O. H. *Estimated Distribution of Minnesota Taxes and Public Expenditure Benefits*. Minneapolis: University of Minnesota Press, 1960.

Brittain, John. *The Payroll Tax for Social Security*. Washington, D.C.: Brookings Institution, 1972.

Davis, Albert, and Shannon, John. "Stage Two: Revenue Turnbacks." *Intergovernmental Perspective* 7, no. 2 (Spring 1981): 18–25.

Due, John F. *State and Local Sales Taxation*. Chicago: Public Administration Service, 1971.

Ecker-Rac, LL. *The Politics and Economics of State-Local Finance*. Englewood Cliffs, N.J.: Prentice-Hall, 1970.

Gardner, Wayland. *Government Finance: National, State and Local*. Englewood Cliffs, N.J.: Prentice-Hall, 1978.

Good, Richard. *The Individual Income Tax*. Washington, D.C.: Brookings Institution, 1976.

Haberger, A. C., and Baily, N. J. eds. *The Taxation of Income and Capital*. Washington, D.C.: Brookings Institution, 1969.

International City Management Association. *Management Policies in Local Government Finance*. Washington, D.C.: The Association, 1975.

———. *Municipal Finance Administration*. Chicago: The Association, 1972.

Investment Banker's Association of America. *Fundamentals of Municipal Bonds*. Washington, D.C.: The Association, 1959.

Lindholm, Richard W., ed. *Property Taxation USA*. Madison: University of Wisconsin Press, 1969.

McClure, Charles. "The New View of the Property Tax: A Caveat." *National Tax Journal* 30 March 1977): 69–75.

———. *"An Analysis of Regional Tax Incidence with Estimation of Interstate Incidence of State and Local Taxes."* Ph.D. dissertation, Department of Economics, Princeton University, 1966.

Mieszkowski, Peter. "On the Theory of Tax Incidence." *Journal of Political Economy* 75 (June 1967): 25–62.

Minarik, John J., ed. *What to Tax: Income or Expenditure?* Washington D.C.: Brookings Institution, 1979.

Musgrave, Richard, and Musgrave, Peggy. *Public Finance in Theory and Practice*. New York: McGraw-Hill, 1980.

Musgrave, Richard; Case, Karl; and Leonard, Herman. "The Distribution of Fiscal Burdens and Benefits." *Public Finance Quarterly* 10 (July 1974).

Mushkin, Selma, and Cotton, John. *Sharing Federal Funds for State and Local Needs*. New York: Praeger, 1969.

Nathan, Richard; Manvel, Allen; and Calkins, Susannah. *Monitoring Revenue Sharing*. Washington, D.C.: Brookings Institution, 1975.

Netzer, Dick. *The Economics of the Property Tax*. Washington, D.C.: Brookings Institution, 1966.

Peterson, George E., ed. *Property Tax Reform*. Washington, D.C.: Urban Institute, 1973.

Phares, Donald. *Who Pays State and Local Taxes?* Cambridge, Mass.: Oelgeschlager, Gunn, and Hain, n.d.

Ross, Irwin. "Higher Stakes in the Bond Rating Game." *Fortune*, April 1976, pp. 132–45.

Scott, Claudia DeVita. *Forecasting Local Government Spending*. Washington, D.C.: Urban Institute, 1972.

Steiss, Alan Walter. *Local Government Finance*. Lexington, Mass.: Lexington Books, 1975.

Stocker, Frederick D. "Diversification of the Local Revenue System: Income and Sales Taxes, User Charges and Federal Grants." *National Tax Journal* 29 (September 1976): 313–22.

Touche Ross and Co. and the First National Bank of Boston. *Urban Fiscal Stress: A Comparative Analysis of 66 U.S. Cities*. New York: Touche Ross, 1979.

Wanniski, Jude. "Taxes, Revenues and the 'Laffer Curve.' " *The Public Interest*, Winter 1978, pp. 3–16.

Index